HALF THE WORLD

EDITED BY ARNOLD TOYNBEE

530 illustrations, 160 in colour

370 photographs, engravings, drawings and maps

HALF THE WORLD

THE HISTORY AND CULTURE OF CHINA AND JAPAN

TEXTS BY   E. Glahn

D. C. Twitchett

Owen Lattimore

Wing-tsit Chan

S. Nakayama

James J. Y. Liu

Zenryu Tsukamoto

Charles D. Sheldon

Carmen Blacker

Donald Keene

Paul A. Cohen

Y. Toriumi

Jean Chesneaux

THAMES AND HUDSON · LONDON

Endpapers: rubbing of a Han dynasty bas-relief from
the Wu family tombs, Chia-hsiang, Shantung. From
Chin-shih-so. Photo R.B. Fleming.

Designed and produced by THAMES AND HUDSON, LONDON
MANAGING EDITOR: Ian Sutton BA
DESIGN: Pauline Baines MSIA
EDITORIAL: Christine Cope BA, Jennifer Rusden BA
RESEARCH: Paul Clifford MA, Elisabeth Croll MA
MAPS: Shalom Schotten
OFFSET ORIGINATION: Gilchrist Brothers Ltd, Leeds
FILMSET by Keyspools Ltd, Golborne, Lancashire
PRINTED in Switzerland by Imprimeries Réunies, Lausanne
BOUND in Holland by Van Rijmenam NV, The Hague

ISBN 0 500 25037 5

CONTENTS

INTRODUCTION

EUROPEANS used to call Eastern Asia 'the Far East'. Even the European settlers in Australia continued to use this term, though Eastern Asia is north of Australia, not east of her, and is near to her instead of being far off. The implication was that Europe was the centre of the World; and, in truth, Europe did dominate the rest of the World for about four centuries ending in the two 20th-century world-wars. China had dominated half the World for more than twenty centuries, ending in 1839, and the Chinese had called their country 'the Middle Kingdom' or even 'All that is under Heaven'. Since the extinction, fifteen centuries ago, of the Roman Empire in the West, no single country has ever dominated the western end of the Old World or the Americas as potently as China has dominated her hemisphere. China's hold on Eastern Asia has not been just political; it has been cultural first and foremost. The East Asian countries that have preserved their political independence—Korea, Japan, Vietnam—have been captivated by Chinese culture; this has been the unifying force in the East Asian half of the World; and it is this that has made it feasible to deal with Eastern Asia as a unity in the present book.

The importance of Eastern Asia in human affairs—past, present, and, we may guess, future too—has become more evident to Europeans now that Europe's brief spell of dominance is over. But China's far older and longer dominance is over too, even in the East Asian half of the World, which was influenced and unified by Chinese culture for more than 2,000 years. Modern technology has knit the whole World together, and, in this comprehensively unified World, neither China nor Europe, nor, for that matter, the United States or the Soviet Union, is now a hub round which all the rest turns. The whole face of the Earth has now been united, not by the dominance of any single region, but by the omnipresence of a common problem. All mankind is now having to cope with the new man-made environment that man has created for himself by the astonishing recent development of his technology.

The impact of modern technology on Eastern Asia is discussed in the last two chapters of this book. The experience of each section of mankind in wrestling with this world-wide problem is a common concern of mankind as a whole. The successes and failures of each region are not only instructive for all the rest; they affect the fortunes of all the rest directly and, at some levels, drastically; and Eastern Asia is so important a part of the World that its vicissitudes in the modern age have a bearing on the future of the whole World, including the Western countries in which the recent acceleration of technological development originated. However, these chapters that deal with contemporary events are only two out of a total of thirteen; for the present cannot be made intelligible unless it is viewed against the background of the past.

Time is of the essence of human life and experience. The past, and our memory of it, always affects our action. In the vocabulary of Buddhism, which is one of the historic religions of Eastern Asia, this momentum of past action is called 'karma'—a Sanskrit word which literally means 'action' but is used philosophically to mean 'the effect of past action on present action'. Karma is a mighty force always and everywhere. It is mighty in the West, which is—or has been—confident of its ability to break with the past, and of its freedom to shape the future. Eastern Asia is not more at the mercy of karma than the West is. Karma is the common lot of all mankind. East Asians differ from Westerners, not in being more subject to karma, but in being more aware that they are subject to it, and their consciousness of this perhaps makes it easier for for them than it is for Westerners to recognize realistically the limitation that karma imposes on Man's power to meet revolutionary changes in his circumstances by taking revolutionary new departures.

East Asians are perhaps also more conscious than Westerners are that the past is not simply a burden but is also a treasure, and this consciousness has been particularly strong in China, 'the Middle Kingdom' of the East Asian half of the World. The Chinese people's sense of the value of their indigenous culture has led them to react cautiously to the two foreign cultures—the Indian and the Western—that have made impacts on Eastern Asia.

Till the 19th century of the Christian era, Chinese culture was the formative influence throughout Eastern Asia. Indian culture, which has been disseminated in Eastern Asia by the Indian religion or philosophy of Buddhism, reached Korea, Japan, and Vietnam via China and in forms in which it had already been given a Chinese impress. For this reason, the present book starts by giving an account of Chinese culture, including Chinese Buddhism, in the first six chapters. The Chinese characters (Chapter I) are something more than a means of communication; they are the expression of an attitude to life, and they have carried this attitude with them into other East Asian countries in so far as they have been adopted there too. The main thread of East Asian history was the political history of China (Chapter II) down to China's sudden catastrophic demotion, in and after the Anglo-Chinese War of 1839–42, from being 'the Middle Kingdom' of Eastern Asia to being a 'native state' at the mercy of the Western powers, of Russia, and eventually also of China's own former cultural satellite, Japan. China's political history is inseparable from Chinese institutions. It has created these institutions and it has subsequently been conditioned by them.

China's northern neighbours, before the eastward expansion of Russia to the East Asian shores of the Pacific Ocean, were the nomadic pastoral peoples of the Eurasian steppes (Chapter III). Pastoral nomadism is now dying out everywhere, but, for about 4,000 years, it was one of the forces that shaped the history of the Old World. The nomads were the first aliens with a distinctively different culture whom the Chinese encountered, and they were a formidable problem for China till as recently as the 18th century. China's relations with the nomads have a longer history than her relations with India, and a very much longer history than her relations with the West.

Human life is many-sided, but our various activities are interrelated. In order to understand any one of them, we have to take a synoptic view of them all. We have to take account of philosophy and religion and science and technology and literature and visual art, besides politics. In this book, visual art is presented in the illustrations, but the other non-political aspects of Chinese culture are discussed in the text (Chapters IV–VI).

The historic cultural unity of Eastern Asia is a product of the radiation of Chinese culture into the East Asian countries on China's fringes (Chapter VII). Chinese culture has been attractive, and China's neighbours have been receptive, but an imported foreign culture seldom maintains itself unmodified, however great its potency and its prestige may be. It has been noted already that China transformed an Indian religion, Buddhism, into something Chinese before she transmitted it, along with the indigenous components of Chinese culture, to Korea, Japan, and Vietnam; and these non-Chinese East Asian countries, in their turn, did to Chinese culture, including Chinese Buddhism, what China had done to Indian Buddhism. They transformed it to fit their own conditions and to meet their own needs.

Japan, for instance, derived her culture from China, but she developed what she had borrowed from China into something so different from the Chinese pattern that the outcome was virtually an original product of the Japanese genius (Chapters VIII–X). The Japanese changed the centralized bureaucratic Chinese system of administration into a feudal system which, in so far as it had any counterpart in Chinese history, was akin to the feudalism of the period of the 'Warring States' which had preceded the establishment of the Imperial regime in China and had

been superseded, not followed, there by this. The forms in which Buddhism became a widespread popular religion in Japan had no counterparts in either China or India. Pre-Meiji Japanese literature was an equally original Japanese creation. Yet some of Japan's cultural imports from China maintained their identity—for instance the Zen (Dhyana) school of Buddhism and the Confucian philosophy, which, like Zen Buddhism, was adopted (in its crypto-Buddhist neo-Confucian form) by the Japanese military class at a late stage in the evolution of Japanese feudalism.

The transformation of Chinese culture on Japanese soil after its transplantation is not surprising; for, at the date of its introduction—the 6th to the 8th century of the Christian era—the indigenous Japanese way of life was not only very different from the Chinese; it was also very much less sophisticated. The success of the Japanese in adopting and adapting one potent foreign culture perhaps partly accounts for their repetition of this achievement in the 19th century when they decided that they now had to come to terms with the Western civilization. Having already once received an alien civilization and having succeeded in adjusting it to their own way of life, the Japanese did not shrink from doing this for the second time. The Chinese, too, had received a foreign civilization once already before they encountered the West; but the Chinese reception of Indian culture in the form of Buddhism had not been so exacting an experience as the Japanese reception of Chinese culture. China had been on a par with India culturally; the spirit of Buddhism was not aggressive; and the indigenous Chinese attitude to life had a facet, represented by Taoism, to which Buddhism was congenial. Thus China was not so well schooled by her past experience as Japan was for the ordeal of coping with the formidably aggressive civilization of the modern West (Chapters XI–XIII).

While this book was being written and was being prepared for publication, the course of human affairs was continuing to accelerate, and their global unity was becoming ever more manifest. This unity had been created by the world-wide expansion of the West Europeans, followed by the outbreak of the Industrial Revolution in Britain and the progressive spread, round the globe, of the mechanized technology of production. From the start, the price of mechanization had been pollution, and the pollution from the smoke of coal-fuel had been reinforced by the still more noxious fumes emitted by petrol-driven vehicles, with the threat of lethal poisoning from the waste products of the fission or fusion of atoms, when atomic power came (as was already probable) to be used on the grand scale for peaceful purposes, not to speak of the ever-present menace of its possible use for war.

Thus Man's relations with non-human Nature had taken an ironical turn. Man had aspired to subdue and exploit the rest of Nature ever since his acquisition of consciousness had made it possible for him to set objectives for himself and to pursue these through successive generations. By the date at which this book was being written, Man had at last achieved an aim that was coeval with humanity itself. He had reversed his original relation with his natural environment. Man's natural environment, instead of Man, had now become the slave; but Man had freed himself from one servitude at the price of subjecting himself to another. Man had conquered his natural environment by calling an artificial one into existence, and this monster, manufactured so improvidently by Frankenstein, was proving to be a more intractable and more ruthless master than the natural environment that Man's handiwork had overlaid, obliterated, and was even threatening to destroy. This was a threat to the survival of Man himself; for his technological *tour de force* had demonstrated a truth that ought not to have required demonstration. Man is an integral part of life in the biosphere that coats our planet—a thin and finite and vulnerable film that is the sole, and the strictly limited, habitat of Man and of all his fellow living creatures.

By the year 1973, the unity of the biosphere, for weal or for woe, had become manifest. The air and sea, on which the denizens of the biosphere depend for their life, are indivisible. The notional frontiers of local sovereign states are no barriers to the global spread of the pollution inflicted on air and water at any point in the biosphere.

The principal perpetrators, and earliest victims, of pollution had been the technologically 'advanced' countries, and, by 1973, one East Asian country, Japan, was the next most 'advanced' country (in this peculiar meaning of the word 'advanced') to the United States. Japan was also the country in which the problems created by industrial pollution were the most acute and urgent. Since the Second World War, the Japanese people had compensated for the shock of a dramatic military defeat by winning an equally dramatic victory in terms of maximizing their G.N.P. The price of this had been a maximization of pollution in Japan. Here a violated Nature had presented her bill for payment demandingly. Already, at the world conference on pollution, held at Stockholm in July 1972, the Japanese delegates had frankly admitted the straits to which Japan had reduced herself by her technological triumph, and they had warned their fellow-men to avoid making the same mistakes.

By that date, both Japan and the Soviet Union, as well as the Western countries in which the Industrial Revolution had started, were deeply committed to the mechanized and urbanized way of life. By contrast, the technologically less advanced countries still retained a greater freedom of manoeuvre. It was still open to these countries to industrialize and urbanize selectively, or even to reject this novel way of life altogether, according to their judgment of what was best for themselves in the light of the 'advanced' countries' experience. Fortunately for mankind, the 'developing' but not yet fully developed section of the human race was still the majority—and this majority included China.

Moreover, on the political plane, human affairs had taken a turn which, at the time of writing, looked hopeful and which might turn out to have been of historic importance. The two 'developed' military and political super-powers, the United States and the Soviet Union, had simultaneously decided to work for a détente in their relations with each other. The same decision had also been reached as between the United States and the potential third super-power, China; and there had been indications that the Chinese Government's attitude towards Japan, too, was becoming less stiff.

The political aspect of human affairs may have changed further between the date of writing of this introduction and the date of publication of this book. But at least one political development could be forecast tentatively. The East Asian half of the World was surely going to pull its full weight once again. Indeed, its weight in world affairs might become preponderant. It would not be surprising if the 21st century proved to be an East Asian century of human history.

ARNOLD TOYNBEE

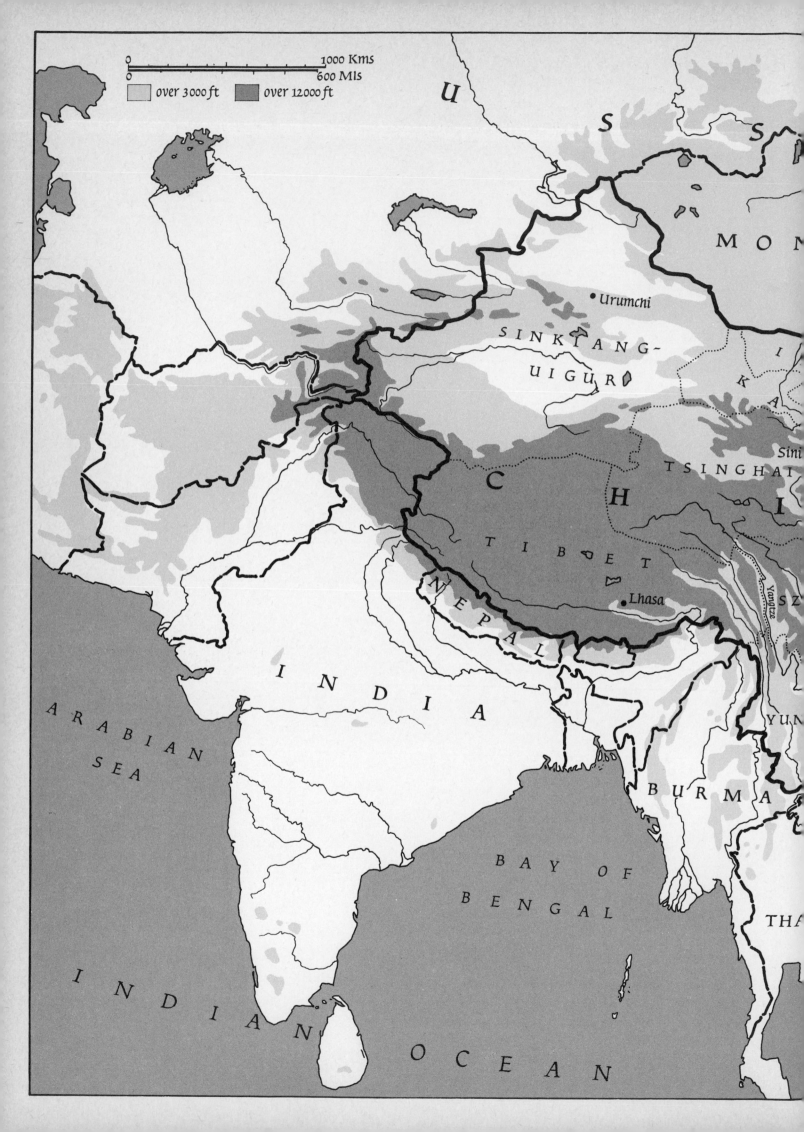

ACKNOWLEDGMENTS

The picture-sections of this book are the responsibility of the publisher. They could not have been produced, however, without the generous help of scholars all over the world, and we should like in particular to thank the following: Takeshi Ogiwara of the Tokyo National Museum; Wang Chih-wu of the National Palace Museum Taiwan; Mr H. Nelson, Dr R. Whitfield, and Mr D. Chibbett of the British Museum; Mr Lust and Mitsuko Ishizuki of the School of Oriental and African Studies Library, London; Wango H. C. Weng; Mr L. Sickman, Director of William Rockhill Nelson Gallery, Kansas; Mr Y. D'Argence of the Avery Brundage Collection, San Francisco; Mme M. Cohen of the Bibliothèque Nationale, Paris; Mr K. Cig, Director of Topkapi Saray Museum, Istanbul; John Massey-Stewart; Mr H. Mitsui, Tokyo; Mrs J. Lo of Princeton University; Mrs M. Tamba of Yokahama; Ling Shu-hua.

The following institutions have also provided us with more than customary assistance: Japan Information Centre, London; Percival David Foundation, London; Okura Cultural Foundation, Tokyo; Service Photographique, Bibliothèque Nationale, Paris; Boston Museum of Fine Arts; Cambridge University Library; Cleveland Museum of Art; Freer Gallery of Art, Washington; National Maritime Museum, Greenwich; Musee Guimet, Paris; Metropolitan Museum of Art, New York; Mitsui Research Institute for Social and Economic History, Tokyo; Royal Ontario Museum, Toronto; Sakamoto Photo Research Laboratory, Tokyo; Victoria and Albert Museum, London; Wellcome Institute of the History of Medicine, London.

Finally, we are deeply indebted to all the authors for their patient advice on the choice of pictures and the wording of the captions. Many of them gave us more of their time and energy than we had any right to ask.

The translations from Chinese poetry quoted in Professor Liu's chapter are taken from the following books, permission to quote from which is gratefully acknowledged:
p. 162 Arthur Waley *The Book of Songs*, George Allen and Unwin, 1937
David Hawkes *Ch'u Tz'u: The Songs of the South*, The Clarendon Press, 1959
p. 163 Ed. Cyril Birch *Anthology of Chinese Literature*, Grove Press Inc. 1965 and Penguin Books, 1967. (This translation from Lu Ch'i *Essay on Literature* by Shih-hsiang Chen was first published by Anthoensen Press.)
Arthur Waley *Chinese Poems*, George Allen and Unwin, 1946
p. 164 J. D. Frodsham *An Anthology of Chinese Verse*, The Clarendon Press, 1967
p. 165 The translation of Wang Wei is by James J. Y. Liu. Arthur Waley *The Poetry and Career of Li Po*, George Allen and Unwin, 1950
p. 166 Arthur Waley *The Life and Times of Po Chü-i*, George Allen and Unwin, 1949

1 SIGNS AND MEANINGS

Chinese writing through four millennia

E. GLAHN

In a sheet of paper is contained the Infinite.

Lu Chi

The art of writing is one of the chains that bind Chinese history together. In the West, language has served to differentiate the local cultures; in China it has been the agent of unity. Because of their language – or, more precisely, their script – the Chinese of today can recognize the inhabitants of An-yang 3,000 years ago as *themselves*, and their history from that time onward as a single process, to a degree hardly conceivable by a Westerner.

The '*art* of writing' is also a phrase that belongs peculiarly to Chinese. The abstract beauty of the script, appreciated from the very beginning, grew into something uniquely important, prized and practised in all its subtlety by every educated man. In China, it is not too much to say, calligraphy was the mother of the arts. The detail opposite is taken from a scroll of the Sung dynasty. Scholars sit at a low table, writing. The scene has almost an air of ritual. Paper is spread on the table, brushes beside it; on the left, an inkstone. Behind the screen at the back a woman ties up bundles of finished scrolls.

The smallest unit in written Chinese is an ideogram with a meaning, not a meaningless phonetic sign (a letter) as in Western languages. Complex words are formed by joining ideograms together, and so the very structure of the language embodies an attitude of mind, a way of thought. Thus the sign for a woman next to that for a child means 'love' or 'good'. 'Bright' is made up of the signs for sun and moon. Such a language is already half way to poetry. Every character is an image in embryo. Writing did indeed attain an almost sacred quality; prayers were written, not spoken; essays, not speeches, swayed politics; book learning was accorded a respect approaching veneration. (1)

16

To consult the oracle the people of An-yang scratched their questions on fragments of bone, human and animal (above far left), heated them, and according to the way they cracked interpreted the answer. Over 2,500 characters are known from this source, more than half of them close enough to modern Chinese to be read. The date is between 1400 and 1100 BC. (2)

Wooden strips used for record keeping (above left) show the script about a thousand years later, in AD 100, painted with a brush. They were held together by a thread through the hole near the top. Paper was invented just about this time. (3)

'In the third month the king issued his command to Jung and the Inner Ministry . . .' reads the inscription inside this bronze vessel (left). It records an award to the Marquis of Hsing in the early Chou dynasty (11th century BC) with characters ('large seal') adapted to the technique of casting in bronze. The sides of the vessel (below left) are ornamented with stylized dragons and birds. (4, 5)

A transition from 'large seal' to 'small seal' script can be seen on stone drums (detail below) engraved with records of royal hunting expeditions in the Ch'in dynasty – the oldest long texts in Chinese. 'Small seal' was the reformed and simplified script imposed by the short-lived Ch'in government. (6)

The dangers of literacy: in 213 BC the first Ch'in emperor ordered the literature of the Chou dynasty to be burnt and its scholars buried alive (above). Such was the importance given to scholarship as the vehicle for ideas. (7)

Printing was invented in China in the 8th or 9th century AD. Even movable type – a process far less useful in China, with its thousands of characters, than in Europe with its twenty-five or so – had been evolved by about 1030. Below: part of the *Diamond Sutra*, virtually the world's oldest printed page, dated 11 May AD 868. The whole text would have been carved on one block, the illustrations on another. Right: a later wood-block used for printing. The Buddhist text at the bottom is made up of strips of characters. (8, 9)

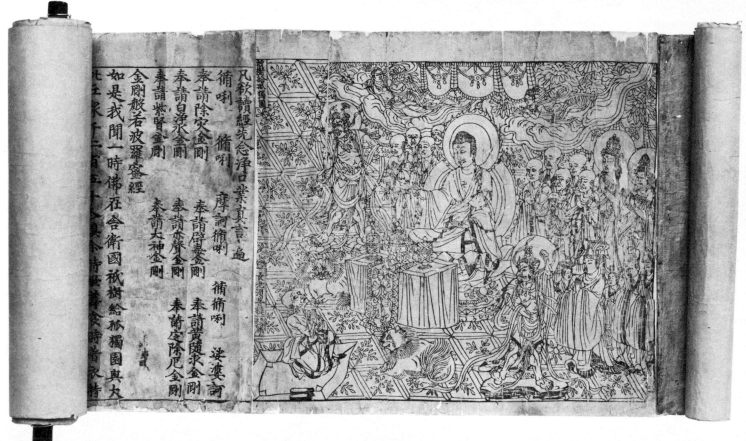

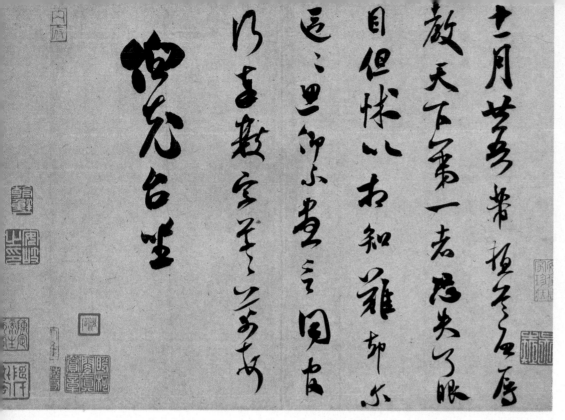

Closest to writing of all natural forms was that of bamboo (right), and the composition of pictures of bamboo with brush and ink became the universal pastime of scholars. The motion of the brush was in the direction that the plant grew, from root to top, from stem to leaf-tip. Each stroke had the same delicate control as calligraphy. In this example, by Hsü Wei (1521–93), writing is added, emphasizing the parallel. (12)

Illustrated scrolls combined calligraphy with watercolour painting. Sometimes these were faithfully reproduced centuries after they had been first created. This example (below right) by Wang Cheng-ming (1522–67) copies a manuscript of two hundred years earlier. (13)

Word and image, poetry and painting, became one. Above and right are shown a letter and a painting by the same artist, Mi Fei, who lived under the Sung dynasty from 1051 to 1107. The letter, done with an ink-laden brush on paper, has a vigour and directness which the West did not discover until the 20th century. (The seals are those of the various owners through the ages.) In the painting (right), the written poem is linked to the painted landscape – two art forms executed with the same tools. A thatched shelter stands under leafy trees; beyond, separated by a misty valley, the peaks of mountains rise mysteriously. (10, 11)

20

海國名卷說求倦畫中顧
色更嬋娟若非酒行來湘浦
枝之葉、自成排嫩、硃、
向上裁信手揚來非
著意違睛是兩忽人猜

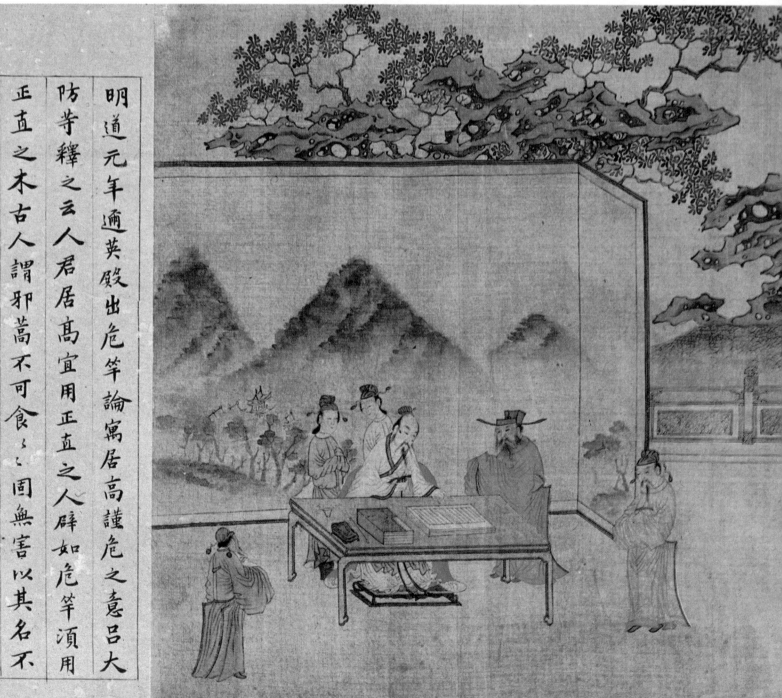

明道元年通英殿出危竿論寓居高謹危之意呂大
防芽釋之云人君居高宜用正直之人辟如危竿須用
正直之木古人謂邪蒿不可食之固無害以其名不

Writing styles could vary according to the nature of the text, just as Europeans can use different manuscript styles or type-faces. These four examples (above) of the same characters written in different ways – running, cursive, square and seal – come from 16th-century versions of the *Thousand Character Essay*, an ingenious composition used by schoolchildren which summarizes Chinese history in a thousand characters, never repeating any twice. (14)

Throughout China an imperial order such as that issued by the Sung emperor Kao-tsung (left) was readily understood, whatever differences there might be in the spoken language. This is one of the great advantages of written Chinese, that it is independent of pronunciation, as in the West written numerals are. (15)

The written examinations, by which the officials of China continued to be chosen until the beginning of the 20th century, were gruelling experiences. Candidates were placed alone in their cells, with brush, ink and paper, to expound their knowledge of the Confucian Classics for days at a time. This row of cells (left) was photographed at Canton about eighty years ago. (16)

Those who could read were, through the examination system, ensured a fair opportunity to rise in government service. Every precaution was taken to make the tests impartial. Success demanded much time and hard work, but was the passport to power and influence. The drawback was that it produced cultured dilettanti, but not necessarily decisive men of action. Here a group of scholar officials talk poetry on a summer evening. (17)

Those who could not read were automatically excluded from the élite. There was no way for them to rise. In this scene, photographed in 1873, a peasant woman dictates to a professional letter-writer who has set up his table in the street. Primary education was as a rule available only to those with money and leisure, so that the child of illiterate parents had small chance of crossing the boundary. (18)

The conquest of illiteracy was one of the first concerns of the Communist revolution. The old complicated characters were drastically simplified, and in the Liberated Areas (above) an attempt was made to write Chinese in the Roman alphabet. Mao Tse-tung also encouraged the writing of plays embodying revolutionary ideals to be performed in the villages. (19)

Modern newspapers use a simplified Chinese script (2,000–3,000 characters) so that the virtue of intelligibility throughout the country is retained – a virtue that would be lost if words were spelled phonetically. Right: a newspaper published on 9 August 1966 containing the directives of the Cultural Revolution. (20)

Education today comes high on the government's priorities. The campaign to teach every child to read makes spectacular headway in the new schools (left). The will to learn is strong and is encouraged as the path to political responsibility. 'If you can read you can write and count as well', says a highly coloured poster (below). (21, 22)

讀了書能又寫能又算

Peasants and workers (left) attend classes at Tsinghua University. It is the aim of modern China to produce, not an intellectual élite as in the days of the empire, but an educated people whose learning is shared by all. (23)

E. GLAHN

The excellence of a piece of calligraphy is determined largely by the quality of individual brush strokes. Here the character 'yung', (eternity), often taken as a model, is analysed into its component strokes. (1)

THE CHINESE SCRIPT consists of characters which are themselves meaningful units of language (morphemes)— monosyllables like 'man' or 'come'—not simply separate sounds (phonemes) like the letters of our alphabet.

The oldest Chinese characters now extant are those cast on ritual bronzes, or written or incised on animal bones and tortoise shells. Most of the characters on the bones are engraved, but some are written with a stiff brush dipped in red or black ink. They are records from the end of the Shang dynasty, *c.* 1400–1100 BC, and were used for divination (see Chapter IV). A large number of such oracle bones have been found at An-yang, the site of the Shang capital, in present-day Honan. The whole vocabulary of these inscriptions is estimated at more than 2,500 characters and about one-half of them can be read and understood today. It is clear that they do not represent the beginning of Chinese writing, but that even at this early date the script had already reached a very advanced stage of development. Of the ritual bronzes some are as old as the oracle bones, but most of them were cast during the Chou dynasty, *c.* 1100–221 BC. They were objects for sacrificial, funeral, and daily use, and were sometimes buried in the graves of aristocratic families. Seals of gold, bronze, jade, turquoise, soapstone, or moulded clay, also occasionally include written words.

The same characters which are used on the bronzes are also used in the oldest literature which belongs to the Chou dynasty—the *Shih-ching (Book of Poetry)* and the *Shu-ching (Book of Documents)*, both from *c.* 800 BC, though preserved only in later copies (see Chapter VI). There are also records of documents from about 400 BC written on bamboo sticks and wooden tablets, but these have all disappeared.

The complicated script was difficult to master, and the small group of learned men who could read and write formed a special group closely identified with the ideals of the reigning dynasty. The very art of writing carried political connotations. When the Chou dynasty was overthrown, therefore, the old literature was seen as subversive. In 213 BC the first Ch'in emperor ordered the destruction of the majority of existing documents and initiated a reform of the characters, which had become complex and over-elaborate. Often the same morpheme could be written with several variant characters. The script resulting from this reform was called *hsiao chuan*, 'small seal', in contrast to the 'large seal' in the bronze inscriptions. The 'small seal' can be seen in stone inscriptions from the Han dynasty (206 BC–AD 221). During this period silk and paper came into more common use, and a flexible brush became the favourite writing utensil. The change in form of the characters was partly due to this new technique and they acquired the shapes that they still have today. The rule, then as now, was that each character should be roughly square.

Characters in combination

In about AD 120, Hsü Shen wrote his etymological dictionary, *Shuo-wen chieh-tzu (Discussion of Simple Graphs and Explanation of Compound Graphs)*. He arranged the Chinese characters in six categories, but he made several mistakes in his explanation of the derivation of many characters because he had access only to bronze inscriptions, not to oracle bones. His system of the six categories, however, can be used with some modifications; even today we do not have sufficient evidence to trace the development of the Chinese script step by step.

The category regarded as the oldest is called *hsiang-hsing*, 'pictographs'. In the modern form of characters in this category it is often still possible to distinguish the original pictures: thus the ancient ☉, for 'sun', is now 日; and ☽ or ☾, for 'moon', now 月. The drawing 𠂁, for a man, is now 人; a child 𡢃, now 子; and a woman 𡥃, now 女. A tree 𣎵, with root and top, is now 木. This method was completely satisfactory for describing concrete objects.

To some extent abstract ideas could be described by drawings. They form the second category, *chih-shih*, 'simple ideographs', and again the ancient drawings are easily recognized today. 一 is the character for 'one', 二 for 'two', and 三 for 'three'. The drawing 二 on oracle bones and bronzes means 'up' and is now written 上. 二, now 下, is the character for 'down'. But the

p 18 (2, 4, 5)

p 17 (1)

p 19 (7)

p 18 (3)
p 18 (4, 5, 6)

土	水	鼎	示	田	就	祖	逆	天	祝

The forms of present-day characters are the result of gradual stylization over many centuries, but often the original can still be recognized. These ten comparisons of oracle-bone inscriptions, going back to 1100 BC and beyond, with modern characters represent earth, water, cauldron, to show, field (showing division), then (man and bowl), ancestor (phallus), to go against or towards, heaven, and prayer (man kneeling before an altar). (2)

possibilities for depicting abstract ideas in simple drawings are limited, so this group is the smallest of the six.

The range was greater when two pictographs were combined to depict an idea. *Huei-i*, 'compound ideographs', constitute the third category. The combination of sun and moon became 明, the character for 'bright', 'luminous'. A woman and a child made 好, meaning 'love', 'good'.

The definitions of the fourth group, *chuan-chu*, 'derived characters', have differed widely. Most scholars regard it as the derivation of characters by graphic inversion. This would explain a character like 尸, a 'corpse', which in a Shang bronze appears as 尸, a man lying down.

The characters in these four groups form, however, only a small part of the Chinese script. They are independent of the actual morphemes in the language, since they could have the same meaning in any other language. In other words, they indicate nothing about the phonetic values of the morphemes at any historical stage of the Chinese language.

Many abstract ideas were too difficult to depict, but it was easy to borrow a character with the same or a very similar pronunciation. Often this meaning entirely replaced the original. The drawing 朱 on oracle bones, 來 in the seal script, was probably a picture of a kind of wheat, and was pronounced lǝg in Archaic Chinese. The drawing was borrowed for the homophonous lǝg, meaning 'to come', which today is written 來, and the meaning 'wheat' became obsolete. This category of characters, the fifth, is called *chia-chieh*, 'loan characters'. In some cases a character is used in both its original and its borrowed senses, an example being 网, Archaic *miwang*, now *wang*. Its basic meaning is 'net' and it is borrowed for the homophonous 'have not'. The original character was therefore enlarged by the signific 糸, meaning 'silk', and is now exclusively written 網 whenever it means a net.

By compounding a new character out of two that already existed, one of which gave the meaning (the signific) while the other indicated the pronunciation (the phonetic) every possible morpheme could be written

Paper and ink came into use during the Han period. Left: bamboo stems are cut and laid down for pressing. Centre: drying the sheet over an oven. Right: carbon deposits and liquid glue have been placed in pottery jars. The mix is then moulded into cakes or sticks of ink and left to harden. The finished sticks are weighed in a balance. (3, 4, 5)

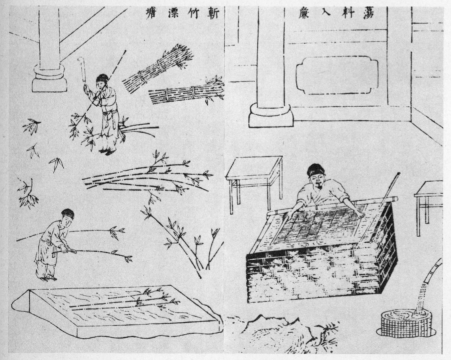

down. In the beginning the pronunciation of the phonetic and the compound character was identical or very similar. But small differences developed and increased in the course of history, so that very often it is no longer possible to deduce the pronunciation of a compound character from the present pronunciation of its phonetic. Such characters form the sixth category, *hsieh-sheng*, 'phonetic compounds'.

The character 方 , 'square', has the modern pronunciation *fang*, and so have most of the compound characters in which it is phonetic. 妨 'oppose', 枋 'timber', 仿 'resemble', and 訪 'enquire' are all pronounced *fang* today. But 滂 , 'heavy rain' (with water as signific) is pronounced *p'ang*, and so is 彷 , 'irresolute walk'. The possibilities were so many that sometimes several characters stand for the same word, such as 坊 , 防 , and 防 , all pronounced *fang* and meaning 'dyke'.

The 'phonetic compounds' are regarded as the last stage in the development of the Chinese script. They form the great majority of the Chinese characters, and it is by this method that new characters have been created since antiquity. In *Shuo-wen chieh-tzu*, four-fifths of all characters belong to this category, and in the 17th-century dictionary *K'ang-hsi tzu-tien* they are as many as nine-tenths. As there was no limit to the possibilities of creating new characters as phonetic compounds, several became rather complicated. The character 讓 , meaning 'thick of voice', contains 36 strokes, but the majority fall within the range of 7 to 17 strokes.

The characters fail to indicate the tone distinctions. In modern Chinese each syllable has a tonal value. In the North Chinese dialect there are four different tones, whereas in Cantonese there are no less than nine. That the spoken language in Chou times had tonal values as well is most likely, but the characters do not reflect them.

Characters and language

One might ask why the Chinese did not long ago reject their complicated script in favour of our marvellously simple writing, which gets along with some two dozen letters. The answer is that the Chinese characters are exceptionally well suited to the very nature of the Chinese language, each character representing one monosyllabic word that often is one syntactic unit. There are no word classes in Chinese. 人 , 'man', can also mean 'to be a man', 'to regard or treat as a man', and 'human'. Nor is there inflexion; 人 means 'the man', 'men', 'the men', 'man's', 'men's'. Whether a Chinese word functions as a noun, a verb, or an adjective; whether it is the subject, the object, or in the genitive case depends on its place in the sentence. Whether it is singular or plural depends on the context.

Written Chinese, irrespective of period or dialect, can always be understood. Texts from the Chou dynasty are read aloud according to the reader's modern pronunciation in Pekinese or Cantonese, whatever his dialect is, and a newspaper or poster can be understood all over the country, which is not the case with the spoken language.

Written Chinese has followed its own course, parallel to and now and then influenced by the spoken language. It derives from the rich Chou literature. Though this is far from being homogeneous (it is written in several different dialects), Chou texts have been first readers for

Chinese schoolchildren up to this century. The Chou language had gone through a long evolution from a more complicated to a comparatively simple stage. Traces of former word classes and disyllabics are few.

Already in the Chou texts we find several disyllabics, consisting of two characters. Examples are 父 母 'father-mother' meaning 'parents', and 君 子 , 'lord-master', usually translated as 'gentleman', the Confucian ideal of man. But each of these characters can appear alone as an independent word.

To show the evolution of the Chinese script a sentence of classical Chinese composed of four characters 'wan pang hsien ming', (the multitudinous nations have laid down their arms), is here written in seven different styles: (a) oracle-bone script and (b) large seal of the Shang dynasty, (c) small seal of the Ch'in dynasty and (d) clerical writing of the Han dynasty. Out of the clerical script developed the three modern forms of Chinese calligraphy – square (e), running (f) and cursive (g). (6)

Encyclopaedias and dictionaries covering a wide range of subjects were frequently compiled as reference works. This late Ming encyclopaedia is made up of objects, maps, charts and tables, each one of which is followed by a brief explanation. (7)

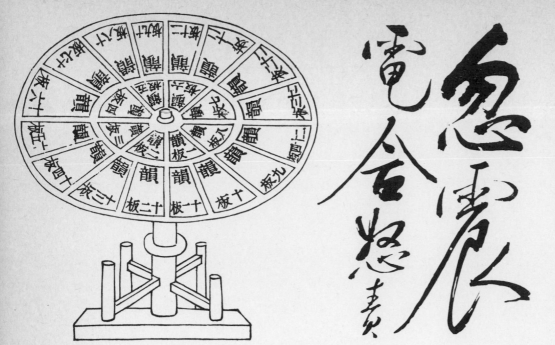

Movable type in wood, porcelain and copper appeared in China in the 11th century. A wheel-shaped case (far left) which could be rotated was invented to store it. It was divided into 24 compartments, and characters were grouped together if they rhymed when spoken, not by any breakdown of their written forms. (8)

Calligraphy was a popular leisure activity and the most prized of arts. Left: an ink squeeze from a particularly fine manuscript written in the cursive script by the poet Su Shih. (9)

The Chinese traditionally divide their words into two groups, *shih-tzu* and *hsü-tzu*, usually translated as 'full words' and 'empty words'. (*Tzu* actually means a written character, and this is further evidence that one character is regarded as representing one word.) 'Full words' are roughly all those which can function as nouns; the rest are 'empty words'. These include pronouns and what we would call particles or function words. Some correspond to our prepositions, others connect sentences, and still others end sentences to indicate statement, continuative action, or question. The two basic relations between words are 'determination', corresponding to modifier and modified, and 'direction', corresponding to verb and object. An example from the philosopher Mencius (Meng-tzu):

滕 小 國 也 竭 力
T'eng small country [statement] utmost strength

以 事 大 國
whereby serve big country

則 不 得 免 焉
then not obtain escape from-them.

'T'eng is a small kingdom. Though I do my utmost to serve those large kingdoms [on either side of it], we cannot escape suffering from them' (Legge's translation). 也 is a final particle which follows a predicate to indicate 'statement'. 竭 力 is a relation of 'determination' (in this case adjective and noun). 以 is a many-sided 'empty word' which is most simply translated as 'whereby', 'by which'. The 事 大 國 which follow it is a relation of 'direction' (i.e. verb and object). 則 is a sentence-connecting 'empty word', which makes the preceding sentence subordinate.

p 22 (16)
p 23 (17)
The Chinese script was first of all indispensable for the administration of the great country, which during the Han dynasty was even larger than today. That it demanded much time and hard work to master did not greatly matter. Literacy, once acquired, was the passport p 23 (18) to power and influence.

Since brush and ink had become the most important p 17 (1 tools in their daily work, the officials took them up as a leisure activity as well. They attached great importance not only to writing the characters correctly, but also to writing them in a graceful, flowing hand in which the various strokes were smoothly run together. The three chief varieties of calligraphy are *k'ai*, 'square', *hsing*, p 22 (1 'running', and *ts'ao*, 'cursive'. Closely connected with p 20 calligraphy is ink painting. When a poem written in (10, 11 artistic calligraphy decorates a painting, three art-forms, all executed with the same tools, are combined.

Chinese poetry exploits to the utmost the lack of word-classes and inflexion in the language. The poems have a laconic brevity which largely discards 'empty words'. Through this terseness the authors have created a style of evocative beauty. Two lines from an eight-line poem by the famous Li Po will illustrate this:

綠 樹　　　　閒 歌 鳥
green tree　　hear sing bird

青 樓　　　　見 舞 人
blue pagoda　see dance person.

Nothing is told about who hears the singing bird or sees the dancing person.

Written Chinese is not, however, a purely visual language. The poems are rhymed, and this is easy, because the range of syllabic finals (vowel, or vowel plus consonant) is limited. The tonal values of syllables have played an important part in the rhythmical patterns of poetry from the time of the T'ang dynasty (618–909) onwards.

Prose literature used many of the same stylistic means as poetry: parallelism, brevity, few 'empty words', and often rhymes. It consisted normally of short pieces of a page or two. Fiction or stories, which first appeared in written form under the T'ang dynasty, were not regarded as proper literature until modern times, nor were novels, which made their first appearance under the Ming dynasty (1368–1644), because both paid more attention to the story than to the style. The difference between the language of the highly artistic literature and the spoken language increased.

Whereas a Chinese character is unambiguous in meaning, the spoken syllables have developed towards greater simplicity of sound, and there are a great number of homophones with completely different meanings today. This has led to the use of an increasing number of disyllabics in the spoken language.

Modernization

Under the impact of the Western countries since the 19th century, the Chinese little by little realized that they had to modernize in order to survive. The traditional examinations in classical literature for admittance to positions in the administration were abolished, and Western literature was translated into Chinese.

The literary May Fourth movement of 1919 had as its programme the creation of a new Chinese literature in *pai-hua*, 'plain language'. This partly follows the line of the formerly disregarded Chinese novels and is partly inspired by Western fiction. Some members of the movement regarded it as a means of awakening the Chinese people, of making them politically aware. But this hope was doomed to failure, since the people could not read and had no possibility of learning to read. To reach the people, Mao Tse-tung in the 1940s encouraged revolutionary authors to write plays which could be performed in the villages.

After 1950 the fight to overcome illiteracy began with the simplification of the most frequently occurring complicated characters, often using 'cursive' forms—an evolution which is still going on. A character like 農, 'farmer', is now 农, and 廠, 'factory', is now written 厂. With a knowledge of about 800 characters, a Chinese can express far more than an Englishman with 800 English words because of the great freedom of combination in Chinese. Chinese literature today is written in the uncomplicated spoken language of the people. Only political slogans are expressed in the terse style of the old literary language, usually in four characters, such as 百花齐放, [Let] hundred flowers blossom'. The characters still remain better suited to the language than any romanization.

But difficulties arose when words and conceptions with no counterpart in Chinese had to be translated from foreign languages. They were first encountered at the introduction of Buddhism into China in the early centuries AD. Proper names and philosophical terms were transcribed phonetically, the characters representing only the sound, not the meaning of the word. The Sanskrit word Mahāmāya was rendered 摩訶摩耶. Today it would be pronounced mo-ho-mo-ye, but would mean 'rub-blame-rub-what', which has no meaning at all. The most common Buddhist transcriptions were gradually abbreviated to disyllabics, a familiar construction in Chinese. Western words have raised the same problems since the 19th century. Should they be transcribed, or was it possible to translate them? A railway train was translated as 火車, 'fire-carriage', but a tank was transcribed as 坦克, *t'an-k'e*, 'be flat-overcome'. For a long time the practice was chaotic, but the tendency is more and more to translate the meaning, and when this cannot be done, as it cannot with proper names, then the most common are abbreviated to disyllabics, such as 英國, *ying-kuo*, 'brave country' for England.

Chinese exported

The influence of Chinese on other languages was far greater than the reverse. In Vietnam, Korea, and Japan the Chinese characters have been the standard script for many centuries, and all current Chinese words became loan-words in these countries, in the same way as Latin words became loan-words in English, only on a much larger scale.

Vietnam was a Chinese colony from 207 BC to AD 939, and during this long period the language of its administration as well as a considerable part of its literature was Chinese. When Vietnam gained its independence in the 10th century, this was mainly a political change, for Vietnam had been lastingly influenced by Chinese culture.

The Vietnamese language belongs to the same language group as the Chinese, the Sino-Austric. It is monosyllabic and the syllables have tonal values. Therefore it was easy to adapt the Chinese characters for purely Vietnamese words to represent either sound or meaning. But the Vietnamese went even further. They created new characters for native words according to the 'phonetic compound' method. These characters do not exist in Chinese and are not understood by a Chinese.

When Catholic missionaries from Europe began to work in Vietnam in the 16th and 17th centuries, they needed a writing system that could be easily taught to a great number of people. A transcription into roman letters was worked out by Alexander de Rhodes, who in 1651 published an Annamese-Portuguese-Latin dictionary in Rome, based on the Portuguese values of the Latin alphabet. This came into increasing use among Christians, but it was not until 1910 that the French administration in Vietnam required all public documents to be transcribed according to the system of the missionaries.

Korea was more or less politically dependent on China from the 1st century BC until the Japanese occupation in 1895. During this long period it was strongly influenced by Chinese culture, and it used the Chinese language both in administration and in literature, much as Latin was used in medieval Europe. The Korean language is fundamentally different from Chinese. It is polysyllabic, and it has word-classes and inflexion.

With Confucianism and Buddhism, Chinese texts in great numbers came to Korea in the 4th century AD, and many Chinese expressions became loan-words in Korean. Some scholars estimate that as much as 90 per cent of the Korean vocabulary today is of Chinese origin. But the Koreans had to write native names with Chinese characters, and thus had to use them for their phonetic values in the same way as foreign loan-words, from Sanskrit or from English, were written in Chinese.

In about the 10th century the Koreans invented an ingenious phonemic script for writing their own language. The phonemes were grouped together in syllables forming a square. The syllables were arranged in series to write a whole word with greater space between the words than between the syllables.

But so strong was the Chinese influence that the Chinese script remained the official one. It was not until after World War II that North Korea abandoned the Chinese characters, and it now exclusively uses its own phonemic script, whereas South Korea still uses many Chinese characters interspaced with Korean writing.

22 (16)
23 (18)

23 (19)

23 (20)
p 24
21, 22,
23)

The case of Japan

Japan was never politically dependent on China, but since the 4th century it has been under a strong Chinese influence, and this grew stronger as Japan adapted the Chinese characters for writing Japanese. Chinese was introduced to Japan through Korea in the 3rd century, and Korean must have been the language through which most of the new techniques of literacy were brought to Japan.

Japanese, like Korean, is as different from Chinese as is English. The difficulties of writing Japanese with Chinese characters are as great as if one were to use them for writing English. The Japanese used the Chinese characters in the same two ways as did the Koreans. They could write the character corresponding to the meaning of a Japanese word, as 人 for instance, for *hito*, 'man'. The use of a Chinese character to represent the meaning of a Japanese word is called by the Japanese the *kun* reading of a character.

All the inflexions and grammatical particles were written with characters whose pronunciation was roughly similar to the Chinese pronunciation of the same characters. The Japanese particle *no*, often equivalent to the English 'of', was written with the Chinese character 乃 , *nai*, meaning 'your'. This phonetic use of the Chinese characters is called by the Japanese *man'yōgana,* after the *Manyōshū,* an 8th-century collection of poems which is written in this way; '-gana' means phonetic script.

After the establishment of direct contact with China from the 7th century onwards, Chinese teachers came to Japan and brought about great changes in Japanese society. Government was reformed according to Confucian ideas, and Buddhism gained an enormous influence at court. A great number of Chinese words were incorporated in the Japanese language. These loan-words were pronounced according to the Japanese conception of Chinese pronunciation at the time and within the limit of sounds in the Japanese language. The 'Chinese' reading of a character is called its *on* reading.

The loan-words came in two big waves. The first (about AD 600) is called *go'on;* the second (about AD 800) is *kan'on. Kan'on* was the pronunciation of Chinese in the T'ang capital Ch'ang-an. Whether *go'on* reflects a dialect or just an earlier stage of pronunciation is uncertain, but the two ways of pronunciation are as different as Dutch and English. Many common loan-words are blends of the two systems. In the name of the old imperial capital Kyoto, 'Kyo-' is *go'on* and '-to' is *kan'on.* It is impossible to know from looking at the characters how they are pronounced.

The standard 'square' form of writing the characters was used in official documents, but letters and poems were written in the flowing, 'cursive' form called *hiragana,* or 'smooth' *kana.* During a short period after 901 the Japanese *kana* syllabary developed as a script deriving from a Chinese origin, a development peculiar to Japan. Simultaneously with the *hiragana* syllabary another similar system was created. Today this is called *katakana* or 'square' *kana. Katakana,* too, derives from *man'yōgana,* but it has developed from segments of Chinese characters rather than from cursive script.

The Japanese syllables are few and simple. Five different vowels and nine initial consonants which combine to make fifty syllables form the whole stock. The final -n is later, and added to the fifty. In *hiragana,* 无 became の , and in *katakana* ノ . At that time *kana* was the normal medium for writing texts in the Japanese language. The early *kana* as well as *man'yōgana* were polyvalent, which suited the aesthetic tastes of the Heian period (794–1185). The simple one-sign-to-one-syllable *kana* which are used today were not standardized until some time after 1868.

The *kana* syllabaries were and are completely sufficient as a phonemic notation for the Japanese language in all its features. Nevertheless even today they are used only as supplementary writing systems in conjunction with Chinese characters.

There are two reasons for this. One is that it was natural to write the great number of Chinese loan-words in Chinese characters. It helped to identify them as loan-words. The other, less logical, reason was the habit of reading Chinese texts as if they were Japanese. During the Heian period, Chinese and Japanese were often treated as if they were the same language and thus the two writing systems became entangled with each other, as indeed they still are today. Heian literature reflects the enormous leisure enjoyed by the upper classes, who seem to have spent their time writing poems and letters which were as ambiguous as possible. Chinese characters, *man'yogana* or *hiragana,* were used to represent meaning or sound at random; the characters were chosen for their aesthetic value or in accordance with the space available.

Today Chinese characters are used for Chinese loan-words and for Japanese words as well. For a Japanese word the character is used as a *kun* writing for that portion of the inflected form which does not change, followed by the inflections written in *hiragana. Katakana* is used mainly for transcribing foreign words, and these are often abbreviated. Thus on a hairdresser's signboard one sees パ ー マ , *pā-ma,* for permanent wave.

The script reform of 1945 aimed at reducing the number of Chinese characters to 1,850. But for a Japanese to be familiar with this number of Chinese characters is a far greater task than for a Chinese to master the same number, since in Japanese most characters have several *kun* and several *on* readings. The character list was edited in haste and is far from sufficient for writing many names, even such common names as Sato and Kamakura. Some characters were abbreviated in accordance with 'cursive' forms. However, these are not identical with the abbreviated characters in the People's Republic of China, and, since they are used indiscriminately together with the old forms, each form has to be learnt. Furthermore, technical and scholarly writing pays no attention to the list.

The temptation to use Chinese characters for ambiguous writing seems irresistible. Especially in personal names it is a game to use uncommon readings of the characters. In cases where readings of names have to be stated clearly, they are transcribed in *furigana,* small *kana* on the right-hand side of the characters. The old system of writing Japanese with Chinese characters has shown itself incredibly durable.

II 'THE MIDDLE KINGDOM'

*Chinese politics and society from
the Bronze Age to the Manchus*

D. C. TWITCHETT

Our celestial empire possesses all things in prolific abundance.

Emperor Ch'ien-lung to Lord Macartney, 1793

'The people are as far from the Emperor as from Heaven', says a Chinese proverb—a saying that highlights the polarity of traditional Chinese civilization: on the one hand the people, peasant farmers working the land, on whom everything depended; on the other the court, the small ruling class headed by the Emperor, with whose actions written history was almost exclusively concerned. This detail from a 17th-century painting shows an encounter that only infrequently took place. K'ang-hsi (on the right), one of the early Ch'ing emperors, goes on a progress and the inhabitants of a poor village come out to greet him.

The two extremes had politically almost no contact. Between them stood the ranks of China's age-old bureaucracy, with its hierarchy of levels, its regulations covering every aspect of life, its resistance to change. Sustained by the Confucian ethical code which itself demanded a rigid social structure and an ordered sequence of duties and responsibilities, the bureaucracy gave to China what always most impressed Western observers before 1911—her stability.

The idea that China remained static and 'stagnant' for 3,000 years is a myth. Dynasties rose and fell; foreign invaders brought upheavals that sometimes lasted generations; science, technology and craftsmanship progressed by experiment and discovery; art styles changed; literature underwent subtle transformations; philosophy achieved new syntheses of ideas—all these will be examined in later chapters. Yet compared with the divided and tumultuous history of Europe, China does indeed present a picture of astonishing continuity. At whatever point in chronology one chooses, the basic features are the same. A few of these 'constants' are represented overleaf. (1)

駕昔邳州水荒

The Emperor ruled by a 'mandate' from Heaven. Above: Chao K'uang-yin, (T'ai-tsu) founder of the Sung Dynasty. (2)

The official (below) belonged to a class of gentlemen-scholars versed in the Classics. (3)

The peasant, representing the vast majority of the population, lived in his own village and knew little of life outside it. He entered recorded history only on the rare occasions when starvation drove him to revolt. His function was to support the land-owning gentry class through rents and the state through services and taxes. His status varied from independent farmer to tenancy and virtual slavery. (4)

The merchant and the artisan occupied the middle places in Confucian society, but in spite of restrictions, they continued to prosper. This detail from a scroll shows shops and tradesmen in Pien-ching during the 12th century. (5)

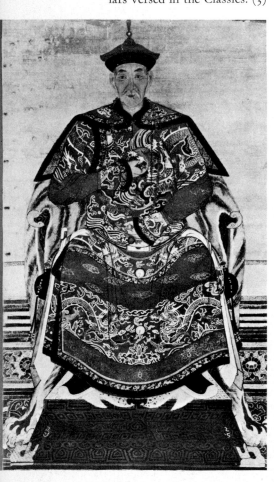

34

Public works were organized by the central government which could thus control the economic life of the country. Among them were canals, vital for both transport and irrigation. A vivid drawing (right) records the digging of a canal at Chung-mon in the 1830s. Hundreds of labourers toil with wheel-barrows and pumps, while the engineer (on horseback) supervises the work from the neck of land still left between the channel and the Yellow River. (7)

A monopoly of salt was one of the methods by which the government gained both money and power. Here bales of salt are being loaded on to boats for transport by river. (6)

Family units not only formed the basic components of society, but in Confucian theory reflected the same relations in microcosm. This family (right) is that of the donor at a 10th-century Buddhist shrine: man and wife in the centre, daughters left, sons right, grandchildren at the bottom. The whole painting is shown on p. 108. (8)

The first dynasty that can meaningfully be called Chinese was the Shang, dated by archaeology to approximately 1400–1100 BC. Already there were sizable cities and a developed state religion; writing was known (the inscribed bones illustrated in Chapter I belong to this period) and craftsmen were capable of superb work in bronze and semi-precious stone. Left: a bronze wine-vessel. Shaped like two rams back to back, it was probably used in rituals connected with ancestor worship. Below: a ceremonial blade of jade, with handle of turquoise on a bronze mount. (9, 11)

The human figure, unknown in Shang art, is still rare in that of its successor, the Chou. This boy on a frog (left) in bronze, dates from the period of the Late Eastern Chou. (10)

The Chou replaced the Shang about 1100 BC. From this time onwards written records prove the existence of a centralized state with a standing army and a civil service. Ceremonial religion seems to have declined but there was a greater awareness of the moral basis of authority. The idea of the 'mandate of Heaven', by which the ruler had to deserve his supremacy by governing well, is first encountered. The Chou nobility spent much of its time hunting or waging war. This painted shell (left) provides one of the earliest representations of the horse-drawn chariot. (12)

A new dynasty, the Han, succeeding the short-lived Ch'in, gave unity to China and inaugurated four hundred years of stable rule. Its founder was Liu Pang, a soldier of humble origins, seen in this 12th-century painting entering the city of Ch'ang-an. Gradually the old nobility was destroyed and a strictly centralized state set up, in which the emperor reigned through officials recruited on merit, not on social position. (14)

The Warring States is the name given to the period 403–221 BC when China was divided into innumerable independent states constantly at war with one another. Yet these years saw the growth of large cities and the evolution of the three great schools of Chinese philosophy, including Confucianism. This detail from a bronze wine-vessel (below) shows figures—possibly mythological—engaged in hunting. (13)

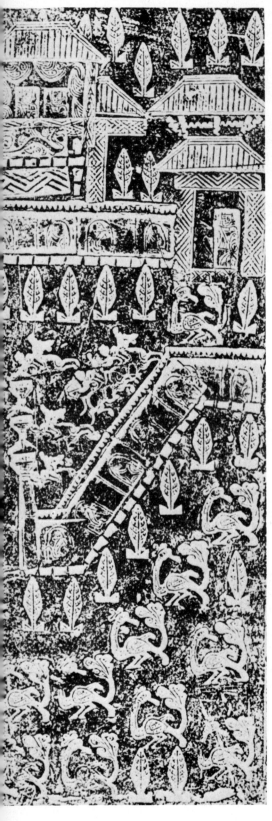

Life under the Han can be reconstructed in vivid detail both through literary sources and through pictures and models. At the time of the first census (AD 2) the population totalled nearly sixty million. The bulk of them lived on the land, in simple one-storey cottages (above left). But in the cities richer citizens were building up to five storeys (above right), with a courtyard in front and wide-spreading eaves. Both these clay models are from tombs. (16, 17)

A garden (left), impressed on hollow tiles forming part of the door panel of a tomb, has been skilfully made up from a dozen or so standard stamps: bird, tree, roof, etc. In the centre is a wall, with gate-piers; at the back, summerhouses. (15)

War was chiefly against the northern nomads and internal rebels. In 147 BC the old rulers of hereditary fiefs rose against the emperor and were finally crushed. In the 2nd century AD a large-scale popular rebellion broke out and in 220 the dynasty collapsed. The battle (below) shown in this woodcut (made from a rubbing) takes place on a bridge and in the water underneath. Weapons include swords, halberds and bows and arrows. (18)

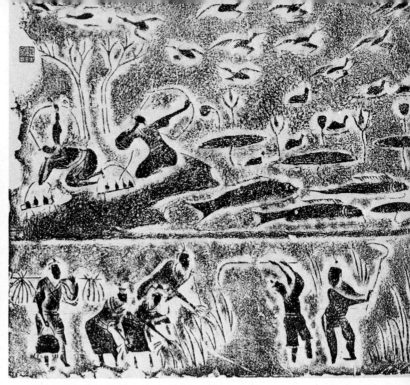

功曹車

沙徹車

賊曹車

Trade and industry: tile and brick rubbings showing scenes from daily life during the Han dynasty. Top left: stalls in a market. Top right: shooting geese and (lower register) reaping and threshing grain. Above left: pounding grain with tilt hammers and winnowing it by some sort of fan-board. Above: extracting salt from brine; the brine is raised from a well by pulleys on the left and conveyed by bamboo pipes to evaporating pans. (19–22)

From their imperial palace the Han emperors presided personally over their vast domain. Every law and every decision was issued on the sovereign's own authority. A conscientious emperor faced an immense load of business; a careless one delegated it to secretaries or to eunuchs. All were surrounded by court ceremonial of increasing splendour. This Han painting shows a scene in front of the palace. By artistic convention the interior audience hall is also visible. In the forecourt the imperial entourage sets off on a journey. (23)

The Han army was a force that no other power in Asia could challenge. The Ch'in had stabilized the northern frontier, built the Great Wall and pressed south as far as Vietnam. Han soldiers (left) completed and consolidated these conquests. (24)

Money came to play a vital part in the economy in Han times. The central administration was concerned that taxes should be paid in full and on time, and the prices of certain commodities, including salt, iron and liquor, were controlled. A surviving cash-box (right) dating from about the 2nd century AD, is made of glazed pottery with applied decoration in the form of coins. (25)

The rise of the T'ang Dynasty came in the 7th century AD, after four centuries of political upheaval. Just as the Han had taken over from the strong but short-lived dynasty of the Ch'in, so the T'ang took over from the Sui, which had similarly re-imposed unity on the country in less than forty years (AD 581–618). The T'ang was consolidated by T'ai Tsung (left), whose reign lasted from 626 to 649.

The T'ang state was run by a bureaucracy even more all-embracing than the Han. County magistrates were obliged to undergo re-examination in the Confucian Classics to decide whether they should be promoted, retained, or dismissed. Here (in a painting from a Ch'ing album) the Emperor Hsüan-tsung (712–756) is assessing the results. (26, 28)

Women enjoyed a position in T'ang society which they were not to regain until the present century. Works of literature, the familiar elegant pottery figurines (left) and the fact that a woman—the Empress Wu—once actually ruled the empire, all go to prove this. (27)

The Emperor Hsüan-tsung, faced with rebellion, fled from his palace in 756, taking with him the beautiful Yang Kuei-fei; but his soldiers, believing her to be involved in the revolt, killed her. In this painting (above) he appears on horseback, right foreground, about to cross a bridge. (29)

T'ang rule disintegrated in the 9th century. Local leaders, nominally Imperial Commissioners, ruled over virtually independent provinces. One of them had his tomb (left) decorated with paintings of his warlike retinue. (30)

Hsüan-tsung's court became a legend in later times. This 14th-century drawing shows his palace at Ch'ang-an, 'the Palace of Great Brilliance'. It is an artistic fantasy, but the palace certainly existed and has been excavated. (31)

T'ang justice was severe but considerably more humane than Han. This drawing of a scene of judgment and punishment in fact represents the afterlife but is a fair picture of a real court. During this period the Chinese legal code spread to Japan, Korea and Vietnam and remained substantially unchanged for five hundred years. (32)

A butcher's shop (late T'ang) from the caves of Tun-huang provides one of our few glimpses into urban life in the 9th century. (33)

Chinese houses of the T'ang period turned their backs on the outside world, just as Roman houses did. The main entrance, on the right, leads to a forecourt from which the main court is entered. In the foreground are stables. (34)

Waiting for the results: Civil Service examinations remained a constant feature of Chinese public life. The position occupied by an aristocracy in Europe was taken in China by the official class. (35)

A golden age of Chinese civilization came with the late T'ang and early Sung, though it corresponded with another period of political disturbance and dynastic change. Left: scenes from a festival at Kaifeng, which became the Sung capital—a later copy of a 12th-century painting. (36)

The Sung came to power after a confused period (907–960) known as the Ten Kingdoms and Five Dynasties. Its founder, T'ai-tsu (see pl. 2), was a general who seized the throne in 960 and reigned for sixteen years, subduing the other states and limiting the power of his own commanders. Right: a Sung official and his attendant. (37)

Domestic life was not dislocated by the dynastic rivalries, and after the T'ang China remained culturally one, even if politically divided. This wall-painting of a family at home comes from a tomb dating from 1099. Husband and wife sit at table laid with cups, saucers and a tankard. Behind them are lacquered screens and servants in attendance. (38)

The Yangtze basin had until the 8th century marked the approximate limit of Chinese culture. The centres of government had been in the north, though the south was already important economically and supplied the north with much of its food. After the 9th century, invasion and unrest caused a flow of immigrants into the southern provinces across the river, part of whose course is shown on this pictorial map. By the late Sung period the south outweighed the north politically, culturally and in population. (39)

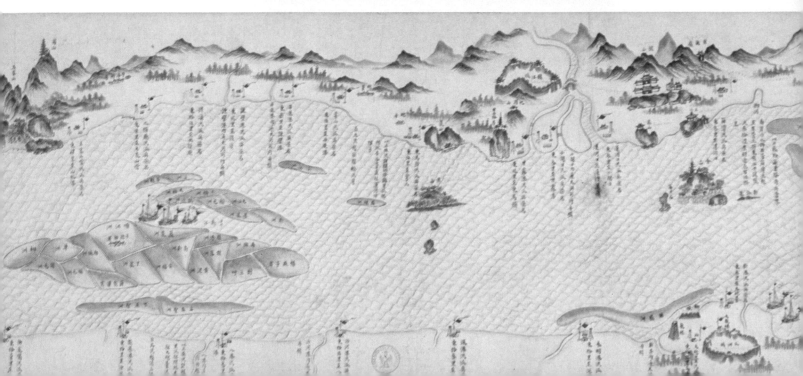

Sung government was more centralized than T'ang had been. All local affairs were strictly controlled from the capital. Left: scene from an Imperial feast given in a fortress after manoeuvres, 11th century. (40)

At the market: riverside stalls sell everything from fish to porcelain. At the bottom a noble lady and her child pass along, carried in a sedan chair. (41)

Rivers and canals were the major means of communication. Boat-building reached a high level of expertise; note the complicated rudder in this example. On the bank a merchant oversees the unloading of his cargo. (42)

The rich lands of the Yangtze basin could support an intensive new agriculture, which in turn fed the new cities of the region. In this painting small, carefully banked rice-fields are built up on each side of a lake. Complex irrigation was needed to keep them flooded to the right depth. On the right four men work a bucket-chain device for raising water, while on the left rice is being dried after reaping and stacked in two kinds of rick.

In the later 13th century, peace was rudely interrupted by the Mongol invasions and for a century (1279–1368) the empire was ruled by Khubilai Khan's alien dynasty. (43)

47

The Ming Emperors, who took over after the Mongol collapse in 1368, concentrated even greater power in their hands than their predecessors. Paradoxically, however, this eventually resulted not in strong government but in weakness and vacillation, since if the emperor was incompetent or unworldly (as was increasingly the case) decisions were left to court officials, and he became a figurehead surrounded by gorgeous ceremonial. This detail from a procession shows the approach of Wu-tsung (1506–21). (44)

Gentry families were the pillars on which society rested. Following a Confucian code, they took responsibility for many aspects of local government, education, public works, and the maintenance of moral standards. (45)

The Ming tombs near Peking, where the emperors were buried from 1424 onwards, are visible records of their splendour. This stone warrior (right) guards the processional way. (47)

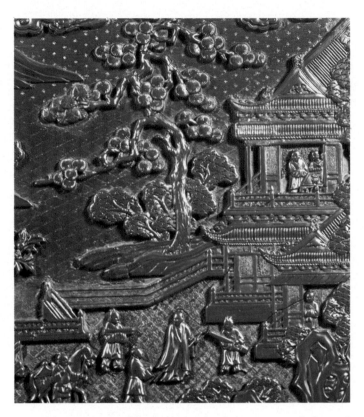

Luxury art: figures in a landscape, carved in red lacquer, early 15th century. (46)

Law and commerce: the lively scene of a magistrates court (below) is painted on the lid of a seal-box, *c.* 1600. Right: a Ming banknote. Excessive use of paper money had been one cause of the Mongols' downfall. (48, 49)

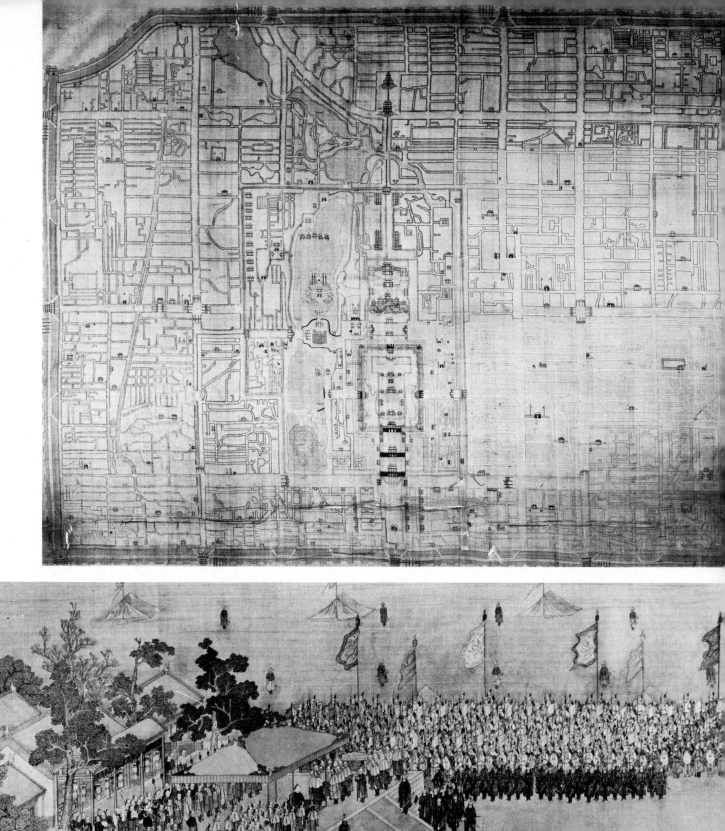

The city of Peking had been the Mongol capital and was adopted by the Ming. The Emperor Yunglo rebuilt it in 1421 as a series of rectangles one inside the other—first the outer walls, then the walls of the Imperial City, then those of the Forbidden City itself. (50)

The early Ch'ing proved to be administrators of genius, and had the advantage of a series of exceptionally gifted and long-lived emperors. Ch'ien-lung, who reigned for nearly sixty years (1736–95) is seen below left reviewing banner troops at Nanking. (51)

A model emperor like Ch'ien-lung would work harder than most of his subjects, dealing personally with every major decision and exhausting a whole team of secretaries. He was also a consummate military commander and in the 'Ten Great Campaigns' stabilized the frontier and suppressed rebels from Turkestan to Taiwan. This painting (top right) shows his camp on one journey to the southern provinces. (52)

The prosperity and peace achieved by the Ch'ing lasted until the middle of the 18th century. Population was rising but agriculture, though making few technical advances, kept pace with it. In this drawing the rice harvest is being brought in and stored. (53)

A crisis approached during the last half of the 18th century. Population now reached over 300 million, and agriculture found it increasingly difficult to provide enough food. The central administration was also weakening, yielding more and more to corruption and inertia. In the countryside unrest increased, leading to both popular movements of revolt and social banditry. Right: a party of bandits with their loot. (54)

Water has been the source of life throughout China's history. But China's rivers are treacherous, subject to flooding and catastrophic changes of course in which millions have perished. Above: building a dyke against the threatening waves of the Yellow Canal in the early Ch'ing period. Below: rice planting and cropping. The rice plant, having been raised from seed, is transplanted in ground flooded to a depth of 2–4 inches (below left). The rice itself is a grass-seed, like wheat, and is harvested (below right) in a similar way. (55–57)

Chinese politics and society from the Bronze Age to the Manchus

D. C. TWITCHETT

The duke of Chou, Wen Wang's fourth son, leads an expedition east; a modern illustration to the 'Book of Documents'. The Chou dynasty is the earliest for which reliable historical data is available. (1)

ALTHOUGH CHINA was the home of one of the very earliest forms of man, Peking Man, Chinese civilization as we know it is not particularly ancient. Evidence of continuous human occupation, and of an unbroken chain of continuous social development goes back only a few thousand years, and the origins of what can confidently be called a 'Chinese' form of culture are quite late when compared with the great civilizations of the Middle East, with India or with Egypt.

What is striking, in contrasting the Chinese record with that of the other ancient civilizations, is not so much its antiquity as its continuity. Our earliest written evidence dates back to the last part of the 2nd millennium BC. Since then we have a historical record which, for continuity, accuracy and reliable chronology, is unrivalled among other cultures. It is remarkable too for its consistency, and for the extraordinary pertinacity of certain basic attitudes which have led some western scholars to erect a myth of the 'unchanging nature' of Chinese society. The myth has some foundation: Chinese history and Chinese society and its institutions have some perennial features, have a pattern of development of their own. In the last three centuries their pace of change, by comparison with the totally abnormal speed of change in Western society since the 16th century, has indeed been slow. But within the framework of its own institutions Chinese history has been marked by dynamic and continual change and development. The 'stagnation' of Chinese society is a myth —whether expressed, for example, by Hegel, in terms of a 'state with no history'; or by Ranke as 'eternal standstill'; or formulated in somewhat more sophisticated terms by Chinese Marxist historians, who tend either to place China in a category of social development different from the norm (characterized by the 'Asiatic mode of production'), or simply to formulate the 'unchanging China' myth in more modern terms, by placing the whole of Chinese history from the 2nd century BC or earlier until the 19th or 20th century in a 'period of protracted feudal stagnation'. It is a totally misleading myth in that it attempts to measure change in Chinese society by a normative model provided by the West since the Renaissance.

If, however, one attempts an analysis of Chinese history in terms of the Chinese tradition, and of Chinese society and institutions, without constant reference to the inappropriate yardstick of Europe, it is clear that China was certainly as dynamic, evolving, changing a society as any other.

One reason for the overall impression of stability and lack of change immediately becomes clear when one considers the nature of the Chinese historical record. More than in the case of any other culture, the modern historian of China is dependent upon a complex, highly developed native historiographical tradition. This tradition has a number of features which dictate the sort of knowledge which we have of China's past. Firstly, it is official history, written 'for the record' by servants of the state. Above all it is 'political history'. It is essentially a record of the exercise of dynastic power by successive royal houses, and of the conduct of their administration. It is didactic history, applying the models of orthodox ethic and morality to the events of the past, destined to provide models of political conduct, both good and bad, for future rulers and for the officials through whom they would in turn rule. It is court-centred, and tells us little of what went on in the vastly varied provinces of the empire beyond the imperial capital. It is concerned exclusively with the conduct of the ruling class, in their role as agents of dynastic power: the ordinary people rarely appear, save as the passive objects of state policy, or when they are driven by hardship to rebellion.

This political record was normally based on records compiled from year to year, or reign by reign, and written for one dynasty at a time. It therefore has constantly seen history in terms of the dynastic span. In recent years its view of the past has been formulated in terms of a recurrent 'dynastic cycle', according to which each dynasty is founded, flourishes for a while, becomes over-ambitious, over-reaches itself, is beset by extravagance and corruption, which in turn lead to excessive demands on the population, resulting in disorder, rebellion and the fall of the dynasty and its replacement by another. Although such a 'dynastic cycle' does have a certain very limited validity it is obviously a very circumscribed view of history. It sees history in purely political terms. It breaks up history into short dynastic time spans which are considered as self-contained, each with its own intern-

According to classical theory, dynasties reigned by the 'mandate of Heaven', and this could be won and retained only by moral virtue. Here the ideal first emperor of the Shang dynasty, Ch'eng T'ang, worships Heaven. When he ascended the throne, says the Book of Documents, 'he was found to be full of benevolence not only towards his human subjects but also towards the animal world.' (2)

A corrupt emperor forfeited the mandate of Heaven and the dynasty could no longer claim its subjects' loyalty. Above: the last emperor of the Shang, the tyrant Chou-hsin, with his concubine, Ta-chi, who is said to have led him into sadism and dissipation. In the foreground is one of her more extravagant ideas, a pond of wine around which the dissolute courtiers reel and stagger. (3)

al pattern of political development, but with little connection with any long-term conception of historical change. Unfortunately traditional historiography rarely attempted to venture beyond the time span of a dynasty, and when it did, tended to view long-term change in such political terms as consideration of the 'legitimacy of succession' of one dynasty after another.

This is not to deny that dynastic periods often have a clear-cut character of their own. It makes perfectly good historical sense to talk about Han or T'ang or Ming China not simply in terms of political continuity and state institutions, but also as clearly defined periods in cultural history with a style and an ethos of their own. What follows is my personal attempt to correlate the traditional political outline of history with a pattern of long-term social and economic secular change.

From legend to history: Hsia, Shang and Chou

Traditional Chinese history began with an era of cultural hero-kings, followed by the 'Three Dynasties' of antiquity, the Hsia, the Shang and the Chou. These periods constituted for later historians and writers on politics a sort of 'golden age' of simple ideal forms of government and social organization to which the man of later and more degenerate times could look back for an inexhaustible fund of models for human conduct. What we actually know about these periods is however very little. About the Hsia we know nothing, save that we have a list of its kings, and that the Chinese as early as the beginning of the 1st millennium BC believed in its existence. Until the beginning of this century, the same could also have been said of the Shang, but here the traditional list of kings and other details of the traditional historical account

were borne out in surprising detail when the site of its last capital at An-yang was discovered and excavated, revealing a vast number of oracles and records inscribed on bones. Half-hearted attempts have been made to equate the legendary Hsia with one or other of the pre-Shang Neolithic cultures revealed by the archaeologists, but there is no measure of agreement about any of them, and at present our detailed knowledge of Chinese history begins with the records recovered from An-yang and other Shang sites which have been discovered subsequently.

The society of Shang was already recognizably Chinese, and already had reached a high level of material culture and social organization. The Shang, to judge from archaeological evidence, had its major centres in northern Honan, while its influence spread out into southern Hopei, Shantung, southern Shansi and eastern Shensi, and to some extent into northern Anhwei. The Shang occupied successively at least seven capital cities, two of which at Cheng-chou and An-yang have been carefully excavated. They were of considerable size, occupying several square kilometres, and consisted of a large nuclear area containing the ritual and ceremonial buildings and the residences of the nobility, surrounded by many separate communities of farmers and of specialized groups of artisans.

p 36 (9, 11)

The written record of the Shang period is extensive. Over 40,000 bone inscriptions have been published to date, varying from single characters to quite long texts. But they are singularly intractable as historical material, being mostly oracular questions on which a king required supernatural advice. They thus give a far from balanced picture of court life since many important routine matters would never have come into question in such a way.

Moreover they are written in a script which is still imperfectly understood, and many of the personal and place names are impossible to identify. Only recently has it become possible to attempt to produce any sort of coherent picture from them. The Shang state seems to have been a loose confederation of clan domains, some of them little more than village settlements. The capital was the 'Great Domain' of the king, who maintained a considerable court of functionaries, and must have been supported by considerable revenues. There is also evidence that the capital city was the centre of a rather extensive network of trade.

With the successors to the Shang, the Chou, we are on somewhat firmer ground, for with the end of the 2nd millennium BC begin the earliest pieces of preserved literature, the *Book of Documents* and the *Book of Poetry*, and the historian also has at his disposal a wealth of detailed inscriptions from ritual bronzes. The Chou had begun as a client state on the western borders of Shang, only partially sharing in the high culture of Shang. Some scholars believe that they were ethnically a distinct people. The Chou conquered the Shang by military force just before the beginning of the 1st millennium BC, and after suppressing a rebellion aimed at a Shang restoration sent expeditions into eastern China. They eventually exercised some degree of sovereignty over a considerably wider area than the Shang, covering all of Honan, Shantung, Hopei, all but the extreme north of Shansi, and the southeastern half of Shensi. The Chou, unlike their predecessors, are known to us not simply by their artifacts, and as a distribution of archaeological sites on the map, backed up by a large but cryptic literature of oracular documents. They have left a literature which enables us to gain a picture of their social and political organization in some detail.

The early Chou state was divided into many domains. Many of these were in the possession of the king and of his clan, and supported him and his court. Others were given as fiefs to the nobility which had assisted him to power, to his most meritorious subjects, and as emoluments to the hereditary holders of certain offices at his court. Enfiefment was a solemn religious act enjoining loyalty to the king upon the enfiefed lord. The king could transfer a domain from one lord to another, and frequently did so. The enfiefed lords in their turn let out some of their domains to their own subordinates.

The king parcelled out sovereignty to this great number of petty lords, delegating to them his royal power, and the term for such enfiefment, *feng-chien*, which in modern times has been used as a translation of our term 'feudalism', came to be used in traditional Chinese political thought to express the idea of decentralized, delegated political authority. He seems, nevertheless, to have maintained a considerable degree of real power in his own hands. Although he depended on his enfiefed nobles to assist him with their levies of troops in time of war, he nevertheless maintained powerful royal armies which could counterbalance any threat posed by a vassal lord against the crown. He levied some forms of taxation and tribute from the various fiefs, and he administered justice. There was almost certainly no law code, but there was a generally accepted body of recognized laws, backed by long usage, many of which were inherited from the Shang.

Warfare was perhaps the most constant strain upon the resources of the state. There were constant campaigns against the non-Chinese peoples who surrounded the Chou domain, and against rebellious local lords. Warfare was largely seasonal, conducted after the year's productive work on the land was completed, though occasionally a campaign might drag on into winter. The armies consisted of a nucleus of nobles fighting from two-wheeled chariots, supported by a throng of peasant foot soldiers. Essential training for war were the great seasonal hunts held in the spring, when the nobles could practise their skills with bow and lance, and the peasants, acting as beaters, could be drilled and become accustomed to disciplined movement. The state was essentially the king's domain, and its government was merely the government of a great domain on a larger scale. A wide range of administrative matters were dealt with by the various personal household officers of the king, much as power was exercised in our own medieval period by chancellors

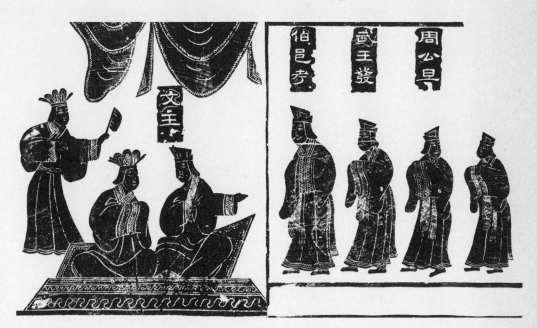

Rubbings from a Han tomb showing Wen Wang (seated, pointing) with his sons, of whom the second, Wu Wang, was the founder of the Chou. (4)

6 (10)

p 37 (12)

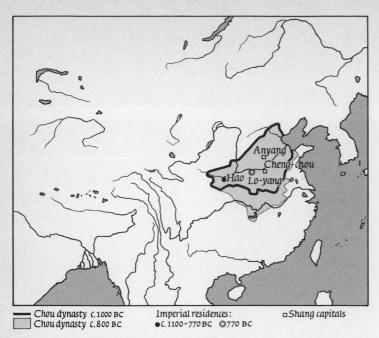

The extent of Chinese civilization during the Chou dynasty. (5)

Chou dynasty c.1000 BC
Chou dynasty c.800 BC

Imperial residences:
●c.1100-770 BC ◎770 BC

□Shang capitals

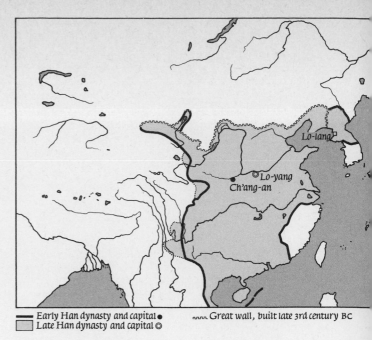

China under the Han dynasty. (6)

Early Han dynasty and capital●
Late Han dynasty and capital◎

ᗤᗤᗤ Great wall, built late 3rd century BC

and chamberlains and lords high steward. In Chou, the steward *(shan-fu)*, master of the royal table, and the intendant *(tsai)* who was the king's agent in charge of his individual domains, acting as a sort of temporary regent while his master was absent, both came to exercise many important functions of state.

Among the documents which have come down to us from this period are a series of pronouncements which embody the conception of political authority current at the time. These documents, later incorporated in a collection of texts known as the *Book of Documents (Shu-ching)* became one of the canonical books of orthodox Confucianism, and the basic ideas enshrined in them continued throughout later history to play an important role in political thought. Most important of these concepts is that of the 'mandate of Heaven' *(T'ien-ming)*. The early Chou kings believed that they had received the approval of Heaven—the supreme deity in their complex pantheon of natural forces, heavenly deities and local gods—to act as ruler over 'all under Heaven' *(T'ien-hsia)*, and to be Heaven's intermediary between Heaven and earth and its people. This was not a Divine Right, nor were the Chou royal house in any way divine, although like many other noble houses they claimed a divine first ancestor. Heaven's mandate could be taken away, should the king either break the pattern of accepted moral conduct expected by Heaven, or treat his people with undue harshness. This theory of the state placed great stress on the continuance of tried and tested institutions, on policy which would not disturb the norms of established order, on compliance with a natural order of human society, which was itself considered as an organic part of the natural order of the universe.

In Shang and Chou times the state was a highly religious one. The kings spent much of their time, and a large part of their revenues, in a complex series of religious rites, sacrifices to Heaven and a whole range of lesser deities, and sacrifices to their own ancestors, for they, like the lords of lesser families, felt themselves temporary representatives not only of the royal succession endorsed by Heaven's mandate, but also as temporarily charged with

the fortunes of their family, which was, like the state, either 'accumulating virtue' through their good conduct of its affairs, or losing it.

After about 800 BC the fervent religious atmosphere of the earlier times was gradually dissipated. No longer were the oracles constantly consulted. No longer was the ceremonial so solemn. No longer were the rites accompanied by massive slaughter of sacrificial victims. No longer were great lords interred along with servants, womenfolk, horses and all the paraphernalia of state pomp. The very idea of Heaven itself gradually changed, from being a wrathful anthropomorphic god personally involved and concerned in human affairs into an impersonal supreme force of nature. But the concept of Heaven's mandate as the justification of temporal authority remained a powerful force in political thought throughout the ages. The exercise of power in accordance with moral ethical norms meeting Heaven's approval, not the use of coercive force, was the way the mandate could be kept. Loss of the mandate by a reigning dynasty was the justification claimed for rebellion, and for its replacement by a new royal house.

The society over which these early kings and their enfiefed vassal lords exercised authority was still a rather primitive one. Archaeological evidence shows that, as in later times, differing social groups at widely differing stages of development lived side by side, and there were clearly wide differences between one region and another. Most of our written evidence derives from the *Book of Poetry*, a collection of poems dating from 1000 to 600 BC, which like the *Book of Documents* later became a canonical text. Many of the later poems in this collection describe everyday life, although this is ordinary life seen through a courtly pastoral convention, rather than folk poetry.

The people seem to have lived in separate communities on the various domains, each of which included not only simple peasants, but the various specialized artisans necessary to local self-sufficiency and the various servants who provided the needs of the lord or his representative the intendant *(tsai)*. In the winter the peasants lived in the walled enclosure of the domain built around the lord's

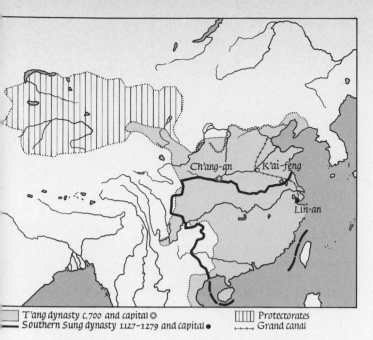

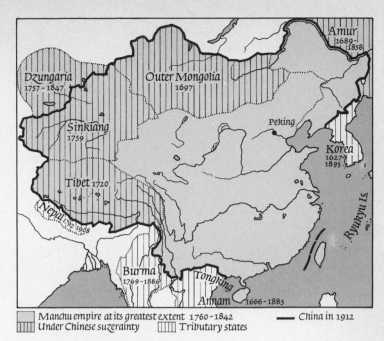

China under the T'ang and Southern Sung dynasties. (7)

China under the Ch'ing dynasty. (8)

residence. In the spring they went out and lived in temporary shacks in those parts of the domain which were to be cultivated. Most land was still cultivated by shifting agriculture, new land being regularly cleared for cultivation and exhausted fields allowed to lie fallow and revert to scrub. Within the areas cleared for cultivation the fields were divided into long strips allocated to the individual peasants, who worked these for themselves, and also worked in common other lands whose produce went to the lord. Work was organized by a domain overseer, and was carried on in common. Techniques of cultivation were primitive, employing a digging stick with a stone point, which was used by a pair of peasants. The staple grains were various types of millet, but a variety of beans and vegetable crops were also grown, and herds of animals were kept in the wild bush surrounding the cultivated areas. Hunting and gathering still provided some large part of the needs, not only of the peasants, but of the noble families.

Various handicrafts were well established. In the capital cities were artisans in bronze, capable of manufacturing vessels and implements whose beauty and craftsmanship have rarely been equalled. But metal was used almost exclusively for ritual vessels, for domestic utensils for the great nobles, and for weapons. Only a handful of bronze tools have been discovered, and these are likely to have been ceremonial in function—early equivalents of the silver trowel with which Lords Mayor lay foundation-stones. If the early Chou nobility was a metal-using culture with a very sophisticated bronze technology, the ordinary population was still living a life little different from that of its Neolithic forebears, using implements of stone, wood and bone and living in semi-subterranean pit-dwellings.

The comparatively strong and stable state of the early Chou seems to have fallen into a decline rather quickly. About 770 a series of internal disorders forced the Chou kings to leave their ancestral homeland in the north-western Wei valley, which was over-run by 'barbarians'— that is people not fully assimilated to the Chinese culture of the time. By the end of the century the Chou, now

settled in the east, around their old secondary capital at Lo-yang, were more or less on a level with their former vassal kingdoms. Soon afterwards they were virtually powerless, still recognized as the holders of religious pre-eminence but increasingly lacking any effective authority.

The Warring States
In place of the comparative peace and stability of the early Chou, there now began a period of constant warfare between the various states which had previously been their vassals. In the period 722–464, the period known in traditional historiography as the Ch'un-ch'iu era, after the name of the chronicle of the period which was attributed to Confucius, there were only thirty-eight years of peace. When effective Chou authority ceased at the end of the 8th century BC there were well over a hundred independent states, many of them miniscule, and before 464 no less than 110 had been extinguished and incorporated into one or other of the major regional states. Actual authority on a regional scale was exercised briefly in the 7th century by the eastern state of Ch'i, centred on Shantung (after 667 BC) and then by the Chin centred in Shansi (from 632), who were recognized as 'hegemons' leading a solemn oath-bound alliance of other states. In the 6th century Ch'u, a southern state with its centre in the Han and Yangtze valleys, focus of a distinct southern style of Chinese culture and thought of by the other states as only partly Chinese, was the paramount military power. But these alliances, for all the solemn oaths with which the parties were bound, often ended with the weaker allies incorporated with the stronger, and the successive hegemonies did little to establish lasting peace or restore a stable political order.

Many of the campaigns were on a rather small scale however, and warfare during this period was not notably destructive. None save the handful of the largest kingdoms had the resources to mount a protracted campaign. The armies comprised a small force of nobility mounted in chariots backed up by an ill-armed crowd of peasants on foot. Warfare was conducted between the nobles according to rigid conventions something like a code of

6 (10)

chivalry, with personal duels between individual champions.

While territorial authority was thus gradually concentrated in fewer and fewer states, Chinese influence was slowly being extended into the north-east and into the south of Manchuria, and into the lower Yangtze valley and the Yangtze delta region. Within the old centres of Chinese settlement there are signs of pressure of population on the land and of the exhaustion of natural resources. Gradually agriculture was becoming more settled, as there was less and less land for the old continually shifting cultivation.

Within the new states, the old feudal hierarchy, based on acts of allegiance and personal links between the king and his noble families, tended to break down and to be replaced by a system in which the families of the great officers who exercised the administrative functions within the states competed for power both with their rulers and with the old enfiefed nobility, sometimes ending in civil war. Over and over again ministers usurped the power of their ruler, allied themselves with other families, and engineered *coups d'état*. Gradually the rulers began to replace ministers who exercised hereditary functions and who had their own groups of client clans, by functionaries recruited for their personal ability from among the lesser members of the aristocracy, the *shih* (sometimes translated as 'knights') who had filled minor positions in government. These, unlike the hereditary ministers, owed their personal loyalty to the ruler, and were not in a position to act as natural leaders of an opposition to him.

By the middle of the 5th century BC the effective powers had been whittled down to seven major kingdoms, and a period of ever more bloody warfare now began. Although during the Warring States period (463–221) there were rather more years of peace than in the earlier period, war when it came was fought, not as a noble chivalric diversion conducted according to set rules between comparatively small forces, but in deadly earnest between massive well trained armies. Three developments changed the face of war: first was the growth of armies of trained infantry to replace the chariot forces of earlier times. The great states, which by now had become far more prosperous, tightly organized and populous, began to recruit and train vast armies of peasant infantry. These were regularly drilled, and adequately armed by a state wealthy enough to manufacture arms on a mass scale. The introduction of the crossbow towards the end of the 5th century, and the gradual introduction of iron weapons made warfare far more lethal. From the 5th century onwards the chariot played less and less of a role in war. Finally, at the end of the 4th century BC, cavalry, practising mounted archery, were introduced from among the Hsiung-nu, China's formidable neighbours in the northern steppe zone. The new cavalry provided a degree of mobility and surprise far superior to the cumbersome chariot forces of earlier times.

Warfare on this scale, warfare aimed at territorial aggrandizement and the annexation of rival states, was only possible in a state with a centralized administration efficient enough to organize the conscription of such formidable man-power, and even more to organize the logistic support and the provision of arms for forces on such a scale. In response to these needs, the various states

began to replace the old feudal system, under which territorial authority was delegated to hereditary nobles, by a system of territorial divisions ruled over by career officials, appointed by the king from among his own cadre of tested administrators. This system of 'counties' *(hsien)* under centralized control was begun in the border states of Ch'u and Ch'in, where the old enfiefed territorial nobility was gradually extinguished. The effective political power at the various royal courts also passed from hereditary ministers to professional political advisers and career functionaries. Further means to a stronger and more efficient state were the systems of centrally controlled taxation and corvée service which now became universal, and the complex systems of codified law designed to impose a rigorous social discipline and a rigid conformity to acceptable norms of social behaviour.

All this impressive, centralized state apparatus depended upon an almost equally impressive increase in agrarian productivity. The introduction of iron about 500 BC meant that Chinese agriculture, which was still virtually unaffected by the millennium of sophisticated bronze technology, went straight from a primitive Neolithic stage to the Iron Age. The Chinese developed from the earliest stage a technique for the manufacture of cast iron implements, which could be easily and cheaply mass-produced both by the state and by large scale industrialists. Besides weapons, archaeology has already retrieved a wide variety of iron implements from this period, spades, hoes, plough coulters, sickles, axes and saws. The use of iron implements meant that much deeper cultivation and much more widespread clearing of forest cover was now possible. Shortly afterwards, in the 4th or 3rd century, animal power also began to be employed in cultivation. New crops, among them wheat, were also introduced, which were more prolific, if less hardy, than the traditional pulses and millets.

The new forms of efficient administration, coupled with these new techniques, led to a rapid colonization of lands which had previously been impossible to farm with the primitive techniques of antiquity. Large-scale mobilization of labour made possible extensive irrigation works, and flood control and drainage projects. State intervention deliberately settled peasants and members of the displaced noble families in newly colonized areas, where their communities were organized to be directly dependent on the state and its local administrative units. The old domain communities with their strong internal coherence and family ties were broken up; the lands which had been cleared for cultivation and worked in common were now broken up into individual holdings, and personal possession of land became the accepted norm.

The economic life of earlier times had been largely confined to small enclosed self-sufficient local communities, whose marginal surpluses went to support the noble ruling class. What little trade there was was confined to the provision of necessities for the few great cities, and was mostly carried on by barter. The only currency was provided by cowrie shells. In the early period, the peasant had met his dues to the lord of his domain by the performance of labour duties. From the 6th century onwards taxation, usually levied in grain, became normal. The peasant who now had possession of his own land in many cases had also lost the protection formerly afforded him by the close community of the domain. Heavy taxation, added to conscription for military service or for corvée labour on public works, aggravated the insecurity of life produced by a still primitive agriculture in a far from favourable environment. The areas of north China in which most of this early history was played out were subject to violent extremes of climate, bitterly cold winters and hot summers, with little rain, and to frequent natural disasters, flood, drought, wind storms, plagues of insects. The individual peasant and his family, as we know from abundant evidence from the 4th century BC onwards, lived a life of constant insecurity, just above the level of subsistence, under the constant threat of indebtedness and the necessity of disposing of his land and of becoming a tenant or a hired hand.

Nevertheless, a far greater surplus of production was available than in earlier times, and trade began to increase rapidly. Communications improved, as several of the states devoted much effort to the construction of roads, and in the south of canals and waterways. These were built primarily for strategic reasons, but were also available for travelling merchants. As the stable internal administration of the few great states improved, the general level of law and order made travel far less risky. At the same time we begin to hear of regional specialization in the production both of natural products and of manufactures, and to have an impression of wide-scale distribution, not only of luxury products, but of more common commodities such as salt and metal implements. The growth of trade was greatly aided by the appearance from the 6th century BC onwards in all of the major states of a variety of copper coinages. By the end of the 4th century, the use of money is mentioned as commonplace in all parts of the country. With the rapid growth of trade a prosperous merchant class made its appearance and individual merchants even played an important role in politics. These merchants were able to achieve power and influence without either owning land and exploiting the labour of its cultivators, or giving service to the state, the acceptable roads to wealth and influence in traditional society and in the new states alike.

Together with the growing complexity of government, the rapid growth of production and population, the burgeoning of trade and industry, and the diversification of society by the growth of new classes of professional administrators, soldiers and merchants, the Warring States period was also marked by the appearance of cities, some of them apparently of considerable size. The capital city of the state of Ch'i, Lin-tz'u in Shantung, was said to have 70,000 households, and contemporary descriptions speak of the richness and variety of city life, the great market places, the multiplicity of trades, and constantly contrast the luxury of the city with the simple frugality of the countryside. Cities had always been of great importance, particularly as centres of administration, as the symbolic seats of authority. The central place of the old domains had normally been a walled defensive site, and indeed the same word, 'I', is used interchangeably for domain and town in early literature, to the great confusion of the modern scholar. Compared with the much smaller and more simple city-plans of early Chou and Shang times, those of the Warring States era were far larger. The

site of Hsia-tu in the north-eastern state of Yen covers about nine square miles; Han-tan in the central state of Chao had a central citadel occupying almost a square mile. Whereas the earlier cities had been simple enclosures surrounded by walls of beaten earth, those of the Chan-kuo period were far more carefully fortified, often with not only a walled central fortress enclosing the administrative buildings, but also with an outer wall and moat enclosing extensive residential areas and specialized quarters for artisans and traders. At least one site in the Yangtze valley has a triple ring of walls.

The importance of cities naturally increased as government became more and more centralized. Throughout Chinese history the city has tended to remain the seat of authority and the centre of state power, rather than a focus of liberty and of forces antipathetic to state power, as in the west. The concentration of power and wealth made them a natural target for warfare, and during the bitter wars of the 4th and 3rd centuries we constantly read of protracted sieges as one state tried to strike at the economic and administrative heart of another.

During these centuries of insecurity, of constant and destructive warfare, of sweeping changes in the forms of government, of radical change in the social order as the old nobility was extinguished and replaced by new classes of wealthy merchants and landowners, of professional soldiers and government servants, of far-reaching changes in the economy and a vast increase in wealth, men were much exercised with the problems of politics and of ethics. During the period from 500 to 200 BC, when established authority had broken down and was being replaced by newer forms, Chinese philosophy enjoyed a golden age, during which the main lines for later development were all laid down.

Many schools of thought arose at this time, but all shared a central preoccupation with ethical problems and with the problems of organizing human society. Many of the early philosophers were themselves practical politicians, or were kept as advisers by one or other of the kings; and the style of Chinese thought, eminently practical and concerned with concrete worldly problems, contrasts sharply with the other-worldliness of Indian philosophy.

Three main 'schools' emerged, examined in more detail in Chapter IV: the Confucians, intensely conservative, believed that man fulfilled himself by playing his allotted role in a rigid order of authority. The Taoists were infinitely more imaginative and speculated deeply over the whole range of philosophical questions. The Legalists shared the authoritarianism of the Confucians, and the belief of the Taoists in the possibility of a social order which would function without deliberate intervention. But since they thought human nature to be basically bad, and rooted in self-interest, they believed that such a society could only be brought into being by the imposition of rigid and severe laws and punishments. They were proponents of naked power politics.

A new order: the Han
Of these rival political philosophies, only Legalism was adopted in practice, and was enforced in all its rigour in the north-western border state of Ch'in. The Ch'in during the latter part of the 4th century BC developed a highly

Left: the harshly totalitarian Ch'in regime aroused bitter opposition. This Han relief shows the attempted murder of the first emperor in 277 BC. The assassin has delivered as a gift the head of a general who had deserted the Ch'in for the state of Yen and as its box is opened hurls a sword at Shih Huang-ti. (9)

Rubbings from Han dynasty tomb-bricks showing minor officials wearing robes and caps and carrying pikes and shields. (10, 11, 12)

centralized state, in which there was no hereditary nobility, in which government was exercised by state servants whose position and promotion were directly dependent upon their services to the state, in which the population, ruled by a harsh and draconian law code, was disciplined and organized for two purposes, to produce revenue through taxation, and to provide manpower for the armies. One after the other, Ch'in extinguished the other states and in 221 the last of the independent kingdoms was destroyed, and Ch'in was ready to organize its new unified empire on the legalist ideal of an all-powerful highly centralized state.

The Ch'in, although they survived only for a few years to be replaced in 206 BC by the Han, set the pattern for the Chinese state of later centuries: the last remnants of the old 'feudal' order, of the ancient nobility, and of the old communal forms of rural society were swept into oblivion. Under the supreme emperor a professional civil service, recruited on personal merit and promoted on personal achievement, ruled over the commanderies and counties into which the entire empire was divided. Direct administrative control reached out from the capital to every corner of the vast empire, backed by the military power of an equally professional cadre of officers and a vast conscript army. With the administrative skills developed in the Warring States period, the Ch'in were able to mobilize vast armies of corvée workers to undertake great public works. An empire-wide system of roads was constructed to enable the government to have rapid communication with its most distant provinces.

The harsh and complex legal code, standardized systems of taxation, coinage weights and measures were applied throughout China. Perhaps even more important in the long term, a standard universal system of writing was adopted. The Ch'in also attempted a high degree of thought-control, deliberately destroying much of the literature of the earlier period which was antipathetic to their system of values. With the arrival of the centralized imperial state, much of the vigour, variety and freedom of earlier Chinese philosophical writing disappears.

Under the Ch'in and the Han, China came to control most of her modern territory. The Ch'in armies established stability on the northern frontier, and the Great Wall was built, at immense cost in human life and suffering, to keep out the nomadic 'barbarians' of the steppe. In the far south Ch'in armies conquered the area around Canton and pressed into northern Vietnam. The Han in their turn completed the conquest of southern China, invaded Turkestan to secure control of the routes to the western world, and established large Chinese settlements in Tongking and Korea. These remained the approximate limits of the Chinese cultural orbit. Only Taiwan, the Ryukyu Islands and Japan were drawn in in succeeding centuries. Later, in periods of strong Chinese power, Chinese armies occupied the steppe areas of Mongolia, Manchuria and Turkestan, and even invaded the impenetrable mountains of Tibet. But these areas, suitable only for a population of nomadic herdsmen, and quite inhospitable for the Chinese type of settled agriculture, were never colonized by Chinese settlers (apart from Manchuria in very recent times) and remained on the margin only of the Chinese cultural sphere, and are therefore relegated to a separate chapter (Chapter VII). The northern frontier was a strict environmental frontier dividing two quite distinct styles of life and types of culture. Tension between the nomad peoples, militarily powerful, but incapable of governing effectively a teeming agrarian population or of controlling China's sophisticated society, and the Chinese, equally incapable of controlling the steppe peoples even when they had conquered them, remained a perennial problem in Chinese politics (see Chapter III). The southern frontier, which presented no such definite environmental demarcation, remained an 'open frontier'. Not only were there no barriers to Chinese settlers establishing their familiar patterns of life in the south; there were also no powerful and well-organized native peoples to present a formidable military challenge as in the north. In the south Chinese settlement, colonization and assimilation of the various aboriginal inhabitants continued steadily throughout the centuries from Ch'in times onwards.

After the Ch'in fell, largely because its ruler had attempted to achieve too many radical changes in too short a time, without thought for the hardships which this imposed on the population, a new dynasty, the Han, succeeded to control of the empire, a dynasty founded not by a member of one of the old ruling houses, but by a soldier of humble origin. Ironically enough, the Han founder who, unlike the first Ch'in emperor, could not simply apply to the whole empire a well-tried state organization, but had to extemporize an imperial administration on the ruins of the Ch'in empire, was forced to revive the system of nobility and to parcel out a great portion of his newly-won empire in hereditary fiefs to

p 37 (14

which he was forced to rule, a bureaucracy which soon developed its own forms of obstructionism, red tape and the formalism which was inevitable in a state which attempted to impose standardized forms of law and administration throughout the empire. To circumvent the delays and frustrations of working through the 'correct channels', emperors constantly had recourse to the use of the members of their own household—often eunuchs—or personal secretarial offices to collect and collate information, draft their edicts and process documents for them. In the later part of the Han period one such secretarial office, that of the Masters of Writing (*Shang-shu*), grew rapidly in size and importance, and its various specialized bureaux became responsible for many policy decisions, leaving only the execution of business to the established ministries.

Such tensions between the emperor and his outer court, resulting in the emperor's reliance upon eunuchs, favourites, members of the families of the royal consorts, or small groups of secretaries and advisers acting as agents of the emperor's personal power were to be a recurrent feature of Chinese political life, and a fertile source both of political tension and also of institutional innovation. Such an entourage did not simply act as the emperor's agents, however. A weak emperor could be isolated in the palace by his 'inner court', be cut off from all other sources of advice and even information, and be brought completely under this entourage's domination. In such circumstances the officers of the regular bureaucracy could only fulfil their functions by allying themselves with one or other of the palace factions. As, during later dynasties, the autocratic powers of the emperor became steadily greater, the institutional checks on his despotic powers were weakened and policy decisions were concentrated in his own hands, the political system became more and more vulnerable to the accession of a weak emperor, who could frustrate the whole business of government by inaction or could be dominated by eunuchs.

Traditionally the Han are held to have replaced the 'Legalist' state of the Ch'in, with its ruthless totalitarianism, by a 'Confucian' state. But in fact their institutions remained closely modelled on those of the Ch'in. The rigour of the laws and the harshness of their application were somewhat relaxed; the underlying authoritarianism, the ideal of a strongly centralized state with uniform administrative practices, remained.

In Han times 'Confucianism' became the predominant philosophy, and was adopted as state orthodoxy, but it was far from the Confucianism of Confucius himself. It was a highly syncretic system, incorporating Taoist cosmological concepts on the one hand and Legalist political ideas on the other. The new system became the basis for education in the state schools at the capital which produced many of the future bureaucrats. In time the basically Legalist state structure came to be manned by a bureaucracy indoctrinated with the new Confucian ideas, and Confucian ethical precepts became the normal stuff of political discourse. But within this new 'Confucian' body of common political theory there remained a stress between the idealist ethics, the belief in moral example and suasion and in the minimum of state intervention inherited from the traditional Confucians, and the

various of his supporters and members of his own family. The recovery of effective central control over these fiefs took the Han many years and led to a great rebellion in 147 BC. But gradually the princes were forced to employ centrally appointed officials in their administrations, and the size of their kingdoms was by degrees whittled down until there was little to distinguish them from the normal commanderies save the hereditary position of the prince.

The Han gradually consolidated their system of government, built up a well-organized bureaucratic hierarchy and established a system of local government which provided them with a firm control over the rural localities of the empire. The Han empire was vast, and immensely wealthy and populous. When, at the end of the Early Han dynasty in AD 2, we have our first series of census figures, the population totalled nearly 60,000,000 persons. The emperor ruled over this vast population with the aid of a bureaucracy some 130,000 strong. But even such an army of officials could not control closely the everyday affairs of such a teeming population. In general the government was concerned primarily with the maintenance of law and order, and with the close control of the people as a source of tax revenues and forced labour, and as potential manpower for war. The local governors in the commandery and county towns could only enforce the policies promulgated by the central government through the co-operation of the leaders of local society, the village headmen and great land-owning families, and were constantly forced to take account of local interests. So long as the countryside remained at peace and taxes were paid on time, the government interfered as little as possible in local affairs, and when in the Late Han period (1st and 2nd centuries AD) the power of central government declined, the real power in the provinces was no longer the civil bureaucracy of the prefectures and counties, but the families of great landowners, who lived on vast estates producing virtually all their needs, and commanded the allegiance of great numbers of tenants, retainers and local client households.

40 (23) At the capital, the emperor presided over a huge personal household and a complex central government. He was the supreme source of authority and the supreme arbiter of justice. An active emperor, such as the first emperor of Ch'in or Wu-ti of the Early Han, dealt personally with a staggering load of routine business. But an activist emperor was always liable to come into conflict with the interests of the bureaucracy through

Han bureaucracy: an important official and his retinue. (13)

practical, materialist opportunist strain and the belief in legislation and institutional solutions stemming from Legalism.

p 39
(20, 21)
Under the Han the economy continued the steady advances already set in motion during the Warring States period. By now permanent agriculture was firmly established in the older settled parts of China. Irrigation and drainage works were carried out widely, and the great northern plain, much of which had been swamp and marshlands in earlier times, now supported an extremely dense population. Agricultural techniques became more sophisticated, and dry-farming methods designed to withstand the climatic regime of northern China were developed. During the first two centuries AD Chinese settlement on an extensive scale began slowly to creep into southern China, and the Yangtze valley began to develop its own distinctive form of agriculture based on rice cultivation. Although farm crops remained very diversified, animal husbandry now played less and less of a part in Chinese agriculture.

The rural population consisted mostly of small nuclear peasant families working rather small holdings of land and living very little above subsistence level. There was a constant tendency for peasants to sell their land under stress of poverty and indebtedness, and for more and more land to be concentrated in the hands of rich landowners. Although the statesmen of Han times were much concerned with the land question, attempts to deal with it by the state were complete failures. Dispossessed peasants were forced either to become tenants of the local landowners, or to move elsewhere in search of land. In the course of the Han period there were considerable movements of population, accelerated by disastrous floods in the most densely peopled parts of the great plain at the beginning of the 1st century AD. Between AD 2 and AD 140, for which years census figures are preserved, there was a marked decrease of population in the extremely populous northern and particularly the north-western areas which had been the cradle of Chinese civilization since Neolithic times, and there was a beginning of extensive settlement in Szechwan and the Yangtze valley. The vast bulk of the population, however, remained in the north.

Trade and industry also continued to develop, encouraged by the centuries of almost unbroken domestic peace. The government, however, saw a contented and passive peasantry as the all-important basis of social stability and the chief source of their agricultural taxes. Confucians and Legalists alike were the proponents of a sort of Physiocratic economic doctrine and were strongly biased against the merchant class, whom they regarded as social parasites, a menace to the stability of rural society, and, as an élite based purely on the possession of wealth, a potential rival to the ruling group. The government now began a policy of deliberate discrimination against the merchants and manufacturers. These were subjected to various legal restrictions and sumptuary laws, were forced to conduct their business under close government supervision, and were frequently subjected to heavy impositions. In addition, Han statesmen began to monopolize certain particularly lucrative industries or areas of trade, for example salt, iron and liquor, to place p 39 (2 them under government control, and to exploit them as a source of revenue. Attempts were also made to devise means of controlling commodity prices, and strict official p 39 (1 control was imposed on markets.

Decline and renewal: the Sui

In the 2nd century the Han fell into a serious decline. A series of ineffectual emperors succeeded one another on the throne, and continual court intrigues between factions backed by the influential families of empresses, by eunuchs and by groups of great landed magnates in the provinces, sapped the morale of the bureaucracy and weakened imperial authority. This was followed by the massive rebellion of the Yellow Turbans, after which the dynasty clung to the vestiges of power only thanks to the support of military dictators. In 220 the dynasty finally collapsed, and until the end of the 6th century China was divided, save for one brief interlude, between rival regional regimes.

During this period the course of history was very different in the north and in the south. South China, apart from the comparatively long-settled region around Nanking and the mouth of the Yangtze, was still largely semi-frontier territory in 220, with many unassimilated aboriginal peoples. Chinese settlement, which had gone on steadily throughout the Han period, was now accelerated by great numbers of refugees, both dispossessed peasants looking for new land and members of the official classes and wealthy members of great families who fled to the south with their retainers and clients in search of a new territorial base. During the ensuing centuries, although political conditions at the courts of the southern dynasties were sometimes extremely insecure and precarious, the region as a whole enjoyed comparatively peaceful and stable conditions. Settlement steadily expanded, a permanent network of local government was extended into marginal areas such as Fukien, the local people were deliberately indoctrinated with Chinese culture. From being a marginal border area hardly assimilated fully to Chinese culture in early Han times, by the 6th century the Yangtze valley had become a rich, productive area, perfectly capable of maintaining a viable independent regime. It developed its own distinct ruling aristocracy who carefully preserved the Han tradition, both in its culture and in its institutions.

Northern China was less fortunate. From the end of the 3rd century it was over-run successively by wave after wave of nomad horsemen from the northern steppe, who devastated the land, sacked the great cities, massacred enormous numbers and depopulated great areas. Militarily the Chinese were no match for them. But the barbarians were completely unable, through lack of experience of a settled agrarian society, to rule effectively the territories which they had conquered. To do so they had to call upon the aid of members of the traditional Chinese ruling class. The nobility of successive conquering peoples repeatedly intermarried with a small group of great Chinese clans, mostly from the north-west, to produce a new semi-barbarian aristocracy which partook of much of the life-style of the alien conquerors. It was from this group that the ruling families of the Sui and T'ang eventually emerged to re-unify China.

Eventually, under the Toba Turks in the 5th century, North China was once again re-unified under a single dynasty, the Northern Wei, some form of stability was restored, and the task of piecing together an administration was begun. Although Toba society was dominated by the tribal aristocracy of the conquerors, who maintained many of their pre-conquest institutions, including widespread slavery, a deliberate decision was taken to set up a stable state on the traditional Chinese model. The bureaucracy was restored, and the government established a set of institutions, designed to meet the circumstances of the times, which proved remarkably durable. A system of land allocation (*chün-t'ien*) was established, under which all registered taxable households received a sizable grant of land, in return for which they became liable to pay taxes and provide labour service for the state.

This land allocation and tax system were taken over with minor modifications by the various short-lived northern dynasties which followed the fall of the Northern Wei, and eventually provided a land and tax system which proved adequate even for the needs of the empire-wide centralized regimes of Sui and T'ang. Equally successful was the military system with which these institutions came to be closely associated. The state maintained a large number of militia units (*fu-ping*) quartered in the countryside, where their members farmed the land and supported themselves. They trained regularly, and did service on guard and garrison duty for short periods at regular intervals. In time of war they provided the government at minimal cost with a very large military establishment which could be rapidly mobilized and organized into an expeditionary army.

There were considerable social changes during this period of division. With the lack of effective centralized administration, local government came to be almost entirely dominated by influential local clans, whose members monopolized public office. Concentration of power and wealth in the hands of the great families was accompanied by the growth of the numbers of their semi-servile dependants. These not only provided them with a labour force to work their estates and clear new lands, but also provided them with an armed force with which to protect their lands during these years of continual insecurity.

The highest positions in the bureaucracy, under both the northern and the southern dynasties, tended to be filled by members of a comparatively small number of great aristocratic clans, who formed a tightly-knit social hierarchy, refusing to marry with members of non-aristocratic families. Chinese of a later period compared the rigidly stratified society of this period with the caste system of India. The members of the local aristocratic clans likewise were sharply differentiated from the common people not only by their wealth, culture, and style of life, but also by legal and fiscal privileges, and by the access to office, which was possible only through the recommendations of the corrupt Recommendation Legates, whose criteria for appointment were limited to the candidate's family connections and the social standing of his lineage.

This was the beginning of the great cosmopolitan period in Chinese history. From AD 200 to the late 9th century there was widespread foreign influence in China. Regular communication was opened by land across Turkestan to the states of Central Asia, to India, to Iran and to the Roman Orient. Shipping brought trade and travellers to Canton from South-east Asia and the Islands, from India and from the Persian Gulf. In the arts, music, ceramics and metalwork new foreign forms, largely from Central Asia, revolutionized native Chinese taste. Vast numbers of foreigners settled in China, with their own quarters in the great cities, maintained their own mosques and temples, and appointed their own headmen. Sogdian and Persian merchants dominated the overland trade from Central Asia. Persian, Arab and Korean ships monopolized the overseas trade by sea. In the 8th century the great ports of Yangchow and Canton each had enormous foreign settlements, Canton being said to have an Arab community of 100,000 persons.

The most potent of all foreign influences however was Buddhism. Appearing for the first time in China under the Han, from about AD 200 Buddhism, introduced from India by way of Central Asia, swept China. Until about AD 1000 China, together with her cultural dependencies Korea, Japan and Vietnam, remained a predominantly Buddhist country. All classes from emperors to peasants were influenced by the new faith, which not only fulfilled a deep spiritual need in a period of total insecurity, but also introduced a new level of sophistication in philosophical thought and in theology (see Chapter IV). The original forms of Indian Buddhism were modified by the native Taoist tradition, which in its turn took over from Buddhism its tradition of monastic life and much of its purely religious content. Even Buddhism, for all its intellectual satisfactions and its complete theology, did not offer a solution to all man's spiritual needs. Most people during this period applied Confucian moral criteria to their public life and family affairs, and tended still to think of the universe in Taoist terms, even though they personally were committed Buddhists.

Buddhism's effects were by no means limited to the realm of ideas. The Buddhists brought with them into China their form of monasticism, and the ideal of withdrawal of the individual from the ties of family and of temporal affairs into a closed monastic community. In time these monastic communities, thanks to the support of the laity and the donations of their supporters, became very wealthy, and the monasteries came to play an ever more important role in society. They held great estates, which were not subject, like the lands of individuals, to subdivision among all the sons at inheritance. They had great numbers of lay-brothers *(po-hsing seng)* and dependent families *(ssu-hu)* and even slaves, who cultivated their lands, tended their flocks, and managed their mills and oil presses. With their reserves of dependent labour, monasteries could clear and exploit forested land and played a considerable part in opening up marginal lands. They also used their accumulated wealth to make loans at interest, they acted as pawnshops, and were an important early source of credit.

In the social sphere, monastic schools played an important role in the spread of learning at every level from the bare ability to read simple words to the highest level of literacy. The monasteries also supported numerous groups of laymen, who undertook many functions in rural society, repairing canals and dykes, keeping up roads, and providing a primitive watch to protect the villages.

Politically the regimes of the various dynasties which followed the Toba Northern Wei in the 6th century were unstable, with murderous court intrigues, frequent purges and emperors given to irrational and arbitrary violence. But the overall power and resources of the state steadily improved, as did its military power. Eventually in 581 a series of court crises in the Northern Chou state brought to the throne one of its noble courtiers, Yang Chien, who established a new dynasty, the Sui, and set about a deliberate programme of reforms in preparation for the restoration of a unified empire embracing the whole of China.

In the space of a few years the Sui produced a new legal code, reformed and rationalized the chaotic system of local government under firm centralized control, strengthened the frontier defences against the Turks and put new vigour into the state's fiscal system. In 589 they turned southwards and conquered the last southern dynasty. The south was placated by very lenient treatment, its ruling class was incorporated into Sui officialdom, and the population, which was deeply Buddhist, was won over by the emperor's public assumption of the role of an ideal Buddhist Saint King, and by his widespread patronage of Buddhist monks and communities. Although the south seems never to have been subjected to the same land and tax systems as north China, it became an important source of wealth and of reserves, and under the second Sui emperor, Yang-ti, a programme of canal construction was undertaken which linked the lower Yangtze with the Huai river and the Huang-ho, enabling supplies from the south to be transported in bulk to the

great new Sui capital Ta-hsing, better known under its T'ang name, Ch'ang-an. A further canal ran from the Huang-ho to near modern Peking, providing a trunk route through the North China plain, and enabling strategic supplies to be shipped to the northern garrisons from the grain-producing areas of the plain.

These canals, which were to be of crucial importance to the T'ang in the 8th and 9th centuries, were constructed in a very short time at immense cost and with the prodigal use of vast armies of corvée labourers, who died by the tens of thousand. Equally large numbers of corvée labourers were employed on the rebuilding of the Great Wall as a defence against the Turks who, in the late 6th century, were immensely powerful, and dominated the steppe from Mongolia far westward into Central Asia. These vast levies of manpower caused untold hardship, and depleted the state's reserves. Unrest became widespread, and was made far worse by the immensely costly series of foreign expeditions, particularly by those sent to conquer Northern Korea from 609 onwards. Within a few years the powerful Sui empire, overstrained by the megalomanic ambition of Yang-ti and the attempt to achieve too much in too short a time, collapsed in disorder. But although it had lasted less than thirty years, it provided its successors, the T'ang, with most of the institutional foundation for their supremely successful dynasty. Although the strain of the Sui's achievements had eventually broken them, their reforms and achievements enabled the T'ang to establish a soundly based regime without themselves undertaking vast public works, and without carrying through radical reforms of the law, of governmental organization, or of administrative practice.

Foundations of the T'ang

The succession of the T'ang did not mean any great change in the nature of the government. The T'ang royal p 41 (2 house, like that of their predecessors, came from the north-western aristocracy, and like them it was heavily intermarried with the nobility of the Turks and other non-Chinese peoples. As under the Sui, the majority of the highest officials were also recruited from the aristocracy, as in previous dynasties. But whereas the Sui court had been dominated by members of the north-western nobility, the T'ang took some pains to give high office also to members of the other aristocratic groups from the east and south, and thus to prevent the north-western families from establishing complete dominance at court. Of the old aristocratic groups only the few chief clans of 'East of the Mountains' in Hopei remained aloof, looking down on the royal house as upstarts lacking in the pure Chinese cultural tradition, and refusing steadfastly to marry with them. The members of all these great clans were immensely wealthy and powerful, and treated the imperial family merely as *primus inter pares*. Unlike the emperors of later times the T'ang emperors mixed frequently with their ministers, and much important government business was decided at informal meetings which were regularly held with the chief ministers.

After the mid-7th century, the T'ang emperors increasingly became aware of the challenge which the great aristocratic families posed to their own authority. The Sui had already experimented, on a very limited scale,

64

with a system of state examinations, based on a curriculum consisting largely of Confucian learning, as a means of recruitment. The T'ang now greatly expanded this system, commissioned standard editions and commentaries on the classical texts to provide orthodox interpretations, and began increasingly to use the examinations as a means of recruiting an elite within the bureaucracy.

Until the end of the T'ang, examination candidates formed only a small elite among the officials, constituting a rival group to the aristocrats. Most of the bureaucracy was still recruited as before by hereditary privilege accorded to the sons of officials of middle and upper rank, and by recommendation as before. However, although the examination system did not transform the ruling class immediately, men recruited through the examination system gradually came to predominate, and members even of the greatest aristocratic clans began to sit for the examinations to achieve membership of the elite marked out for rapid promotion.

From this time onward the education of the upper classes tended to become more and more bookish and literary. The martial arts, horsemanship, archery, swordmanship, and hunting, which still played a large part in the life of the T'ang nobility, were no longer so much cultivated. This had as a side-effect an increasing distinction between the military and civil branches of official service.

The T'ang did not, in their early years, make many changes and innovations in the structure of government which they inherited from the Sui. The period is, however, recognized as one of the high-points in the history of Chinese administration, important both as the time when Chinese political institutions began to take on the general form in which they endured into our own century, and also as the period when Chinese law and government imprinted its indelible mark on the institutions of the states within China's cultural orbit. The T'ang finally established China, not merely as a source of culture, but as the spiritual centre of the East Asian world; it also made it the centre of a cultural world of states organized along similar lines, with common bureaucratic practices, a body of common laws, and sharing a common tradition of 'Confucian' political theory. Members of the ruling houses of the Korean states, the petty kingdoms of Manchuria and of Central Asia came to China to study. Japanese embassies brought students and monks to study in the T'ang capital.

The shape of later Chinese relations with the outside world also begin to appear in this period, and the emperor began to take in earnest his theoretical supremacy, formulated in early times, as the acknowledged 'Son of Heaven', over other rulers, all of whom, whatever their actual relative power, owed him a theoretical allegiance. But this theory covered a wide range of actual relationships.

Although the T'ang maintained continual domestic peace for the first century of their era, and the country grew prosperous as never before, the imposing edifice of state was in fact under very severe tensions. The institutions and forms of government which it had inherited from the Sui, particularly its taxation, land, and military systems, were essentially up-dated and modified versions of the system of government developed in northern China from the 5th century onwards. They were designed to provide uniformity of administrative practice, irrespective of variations in local conditions. When the T'ang imposed these institutions on the whole of their empire, households in the tropical south and on the borders of the northern deserts were subjected to exactly the same rules and procedures. These local differences were still further magnified by the fact that, until the Sui unification, southern China, although comparatively thinly peopled, was economically more advanced than the north. A money economy was better developed there; trade and commerce were more important; and the southern governments depended on taxes and commerce, taxes assessed on production, property, and wealth.

The breakdown of centralism

The early T'ang government was simple and economical. The bureaucracy was kept as small as possible; many routine tasks were entrusted to taxpayers as a form of labour service; the military establishment was kept at a minimum by the use of the militia system. But gradually this situation changed. Border troubles with the Tibetans in the west, the Turks in the north and the Khitans in the north-east, coupled with the expansion of permanent T'ang occupation far into Central Asia, made a permanent defence establishment imperative. At home, particularly under the Empress Wu, the bureaucracy rapidly increased in size and complexity, and many new public works were put in hand.

Expenditure increased rapidly, threatening to outstrip revenues. The tax system came under great pressure, and various new levies were imposed. At the same time the land allocation, which, it seems, was never enforced in southern China, was also put under great pressure, as in many parts of the north the major social problem was no longer the bringing of land under cultivation, but a chronic shortage of land for allocation.

Signs of strain were already apparent by the end of the 7th century. The costs of the military establishment soared, now that it was forced to maintain large forces of semi-permanent garrison troops on the frontiers rather than to depend on the militia system, which had fallen into a rapid decline. Attempts to make the frontier garrisons self-supporting by settling them in 'military colonies' met with only partial success. In the interior of the country great numbers of peasants fled from the areas in which they were registered, in the face of an increasing shortage of land, encroachment on their lands of powerful neighbours, and heavy taxation and labour services. Many of them fled to the Yangtze and Huai valleys to settle on vacant lands, accelerating the tendency for the south to grow at the expense of the old centres of Chinese culture in northern China. The government made several attempts to restore their control over population registration and disposal of lands in the early 8th century, but it was already clear that there was an irreversible tendency towards official recognition of the right to own and dispose freely of landed property, which the *chün-t'ien* allocation system was increasingly unable to control.

The 750s began badly, with military disasters in the far west, where Chinese armies were routed by the Arabs on the Talas river, and in the south-west where a massive punitive expedition sent against the newly risen state of

Nan-chao in Yunnan was virtually annihilated. The factional strife at court was intensified, and the emperor more and more withdrew into Taoist mysticism and personal luxury. Eventually An Lu-shan, the most powerful of the northern military governors, rebelled, and plunged China into seven years of bloody and destructive civil war.

p 42 (29)

The T'ang royal house survived this catastrophe, but only with difficulty, and at the expense of lasting and far-reaching changes. The most important of these changes was that, in order to survive, the country was divided up into provinces to which the central government delegated many powers which they had previously jealously preserved in their own hands. The provincial system which had enabled An Lu-shan to rebel was now extended to the entire empire.

The degree of autonomy varied greatly from one province to another. North-eastern China, heartland of traditional culture, and until now the most populous and productive region of China, was divided among three or four provinces, which until the end of the dynasty remained to all intents and purposes independent states acknowledging only nominal sovereignty of the emperor. An attempt to re-establish control over them in 781 was a disaster, and brought about a civil war even more destructive than the An Lu-shan rebellion. The northern frontier provinces, and the rich central province of Honan, were divided up into heavily garrisoned military commands. Only the southern provinces and Szechwan remained loyal, regularly contributed revenue, and retained civil administration as before. Though temporary, the semi-independence of the provinces, by which each province agreed to contribute a predetermined quota of revenue, but was given wide freedom in the ways in which these revenues were to be raised, marks a very important turning-point in administrative history.

From this time onwards the government abandoned the traditional principle of universal and uniform head taxes and uniform administrative procedures which had been the accepted norm since the beginnings of the unified empire. They also abandoned the concept of a minute registration of the population down to the last individual, and the centralized control of fiscal affairs reaching down to the individual household. With the establishment of local quotas, the incidence of taxation came to vary widely from one district to the next. As government became more and more complex over the ensuing centuries, this variety of local practice spread into all fields of government activity, into justice, education, and military affairs, until in Ming times it is almost impossible to describe a 'national' system of government, sometimes even difficult to generalize for a single province.

p 43 (22)

This reversal of the long-standing attempts at codified practice and uniformity was also carried into the field of law. In early T'ang times great efforts had been made to codify centrally, and periodically to update, both penal law and administrative practice. After 737, however, the *Code* was never revised, and remained in much the same form for the next five hundred years. Its place as the crucial central body of law was gradually taken by collections of edicts and other legislative acts.

Provincial autonomy and decentralization did not go unchecked. From the end of the 8th century a great effort

66

was made to restore the authority of central government over official appointments, over the control of finance, and over military affairs. The attempt was successful, except in the extreme case of the north-east. The provinces were gradually fragmented until they were no longer viable as independent units, and were again subjected to centralized government control, a process which was finally completed only under the various regional states into which China was divided during the Five Dynasties period. This restoration of central authority, however, was not without its price. One of the principal needs of central government in the late 8th century was for a powerful central army which could be readily deployed against mutinous provinces. To ensure firm imperial control of the new 'Palace armies', established to meet these needs, these were gradually placed under the control of eunuchs.

In the 9th century the eunuchs, their influence based upon their monopoly of military power, began to play an ever-increasing part in court politics. After the brief 'restoration' of T'ang authority under Hsien-tsung (805–20), T'ang court politics is a squalid story of plot and counterplot, in which the eunuchs and their allies at court enthroned, dominated, and murdered one weak emperor after another. The bureaucrats and the educated elite, realizing that the civil bureaucracy no longer made policy, tended more and more to be disillusioned with politics and in many cases withdrew from official life.

p 42 (3

Although court control was to a certain extent restored, effective, day-to-day administrative authority remained in the hands of the provinces. The lack of effective central authority and the breakdown of uniform national administration had extremely important effects on society as a whole. The provinces of late T'ang times, especially in northern China, were staffed to a large extent by the military subordinates of the governor or by local people chosen for their specialized experience and skills. Many of the soldiers were of very humble origins indeed, a large proportion being non-Chinese cavalrymen. Many of the employees of the specialized finance commissions, and the financial experts in provincial government, came from the merchant community, whose members had normally been barred from official service. The influx of such people into the governing elite probably brought about a degree of social change, and new chances of real upward social mobility, much greater than that effected by the examination system.

The breakdown of authority also caused other social changes. Many of the poor peasants who had managed to cling on to their lands were now forced, either by economic pressures or by the desire for the protection of a powerful patron, to accept a subordinate position as a tenant of a local landlord. The tacit abandonment of the government policy of land allocation meant that anyone with money or power could build up estates for himself, and the great land-holding *(chuang-yuan)* became a normal feature of rural society. The new provincial elite, coming from poor origins, were avid for the possessions in the form of land which would provide them with an economic basis for their family fortunes and also with an assured position in local society. In the 8th century such men could, for the first time, build up estates easily and legally, either by taking possession of abandoned land or by

The government retained a monopoly on the sale of salt. In this woodcut sea-salt is being processed. On the right sea-water is ladled into barrels, then carried to a cauldron (stoked with wood) and the refined salt is then packed in sacks. An official supervisor watches from the house behind. (14)

purchasing the lands of impoverished peasants. Their opportunities were redoubled when, in the 840s, the government imposed a rigorous suppression of the Buddhist monastic foundations, laicizing hundreds of thousands of monks and nuns and selling off the vast estates which the monastic communities had accumulated.

Tenancy had always existed, but the tenants who worked these new great estates were bound to their landlord not simply by an economic agreement between legal equals, but by a long-term contract placing the tenant in a position of legal subservience to his landlord. This system was intensified under the Sung, when tenants were often not only required to pay rent, but were expected to perform all sorts of customary duties on behalf of their landlord, and to pay him an amercement when their children married. Moreover, they could be disposed of together with the land on which they worked. Slavery too seems to have increased, although it remained insignificant. Social instability was increased by the final disappearance of the old aristocracy in the late 9th and 10th centuries.

Cities and trade

The fragmentation and dispersal of political authority among the provinces also had important effects on the economy. The provincial capitals grew into regional metropolises, with a great concentration of officials and with a high level of commercial activity. The economy began more and more to depend on money. Silver became the normal medium of exchange for large transactions, and a flourishing class of silversmiths grew up, who assayed silver for transactions and acted as bankers and as sources of credit. Primitive 'proto-banks' began to appear in the great cities. The volume of trade expanded rapidly, and increased still further as more and more of the population moved to the more fertile and productive south, where new intensive methods of rice culture, irrigation works, and an ever-increasing range of crop varieties produced larger and larger agricultural surpluses. The south was the centre of the two richest

groups of merchants, the salt merchants, operating as agents of government within a government monopoly, and the tea merchants from Kiangsi. The great city of Yangchow, where the canal joined the Yangtze, became the commercial metropolis of the south, and the seat of the Salt Commission which administered the finances of southern China. But other cities also boomed; Pien-chou, the canal point near the junction with the Huang-ho and the collecting centre for the great plain; Chiang-ling on the upper Yangtze; Ch'eng-tu the capital of Szechwan; and Canton, the great centre of overseas trade, all became great urban centres. But they were urban centres with a difference. Unlike the vast capital cities of former times, they were not predominantly administrative centres, although each was in fact a provincial capital. They were primarily commercial cities, regional economic capitals at the centre of a network of trade and commerce which stretched out through the prefectural and county towns, with their official markets, to the ever-increasing number of small rural market centres and periodical markets, which provided most of the needs of the innumerable self-contained and virtually self-sufficient market areas into which China was broken up.

Urbanization affected the countryside as well. Where until T'ang times there had been very few urban settlements intermediate between the county and prefectural cities, the walled defensive centres of administration, and the villages, there now grew up great numbers of new small towns. Some of these, originally market settlements, were used by the provincial governors as out-stations of their regime, or as minor garrison centres. Villages came increasingly to be dependent upon a local administrative centre in the county town, but at the same time to form part of an economic district centred on a local market town. These rural marketing areas gradually became a permanent component of local society, the area which formed the social horizon of the average peasant, within which he procured the necessities of life, disposed of his surplus products, hired out his labour, formed his marriage links. These units proved remarkably long-lived,

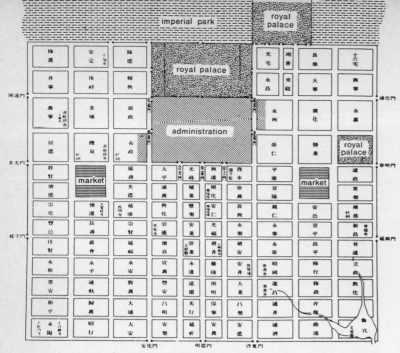

The T'ang capital of Ch'ang-an, a plan reconstructed from excavations. In the 8th and 9th centuries this was one of the largest cities in the world, with over a million inhabitants. It was laid out on a chequer-board plan, and divided into closed wards which were locked at night. The imperial palace, from which every aspect of urban life was supervised, is in the north. (15)

and many lasted from the Sung into our own time. As natural economic and social units they frequently formed the nucleus around which collectives and communes were built under the Communist regime.

The government was faced with this burgeoning of trade at a period of weakness. The repressive measures by which successive regimes had attempted to control merchants and trade were already strained, and now broke down. In the capital cities the old enclosed markets and wards could no longer be maintained; the strict curfew was no longer imposed. Settlement spread beyond the city walls, where new suburbs, markets and amusement centres *(wa-tzu)* grew up. The strict sumptuary laws were tacitly abandoned, the restrictions on the holding of land were relaxed. The government's attitude changed from a conviction that merchants were a potential source of mischief which must be contained, to the realization that they were a source of revenue which should be tapped.

In the years following An Lu-shan's rebellion, the government had adopted the monopoly of salt production as a major source of revenue. By strictly controlling salt production and selling salt to the merchant distributors with the addition of a high surcharge on the costs of production, the government was able to collect tax indirectly, through merchants, even from the provinces where their authority was at best nominal. This policy led on to attempts by the government to monopolize, or to control directly, a wide variety of profitable trades and industries. Salt, wine, tea, alum, lacquer, building timber were all at one time or another subject to such government monopoly or intervention. In later times, mining also was frequently placed under government monopoly or control. The government also began to devise urban taxes for deriving revenue from the wealthy commercial community, which under the old tax and labour service system had escaped very lightly. *Ad valorem* taxes on

sales, transit taxes, and percentage levies on all transactions became important sources of revenue.

At the same time the merchant community itself began to develop institutions and an identity of its own. There had already existed associations of merchants dealing in the same trade, who had registered members and acted as spokesmen with the local authorities, but had little power. These associations *(hang)* gradually grew more and more powerful from the 10th century onwards. By the 16th century the *hang* had grown into a sort of guild, forming a closed community of merchants of the same trade, which restricted its membership, was officially recognized for taxation purposes, and often had a religious cult of its own. But although trade guilds, associations of merchants from the same home area, and other groupings came to play an important part in the organization of urban life, they remained politically powerless. No Chinese government ever granted a guild any charter or freedom. The guild was used as an agent of government, to collect taxes and help regulate trade. But it was accorded no privileges in return. Indeed, no citizen body or urban community was recognized by the government.

The citizens nevertheless gradually began to develop a strong sense of identity, particularly under the Sung, when, with the establishment of the capital at Kaifeng, the metropolis was for the first time essentially a bustling commercial city, centre of a large industrial complex, rather than a symbolic centre of political power. The citizens of both Kaifeng and the southern capital Hangchow which succeeded it when the Sung were forced to abandon northern China, were extremely proud of their city, and a series of fascinating books survive describing in minutest detail the richness and variety of life, the immense diversity of trades and occupations, the rich profusion of goods for sale, the pleasures of the gay quarters of these cities.

p 44 (
p 46
(41, 42

The merchants of late T'ang and Sung times sometimes grew immensely wealthy, and after the 8th century the rigid social discrimination against them gradually broke down. It remained normal, however, for the successful merchant not to re-invest his profit in his business but to attempt to buy his way into the 'gentry' class, either by buying estates and becoming a country landowner, or by purchasing minor office or graduate status, or by educating his children to take the examinations and become members of the scholar official class. Trade and commerce were conducted on a short-term basis, with quick returns, very high rates of interest, and a high degree of risk.

All these social changes continued from 750 until the 13th century, and were facilitated in the early stages by the relaxation of central authority and the fragmentation of power under the late T'ang and the Five Dynasties.

A changing pattern: the rise of the Sung
Perhaps the most fundamental change which took place during these centuries, however, is the complete change in the balance between north and south in Chinese life. Until the 8th century, the majority of the Chinese population had lived to the north of the crucial environmental divide which follows the line of the Huai-river and the Chin-ling mountains. As we have seen, there was already a steady migration of people to the south in early T'ang

times. This accelerated sharply after An Lu-shan's rebellion, and between 750 and the end of the 11th century the distribution of the Chinese population underwent a complete change. Until the early T'ang the old traditional centres of civilization in the north had remained very populous, but these now declined sharply. In a period when the total population rose from about 50 million to 100 million persons, the population of the north-eastern plain fell by half, while the north-west remained stationary. The population of the south however, particularly that of the Yangtze and Huai valleys, increased severalfold, and the southern provinces of Hunan, Kiangsu, and particularly Fukien were now settled heavily for the first time. By the 11th century the north, in spite of the capital's still remaining at Kaifeng, was falling behind the south in population, productivity, wealth, and even in education. The decline of the north was mainly the result of political conditions. During the T'ang period it had been devastated by several destructive wars and rebellions, and these tribulations were followed by a period of extreme political instability during the Five Dynasties, as one short-lived regime succeeded another in the north-east. During these troubled years the area around Peking was occupied by the Khitan kingdom of Liao based in Manchuria, and remained out of Chinese control for four centuries. The far north-west too was invaded by another powerful and well organized non-Chinese state, the Tangut Hsi-Hsia, and all the T'ang dominions in Central Asia were lost. In contrast to this, southern China enjoyed comparative calm and prosperity.

It was, however, one of the northern regimes, the Sung, that eventually restored a unified centralized government to the whole of China.

As in the case of the T'ang and the Han, the ground had been prepared for re-unification under a preceding dynasty. The Sung's precursors were the Later Chou, who, during their brief nine-year period of power, had built up a powerful military establishment which the Sung took over and employed in their campaigns of unification. They had also carried out extensive reforms of administration, had undertaken the rebuilding of the new capital Kaifeng, had taken new measures against great landlords and the monasteries, had attempted to equalize the incidence of taxation, and had destroyed the last vestiges of the power of military provincial governors within their borders. The Sung built on their achievement, and over the next twenty years gradually incorporated the formerly independent states of southern China and the north-west into their empire and established once again a stable and powerful centralized state.

The organization of this new state was somewhat different from the T'ang's. The central government was modelled on the provincial administrations of the late T'ang military governors. The emperor ruled through a central Secretariat headed by a council of state of Chief Ministers and assistant councillors, some civil and some military. These councillors were responsible for the formulation of policy, in which they were assisted by the Han-lin scholars. Executive administration was divided clearly into three separate spheres: military, financial, and general civil administration, each of which employed its own cadre of officials and provided specialist careers leading to the highest posts in government. In local administration the county and prefecture were once again re-established as the major local administrative districts. The late T'ang provinces had been whittled down to the size of single prefectures. In their place the empire was now divided into some fifteen or twenty 'circuits', whose intendants were responsible to the capital for the administration of specified types of governmental business in the prefectures and counties in their area. These circuits were designed to exercise a supervisory rather than an executive function. There was no single intendant in control of the whole of the circuit's business. Separate individuals were responsible for fiscal, judicial, military, and transportation matters.

The Sung bureaucracy

The Sung bureaucracy was considerably more numerous than that of T'ang times, both at the capital and in the provinces, and it more than doubled in size during the first century of Sung. The network of local administration steadily grew denser as the dynasty went on. The central government gradually regained its power of appointment to all posts in the local administrations, and thus restored a degree of professional uniformity to the bureaucracy which had been lost since the 8th century.

In this bureaucracy the examination candidates soon came to predominate completely, in every field save the military. The military service was theoretically separate from, but equal with, the civil service, but it was in fact very much less highly esteemed. The very lowest rungs of the bureaucratic ladder, the offices 'outside the current of promotion', were filled by the very numerous clerical service. In early Sung times roughly half of the ranking civil bureaucrats were recruited through the *chin-shih* examinations. The graduates were far more numerous than under the T'ang, or indeed than under any later dynasty. This meant that the examination graduate, unlike the select few *chin-shih* in T'ang times, was no longer a marked member of an elite within the bureaucracy, destined for rapid advancement and consciously groomed for high office. However, under the Sung the graduates still filled most important offices and provided almost all of the members of the central government. Competition was intense; an average of less than 10 per cent of the qualified candidates passed the final palace examination. In one year no less than 97,000 candidates competed, of whom only a thousand were given degrees.

The average age of graduation also tended to rise. A T'ang scholar might have taken his *chin-shih* in his mid-twenties, but his Sung equivalent would take his examination at about thirty-six. Many men tried repeatedly, sometimes as many as fifteen times, eventually graduating in their fifties. The availability of schools and educational standards varied widely from one province area to another. A great proportion of successful candidates came from the metropolitan area and from the Yangtze region, Chekiang, and Fukien, and these threatened to swamp the civil service. Eventually a provincial quota system had to be devised to ensure equitable representation within the ranks of the bureaucracy for every region of the empire.

Not all Sung statesmen were contented with the examination system. Reformers such as Fan Chung-yen and Wang An-shih urged that the examinations should stress practical skills, judgment, and statesmanship rather than sterile classical erudition. But these pleas fell on deaf ears. If anything, the Sung examination became steadily more stereotyped and less practical. Freedom of entry, moreover, was more apparent than real. An educational process which continued until the candidate was in his thirties or even later demanded a good deal of money and leisure, far beyond the reach of any but the well-to-do. A candidate from a family with a long tradition of learning and with adequate means for his support was at an advantage from the beginning. Most of the rest must have come from the educated elite, but there was, nevertheless, an appreciable majority whose immediate ancestors were not officials, and it is clear that the examinations were drawing on a totally different social group than had been the case in T'ang times.

p 45 (38) The maintenance of the social and economic standing of a family or lineage was very difficult. The lack of any system of primogeniture meant that the family property was divided among all male descendants at each generation. In a society in which concubinage was commonplace, this meant constant fragmentation of property, often among a large number of sons, property which could normally be renewed only out of the fruits of office. In the Sung period a great awareness of the needs for a close community of family members led to new stress on family institutions. Ancestral ritual was made more complex and the ancestral cult more strictly observed; the compilation of genealogies became widespread; clan schools were set up to prepare the clan's children for the examinations which led to an official career; and a system of charitable trusts was developed on the model of the perpetual corporations formed by Buddhist monastic communities, which enabled part of a clan's wealth to be invested in the name of the clan cult-community and thus be freed from the threat of division on inheritance. Such trusts gave large clans some measure of security for their poorer members against poverty, helped pay the heavy burden of marriage and funeral expenses, and also made funds available for the education of sons, and for the considerable expenses incurred in taking the examinations. In spite of these measures, and the degree of stability which they restored to the ruling elite, the members of even the most powerful Sung families depended to a far greater extent than their predecessors upon their office and their official salaries.

During the 11th century the need for widespread administrative reform split the bureaucracy into rival reformist and conservative factions, and introduced a new element of violent partisan politics into Sung government, poisoning the atmosphere of the court for half a century and more. The social problems facing Sung government, for all the expanding economy and growing wealth of the country, were pressing ones. The plight of the small peasant farmer grew worse, as great landed estates became more and more numerous. The great landowners not only accumulated more and more lands, but their owners were able to invest in expensive reclamation and irrigation works, to purchase the many improved implements which were coming into use, and to afford to their tenants a measure of security against bad times which the poor peasant was denied. This gulf between the wealthy and the rural poor was constantly

widening. Government policy never succeeded in dealing with the agrarian problem.

But the besetting problem of the Sung was that of its foreign relations. After the unification of the country the Khitan state of Liao retained control of the north-east, and there was continuous fighting on the northern border, which only ended with the treaty of Shan-yuan in 1004. Even after this the Sung had to recognize the equality of their neighbours, and pay them vast sums in subsidy. In the 1030s an equally destructive and long-drawn war began in the north-west with the Hsi-hsia, and this ended in a similar way.

In the 12th century the Liao were replaced as the power in Manchuria and the north-east by the Jurchid Chin dynasty, who had been encouraged and aided by the Sung to destroy their old enemies. The Sung had already been weakened by the outbreak of peasant risings in Chekiang, Kiangsu and Shantung. The Jurchid, having destroyed the Liao in 1125, now turned on the Sung and drove them ignominiously out of northern China. The Sung withdrew to the Huai and Yangtze valleys, and their capital was transferred from Kaifeng to Hangchow in the Yangtze delta. In the south the Sung survived until 1278. But they were no longer the politically dominant power in China. Northern China fell under a harsh alien domination which was to last for more than two centuries.

The Southern Sung

This loss of the north, bringing with it the loss of half of the Sung's population, the complete eclipse of many of the greatest clans, and the ruin of the vast commercial and industrial complex centred on Kaifeng, was far more than a mere military defeat. It dealt a tremendous blow at Chinese self-confidence, and was a trauma which brought about a new attitude on foreign matters. The Jurchid conquest obsessed the historians of later ages even more than the far more destructive Mongol conquest which succeeded it, and it was a key factor in the growth of the defensive xenophobia which more and more came to dominate Chinese thinking. The confident assimilation of all kinds of foreign influences under the T'ang was replaced by the emergence of a sharp racist feeling about China's northern neighbours, and by an ultra-defensive attitude.

The loss of the north also completed the dominance of the south, in almost every sphere of Chinese life, which had been growing since mid-T'ang times, although the Chin was by no means the negative régime which loyalist Sung writers would have us believe. For the first time not only was southern China the economic heart of China, containing well over half of its total population, but it also became the cultural centre of the empire and the seat of political power. The rich lands of the Yangtze p 47 (valley, their productivity multiplied by new techniques, widespread irrigation, new crops, and quick-ripening rice, produced wealth ample enough to maintain the great new cities of the region, and to sustain a vast diversified commerce, which was rapidly developing a 'national' market in many commodities. It also enabled the Southern Sung to maintain enormous armies for defence against the Chin and, for the first time in Chinese history, to build and maintain a great navy.

Under the Sung, China became a great sea power. Under the T'ang, sea-borne trade had been carried largely in Arab ships to the south, or in Korean ships to Japan and the north; but now Chinese shipping from Fukien and Canton sailed regularly to South-east Asia, India, and the Persian Gulf. The defection of the Sung navy was an important factor in the Mongol conquest, and enabled the Mongols to undertake their massive, if abortive, invasions of Japan. The apogee of Chinese sea power was reached under the early Ming, when in the first quarter of the 15th century Chinese fleets under the great eunuch admiral Cheng Ho sailed all over the Indian Ocean, as far as the East African coast. These enterprises, however, were brought to a sudden end, partly because of their ruinous cost, but partly again as a result of the increasing inward-looking defensive 'fortress mentality' which came to characterize Chinese strategic thinking. In and after the 15th century, naval policy reverted to the most limited form of coastal defence. The idea of a positive naval policy was forgotten, and the powerful Chinese navy ceased to exist, just at the period when new rivals, the Western powers whose military superiority was essentially sea-borne, appeared on the scene.

In spite of its political weaknesses, the Sung age was perhaps a high point of Chinese culture. Literature, the arts, technology, and science all reached a peak of development. Education was more widely available than ever before. Printing made the mass production of books on all sorts of subjects a simple matter. The central government and local officials commissioned a wide variety of books ranging from technical manuals to editions of classical literature and vast literary compilations. Not only did the traditional elite arts flourish, but such popular arts as the theatre and fiction began to flourish, while printing made available cheap books to the large reading public of the cities who were uneducated by the standards of the traditional literati, but who provided an insatiable market for almanacs, cheap books, plays, fiction, popular encyclopaedias, practical handbooks, and popular histories.

The Southern Sung era was a time of increasing authoritarianism. Not only did government become more oppressive and more autocratic in practice; a new form of Confucianism, a mixture of Confucianism with Taoist cosmology and with concepts from Buddhism, provided a new orthodoxy in the shape of Chu Hsi's philosophy. This orthodoxy rapidly began to permeate both the school curriculum and the examination system, and the requirement of exact ideological conformity to this orthodox system rapidly began to become mandatory. Neo-Confucian orthodoxy, for all its systematic formulation and its metaphysical pretensions, stressed, above all, subservience, obedience, and loyalty to one's superiors, whether parents, elders, superiors in office, or the ruler.

The Mongol invasion completed the trauma about foreign relations which the Jurchid invasion had begun. It took place in two waves. The first wave, which engulfed the Chin empire of northern China, took place while the Mongols were still a unified world empire, and northern China suffered the barbarity and destruction which accompanied the Mongol conquests elsewhere. Much of north China was depopulated, great areas were converted into pasture, the once prosperous farmlands were divided up into appanages for the Mongol nobility, a large part of the population was enslaved. Under the Chin at the end of the 12th century the north China plain had already suffered terrible disasters from flooding when the Huang-ho changed its course, flowing into the sea to the south of the Shantung peninsula and no longer in the vicinity of Tientsin. Millions had died, millions more had been made homeless, and vast areas of the most fertile farmland ruined. The Mongol conquest completed the ruin of the north. It took many centuries to recover.

Pax Mongolica
Southern China escaped comparatively lightly. By the time the Mongols seriously began its conquest they had already been in China for thirty years or more, and had begun to employ Chinese advisers to cope with the problems of administering the vast agrarian population. The Mongol empire had split into separate khanates, each of which had begun to develop in its own way. Khubilai, under whom the conquest of the south was completed, was strongly influenced by Chinese advisers and ruled as much as a Chinese emperor as a traditional Mongol Khan. The severe policies imposed in the north never affected southern China to anything approaching the same extent. The Mongol conquest thus exaggerated the existing imbalance between north and south.

The Mongol conquest was a totally new experience for the Chinese in many ways. Never before had the Chinese been so completely outclassed militarily by a foreign conqueror on their own ground. Never before had the whole of China fallen under foreign domination, and moreover become a component of a still larger world empire. Never before had a foreign conqueror been so successful in adopting those Chinese techniques and those Chinese assistants which it required to rule the country, while still remaining totally alien. The Chinese confidence that in time they could absorb any of their conquerors by virtue of the 'transforming power of superior Chinese culture' was shattered.

The Mongol conquest was, however, not entirely negative in its results. The Pax Mongolica extending across the steppe to the threshold of Europe meant that travel between China and the West was easier than ever before. Marco Polo was only one of the great numbers of Westerners who made the long journey to the Far East. In their administration of China, the Mongols employed indiscriminately all sorts of foreigners, Jurchid officials taken over from the Chin state, Uighur and Central Asian merchants who became tax-farmers for Chinese provinces. In return, a great tide of Chinese technical and scientific inventions flowed to the West, including printing and gunpowder. This interchange of people and ideas was not a contact between equals. In the 13th century China was far richer, more productive, infinitely more populous, more advanced technologically, and far better governed and more orderly than Europe. Marco Polo's astonishment at China's vast size and wealth, at the splendour of its cities, was not merely the astonishment of a man observing a totally alien society. He, a citizen of one of Europe's most prosperous and sophisticated societies, stood in awe at the sight of a civilization in almost every way far more advanced than his own.

This Ming map of China shows the country with a considerable degree of accuracy. The thick dark line top left is the Gobi desert. The Great Wall, the Yellow River (disgorging south of Shan- *tung) and the Yangtze are all clearly visible. On the far right are Korea and a small part of Japan; at the bottom Annam (Vietnam). Names inside squares are provincial capitals. (16)*

Eventually in the 14th century the misrule of a series of demented emperors and the savage and indiscriminate coups and purges into which court life declined after Khubilai's death, the mismanagement of the country's finances, which were brought to the brink of ruin by excessive issues of paper money, and a series of costly military failures, brought about the fall of the Mongol dynasty in the face of a wave of popular rising. The Mongols, still basically un-sinified, withdrew to their steppe home, and there remained a powerful force for some centuries.

With their defeat China was once again, for the first time for four centuries, united under a Chinese dynasty, the Ming.

A new dynasty: the Ming

T'ai-tsu, the founder of the Ming dynasty, was a man of humble origins who had risen by sheer force of character to be a rebel leader. The dynasty which he founded was marked indelibly by his own harsh, pathologically suspicious and autocratic character.

p 48 (44) Institutionally the Ming carried further the tendency towards ever greater concentration of authority in the throne which had persisted since the late T'ang period. Although T'ai-tsu's regime was a self-conscious 'restoration' of the great institutions of the past, in particular of those of the T'ang, there was an important difference in

that the central Secretariat and the advisory and policy-making ministries of the central government were still further whittled away, until in 1380 he abolished both the central Secretariat and the office of Chief Minister, thus leaving the bureaucracy without their chief policy-making office and without their principal spokesmen. The central bureaucracy was left as a purely executive administration consisting of six ministries modelled on those of T'ang times. These, however, were responsible, not to any central ministry, but to the throne. All important policy decisions were taken by the emperor. This is not to say that the emperor merely exercised power in a purely arbitrary manner. T'ai-tsu and his immediate successors took counsel with their greater ministers and with the highest officers in the Han-lin Academy, which acted as their secretariat. Decisions of crucial importance, especially those involving war, were discussed at a formal court conference attended by the heads of the chief ministries and other offices of the central government. But, nonetheless, the new system placed a huge ultimate burden of responsibility and a vast load of day-to-day routine business upon the emperor himself.

After the middle of the 15th century the intimate conferences between the emperor and his chief ministers and Han-lin Secretaries came to an end, and from about 1465 until near the end of the dynasty successive emperors—still in theory bearing personal responsibility for everyday decisions—gave audience to their chief ministers only very rarely. The routine handling of affairs was carried out within the executive ministries, or by the Grand Secretaries, some of whom came to hold great power for long periods. They themselves, sometimes in consultation with other high officials, would draft legislation, when necessary, for the emperor's formal approval. The emperor could still reject or revise such proposed edicts if he wished. But the later Ming emperors mostly were happy to rubber-stamp the policies suggested to them or even to leave the decision to the chief of their eunuch attendants, who thus acquired the power to affect policy, in addition to controlling the emperor's channels of information.

The increasing authority of the emperor was thus not necessarily a cause of a more dictatorial state, or of a managerial despotism. It could equally easily lead to a power vacuum at the centre, a vacuum which had to be filled either by members of the bureaucracy, acting without formal institutionalized authority, or by the eunuchs, who were subject to none of the pressures towards conformity and to none of the ideological constraints of Confucian ethic which directed the actions of the civil officials. It says a great deal for the effectiveness of the bureaucratic machine that the normal functioning of government continued.

The despotism of the Ming emperors was only partly the result of the new institutional arrangements. Its manifestations were not so much felt in the personal intervention of the throne in government as in the new atmosphere and ambience of court life. The first emperor had already established his own ethos of government by terror. Thousands of officials and members of the old ruling class of his own home region of Chiang-nang were executed or suffered purges, forced exile, and deportation. Life for even a high-ranking official at court was precarious, liable to be brought to an untimely end for some imagined slight. Thousands of his officials were executed or publicly humiliated. Censors and eunuchs were employed in constant investigation and purges. The bureaucracy now began to treat the throne with an exaggerated servility.

The bureaucracy too lacked the unity of interest and *esprit de corps* which its predecessors had possessed. Their powers were eroded at the top by increased imperial authority. Their authority was rivalled by an 'inner court' —the eunuchs, and the Han-lin scholars, who came to form a sort of inner cabinet, the Grand Secretariat, whose members held only low formal rank and whose influence derived from their employment as the emperor's personal aides. Their own cohesion was further destroyed by the informal but none the less real division of the bureaucracy into a central and a provincial service. The ever increasing postponement of the age at which a man could hope to pass the examinations meant that the active life which an official could expect became shorter. The official body was, moreover, riddled with partisan cliques, the importance of which increased as the insecurity of official life grew ever more extreme.

In the provinces, too, the growth of bureaucratic complexity made itself felt. The Ming took over and modified the Mongol system of dividing the country into provinces, each of which was a sort of branch in miniature of the central government. These new provinces *(sheng)* became very powerful and developed a high degree of local independence of administration. The operation of policy became more and more diversified from one region to another. But the Ming local official had far less real authority, far less latitude for action, than his predecessors. Normally holding office for only a short tenure, having to operate through the permanent body of grasping and corrupt subaltern officials who clustered in every government office, and depending for the execution of many routine tasks upon the local gentry, the Ming local magistrate was also forced to operate in a strait-jacket of complex administrative precedent and written rules.

p 48 (45)

The society which supported this vast ramifying system of government remained not dissimilar to that of late Sung times. In the countryside landlordism on a large scale continued to grow, particularly in the Yangtze provinces and the south. In the north much land which had been abandoned under the Mongols was brought back into cultivation. But neither great estates nor semi-servile tenancy were important there. Until this century north China has been a region of independent peasants, while the south has been characterized by a high incidence of tenancy. Although the more extreme forms of semi-servile tenancy of later Sung times were to some extent ameliorated, the condition of many tenants was very poor, and the late Ming saw a considerable number of popular revolts of tenant farmers and 'servants' (i.e. virtual serfs) in the south-east, where the incidence of tenancy was highest.

The gradual commercialization of agriculture continued, and a large-scale national market developed in grain and in cotton, which had been introduced under the Mongols and rapidly spread over much of China. The Yangtze delta area, once a grain surplus producing area, could no longer support its large urban populations, and grain had to be imported from the middle Yangtze provinces of Hunan and Hupei, while cotton for the spinning and weaving industry was imported from Hopei and Honan.

The economy not only had to produce revenues to maintain the enormously expensive state apparatus and a huge defence establishment. It also had to cope with an increasing population. During the Ming period the population doubled. Part of this increase was taken up in repopulating the north, which began to recover from its four centuries under foreign rule. But the pressure on the land began to be extreme in many parts of central China. The productivity of agriculture certainly improved considerably in the face of this challenge. But the major technical innovations of Sung times, in early ripening varieties of wheat and rice, double cropping, fertilization, irrigation techniques and new implements, were not greatly improved upon. Some marginal improvement was effected at the end of the Ming period by the importation of new food crops from the New World—maize, ground-nuts, and sweet potatoes, which made possible the profitable cultivation of lands whose use was only marginal with the traditional forms of agriculture. But basically the main changes in agriculture after Sung times were the increasing commercialization of farming by the production of cash crops and the increasingly intensive

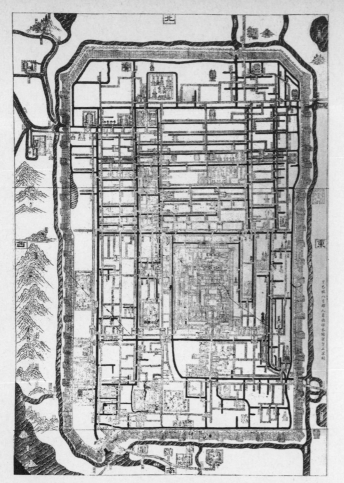

Plan of Soochow, carved in stone in the 13th century. The Grand Canal flows in at the north-west corner and out at the south, providing water for the city's numerous canals. (17)

Nanking: a Ming woodcut shows life inside the city wall (the embattled line at the back). Temples, houses, markets and gardens form a picturesque, well-watered landscape. (18)

use of the land by double or multiple cropping and great labour-intensity.

The growth of the great cities, the increasing urbanization of small market towns, the increasing prosperity of the urban merchant and manufacturing class continued trends that had set in under the Sung. The volume of trade increased steadily. Towards the end of the dynasty there began a steady inflow of silver from the Spanish dominions in the Americas, which provided a more adequate currency than ever before. The great merchants p 49 (46) of Hui-chou in Anhwei, dealers in tea, timber, lacquer, and ceramics and also famous as bankers, the immensely wealthy shipowners and overseas merchants of Fukien, the textile merchants of Kiangsu and Nanking, the merchants of Shansi, all formed commercial elite groups whose wealth and style of life rivalled that of high officials. In the intensely commercialized and industralized cities of the Yangtze delta an identifiable urban labour class began to appear, and the last years of the Ming added urban unrest and workers' risings to the normal rural peasant and tenant insurrections and refusals to pay rents.

The strains of the late Ming are still imperfectly understood. But there can be little doubt that misgovernment played a very large role. The already onerous taxation system was made still more unbearable by additional taxation, labour duties, and levies imposed by the eunuchs, who by this time numbered something like 70,000, as against only some 15,000 regular civil servants. No doubt these purely economic pressures played an important role in producing unrest and disaffection in the countryside. But late Ming governments also effectively alienated a large part of the educated elite through whom they had to rule. The ever increasing arbitrariness of government and the dominance of the eunuchs were themselves abhorrent to the scholar class.

The Manchus: end of a tradition

By the beginning of the 17th century the Ming regime was continually in a state of crisis, and it was merely a question whether it would be destroyed by internal insurrection or by attack from outside. The people who eventually liquidated the Ming were the Manchus, the descendants of the Jurchid, who had established a powerful state on Chinese lines in southern Manchuria. Like the Khitan and the Jurchid before them, the Manchus invaded China, not as a nomadic steppe people coming from a totally alien environment where settled agriculture was impossible, but as rulers of a strong established state which already included large numbers of settled farmers of Chinese origin and had already developed a semi-Chinese style of administration. The Manchus were not only a formidable enemy in military terms. They were also the best organized enemy China had faced, an enemy in whose employment there was already a large cadre of defecting Chinese officials.

When in the 1640s massive internal rebellions threatened to destroy the Ming in any case, the Manchu forces were poised on the border, and they over-ran the whole country with comparatively little opposition. The Ming loyalist forces resisted for some years in more and more remote areas of the south, but they were finally destroyed.

It was under the Manchu Ch'ing dynasty that traditional China achieved its final form. The form of government which they introduced was carefully designed to balance the power of the Manchu and Chinese officials, but in its general lines it followed the Ming model and retained the highly centralized autocratic form developed by their predecessors. Unlike the Ming, however, the Manchus were extremely lucky with their emperors. Under three of the greatest rulers in Chinese history, the K'ang-hsi, Yung-cheng and Chien-lung emperors who occupied the throne in succession from 1661 to 1796, all men of extraordinary energy and outstanding talent, the personal power of the emperor was cemented even more firmly than before.

The achievement of the early Manchu period was very great. At home it was a period of stability, peace, and prosperity, and, although the Manchus' presence was irksome and their privileges offensive to the Chinese, they assimilated to Chinese culture more rapidly and more completely than any of their predecessors and went to great lengths to win the support and allegiance of the scholar gentry. Of all the dynasties of conquerors which have ruled China, theirs was undoubtedly the most successful and the most constructive.

One field in which they were extremely successful was in their conduct of foreign affairs. In a series of brilliantly conceived military campaigns the Manchus restored Chinese sovereignty over all the areas which had traditionally formed a part of Chinese territory, including Manchuria, which was retained as their homeland and barred to Chinese settlement, Mongolia, Turkestan and much of Central Asia, and for the first time Tibet. Beyond these areas, which were occupied by Manchu armies and controlled from Peking, there was a ring of states which acknowledged China as their titular overlord and sent tribute missions to the court. But the campaigns which established the Manchu empire, with large forces ranging far into Inner Asia, into such distant and inaccessible regions as Burma and Nepal and Vietnam, were enormously and disproportionately expensive.

This expense had to be met from the antiquated and ineffectual system of taxation depending very heavily upon land taxes, which had been pegged early in the eighteenth century. A great proportion of the revenues which were collected was dissipated either through the inefficiencies of government and the lack of an accounting system or through corruption at every level in administration. By the end of the 18th century the finances of what was still the world's richest and certainly its most populous empire were very shaky indeed.

The Ming potter at work. On the right is a heap of white clay from which porcelain is made. The man in the foreground is throwing a pot on the wheel; the one behind finishes another with a small knife. (19)

Tree felling: in the middle two trees are chopped down with axes. In the foreground the trunk is trimmed. Note, bottom left, the official supervisor speaking to the workers who, according to custom, kneel before him. (20)

Ming coins were made of copper with square holes in the middle. Here the matrices are laid out in a grid on the right and covered with sand from the heaps behind to form moulds. The metal is

heated in the furnace (centre) and poured into the moulds (upper left), which are fastened together and stacked upright. The finished coins emerge in strips and have to be cut apart. (21)

Inefficiency did not make itself felt only at the financial level. At every level of local government, administrative inertia had begun to limit the effective functioning of the administrative machine. Even more than in earlier times the recruitment of officials through the examination system placed great stress on conventional humanistic education and ideological conformity, rather than on real imagination and originality. Moreover, technical competence and specialized knowledge, which were increasingly required as society became more complex and diversified, were looked down upon as something appropriate only to underlings. Although some attempt was made to provide the new official with some in-service training in general administrative routine, specialist knowledge was picked up haphazardly in the course of an official's duties. The official decided disputed cases by applying the moral lessons of his humanist Confucian education, while most of the routine business, whether in legal cases, tax-collection, or the organization of social services was performed by the huge army of professional secretaries, low-grade clerks, and minor underlings. The latter neither shared nor cared for the Confucian training of their masters, but kept the administration moving by the constant practice of graft and bribery and by their own knowledge of custom, precedent, and local conditions. Corruption, either accepted by tradition in the form of 'conventional fees' for every conceivable action or sheer illegal graft, riddled the whole administration, from the clerks, who being unpaid had to accept such payments or starve, to the imperial favourites such as Ho Shen, who in the last

days of Chien-lung, when the emperor's powers were failing, built up a colossal fortune by means of graft and patronage on a national scale.

In spite of the shortcomings of government and in spite of the expense of its foreign adventures, China in the 17th and 18th centuries was immensely wealthy and productive. Trade continued to burgeon throughout this period, and the merchants continued to prosper. To the Hui-chou merchants, the Shansi merchants, and the industrialists of the Kiangsu who were already powerful in late Ming times there were now added the immensely wealthy salt merchants of Kiangsu and the merchants who dealt with overseas trade at Amoy and traded with increasing numbers of Western merchants at Canton. These great merchant princes had much influence with the official class, and could now rather easily gain acceptance as members of the 'gentry' by purchasing official status as graduates, a practice which in the 19th century came to be abused on a massive scale.

The guild organizations of merchants in individual trades grew steadily more efficient. Merchants organized the transport of goods and their insurance in transit on a wide regional scale. Every great city had associations of persons from specific provinces or cities, which provided lodging and some security in a strange city. Associations of manufacturers, with regular systems of apprenticeship, began to appear. A strong monetary system was established, backed by abundant supplies of foreign silver, though continually hamstrung by the shortage of copper for coinage, and there were well

Ch'ing 'banner troops' were first organized in the Manchu home-lands, and took their name from the coloured flags under which they were grouped. After the Manchus conquered China they were regarded as picked soldiers to strengthen the army, but by the 19th century (above) were no longer effectual as a fighting force. (22)

organized native banking and credit systems. Handicraft industry in every variety produced an enormous range of commodities. When the emperor informed the first Western envoys to Peking that China had no need of their manufactures, he was speaking the literal truth.

p 52 (56, 57) All this commercial activity, and the state structure too, rested upon the country's agriculture. Here, as under the Ming, there had been little technological innovation. The increasing population had to be supported by increasing the area under cultivation, or by the more and more intensive cultivation of existing lands. Under the Ming it had been possible to accommodate the increase by resettling the north, by bringing into cultivation marginal lands in the south, and by cultivating uplands. But the population, which had doubled under the Ming and had reached about 150,000,000 in 1600, continued to grow at an ever-accelerating pace. By 1800 it had reached 320,000,000. On the eve of the Taiping rebellion in 1850 it was over 400,000,000. By the middle of the 18th century the population had already reached the optimum which could be supported by traditional agriculture. Further expansion depended solely upon more and more intensive use of labour on the land, and diminishing returns for labour had set in. The standard of living began inexorably to deteriorate.

At the end of the 18th century the state of the economy, outwardly so prosperous, was in fact already precarious. It was made still more so by the changes in the pattern of foreign trade which followed the introduction of opium by foreign merchants. During the earlier periods foreign trade, mostly in tea, silk, and porcelain, for which there was a large European market, had brought in a steady flow of foreign silver. In the first decades of the 19th century, after the spectacular growth of the opium trade, the balance of trade was reversed, and silver began to be exported in large quantities, with disastrous effects on the currency and the economy as a whole, particularly in southern China. By the mid-19th century, over-population and poverty had reached such a point that only a radical technological breakthrough of some kind could have saved the Chinese economy.

By the end of the 18th century, then, China had reached p 51 (54) a crisis point in almost every sphere. The economy was yielding to the relentless pressure of population increase. The dynasty, so far sustained by a succession of extra-ordinarily active and able emperors who had been able to operate effectively the centralized system where all important and many routine decisions had to be made by the ruler in person, now had to function without a strong hand at the helm, and without any institutional arrange-ments which would have provided an alternative source of authority. The bureaucracy, weighed down by ad-ministrative inertia and hampered by immemorially old formalities, continued to go through the motions; but, staffed, as it was, by scholars whose entire education was conservative and conformist, it did not have the means or the will to make necessary innovations or to respond to change or to new situations. Radical innovation was needed in the political structure, which had provided the longest record of orderly government in any civilization

The later 19th century saw China beset with a host of internal problems, largely due to the inefficient Manchu administration.

Famine ravaged the provinces. Here peasants of Wenchow seize a cargo of grain in defiance of the local authorities. (23)

but was now hypnotized by respect for past achievements and bogged down in established precedent; in the economy, which, although up to this point remarkably productive and versatile, was no longer able to support a rapidly growing population without a steady decline in living standards; in technology, where innovation was frustrated by a superabundance of available labour; and in the ways of thought of the educated elite, which were inextricably committed to the social and political status quo.

The resultant stresses were already beginning to appear at the end of the 18th century in the traditional guise of a mass rebellion—that of the White Lotus secret society. But at the end of the 18th century an additional stress was added to the situation, this time from outside, in the shape of the new industrialized expansionism of the Western powers. This had a tremendous impact upon China. But because it was a novel stress—the impact for the first time of an alien culture which was the equal of, and in many respects superior to, that of traditional China—it has been greatly over-emphasized, by Chinese and Western historians alike. Much of the sorry failure, humiliation and terrible suffering which late 19th century China had

to endure came from internal problems—famine, widespread social unrest, political dissatisfaction with the increasingly corrupt and incompetent Manchu regime, a succession of massive and immensely destructive internal rebellions—which arose out of China's own existing weakness. Even without the appearance on the scene of the Western powers, the 19th century would certainly have seen a massive upheaval in China's institutions. The pressures from the Western powers ensured that this upheaval would be aggravated, and also ensured that it would be impossible for China to settle her own crisis, as she had dealt with so many crises in the past, on her own terms, by her own traditional methods.

It is a moot point whether, in fact, the traditional forms would have been able to achieve more than a holding operation. This was attempted, with some measure of success, in the T'ung-chih restoration of the 1860s. But things had probably reached a point by the middle of the 19th century at which, even if China had remained insulated from the rest of the world, master of her Far Eastern *oikumene*, she could no longer have dealt effectively with her massive accumulation of problems without a sharp break with the past.

78

III BEYOND THE WALL

China's relations with her northern neighbours

OWEN LATTIMORE

The Hsiung-nu move on the feet of swift horses, and in their breasts beat the hearts of beasts. They shift from place to place as fast as a flock of birds, so that it is extremely difficult to corner them and bring them under control . . . It would not be expedient to attack the Hsiung-nu. Better to make peace with them!

Han An-kuo, minister of Emperor Ching of the Han

The Great Wall marks a frontier that goes back to the very dawn of China's history—the frontier between settled arable farmers and pastoral nomads. To the south arose the flourishing civilizations of the Shang and the Chou; to the north the mobile tribes with their simpler way of life and their property in cattle posed an ever-present threat.

The Wall was the achievement of the amazing Ch'in Dynasty, who in the space of twenty years probably did more to transform China than any subsequent regime. Before 228 BC, separate states along the northern border had constructed defence works against barbarian raids. The Ch'in, between 228 and 210 BC, caused them to be connected and completed until they formed a continuous line over 1,400 miles long—the distance from Paris to Smolensk or New York to Kansas City—running east–west from the sea just north of Peking to the edge of the mountains of Central Asia. The materials are earth and stone faced with brick; the height varies between 20 and 30 feet and there are square watch-towers at close intervals, on which fires were lit in emergencies. Along the top is a path 10–12 feet wide, protected by crenellated parapets. Since the course of the Wall was determined by defensive considerations, it normally follows the crests of hills, snaking across the country almost like a feature of nature. It is China's oldest architectural monument and her most spectacular.

The Great Wall encourages the impression that Chinese and barbarians remained hermetically sealed off from each other. This was by no means the case. Not only was it frequently breached by invading armies, but a constant ebb and flow of trade and tribute passed through it. The direction and volume of this flow are indications of the changing relationship between China and her northern neighbours. China did not automatically enjoy the advantage. Provincial governors were often obliged to pay for their peace and quiet by awarding subsidies to troublesome chiefs.

The north was a breeding ground of conquerors— the Khitan, the Jurchid and the Mongols all founded dynasties. Finally came the Manchus whose reign saw the end of imperial China. Each of them had partially imbibed Chinese civilization in their homelands and came not simply as barbarians but as a ruling class ready to preserve the institutions which they found. None of them broke the continuity of Chinese civilization. All China's conquerors ended by being conquered by China. (1)

The northern nomads occupied the whole of the Central Asia steppes from China to Russia, at intervals erupting with equal violence into the histories of both East and West. The Mongols provide the most extreme example. For a few astonishing years in the 13th century they occupied both Peking and Budapest.

The steppes were a training ground for war. As far back as Chou times nomad cavalry had forced the Chinese to abandon their chariots and reorganize their army, and the hunting tradition (left: a scene of about 1400) survived the rise and fall of the Mongol dynasty in China. (2)

Nomadic life has changed between prehistoric times and the present century, but many elements have remained constant. This 14th-century miniature (centre left) shows some common scenes in camp: one man washing clothes, another blowing a fire to make a meal, another attending to a saddle. Horses and weapons complete the picture—the hardy Asiatic horses that were the Mongols' most prized possessions and the bows and arrows at which they were unsurpassed. (3)

The road to Persia lay through the lands of the nomads and they eagerly seized the chance of profiting by the trade. Below left: a Persian emissary to T'ang China. Below: travellers crossing the desert during the 14th century, when Mongol rule made east–west contacts easier than before. (4, 5)

The descendants of the Mongols still pursue the old way of life. Here a group of nomads in the Gobi region pause with their sheep, camels and horses on their way to fresh pastures. (6)

Barbarian alliances were a normal feature of Chinese diplomacy, one tribe being subsidized to defeat the others, a process sometimes glamorized by Chinese historians. In the 7th century the Uighurs, a tribe of Turkish origin, having sacked the town of Lo-yang, were persuaded to ally themselves with China to defeat other Turks in the Tarim basin. This coup was attributed to the personal courage of a T'ang general, Kuo Tzǔ-i (below), who entered their camp unarmed and received their homage. (7)

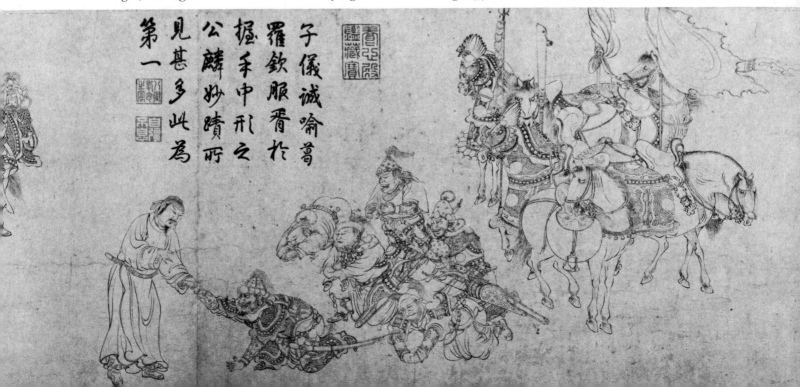

A nation of warriors: when this horseman was painted, *c.* 1400, the great age of Mongol expansion was over and they had been driven out of China by the Ming. He is about to plait the tail of his war-horse. Most of the artistic conventions here are Persian, but the spiral patterns on the belt are Chinese. (8)

In Chinese eyes the early Mongols were primitive and slightly grotesque people, though their skill in horsemanship won respect. This drawing on silk, by the Chinese artist Chao Kuang-fu, shows Mongol royalty in the 10th century. (9)

Genghis Khan (the modern Mongolian spelling is Chinges) assumed leadership of the Mongols in 1206 and immediately turned a loose confederation of tribes into a strong feudal state with a mission to conquer the world. Five years later he attacked China and in 1215 captured the capital, the site of Peking. A Persian miniature (above left) gives an idea of the exotic splendour of his court. Above right: the Mongol army besieging Ch'eng-tu. (10, 11)

Khubilai Khan (right), Genghis's grandson, completed the conquest of China, replacing the Sung by his own dynasty, the Yuan, and even attempting invasions of Japan and Java. Khubilai's China is well known in the West from the descriptions of Marco Polo and other travellers. Most of the splendours they admired were in fact due to the Sung rather than to Khubilai, but he was a cultured and sensitive man who appreciated what he found and built upon it. Even so, Khubilai preferred to administer his empire through non-Chinese, and in fact probably never learnt the Chinese language. (12)

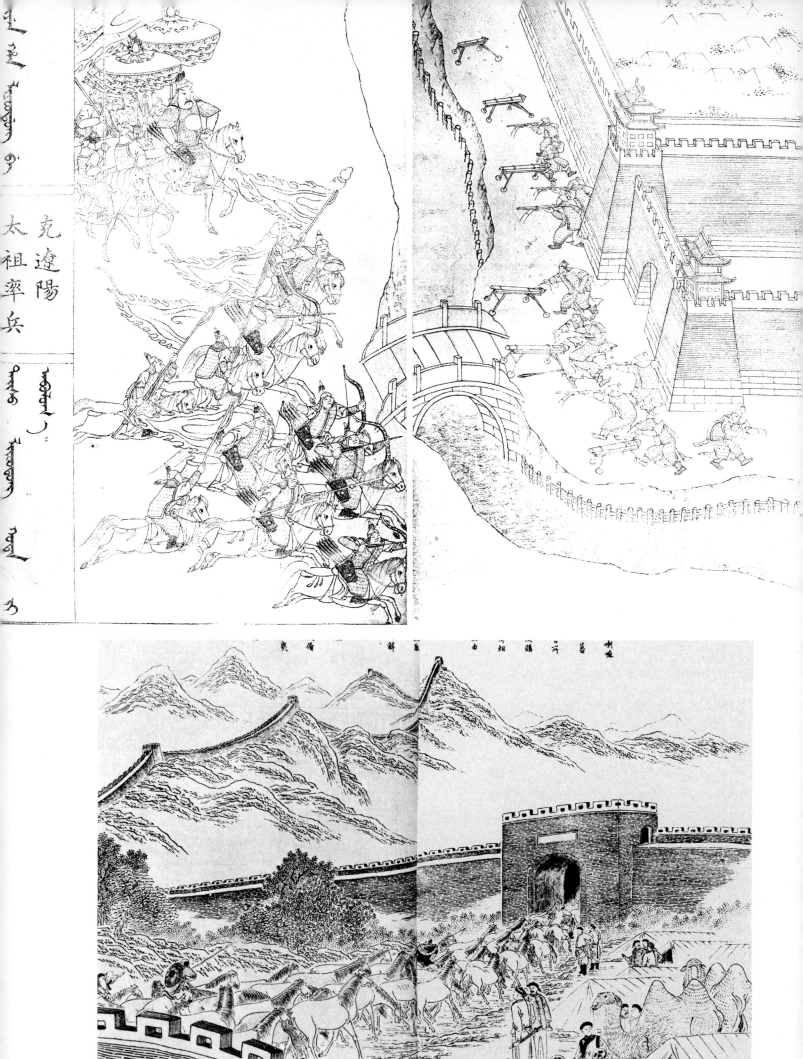

克遼陽
太祖率兵

The last conquerors to penetrate China from the north were the Manchus. Like the Mongols, they were a loosely organized group of tribes forged into unity by a single dynamic leader. The Genghis Khan of the Manchus was Nurhachi (later called T'ai-tsu, 'Great Progenitor'). Born in 1559, he rose to power in the service of China,

Horses from the steppes had always been among the main items of trade through the Great Wall, and this continued after the Manchus had taken over in the mid-17th century. This drawing (left) belongs to the 19th century, but the scene it shows had not changed for many centuries. (17)

learning much from the Ming administration and himself employing Chinese advisers. In 1618 he attacked China. In this series of drawings Nurhachi is seen on horseback on the far left, as his soldiers storm a town. The Chinese already had guns, but they were as yet no match for the Manchu arrows. (13–16)

In their days of power the Manchus looked back to their 'heroic' age with a certain nostalgia, perpetuating the warrior tradition in their art after it had changed in reality. Below: an 18th-century general, Ma-ch'ang, is still portrayed in the old epic style as a horseman with bow and arrows. (18)

Reversal of roles: before 1644 the Manchus had presented horses as tribute to the Ming emperors. Now, seated upon the throne themselves, they received the same offerings from the tribes that remained beyond the Wall. Here Ch'ien-lung (1736–95) receives Kazakh envoys. (19)

Modern Mongolia is not entirely cut off from its past. Nomadism has become a form of 'ranching' and automobiles are used as well as horses, but in many areas pastoralism is the way of life, and traditional crafts—such as tent-making—are still necessary. This naive painting of a village was recently exhibited at Ulan Bator. The Cossacks began their expansion into Central Asia at about the same time as the Manchus were conquering China. Incorporation into the Russian Empire followed in the 19th century. (20)

OWEN LATTIMORE

China's relations with her northern neighbours

AN ANCIENT POLARIZATION between two economies, two ways of winning life from the terrain occupied by a society, accounts for the long-enduring tensions on China's northern frontier. By the second millennium BC, when the Bronze Age emerged out of the Neolithic Age, the Chinese of north China had evolved a distinctive agriculture. Even with stone tools the soft loess soil of the middle Yellow River (Huang-ho) region was easy to cultivate. Although the rainfall was erratic, there was water in the valleys of the streams flowing into the Yellow River, and—again because of the softness of the soil—ditches could be dug for irrigation on a small scale. The consequence was that those villages which practised the most intensive agriculture prospered most and grew fastest.

Rival economies

Farther north, beyond what came to be the Great Wall frontier, but south of the Gobi zone, there was less rain, and the streams were not so suitable for agriculture. Both north and south of the Gobi zone, those communities prospered most which made progress in the handling of larger numbers of livestock, and in the forms of social and political organization best suited to the pastoral technique. These were: wide dispersal (an 'extensive' economy contrasted with the Chinese 'intensive' economy), and a disciplined procedure for grazing each kind of livestock (sheep and goats, cattle, horses, and camels) on the most suitable pastures, and for controlling orderly movement between seasonal pastures. It must be emphasized that the 'nomadism' of such communities does not mean erratic wandering. The concept of territory, of a specific orbit of migration from seasonal pasture to seasonal pasture, with a clan or tribal organization to maintain the claim to the orbit of migration, is as early among nomads as the concept of the village domain is among farming peoples.

Bronze, which came into use among Chinese and nomads at about the same time, did not greatly change the technology of production, since there was not enough of it available to make farming implements on a large scale. There was, however, enough to make superior weapons. It therefore speeded up the emergence, among the more or less undifferentiated warrior-levies of the Stone Age, of a military-aristocratic elite, a ruling class capable of perpetuating itself, and of creating increasingly

Tribesmen from the northern frontier. The Hsiung-nu, with their composite bows which could be aimed from the saddle, were extremely mobile. They formed a tribal federation which spread from Manchuria to Turkestan and was a constant threat to the Han dynasty, raiding and looting in North China and on one occasion getting within sight of the capital. (1)

large political units. Cities came into being which, in China, drew tribute from subordinate villages. They were not 'city-states' like those of the Greeks, but they were cities which were the capitals of states. In the northern steppes, where a similar development occurred, there was no similar growth towards an urban-rural complex, because, in order to collect their tribute, the members of the ruling class had to move about, in contact with their mobile subjects.

In both societies, therefore, there was a parallel development. In both, the ruling class, the core of the society, sought to expand into and appropriate as much as possible of its own kind of optimum territory: for the nomads—the richest and seasonally the most dependable pastures (especially the most sheltered winter pastures); for the Chinese—the terrain most suited to an intensive agriculture aided by irrigation, making possible a denser grouping of villages and larger cities, with an artisan population fed by the grain tribute of the villages.

But there was also an increasing tension between the two societies, expressed in the increasing inequality of the terms of trade. Both the nomadic economy and the village farming economy are, when restricted entirely to their own resources, self-sufficient. As the Chinese society matured, however, it produced both a greater and a more diversified surplus, enough to satisfy not only the requirements of survival but the luxury demands of the ruling class. It was out of this 'essentials plus luxury' adequacy that there grew the solid, imperturbable self-satisfaction of the Chinese: the conviction that the Chinese civilization provided everything that was worth having, and that nothing imported from abroad was really worth, economically, what China would have to pay for it in the way of exports.

For a nomadic society, on the other hand, it was possible to produce a surplus of necessities but not a surplus (or a sufficient diversity) of the conveniences and luxuries that a ruling class, as it prospers, increasingly demands. Even at a level above necessity but below luxury there was always a demand for grain among the nomads. It

81 (1)

p 82
(2,3)
p 83 (6)
p 84 (8)

was not a necessary supplement to their meat-and-milk diet, but it was handy to have in reserve, especially in seasons when the herds were in poor condition. Nor was cloth, and still less silk, a necessity; skins and furs would do. Nor was even iron a necessity; nomad smiths could turn out weapons and tools of high quality, but their production was necessarily small, and it was easier to buy in quantity from the Chinese.

From a very early period, therefore, the nomads of China's northern frontier wanted more from the Chinese than the Chinese wanted from them. The Chinese preferred to make clothes from hemp (later cotton), and silk; there was never more than a very small demand for wool. Nor did they need much mutton and beef. The Chinese preferred pork and fowl (pigs and chickens were the village scavengers), and they had plenty of fish. Nor could the nomads produce enough treasure like gold and jade to provide an effective balance of payments. It is true p 87 (17) that there was always a market for horses, not only mares for the breeding of mules, but remounts for the Chinese Imperial Cavalry. (Trade in military supplies with potential enemies was always as characteristic of pre-industrial as it is now of industrial societies: American Indians shot American settlers with guns bought from American traders.) But it is a recurrent theme in the Chinese documents that the nomads wanted to sell, or to deliver as 'tribute', more horses than the Chinese wanted to accept.

The tributary relationship between the nomads and the Chinese empire continued into modern times. In 1884 the Mongol princes presented to the Ch'ing court as tribute one hundred camels and four hundred horses, seen here entering Peking. (2)

The politics of inequality

Economic imbalance was a stimulus to political action. Military pressure in the form of frontier raiding could encourage Chinese officials to grant subsidies to tribal chiefs, in the form of trade-goods and trade-permits (euphemistically known in the Chinese tradition as 'permission to present tribute'). Goods thus acquired could be passed on in more distant inter-tribal trade. Many 'international' merchants from India, Bactria, Iran, and Parthia engaged in this trade. The great 'Silk Road' that linked China with the Mediterranean was not pioneered in a Chinese effort to unload surplus Chinese silk on a wide market. That is a modern-minded assumption which dies hard. The record of the Chinese diplomatic explorer Chang Chien, whose name is associated with the origins of this trade-route, tells us that his mission was to find allies who might help the Chinese to turn the flank of the troublesome Hsiung-nu in Mongolia: if they were granted trade privileges which were refused to the Hsiung-nu, that would make trouble among the tribes and relieve the pressure on the Great Wall. p 82 (4, 5)

It is important here to consider circumspectly the Chinese documents on which we chiefly rely. Like the Roman historians, the Chinese conventionally assigned to 'barbarians' no higher motive than rapacity. Here again, however, the truth can be seen through the conventions. The inequality of the terms of trade set in motion a complex of processes. A chief who had forced a provincial governor on the frontier to buy him off for the sake of peace and quiet could, by distributing rewards, increase his tribal following. A rival chief could then offer, if the Chinese would treat him properly, to attack the chief who was growing too dangerously powerful. One must not be misled by ideas of patriotism of a modern kind. In times of trouble, grain-growing peasants often accepted the protection of barbarian warriors. Conversely, defeated barbarians were often 'accepted' by the Chinese and allocated frontier territories where they served as auxiliary troops, loyal to the Chinese state rather than to their tribal kinsmen for as long as that particular situation lasted. p 83 (

By the 10th century this interaction of processes had reached a high level of complexity and of political sophistication. Between the fall of the Han dynasty (whose rule of 400 years may be called China's Roman Empire period) in 220 and the founding of the equally great T'ang dynasty in 618, China had passed through its equivalent of Europe's Dark Ages; but for the student of world history the important thing to note is that this 'equivalent' was no equivalent. When the barbarians broke through to the Mediterranean, Rome was finished, because it had no hinterland. (Byzantium, because it had enough hinterland in Anatolia and the Near East to combine with sea power, survived as a lesser but highly civilized empire for another thousand years.) One of the keys to China's history is that China had in the south an immense hinterland. Here the 'barbarians' were not mounted warriors, capable of wide movement, but jungle-bound tribes, each limited to a few valleys. They were, moreover, already cultivators, and they lived in a rich terrain. By the introduction of superior techniques brought from the north they could be 'converted' into Chinese, the rate of production could be raised, and new

81 (1)

The Khitans, a semi-agricultural, semi-nomadic people from South Manchuria, extended their power over Mongolia and eventually part of North China, where they founded the Liao dynasty, making their capital at Peking. The Sung dynasty to the south was unable to dislodge the Khitans from North China and were forced to pay annual tribute to the Liao. The Jurchid peoples (right) drove the Sung dynasty from their northern capital of Kaifeng into South China and founded the Chin dynasty. Later the Manchus sprang from the Jurchid tribes. (3, 4)

states which perpetuated the classical traditions of north China could be built up rapidly. Retreat from the north was in fact transmuted in large part into conquest of the south; and this retreat-conquest went far beyond the disorderly flight of terrified peasants. The movement was in the main directed by representatives of the 'great houses' of north China, who did not come to terms and take service (as some of their kinsmen did) under the steppe conquerors, but organized their own peasants and dependents, moved south, and carried their institutions with them.

Tenth-century China, therefore, was a China with a new centre of gravity. Chinese control beyond the Great Wall, by any combination of war and diplomacy, was no longer possible, but for several centuries there was to be a flourishing Chinese state, centred on the Yangtze Valley, with a zone of expansion to the south. The economy improved—with, for example, the importation of higher-yielding strains of rice from what is now Laos, Cambodia and Vietnam. New hillside crops, above the rice-paddies, were also developed. Art and literature attained levels that have been famous ever since. Philosophers reconsidered and revised the Confucian tradition. A strikingly 'modern' mentality began to show itself: in the observation of nature, learned men, instead of merely recording marvels and mysteries, began to compile classificatory lists of plants, animals, and minerals, and to note relationships, causes, and consequences. In the economy, finally, there began to appear what Chinese historians of today call 'sprouts' of true capitalism— venture and entrepreneurial capitalism, that is, as compared with the medieval norms of barter and usury trade in food and everyday commodities, and scarcity trade in luxuries and rarities.

Frontier history was an important factor in the development of this new China far south of the frontier, but the operation of the frontier factor has been insufficiently understood. In the 10th century, power north of the Great Wall shifted decisively from the west to the east, from western Mongolia, where the steppe-pastoral economy prevailed, to eastern Mongolia and Manchuria.

The key to the shift was south Manchuria, which, though excluded from 'China proper' by the Great Wall, had always been peopled by Chinese. Here the monsoon rainfall was more regular than in the rest of north China. Grain crops were heavy and provided food for fairly large towns and even cities, with artisans producing wares for trade with the steppe tribes. Surplus grain could be floated in barges down the lower Liao river, and then by a short sea transit to the Shantung peninsula and the ready market of north China. In this region a tribal people, the Khitan, were able to attach their mobile cavalry power to a solid agricultural and urban base and, drawing on the experience of previous half-barbarian dynasties in north China within the Great Wall, to progress from tribal to dynastic politics.

Outsiders

This question of 'drawing on previous experience' is worth a note in passage. In the periodization of Chinese history by dynasties, peoples like the Khitan who founded the Liao dynasty (907–1114), the Jurchid who founded the Kin or Chin dynasty (1115–1234), and the Mongols who founded the Yuan dynasty (1206 in Mongolia, 1279 in China, to 1367) seem to appear suddenly. If we search the records of earlier dynasties, however, we always find that these names have been known for centuries. They are first the names of clans or sub-tribes, which subordinate to themselves tribes that had formerly been important, and at last become 'great'—just as the Huns of Attila, by the time they became 'great', had brigaded Goths and others under their battle standards. The point is important. No really 'raw' barbarians ever achieved either total or even partial conquest of China: all leaders of conquerors came from families or clans which had had at least several generations of experience in dealing with Chinese officials and the Chinese state; they knew their history and they knew what they were doing.

Although they knew what they were doing, they were never able to accomplish what they set out to do. All barbarian conquerors of states within China—or, like the

p 85
(10–12)

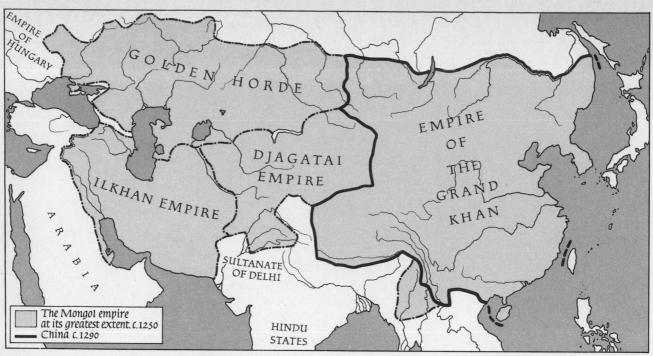

The Mongol empire at its greatest extent. China, as one of its Khanates, was incorporated into the empire. (5)

Mongols and the Manchus, of the whole of China—began with the same idea as the Normans in Saxon and Celtic Britain: an elite linked together by a blood-kin loyalty of a clannish quality (for which reason the notion of 'race' is here anachronistic) that included both the aristocracy (the 'upper elite') and the rank and file. To symbolize this clannishness, attempts were made to preserve the language of the conquerors and to prohibit or limit intermarriage; but because men of the conquering people normally took women of the conquered people as primary or secondary wives, and the 'ban on intermarriage' applied in reality only to giving women of the elite to men of the subject people, and because children learnt first and best the language of their mothers, the language of the conquered always prevailed.

To narrow the analysis to the social absorption of the conquerors, however, is just that: it is too narrow. In frontier history the economic factor is the one that has been most neglected. Contemporary Chinese historians are interested in periods in which, they say, 'sprouts' of capitalism showed themselves, only to wither later: periods, that is, in which a post-feudal economy began to emerge, but true entrepreneurial capitalism failed to establish itself, because it was unable to throw off feudal and bureaucratic controls. The most important of these periods were those of the Northern and Southern Sung, when most of north China was ruled by invaders, and that of the Ming, which began triumphantly with the overthrow of Mongol rule, but soon came under heavy pressure along the Great Wall frontier, and at last was itself overthrown by the Manchus. (The official date is 1644, but the process of Manchu conquest had begun more than half a century earlier.)

Even the Chinese historians, however, do not seem to have appreciated to the full the way in which frontier pressure operated as a factor in the Chinese economy. Most historians—Chinese and non-Chinese, Marxists and non-Marxists—hold that the Chinese society, whether we call it 'feudal' or 'bureaucratic', was inimical to business enterprise. Regulation of the state, as we saw in the last chapter, was the prerogative of bureaucrats who were in the main recruited from landholding families prosperous enough to save their sons from field labour, and to provide them with tutors so that they could pass the state examinations. A landlord-bureaucracy of this kind was self-perpetuating, if it took precautions against the rise to power of any competing class. It tolerated merchants as distributors of the landlord's products—grain, tea, silk—but allowed them no control. Salt, a national necessity, was a state monopoly, administered by the anti-merchant bureaucracy. The actual producers and distributors of salt, operating under licence, could individually get rich, but they could not win control or establish a merchant monopoly challenging the state monopoly.

Frontier pressure was the one force that could distort this pattern. The Northern and Southern Sung dynasties paid tributes of hundreds of thousands of ounces of silver and hundreds of thousands of rolls of silk to the barbarians of the Liao and Kin (Chin) dynasties. Under the Ming dynasty undisguised tribute was not paid, but the weakening of the Ming in the late 16th and early 17th centuries was marked by increasing demands from the Mongols and Manchus for more frontier fairs and market towns. Here the barbarians brought what was formally called 'tribute'; but the privilege of 'presenting tribute' was always accompanied by a privilege of private trade for members of the 'tribute mission'. In fact, it is one of the key indices of Chinese economic history that, instead of periods of strength in China being marked by increased demands for real tribute to be paid by the barbarians, periods of weakness in China were marked by increasing demands from the barbarians for the right to present more fictitious tribute. In other words, political pressure and the threat of military action enabled the barbarians in such periods to improve the terms of trade in their own favour.

p 88 (

92

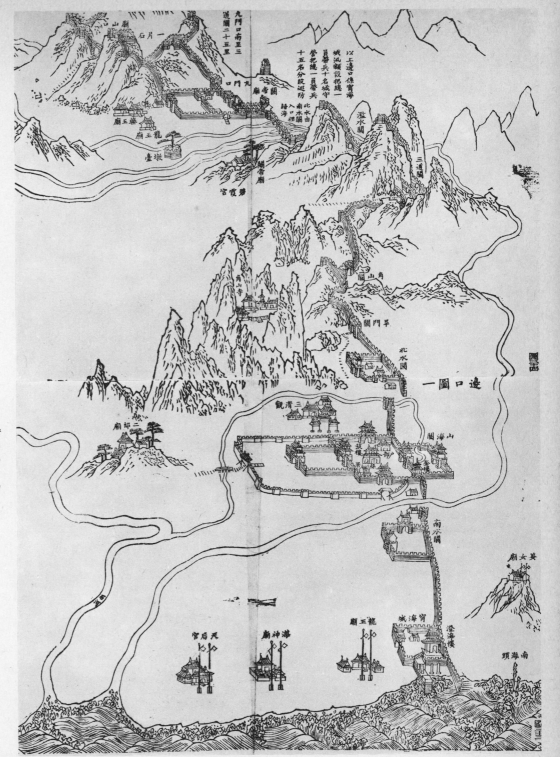

At the Shanhaikuan (right) the Great Wall meets the coast. This pass, the gateway from Manchuria to the North China plain, has always been of strategic importance in Chinese dealings with the northern nomads. (6)

Under either system—real tribute paid by the Chinese or fictitious tribute paid by the barbarians—the wealth of the barbarians was increased, and this led to demands for more and more supplementary trade. As the Chinese merchants were the indispensable collectors, transporters, and deliverers of the commodities demanded by the barbarians, they were in a sense under the patronage and protection of the barbarian rulers or chieftains. This made them more independent of the landlord-based bureaucracy, better able to resist being 'taxed to death' by the Chinese state, and better able to diversify their enterprises and to invest their profits in new ways. It would seem a necessary conclusion that there was a direct connection between periods of frontier barbarian ascendancy and periods of the 'sprouts of capitalism' in China.

Russia looks east

With the coming of the Manchus there was a partial continuation of the old frontier tradition, accompanied by vast changes. Although the Manchu conquest is often treated as if it hinged on a single act of breaking through the Great Wall (or, rather, being let in through the Wall by a traitorous Chinese general), it took in fact six decades: from 1583, when the Manchus proclaimed their imperial aspirations, to 1644, when they set a child emperor on the throne in Peking. The conquest therefore fell within that miraculous period when a true world history of all the continents was created. In 1588, with the defeat of the Spanish Armada, power began to shift from the Spanish and Portuguese to the English, Dutch, and French. In India, as the Mogul dynasty declined, the English and

p 87 (13–16)

French began their long rivalry for its heritage; in America they undertook the vigorous colonization of the Atlantic states and Canada. In the same period the Thirty Years' War redistributed power in Northern Europe, the Japanese withdrew into seclusion, and the Cossacks began their fantastically rapid exploration and conquest of Siberia.

Because of the conventional lack of cross-reference between the histories of Europe, Russia, and Eastern Asia, it is easy to overlook the importance of the fact that the Russians were reaching the Amur and the Ussuri in the very decades when the Manchus were depleting the tribal manpower of north Manchuria by mobilizing it for the coming conquest of China. They were also mobilizing the manpower of southern Mongolia—the modern Inner Mongolia, from the Ordos through Chahar to Manchuria—partly by conquest and partly by a skilful diplomacy, winning over important Mongol chieftains as allies, and strengthening the alliances by giving them Manchu princesses in marriage. In this opening period, the Russians, because of the small, far-ranging bands of Cossacks, were also thought of as a tribal people. In fact the Manchus and Chinese, hearing the name 'Russ' from Tungus tribes in a form which in the Chinese pronunciation became 'Lo-ch'a', and from the Mongols in the form 'Oros', which in the Chinese pronunciation became 'E-lo-ssu', thought for a time that there were two new barbarian tribes appearing on the horizon.

These tribal associations, if transposed into a modern cliché-idiom, make it easy to treat the entry of the Russians into Chinese history as merely the latest chapter of ancient trans–Great Wall history. The comparison can be made much too glib. In the first place, the Cossacks represented the first example of technological superiority approaching China from the north. They were armed with muskets and with at least some artillery at the very time when the Manchus (though they, too, had some firearms, acquired first from the Chinese and then from the Jesuits) had set out on the last bow-and-arrow conquest of China. (This fact alone meant that the Manchus, the last dynasty to establish itself in China in the traditional, 'classical' manner, could not possibly fall, when the time came for it to fall, in the old manner.)

p 87 (18)

In the second place, the Russians were the most versatile people who ever played a part in tribal history and Chinese frontier history. The Cossacks were not only superb horsemen but superb boatmen and woodsmen. If, on horseback, they reached a river that looked promising, they were capable of light-heartedly abandoning their horses, felling and sawing timber, building boats, and floating off down the river—which, in Siberia, meant floating toward the north. On such a voyage, if it later looked promising to strike out into the forests or tundra away from the river, they would with the same audacity abandon their boats, get hold of horses, reindeer, or dogsleds, and start a fresh venture.

In the course of these forays the Russians built up a terrible record of brutality in their handling of tribal peoples; but one must go beyond that. In the late 1500s

it would be as absurd to expect 'gentlemanly behaviour' from Cossack adventurers as from Spanish Conquistadores or those pious pioneers who in New England

> *. . . first fell on their knees*
> *And then fell on the aborigines.*

More pertinent to the making of history was the flexibility that went with the Russian versatility. In the course of ages, south Russia and the Cossack homeland had been repeatedly invaded and partly ruled by Turkish peoples, not to mention the period of Russian subjection to the 'Tatar yoke' of the Mongol conquest. Alternating rule was an idea familiar to Russians. At one time Asians might rule Slavs, at another time Slavs rule Asians. Consequently, class was more important than race. Ruling-class Russians intermarried with ruling-class Asians, and subject-class Asians with their Russian class equals. When, therefore, the Russians encountered in Siberia and Central Asia peoples who had not yet reached the political level of nationhood, the end-result might be Russian conquest and rule, but on the road to that end-result many tribal chiefs and sub-chiefs voluntarily entered the Russian system. The Kalmuk Mongols of the Lower Volga were cheerful feudatories of the Tsar, and took part in the Russian conquest of the Caucasus. During the Russo-Japanese war, a 'Russian' cavalry officer who made a name for himself by cutting his way out of a Japanese encirclement was Prince Gantimur: he was the descendant of a Daghur Mongol chief, who, in the 17th century, when the Manchus conquered his homeland, had migrated to Siberia to take service under the 'White Khan' of the Russians, rather than submit to the 'Holy Khan' of the Manchus.

Equally important, perhaps even more important, was the many-sidedness of Russian economic activity. At the time of the formation of the Sino-Russian frontier, the Russian economy was backward if compared with Western Europe, but it was at a level which in Asia permitted fusion rather than stark superimposition. Both in Central Asia and in China itself there had been an immemorially old confrontation between an intensive irrigational agriculture and an extensive pastoral economy. The exchange of commodities between these extremes was limited, as has been argued above. The Russians, however, were accustomed to an extensive rainfall agriculture rather than an intensive irrigational agriculture. They could therefore profitably combine the use of livestock with plough-farming, whereas the hoe-farming of irrigational agriculture could not. On the Chinese side of the frontier zone, agriculture excluded the pastoralist. On the Russian side, it included him. The 'terms of trade' were better for the nomad when he could deal with the Russians than when the only possibility was to deal with the Chinese or the Central Asian oasis-khanates.

p 88 (2

It is beyond the scope of this chapter to project this historical account into an analysis of the contemporary relationship between Russia and China; but surely any casting of accounts made today ought to include what can be learned from the historical record.

IV THE PATH TO WISDOM

Chinese philosophy and religion

WING-TSIT CHAN

When the superior man has studied the Way, he loves men.

Confucius, *Analects*, 17/4

He who exerts his mind to the utmost knows his nature. He who knows his nature knows Heaven. To preserve one's mind and to nourish one's nature is the way to serve Heaven.

Mencius, *The Book of Mencius*, 7A/1

Faith and reason, philosophy and religion, are concepts which Western thinkers have on the whole tried to keep apart. Where a close connection has existed, as in Christianity and Islam, it is religion which, by becoming more and more intellectualized, has produced its own philosophical system. In China, the very reverse has been the case. Not only is the distinction between the two very much harder to draw, but the process of development has been inverted. Confucianism, Taoism and Buddhism all began as philosophies and branched off to become religions as well. It is as if Plato and Aristotle had been deified and worshipped for two thousand years, gathering round them a host of subsidiary gods and rituals from folk-beliefs and superstition.

Among the most ancient, and still the most popular, of these subsidiary figures are the so-called Kitchen Gods. Every household had its tutelary deity who presided over the hearth. This painting (opposite) shows one of them with his consort. Every year he was believed to ascend to the legendary Jade Emperor in heaven and report on the way the family had conducted itself, interceding for it and winning special favours. At the top is a calendar noting dates important in the agricultural year. The inscriptions at the sides say, 'Go up to heaven to say good words' and 'Return to the shrine to bestow blessings'. On the left is the word 'evil', on the right 'good'. The whole system clearly goes back to a primitive cult, but from early times it became associated with Taoism, the Jade Emperor taking his place alongside Lao-tzu. (1)

Confucius (the Latinized form of K'ung-fu-tzu, 'Grand Master K'ung') lived from 551 to 479 BC in Shantung province. As a minor official, magistrate and adviser to local rulers he made no great impact, but he attracted a group of followers who noted down his sayings and from them constructed a systematic philosophy which was to be basic to all future Chinese thought. Human relations, said Confucius, should be governed by moral principles, not by force or privilege; every rank and position should carry with it its duties and responsibilities. In the society he envisaged opportunity would be equal and power exercised only by the virtuous. Confucius's followers, who included Mencius and Hsün-tzu, extended and elaborated his teachings. (2)

The family unit was for the Confucians the basic brick from which society is built, embodying all the values that are essential to the state. In this painting from the 12th-century *Book of Filial Piety* children pay their respects to their parents. In the same way the citizen should respect the ruler, and the ruler govern by virtue and proper ceremonies. Titles must correspond to functions and deeds to words. (3)

A new Confucianism arose in the 11th century, in response to the challenges of Buddhism and Taoism. It was a highly sophisticated creed, made up of ideas that would certainly have puzzled Confucius himself. Among its leaders was Chu Hsi (left), who died in 1200. The centre of his system was a concept that can only be called theological – the Great Ultimate, which brings together principle (the eternal essence of things) and material force (physical substance) – but in trying to reach understanding he advocated rational techniques which in many respects foreshadow the scientific method. Chu Hsi's version of Confucian teachings served as the standard interpretation for the next 800 years, his influence extending to Korea and Japan. Here he appears in the attire of a plain citizen; he was dismissed from his position of lecturer before the emperor because of his attacks on a corrupt prime minister. (4)

Is Confucianism a religion? That depends on what is meant by religion. The distinction, for instance, between venerating one's ancestors as moral guides and worshipping them as supernatural beings is in practice often a subtle one. (The same problem has arisen in the Christian religion with regard to saints.) Honour to ancestors was strongly inculcated by Confucius, and political authority paternal authority writ large. Left: members of the imperial family bringing offerings to a family shrine. The plaques at the top record the names of ancestors whose spirits were believed to watch over the living. Such traditional ways of thought are still strong, and even in modern China (above) offerings of food are laid before the gravestones of the dead. (5, 6)

99

Confucian learning became the passport to success in China, since the civil service examinations were largely based on it. The Confucian Classics consisted of ancient works supposedly edited by him, and those of his immediate followers. These books became the ideology of government and the scholar-bureaucrats who studied them became the most influential class. In this detail from a Ming painting (above) four scholars greet each other as they enter the Imperial Palace. (7)

Women's subordination to men was an axiom of Confucianism, since society, from the family up, was male-dominated. From Sung times onwards they were practically confined to the home (left, detail from a Ch'ing painting), without property of their own or the right to remarry if their husbands died. Fashions such as binding the feet might win admiration and social position, but only emphasized their dependence. (8)

The Yin-Yang, one of the basic concepts of Chinese philosophy, is wholly abstract, yet has traditionally been represented symbolically: two mouchette-shapes, one light, one dark – the form of each defining that of the other – which together make up a perfect unity, the circle. In the same way, the universe and everything in it can be understood as the interaction of contrasting forces or elements, the dark Yin and the light Yang – words whose particular connotation will depend on the particular 'unity' being analysed. Right: sages study and meditate upon the Yin-Yang symbol. (9)

一青山一鹿帶鞍坡破下有一女子卧

木易若逢山下鬼火金

定於此處喪連環

Lao-tzu (left), traditionally a contemporary of Confucius, formulated a philosophy – Taoism – which begins from a completely opposite point of view. Virtue, for him, was not a system of rule-keeping but a matter of instinctual inner harmony. Confucius produced good citizens, Lao-tzu saintly mystics. Where the Confucian played his part on the stage of life, the Taoist retired into solitude, to Nature, to meditation. Two typically Taoist paintings are shown here. In the early 13th-century *Hermit Fishing* (below) by Ma Yüan, the philosopher pursues the path of tranquillity and non-action. In *Dreaming of Immortality in a Thatched Cottage* (bottom), of the 16th century, another sage, asleep at a table in the centre, sees himself as an immortal floating over the landscape. (10–12)

閶来隱几枕書眠夢入
壺中別有天彷彿未
親面目大還真訣得
親傳晋昌唐寅為
東原先生寫圖

102

Taoism's fate as a religion was to be even more ironic than that of religious Confucianism. Astrology, alchemy and a host of other absurdities reduced its pure doctrines to superstition, and it became associated especially with secret societies and political plots. This enigmatic page (left) of about 1870 is a concealed prophecy of the fall of the Manchu dynasty. The apparently descriptive caption on the left contains the words *an* (saddle), *lu* (deer) and *shan* (mountain), the name of a rebel general An Lu-shan in T'ang times (see p. 42). The lady is Yang Kuei-fei, the story's tragic heroine. (13)

Wayside altars to Taoism's innumerable gods dot the Chinese countryside (below). In them paper money is burnt as an offering to local spirits of the fields. (14)

Popular gods, grotesque creatures of half-serious, half-playful significance, like the elves and fairies of Western folklore, form part of the motley Taoist pantheon. Above: a door-guardian, one of the Men-shen, deified generals of the Shang dynasty, images of whom are hung on the door at New Year to ward off evil and bring blessings. (15)

The War God, Kuan Yü, goes back to a military hero of the Three Kingdoms period (born in AD 162), round whom stories gathered. In a characteristic way he can also act in a variety of other capacities, according to the locality or the special desires of the worshipper. In some places he was regarded as the God of Literature because he could recite Tso's *Commentary on the Annals.* (16)

Chung K'uei, 'Great Spiritual Chaser of Demons for the Whole Empire', protects his votaries from evil spirits, one of whom, carrying a light behind him, he has subdued and forced to act as his attendant. In this print he can be recognized by his blue cap, his dishevelled hair and the hairstrings which fly apart with loose ends. (17)

Longevity, Wealth and Happiness – the Three Blessings. The bald-headed God of Longevity holds a peach, symbol of long life, to be attained by religious devotion, represented by the scroll (of scriptures) and the gourd (holding medicine for the sick) on the staff behind him. In the centre is the God of Wealth. Of the blessings that the God of Happiness brings, the best is children. (18)

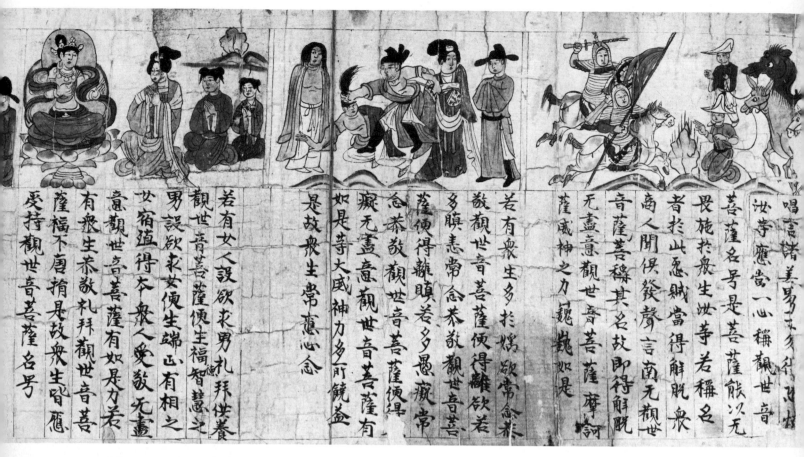

唱言諸善易士多行
泯尋應當一心稱觀世音
菩薩名号是菩薩能以無
畏施於衆生汝等若稱名
者於此怨賊當得解脫衆
商人聞俱發聲言南無觀世
音菩薩稱其名故即得解脫
無盡意觀世音菩薩摩訶薩
薩威神之力巍巍如是

若有衆生多於婬欲常念恭
敬觀世音菩薩便得離欲若
多瞋恚常念恭敬觀世音菩
薩便得離瞋若多愚癡常
念恭敬觀世音菩薩便得
離癡無盡意觀世音菩薩有
如是等大威神力多所饒益
是故衆生常應心念

若有女人設欲求男礼拜供養
觀世音菩薩便生福德智慧之
男設欲求女便生端正有相之
女宿植德本衆人愛敬無盡
意觀世音菩薩有如是力若
有衆生恭敬礼拜觀世音菩
薩福不唐捐是故衆生皆應
受持觀世音菩薩名号

The roots of Buddhism in China go back to the 1st century BC, though it was not introduced officially for another 200 years. At first its ideas found a place within the loose structure of Taoism, but by the 5th century AD it was a powerful force in its own right. Between 255 and 601 the *Lotus Sutra* was translated into Chinese three times, that of 406 being the most popular. Chapter 25, which related the miracles of the Bodhisattva (or saint) Kuan-yin, proved especially influential, and is illustrated on a silk painting found in the caves of Tun-huang (above). The next major step was in 645, when Hsüan-tsang returned to Ch'ang-an from India, bringing with him authentic versions of seventy-five Buddhist scriptures and a multitude of sacred images (below). Here the party is seen arriving at the temple, the road lined with priests and worshippers. (19, 20)

The pilgrim's return: another version of Hsüan-tsang journeying from India laden with Buddhist scrolls. The whisk in his left hand is to wipe away evil desires. (21)

The way to Buddhahood (right): episodes in the life of the Buddha Sakyamuni. He bids farewell to his groom; two gods and the 'five companions' visit him; he begins the life of austerity. (22)

Buddhism translated into the context of China underwent developments unknown in India. Kuan-yin, the Buddhist saint seen in pl. 19, was received into the Taoist pantheon as a female Goddess of Mercy. In this painting from the Tun-huang caves (left) we see the whole scene of which pl. 8 on p. 35 was a detail. A family, women on one side, men on the other, pay their devotions to Kuan-yin who sits enthroned above them. The inscription dates it precisely to 27 August AD 983. They pray 'that children and grandchildren may abound, that for ten thousand years and a thousand seasons there may be riches, dignity and prosperity'. (23)

Rebirth in the 'Pure Land' was promised by the Bodhisattva Amitabha (who in Japan became Amida, see p. 231). Again the great Buddhist shrine of Tun-huang provides the most splendid representations (right). In this 8th-century fresco Amitabha is seen teaching, surrounded by other Bodhisattvas and monks. His throne is a lotus, resting on a pedestal which is the world. (25)

Torment in Hell is the corollary of bliss in paradise, though both were foreign to Buddha's own doctrine. In this scene, also from Tun-huang, devils round up shackled sinners while another man roasts in eternal fire. (24)

The Buddhist message made peaceful progress in China. There was no violent clash between Buddhism and the other two faiths (as there was in the West between Christianity and Islam), and Buddha, Confucius and Lao-tzu are often represented together in amity. Buddhist ideas such as tranquillity, the suppression of desires and the way of non-action came very close to Taoism. But friction arose over the relation between religion and the state (Buddhism separating the two, Confucianism bringing them together) and over the nature of the soul (transmigration being alien to both Confucianism and Taoism).

The political situation was also important. In AD 221 the Han Empire broke up into the Three Kingdoms. The northern Wei dynasty, less bound to Confucian traditions, promoted Buddhism as a state religion. The caves of Yün-kang are its memorial. Left: a Buddha, probably Sakyamuni, about forty feet high, with attendant. In the photograph of the whole cliff face (below) this cave appears on the extreme left. The date is between AD 471 and 499. (26, 27)

Buddhist art also underwent transformation when it migrated to China. The Indian stupa became the Chinese pagoda, an architectural type originally evolved in wood but later built in stone or brick. The 10th century saw the introduction of the octagonal pagoda divided into three distinct parts: a base, a body with projecting eaves, and a crown. In the slightly later pagoda of T'ien-ning-sse at Peking (right) the base is carved with giant, threatening door-keepers and there are thirteen roof-projections. The interior was a shrine for images. (29)

Youth and age are portrayed with a realism rare in Chinese Buddhist art in two 6th-century painted clay figures at Tun-huang. They represent the youngest and oldest disciples of the Buddha. (28)

祭神

一年農事週民庶皆安逸歌謠
遍社村共享昇平世五風君德
生十雨蒼天濟當年后稷神留
與後人祭

欽天監五官臣焦秉貞畫
鴻臚寺序班臣朱　圭鐫

Alongside the great religions, often assimilated to them but always drawing strength from sources that were fundamentally their own, ran the primitive fertility cults that had existed from the dawn of Chinese history. Here, in the late 17th century, a farmer and his family return thanks before a small altar with candles for a successful harvest. It is a ceremony that might have been given the trappings of Buddhism, Taoism or Confucianism (or indeed Christianity) yet needed none of them. (30)

112

WING-TSIT CHAN

Woodcut icon of the patron saint of all artisans and engineers. Icons like this one were pasted onto the walls of workshops, with incense sticks burning in front of them. Attendants in the foreground carry the tools of the trade, those behind hold technical treatises. (1)

Two DOMINANT NOTES run through Chinese philosophy and religion, namely humanism and syncretism. This is an oversimplification, of course, but it is essentially true.

Anyone studying the history of Chinese thought is likely to be struck by the early growth of humanism. The life of the Chinese in the Shang period (*c.* 1700–*c.* 1100 BC) was dominated by spiritual beings. Nothing of any importance would be undertaken without first consulting them, especially ancestors, and the god Ti, who was probably the greatest of ancestors. Questions and reports would be written or carved on tortoise-shells or animal bones, heat would be applied to them, and priests would then study the cracks to find out the wishes of spiritual beings. Usually such divination was practised every ten days. It was evidently a major activity, for sacrifice and divination are the two main topics in the inscriptions on the oracle bones. Needless to say, the sacrifices were performed for the purpose of securing rewards and averting punishments.

During the transition from the Shang to the Chou (*c.* 1100–221 BC), however, radical changes took place. Ti, basically a tribal god, became Shang-ti, the Lord on High, or T'ien (Heaven), the God for all. The doctrine of the mandate of Heaven developed, most probably to justify the Chou's seizure of power on the ground that it was Heaven's will. Significantly, the justification rests on the concept of virtue. Both the *Book of Documents (Shu-ching)* and the *Book of Poetry (Shih-ching)* repeatedly sound the note that the Chou received the mandate because of the moral excellence of its founders; for Heaven, it is said, always favours the virtuous. Because of their virtue, ancestors became 'counterparts' of Heaven. Primitive religion persisted, but, for the enlightened, religious sacrifices had lost their magical efficacy and acquired an ethical meaning. They were regarded as expressions of moral feelings, especially that of filial piety towards parents. Survival after death, too, was interpreted in moral terms. There had been a widespread belief in *hun*, or the heavenly component of the soul (that is, the spirit of man's intelligence and power of breathing), and in *p'o*, or the earthly component (that is, the spirit of man's physical nature). By the 7th century BC, however, the previously prevalent belief that after a man's death *hun-p'o* survives and con-

tinues to do good or evil was superseded by the conviction that immortality consists in virtue, achievement, and wise words. Man's virtue thus became the central basis of religion. This is the meaning of the saying in the *Book of Rites (Chou-li)* that the people of Shang honoured spiritual beings, whereas the people of Chou honoured ceremonies.

This is not to say that the Chinese had ceased to depend on spiritual beings. Divination continued, now with the use of stalks. Religious sacrifice became an important function of the government. But when prayers for rain did not result in rainfall, the request for help was directed to irrigation experts. Ability was in demand, and in the 7th century BC a poor commoner, perhaps a slave, could reach to high office. This is just one example of the increasing reliance on man. The new feudal society of Chou required human talents to build cities, expand trade, and conduct diplomacy and warfare among the feudal states. Thus man emerged as the controller of his own destiny. According to Tzu-ch'an (?580–522 BC), whom Confucius greatly praised, 'The way of Heaven is far away, but the way of man is near.' The tide of humanism was rising fast.

Confucius

Confucius (551–479 BC), whose family name was K'ung and private name Ch'iu, was the first Chinese philosopher and the greatest Chinese in history. He moulded not only the civilization of China but the civilizations of Korea, Japan, and to some extent Vietnam also. p 98 (2)

He was born in a poor family in what is now Shantung Province. His father died when he was very young. He was married at about nineteen and had a daughter and a son. In his early twenties he was a minor official in his native state of Lu. At fifty-one he became a magistrate, and later minister of justice. Failing to carry out his political reforms, he set out to travel from court to court hoping to convert feudal rulers to his ideals. These travels lasted for about fourteen years. Ultimately disappointed, he returned home to teach and write.

He was actually returning to his main profession, for throughout his life he had been a teacher. In his late twenties he had begun to attract followers, and he had

論語公冶
齊景公問政
問曰昔秦穆公國小
處附其霸何也孔子
曰秦國雖小其志大
處雖僻行中正身舉
五羖爵之大夫以與
之致爵之大夫以與
之雖王河也景公
說

pupils with him during his government service and travel. Thus he was China's first full-time, professional teacher, and the first to take his school with him while travelling. Also, he was the first to teach 'literature, principles of conduct, loyalty, and faithfulness' and 'poetry, history, and the performance of rules of propriety', that is, moral education, instead of purely vocational subjects. Equally important, he was the first to open the door of education to all, declaring that 'In education there should be no class distinction.' For his pupils and later for all Chinese, he was K'ung-fu-tzu (Latinized, Confucius), or Grand Master K'ung.

While conservative in certain respects, Confucius was radical in transforming a number of traditional ideas. The first and most fundamental is *jen* (humanity, human-heartedness, goodness, love). Hitherto it had meant the specific virtue of benevolence or kindness, but Confucius reinterpreted it to mean universal virtue, an entirely new concept in the history of Chinese thought. He talked about *jen* more than anything else. The word appears 105 times, more frequently than any other word, in the *Analects*, the anthology of his sayings and deeds. All his teachings may be said to centre on this idea of humanity. It makes a man different from an animal. It is the root of all particular virtues such as filial piety and brotherly respect, loyalty and faithfulness. A man of humanity 'loves men'. Negatively, he 'does not do to others what he does not want others to do to him'; positively, 'wishing to establish his own character, he establishes the character of others, and, wishing to be successful, he helps others to be successful.' A person who acts up to this ideal is the 'superior man', the *chün-tzu*. Before Confucius, *chün-tzu* meant the son of a ruler, the implication being that nobility was a matter of social origin. But for Confucius the *chün-tzu* is the moral man whose nobility is that of character and not of blood. He is a man who is 'wise, humane, and courageous' and who 'learns the truth and loves men'. Confucius distinguished sharply between the superior man and the inferior man. The superior man understands what is right and reaches after higher things, whereas the inferior man understands only what is profitable and reaches after lower things. But anyone can become a superior man and—after that—a sage. This was a new idea of equality, and eventually it shook the foundations of feudalism based on class distinction by birth.

Personal perfection, however, is impossible without a good society. Confucius was therefore always careful to stress this interdependence. It is significant that the word *jen* means both the individual man and also man-to-man relationship, or society. Since man's first society is the family, in which he has his own specific status but is always in relation with others, Confucius strongly stressed the family, and since man's first relation is with his parents, he strongly stressed filial piety. For Confucius the state is an enlarged family, and the ruler, being parent to his people, should take care of them, be kind to them, and set moral examples and exert moral influence on them. In the days when force, law, and punishment were the chief weapons of control, he advocated rule by virtue and ceremonies, that is, proper behaviour. In the days when feudal origin guaranteed people government positions, he repeatedly pleaded with feudal lords to 'raise the virtuous to high positions'. In the days when the right to rule was hereditary, he urged rulers to imitate the legendary Emperors Yao and Shun, who transmitted their thrones to virtuous ministers and not to their own sons. In these ways Confucius revolutionized traditional concepts of government and established political ideals for China in the centuries to come. In his view, titles must correspond to their functions, deeds to words, and authority to virtue. This is his famous doctrine of the 'rectification of names', another innovation in Chinese history.

As a result of his central concern with man and with human relations, Confucius carried Chinese humanism to a climax. He boldly declared, 'It is man that can make the Way (Tao) great, but not the Way that can make man great.' His humanism seems to be uncompromising, but he was at the same time intensely religious. It is true that he did not care to discuss spiritual beings or the problems of life and death, but he praised Heaven (T'ien), testified to its greatness, and declared that at the age of fifty he knew the mandate of Heaven. When he was in danger, he declared that his moral nature was an endowment from Heaven and that a political enemy could not harm him. But he also said that Heaven does not speak, and that, nevertheless, all things flourish. Heaven ceased to be an anthropomorphic god and became the spiritual and moral Supreme Being who reigns but does not rule, leaving the Moral Law to operate by itself and allowing man to

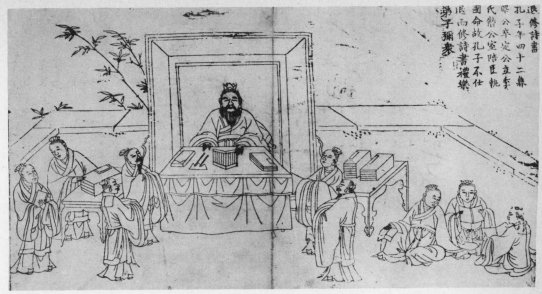

Though as a politician Confucius was largely a failure, as a teacher he was a great success. To counter the prevailing anarchy, he instilled into his pupils the high moral values which he believed were current in the golden age of the early days of Chou rule. In this print he is shown editing the Classics (Poetry, Documents, Ceremonies and Music) and handing them down to his followers. (3)

assume responsibility for human affairs. Here is another departure from tradition. When Confucius quoted the ancient saying 'Respect spiritual beings but keep them at a distance', he was merely saying that man must not depend on spiritual beings as people had done in the Shang Age, and yet man must honour spiritual beings as a token of respect.

Followers of Confucius developed his thoughts in various directions. This is illustrated by two different, but complementary, works: *The Great Learning* and *The Doctrine of the Mean*.

The Great Learning, which is attributed to Confucius's pupil Tseng-tzu (505–*c*. 436 BC), teaches the 'eight items': investigation of things, achievement of knowledge, sincerity of the will, rectification of the mind, cultivation of the person, regulation of the family, ordering of the state, and bringing of peace to the world. Confucius's equal emphasis on the individual and on society is here systematically formulated. This short treatise sets a definite procedure, offers a priority of values, and, as we shall see, lays the foundation for important theories in Neo-Confucianism.

The Doctrine of the Mean, which is attributed to Confucius's grandson Tzu-ssu (?483–402 BC), adds a new dimension to Confucian teachings by dealing with religion and metaphysics. It is the most mystical among the Confucian Classics. Human nature, which Confucius seldom talked about, is here conceived of as being an endowment from Heaven, and as being revealed through two states— of equilibrium before the feelings have been aroused, and harmony after they have been aroused and been ex-

pressed in due measure. The Way of Heaven, which Confucius had avoided discussing, is here described as unceasing, eternal, evident, and transcending space, time, substance, and motion. It is the way of sincerity (or reality). When a person is sincere in the sense of being true to his nature, he can fully realize it, can fulfil the nature of others, and can ultimately form a trinity with Heaven and Earth. The foundation is here laid for a dominant theme in the history of Chinese thought, namely the unity of Heaven and man. As the title of the treatise indicates, it elaborates the Confucian teaching of the Mean. But, in addition to moderation, the Mean here denotes harmony and synthesis. Words and acts must agree. 'Honouring the moral nature' and 'following the path of inquiry and study' must go hand in hand. Both the self and all things should be completed, for the Way unites the internal and the external, and culminates in the oneness of Heaven and man.

The first Confucians: Mencius and Hsün-tzu

The Great Learning and *The Doctrine of the Mean* may have paved the way for the teachings developed by Mencius and Hsün-tzu, respectively. These two philosophers represent the two wings of ancient Confucianism, the idealistic and the naturalistic, although this is a moot point, since not all scholars agree that the two treatises antedated these two thinkers. But in any case Mencius (Meng K'o, ?372–289 BC) carried the teachings of Confucius a great step forward. Confucius had merely said that by nature men are alike but that practice makes them different. Mencius, however, definitely said that man is

This rubbing from a Han tomb depicts some of Confucius's disciples including Tzu Lu (second from right) and Tseng-tzu to whom is attributed 'The Great Learning.' The youngest is probably Yen Hui, Confucius's best and favourite pupil, who died at thirty-two. (4)

born good. From the facts that all children love their parents and that people instinctively rush to save a child about to fall into a well, Mencius concluded that human nature is originally good, that man possesses the feelings of commiseration, of shame and dislike, of respect and reverence, and of right and wrong, which he called the 'four beginnings' of humanity, righteousness, propriety, and wisdom, and that man has an innate knowledge of the good and an innate ability to do good. Thus man is 'complete in himself'. If he develops his nature to the utmost, he will be able to serve Heaven and to achieve his own destiny. Evil is due to man's neglect of his own endowment. He should 'seek the lost mind' and 'recover the original mind'.

Of the four virtues, humanity is the basic one, because, if we have it, the other three will follow. Mencius usually mentioned humanity and righteousness together, to underline the idea that humanity means love for all, while righteousness prescribes the specific measure of its application. For this reason he taught 'love with distinctions', meaning that love must be applied differently in different human relations. Of these, that between parents and children is the most fundamental, and therefore he underscored filial piety more strongly than even Confucius. He vigorously attacked two philosophers—Yang Chu (?440–360 BC), who, he said, was all for himself and thus neglected society; and Mou-tzu, who loved universally without distinction and thus underrated the specific relationship between parents and children. What Mencius insisted on was the Confucian balance between the individual and society.

On a social level, Mencius advocated 'humane government', and he was the first one to use the term. The ruler must have a compassionate mind that 'cannot bear the suffering of the people'. He clearly differentiated the kingly ruler, whose standard is righteousness, from the despot, whose standard is what is profitable and advantageous. A true king has the mandate of Heaven to rule, for Heaven represents the will of the people, since 'Heaven sees as the people see and hears as the people hear.' In a State the people are more important than the ruler or the territory. An evil ruler should be removed, through revolution if necessary.

Hsün-tzu (Hsün Ch'ing, also known as Hsün K'uang, ?313–238 BC) differed from Mencius in almost every respect. For him, human nature is originally evil because desires lead to greed and strife. So far from being a purposive spiritual being, Heaven is simply Nature; it operates almost mechanically; its operation has no relation to human behaviour. Instead of moral examples and moral persuasion, Hsün-tzu recommended government by law. In his eyes ceremonies are not expressions of moral feelings, as they are for Confucius and for Mencius, but are methods for regulating people's conduct. For Mencius, discipline comes from within, for Hsün-tzu from outside. His emphasis on law and on external control probably contributed to the development of the Legalist school. He was the most tough-minded and most naturalistic among ancient Confucianists, and also the most logical. In his philosophy the Confucian doctrine of the rectification of names goes beyond the relation between ranks and titles, and deals with systematic classification, with the analysis of causes, and the like. But in

Lao-tzu was keeper of the archives at Lo-yang, capital of the Chou dynasty, where he is said to have been visited by Confucius. The interview was not very successful, Lao-tzu admonishing him to 'get rid of your air of pride and many desires'. It made the orthodox sage compare him to a dragon that 'rides on the winds and clouds and ascends to heaven'. Confucius is offering a pheasant as a gift. (5)

spite of his opposition to Mencius, Hsün-tzu was a genuine Confucianist, for his objective was the Confucian sage and the Confucian society of harmonious relations.

The opposition: Lao-tzu and Chuang-tzu

While Confucianism was developing, a strong counter-current was already under way. Like Confucianism and most of the 'Hundred Schools' in Ancient China, this other school offers a Way (Tao) of life; but its Way was so distinctive, being in many respects opposed to that of Confucianism, that the school came to be known as the Taoist school. In Confucianism the Way is the way of man, but in Taoism it is the way of Nature. The Taoist school opposes the Confucian doctrines of humanity and righteousness, filial piety and loyalty, and ceremonies and social distinctions. And yet the two currents cross each other at many points, as we shall see.

The *Lao-tzu*, also called the *Tao-te ching (Classic of the Way and Its Virtue)*, is popularly called the 'Five-Thousand-Word Classic', but it actually contains from 5,227 to 5,722 words (the number depends on the edition). It is the most influential book in Chinese for its length, and certainly it is the strongest competitor with the Confucian *Analects* for ranking as the most important book in Chinese history. Tradition has attributed it to Lao-tzu, who is usually taken to be a senior contemporary of Confucius, and whose surname was Li and personal names Erh and Tan. But the earliest biography of him in the *Shih-chi (Historical Records)* of 91 BC also contains accounts of Lao Lai-tzu, another contemporary of Confucius, and Tan, a historian of the 4th century BC. Many modern scholars infer from these accounts, and also from the terminology, ideas, and style of the book, that Lao-tzu is not its author, or that both he and the book are of the 4th century BC. The probability is that the work is a product of a long evolutionary process ending in its acquiring book form in the 4th century BC; but its basic ideas, and even some actual passages, may well go back

p 102
(10)

to Lao-tzu. In any case, Confucius and Lao have been revered by the Chinese as the two greatest sages in Chinese history.

The best description of the school, and also the earliest, is that in the *Chuang-tzu*. It says: To regard the fundamental as the essence, to regard things as coarse, to regard accumulation as deficiency, and to dwell quietly alone with the spiritual and the intelligent—herein lie the techniques of Tao of the ancients. . . . Weakness and humility are the expression, and openness and emptiness that do not destroy anything are the reality. Tao (the Great One) is described in the *Lao-tzu* as the natural (*tzu-jan*, literally self-so), the eternal, the spontaneous. It is simple like an uncarved block. It is the Mother of all things, the highest good, producing, supporting, and benefiting all things, and always returning to the root. It is real but nameless, evident but indescribable. It produces the one, which generates the two (Yin-Yang, i.e. the weak and the strong forces in the universe), which produces the three, which in its turn gives rise to all things. Most important of all, it is non-being: that is, not a particular thing but the source of being. In it all the key elements and basic patterns of later Chinese cosmology and metaphysics are to be found. When heaven and earth, and kings and dukes, obtain Tao, their courses will be smooth and correct.

p 102 (11)

The Taoist life is one of simplicity, weakness, purity, harmony, and tranquillity. It is one of humility, lowliness, and vacuity. The Taoist has no selfishness and few desires, avoids strife, and rejects profit and excess. He repays hatred with virtue. Most of all, he pursues the course of *wu-wei*, or non-action. The ideal examples are water, the mother, the female, and the infant, all models of tenderness. Such a philosophy might seem quietistic and negativistic. It has been so understood and it has had such an effect, but it should not be forgotten that water eventually dissolves rock. In a sense, non-being is what is most real and most useful. The most useful part of a cup, for example, is where there is nothing. 'Non-action' is not to be taken quite literally; it does not mean defeatism or withdrawal but simply being natural, taking no *un*natural action: that is, following the natural process of Tao. To be natural does not mean to do nothing; it means to 'produce things but not to possess them' and to 'lead things but not to master them'. Tao 'always leaves things alone, and all things will change by themselves.' 'The sage-ruler takes no action and thus the state is in order.' In fact the best government is one of which the people are unaware. We have here the strongest statement of *laissez-faire* government.

The quietist element in Taoism should not blind us to the social and radical character of Taoism. The *Lao-tzu* is, after all, principally concerned with the sage-ruler. Ideal government is as much the main theme as individual perfection. Taxation, punishment, and war are as severely condemned as superficiality and hypocrisy. While challenging Confucianism, Taoism also supplements and reinforces it. Its ideals of sagehood, personal cultivation, and social order are at bottom similar to the ideals of Confucianism. 'Supreme humanity and righteousness' are as truly Taoist values as they are Confucian. It is difficult to find a Chinese who is exclusively Confucian or Taoist.

A Ming portrayal of Chuang-tzu. According to one story, when invited to become prime minister he declined and said: 'Instead of an ox richly decorated only to be sacrificed in a temple, I prefer to remain a lowly pig.' (6)

Chuang-tzu (Chang Chou, born about 369 BC) stands to Lao-tzu in the same relation as Mencius stands to Confucius. As Mencius advanced Confucius's doctrines, so Chuang-tzu improved on Lao-tzu. He did so in at least five respects.

First, whereas Lao-tzu emphasizes that Tao is one, Chuang-tzu stresses that it is one that embraces all differences and conflicts. According to his famous theory of 'the equality of all things', a large mountain is as small as the tip of a hair. Beauty and ugliness, life and death, possibility and impossibility, and success and failure are all identified with each other in the unity of Tao. They are identical or equal because they 'produce each other', succeed each other, are only relative, or are merely products of subjective judgments. Chuang-tzu's dialectic resembles Hegel's: 'there cannot be the "this" without the "that", or the "that" without the "this", and the opposition has to be resolved, only to result in another "this"'. Only in Tao will all antitheses and contradictions be resolved into the harmonious Great One.

Secondly, Lao-tzu had emphasized the eternity and constancy of Tao. For him the note of change is a minor one. For Chuang-tzu, however, the universe is a process of unceasing transformation. 'Time cannot be arrested', and things go on 'like a galloping horse'. In this dynamic process of constant flux, things develop from small organisms to insects, to the horse, and finally to man. He asks whether in this 'evolution of Nature' there is a directing agent. Even if there is one, he says, there is no evidence of its existence.

Thirdly, according to Lao-tzu, non-action means following Nature, whereas, according to Chuang-tzu, it means following Nature by self-transformation. One should know one's own capacity, nourish one's nature, and adapt oneself to the environment. An eagle should soar to the sky, but a dove should fly only a small distance. It would be the greatest folly to shorten the crane's neck because it is too long or to lengthen the duck's feet because they are too short. One should 'fast one's mind', 'forget time and conventional moral principles', and rise above considerations of self, achievement, and fame. In these ways one can achieve peace of mind and freedom of spirit, 'roam the universe', and 'become a companion of Nature'.

117

Fourthly, Chuang-tzu is much more individualistic than Lao-tzu. There is a special chapter in the *Chuang-tzu* on kingly government, and his ideal is 'sagacity within and kingliness without', but he does not concern himself with social and political questions as much as Lao-tzu did.

Finally, Chuang-tzu is much more mystical and transcendental than Lao-tzu. He wants to 'travel beyond the mundane world', become 'one with all things', 'exist together with the universe', and be a 'spirit man' who rides on the sun and moon and remains unchanged by life or death. The combination of Chuang-tzu's romanticism, mysticism, philosophical transcendentalism, and poetic imagination has never been surpassed in Chinese history.

Darkness and Light: the Yin-Yang school

p 101 (9) The Yin-Yang doctrine is based on the simple idea that all things, events, and situations are interactions between two forces, or elements: namely, Yin, literally 'the dark side of a hill', which is characterized by darkness, tranquillity, and weakness, and is represented by earth, the female, the son, winter, water, going, sorrow, death, etc., and Yang, literally 'the bright side of a hill', which is characterized by brightness, activity, and strength, and is represented by Heaven, the male, the father, summer, mountain, coming, joy, life, etc. The theory probably originated at the beginning of the 1st millennium BC. In time it became an integral part of all schools of thought and religious systems, and brought them into a great synthesis. According to the Yin-Yang theory, all things are relations, for the universal forces operate in all of them. Their interaction causes the beginning and ending and the rise and fall of all things. Because their interaction is regular, the universe is an ordered one, and because their interaction is incessant, the universe is ever-changing and dynamic. By the same token, the status and future of one thing can be determined by those of another. In other words, mutual influences are predictable, measurable, and controllable. Man and Nature are intimately related. They correspond to and affect each other.

By definition, Yin and Yang are opposites. To resolve their conflict there were several approaches. One was for Yang to overcome Yin, as in the case of good overcoming evil. Another was rotation, as in the alternation of day and night. But the most widely adopted approach was that of synthesis. Yin and Yang can be brought into a harmonious whole because they are looked upon as implying, requiring, penetrating, and embracing each other, as in the marriage of a man and a woman.

The development of the Yin-Yang concept in the early years of the 1st millennium BC was contemporaneous with the rise of the Five Elements, or Five Agents, school. According to its theory, the five agents metal, wood, water, fire, and earth have their counterparts in all things: the five colours, five virtues, five legendary emperors, five periods of time, etc. The important point is that the Five Elements operate in rotation. They run in cycles, one succeeding another. Tsou Yen (305–240 BC), the chief representative of the school, is believed to have brought the two movements together, with the Five Elements elaborating the two forces of Yin and Yang. Whether two or five, they are forces that operate in an orderly and dynamic fashion, harmonizing contradictions and combining multiplicity into a unity. Just as Yin and Yang interact, so the Five Elements produce and overcome one another. The theory of correspondence has provided the foundation for the doctrines of correspondence of man and Nature, the unity of Heaven and man, and the harmony of opposites taught in various schools; and the theory of rotation gave rise to the cyclical interpretation of history, change, movement of Tao, etc.

Moists, Logicians and Legalists

Like most other schools, Moism was dedicated to solving social and political problems. Its founder, Mou-tzu or Mo Ti (?468–376 BC), once walked for ten days and ten nights to try to dissuade a feudal lord from making war. But, whereas the Confucianists centred their ethics on humanity, the Moists centred theirs on 'benefits'. Their slogan was 'Promote welfare and remove evil'. They attacked music festivals, religious rites, and war because these destroy population and wealth, which, for Moists, were the two greatest benefits. For the same reason, they denounced belief in fate but encouraged belief in spiritual beings. The criterion was whether belief would bring 'benefits to Heaven, to spiritual beings, and to all men'.

The best way to bring about the greatest amount of benefits is to love other people's parents, families, and countries as one's own. This doctrine of universal love was peculiar to the Moist school, and it presented a strong challenge to other schools, especially to the Confucian doctrine of love with distinctions. According to Mou-tzu, we should love everyone because this is the will of Heaven, for Heaven wants to benefit everyone. One must therefore completely obey the will of Heaven. On the political level, one must 'agree with one's superiors'. Obviously the interest of the group overshadows that of the individual, but ultimately the greatest benefit for the individual will be attained through universal love and agreement with the ruler.

It may look as if Moism is purely utilitarian, yet it is not. It strongly emphasizes righteousness. However, Mou-tzu criticized the Confucian doctrine of humanity and righteousness because, he said, the Confucianists failed to realize that these originated with Heaven. Thus the Moist school put its ethics on a religious basis. It was the only ancient Chinese philosophical school that did so.

Was the Moist school a religious sect? It is perhaps going too far to say that Mou-tzu was the founder of a religion; but his three hundred followers were ascetics and could have been a religious society or some fraternal order representing the working class as opposed to the Confucian elite. They also developed an elementary system of logic involving definitions, discussions on names and knowledge, and seven methods of argumentation. Mou-tzu himself taught the 'three tests' of a basis, an examination, and a practical application. These tests led him to support the popular beliefs in fate and in spiritual beings.

The school died out after the 3rd century BC—most likely because its way of life was too ascetic, its logic too hair-splitting, its doctrine of universal love too one-sided, and its utilitarianism, while humanistic enough, too crude.

Another school that did not last was the School of Names. It concerned itself not merely with the problem of the relation between names and reality. Many other schools did that; but the Logicians also discussed such metaphysical problems as existence, relativity, space, time, quality, and causation. The ten paradoxes of Hui Shih (380–305 BC) deal with similarity and difference, the finite and infinite, the 'great unit', 'small unit', and the like. The six essays of Kung-sun Lung (b. ?380 BC) deal with such questions as the nature and relationship of stone, whiteness and solidness, things and their 'marks', classes of things, and change. The twenty-one paradoxes of the Debaters declared that 'Fire is not hot', 'The wheel never touches the ground', etc. Generally speaking, Hui Shih emphasized change and relativity, whereas Kung-sun Lung emphasized permanence and absoluteness. They did not develop any syllogism or formulate any law of thought. The school is the only one of the Hundred Schools that was completely rationalistic, that entertained an entirely objective attitude, that followed a strictly logical approach, and that was interested in knowledge for its own sake. Because it was devoid of humanistic interest, it exerted little influence in its own time and disappeared after the 3rd century BC—in sharp contrast to the Yin-Yang school, which penetrated other schools and has continued to be influential to this day.

The Legalist school (Fa-chia) rejected the Confucian moral approach, the Taoist naturalistic approach, and the Moist religious approach in favour of a realistic approach aiming at the concentration of power in the hands of the ruler. The movement is traced to Kuan-tzu (Kuan Chung, b. 645 BC), prime minister of Ch'i, whom Confucius highly praised (but the book *Kuan-tzu*, in which law is advocated as the chief instrument of rule, is spurious). Generally speaking, there were three tendencies in the movement: that of law *(fa)*, in which the ruler issues laws for the people to obey; that of technique *(shu)*, that is, statecraft and methods used by the ruler to control his ministers and people, advocated by Shang Yang (Kung-sun Yang, Lord of Shang, d. 338 BC); and that of power *(shih)*, advocated by Shen Tao (?350–275 BC), who studied how the ruler is to achieve power, to take advantage of circumstances, and to make use of certain natural tendencies. Han Fei (d. 233 BC) combined all these features and became the leading figure in the school.

The school offers no original philosophical ideas and lacks philosophical content, but its spirit is both radical and new. It accepts no authority except that of the ruler, worships no historical heroes, depends on no precedents, looks to the present rather than the past, denounces Confucian moral platitudes as idle talk, insists on objective standards, and demands concrete results. It acts according to changing circumstances and insists on a strict correspondence between name and reality. Laws must be written, uniform, publicly proclaimed, applicable to all, and supported by generous rewards and severe punishments. Wars and regimentation are considered to be necessary instruments. The individual is totally subjugated to the state. The application of law to all men suggests the idea of the equality of all men; but the Confucian doctrine of raising men of virtue to high governmental positions is obviously regarded as risky. The Legalist school offers no theory of human nature, but its assumption is that man's nature is evil. Hence the requirement of government control and the rejection of the theory of government by moral influence and ceremonies. Han Fei

and Li Ssu (d. 208 BC), the prime minister of Ch'in (221–206 BC), were Hsün-tzu's pupils. His emphasis on law may have influenced them, but the school's anti-moral ideology would have shocked Hsün-tzu and also Kuan Chung. Han Fei offered his service to Ch'in, but through Li Ssu's intrigues he was forced to commit suicide.

The Legalists helped the state of Ch'in to unify China in 220 BC and to set up the most highly regimented state in Chinese history. Thought, like everything else, was tightly controlled. The infamous book-burning of 213 BC drove all other schools underground, and many—including the Moist—into oblivion. The Ch'in's ruthlessness brought about its downfall. It is the shortest-lived dynasty in Chinese history.

The Han Dynasty: Confucianism supreme

After the collapse of Ch'in in 206 BC, several schools re-emerged, producing a syncretism which became the most outstanding characteristic of Han (206 BC–AD 220) thought. Many thinkers drew their ideas from several sources, and their adherents were called 'Mixed Schools'. Of these the most famous was Huai-nan-tzu (Liu An, d. 122 BC), who, because his basic concept is Tao, may be considered a Taoist. He conceived of the universe as evolving through seven time-periods in which material force *(ch'i)* produced all things in successive stages. The universe is the macrocosm, while man is the microcosm. In Confucianism, human nature was the focus of discussion, and it has remained so ever since. For Tung Chung-shu, nature is good while feelings are evil; for Liu Hsiang (77–6 BC), nature is evil but feelings are good; for Yang Hsiung (53 BC–AD 18), human nature is a mixture of good and evil; and, for Wang Ch'ung, nature is good in people who are above average, but evil in people below average, and mixed in people of the average level. These are obvious attempts to synthesize the opposite theories of Mencius and Hsün-tzu.

In the *Book of Changes*, the Yin-Yang element is exceedingly strong. Its different parts have been attributed to ancient sages, including Confucius. It is a product of many hands in different periods earlier than the Ch'in Age, but its philosophy flourished under the Han. According to it, the Great Ultimate produces the two material forces of Yin and Yang, which give rise to the Four Primary and Secondary Forms, which in turn produce the Eight Trigrams, which in their turn engender all things. In other words, the universe is a natural cosmological evolution. By virtue of the harmonious and regular interaction of Yin and Yang, it is a well-ordered and dynamic process of change. Spirit is understood, not as spiritual beings, but as the mysterious force underlying the universal process of change. The principles governing the process are those of the mean and correctness, and therefore whatever proceeds from change is good. The book's moral tone has made it a Confucian Classic, but its naturalism endears it to the Taoists too.

The Yin-Yang element is particularly prominent in Tung Chung-shu (c. 176–104 BC) also. He equated nature with Yang and feelings with Yin. By arranging all things in correspondence with Yin and Yang and the Five Elements, he reduced them to numbers. History moved in cycles, and Nature and man form a correspondence of macrocosm and microcosm in exact numerical details.

Here Tung introduced a new note, that of activation. Because of this correspondence, man and Nature activate as well as influence each other. According to Tung, things of the same kind have the energy to set one another in motion. The result is not just the well-ordered universe of the Yin-Yang school or the changing universe of the *Book of Changes*; the result is an organic whole.

Tung's theory produced an extremely important effect in Chinese history, the supremacy of Confucianism. In the early decades of the Han dynasty, Taoism and to some extent Legalism prevailed. But neither the Taoist doctrine of non-action nor the Legalist policy of government control was satisfactory to the Emperor Wu (*r.* 140–87 BC), who had vastly expanded the empire. He had ordered that able scholars should be recommended to him from various parts of the country. In 140 BC he asked these scholars for opinions on the mandate of Heaven and related questions concerning government. Tung replied that Heaven always punishes man for his evil with catastrophes, but that man can always influence Heaven by his moral conduct. He also told the emperor that the fall of Ch'in had been due to its severity in meting out punishment, and that therefore government should be by moral examples and moral influence, and that virtuous men should be recruited to serve in the government. He specifically recommended that all doctrines not included in the Confucian Classics or contrary to the teachings of Confucius should be prohibited. He impressed the emperor so much that he was appointed prime minister of a state, and, among the hundred and more recommended scholars, only the Confucianists were retained.

In 136 BC Confucianism was declared supreme. Non-Confucian teachings were banned, and five doctoral chairs were founded for the Five Classics: namely, the *Book of Documents*, the *Book of Poetry*, the *Book of Changes*, the *Book of Rites*, and the *Spring and Autumn Annals*. From now on, Confucianism was the established ideology for Chinese government, society, and education. Confucian scholars manned the governmental bureacracy, the Classics became the basic texts for schools, and a knowledge of them was required of all government officials. In addition, the Classics were regarded as the standard of right and wrong, and they acquired a sacrosanct authority comparable to that of the Bible in the West.

Apart from the fact that the Confucian school had the best political literature, system, and personnel to offer to the government, there is no doubt that its doctrine of honouring the ruler and driving off barbarians, its teaching of loyalty and filial piety, and (still more important) Tung Chung-shu's theory that the ruler, the father, and the husband are the 'three bonds' or standards of the minister, the son, and the wife, respectively, were attractive to Wu and to later rulers.

In the 1st century AD the belief in the correspondence between Nature and man led to the appearance of a vast body of apocryphal literature. These works were supposed to serve as warp for the woofs provided by the Confucian Classics. They contain a great wealth of materials on myths, portents, and prophecies purporting to reveal the hidden meanings of the Classics. The great number of catastrophes and anomalies recorded in the Classics, and many more that were newly manufactured, were interpreted as warnings to the ruler. Many historians have conjectured that this movement started because Confucian scholars wanted to check the growing power of the emperor. Since strange phenomena were open to diverse interpretations, free discussion and open criticism of the government were inevitable. The ruler was now held responsible to Heaven, whose will—hidden in the Classics—only the Confucianists could discover and understand. The doctrine of the mandate of Heaven thus became the scholars' weapon to check the government.

Unfortunately the belief in the mutual influence of Nature and man degenerated into all sorts of superstition. Wang Ch'ung (AD 27–100) reacted strongly against this. He insisted that prodigies are natural occurrences. T'ien (Heaven) is simply Nature, not the Lord on High. It is not purposive, and it takes no particular action for or against man. Man does not become a ghost after death, much less a ghost that can influence people's lives. He insisted on the presentation of concrete evidence before any belief can be tolerated, and he found no evidence for the existence of spiritual beings. His naturalism, critical spirit, scepticism, and rationalism opened up a new era in Chinese intellectual history. In a way, his rationalism prepared the ground for the development of Neo-Taoism.

Taoism becomes a religion
Neo-Taoism developed in two different directions in the Wei-Chin period (AD 220–420), the philosophical and the religious. Philosophically it concentrated its interest on reality beyond space and time, and for that reason it came to be known as Hsüan-hsüeh *(Profound Studies or Metaphysical Schools)*, better known as Neo-Taoism. The philosophies were set forth in the commentaries on the *Book of Changes*, the *Lao-tzu*, and the *Chuang-tzu*, the so-called 'three profound studies'. In his commentaries on the former two, Wang Pi (AD 226–46) postulates 'original substance', or non-being, by which he means original pure being that transcends all distinctions and descriptions. It is the universal principle *(li)* that unites all particular concepts and events. As such it is one, strong, and always correct. In his commentary on the *Chuang-tzu*, Kuo Hsiang (d. 312) took the opposite view. For him, Tao, or rather Nature, means that everything has its specific being, is self-contained, and transforms itself according to its own principle. In other words, principle is transcendental for Wang Pi but is immanent for Kuo Hsiang. As intellectual currents, these movements were small, but they elevated Chinese philosophy to a truly metaphysical level and turned the idea of principle, which had already become increasingly important in earlier schools, especially the non-Confucian, into a key concept that was to become dominant in Buddhism and central in Neo-Confucianism.

The story of the religious development of Taoism is a strange one. Since Taoism is rationalistic and even atheistic, it might have been expected to be the least likely of all the philosophies to branch off into a popular, animistic religion; but that was what happened. From very early days there had been a movement of priest-magicians who prescribed formulas for everlasting life and shamans who offered rejuvenation, inner power, and superhuman ability through divination and the use of charms. The belief in immortals was widespread. By the 1st century BC the legendary Yellow Emperor and Lao-tzu were being worshipped together for these purposes. In AD 143 a rebel leader, Chang Ling, an expert in faith-healing, collected five bushels of rice from each of his followers, exhorted them to read the *Lao-tzu*, and thus founded the Way of Five Bushels of Rice. He was called the Heavenly Teacher, a title that a 37-year-old junior college student inherited as the descendant in the 64th generation in 1970 in Taiwan. Lao-tzu and Chuang-tzu would never have expected that their references to 'everlasting existence', 'the spirit of the valley that does not die', 'death but not decay', and 'an immortal in the mountain', would open a new chapter of this kind in Taoism.

Historically the religion grew along two lines. One was the Way of the Heavenly Teacher. This prevailed in the north. It aimed at driving away evil spirits, warding off catastrophes, and obtaining the blessings of health, wealth, and happiness. It had a great number of gods, elaborate rituals, and charms of all kinds. In fact, it was a folk religion of sorcery and witchcraft. Ignored by Taoist scholars, the religion lacked philosophical content, though it promoted such Taoist ideals as purity and tranquillity. In the 5th century, K'ou Ch'ien-chih (d. AD 423) gave it a better organizational structure, regulated its ceremonies, fixed the names of gods, and formulated some sort of theology. It became so powerful and influential that it was made the state cult in AD 440.

The other line was the cult of immortals. This, too, prevailed chiefly in the north. It aimed at physical and mental health, the restoration of youth, and everlasting life on earth. To these ends, concentration of thought, breathing exercises and control, physical exercises including extending the body, massage, bathing, diet, medicine, and sex techniques were practised. The most important method, however, was alchemy. In internal alchemy, the goal was to concentrate and refine one's essence or semen, vital force, and spirit through pills, breathing exercises, and cultivation of the pure vital force; in external alchemy, fire was used to turn sulphides of mercury into gold. Since gold is unchangeable and ever-lasting, drinking gold fluid was held to prolong life. In both cases the effort was to co-ordinate all elements in the universe, in the person, and in sun and moon, into correct and harmonious relations, so as to achieve correctness in one's nature and destiny. A formulation of these ideas and techniques is found in the *Ts'an-t'ung-ch'i* ('The Three Ways Unified and Harmonized') attributed to Wei Po-yang (*fl.* AD 147–67), from whom the basic ideas may well have been derived. The book formed the basis of the *Lung-hu* ('Dragon and Tiger') *Scripture* of unknown date, the *Huang-t'ing* ('Internal and External') *Scripture* (3rd century), and the *Yin-fu* ('Secret Accord') *Scripture* of the 8th century.

The theory of immortals and of techniques for alchemy were elaborated by Ko Hung (AD 284–363) or Po-p'u-tzu (Philosopher Who Embraces Simplicity). He argued vigorously for the existence of immortals. Denouncing magic, witchcraft, prayers, and dependence on spiritual beings, he emphasized the cultivation of one's nature. In addition to supplying detailed formulas for alchemy, he devised a merit system according to which a specific good or evil deed will increase or decrease a specific number of days in one's life span. Although a Taoist, he enthu-

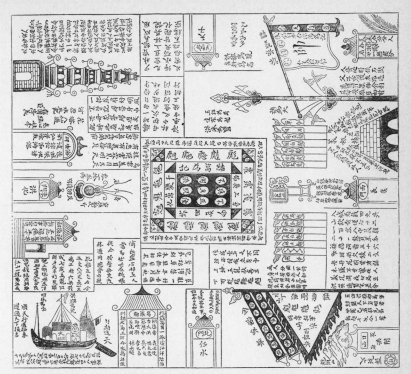

Religious Taoism has often become associated with secret societies and popular revolt. This is part of the credential of a member of the Triad Society, whose main object was to overthrow the Manchus and restore Chinese rule. One of its branches in south China played an active, though minor, role in the revolution of 1911. (7)

siastically promulgated Confucian ethics. The efforts at alchemy did not bring earthly immortality, and the search ended about the 7th century. This pseudo-science made some positive contributions to scientific development. In fact, it resulted in some scientific discoveries. Though its science is primitive, it demonstrates that science and religion are not in conflict. According to some, the Taoist philosophy is more conducive to science than the Confucian.

On the popular level, the Taoist religion grew and spread as a great reservoir of ignorance and superstition as well as a vast ocean of piety and devotion. It greatly expanded as a result of official patronage from the T'ang (618–906) and the Ming (1368–1644) rulers. Since 1000, the religion has been divided more or less into two sects. The southern sect, called the True Unity Sect, flourished south of the Yangtze. It was probably founded in the 10th century, though its roots go further back. Its goal is to preserve one's nature, chiefly by one's own power but sometimes by the use of charms and magic. Its priests marry, stay at home, and regard the Heavenly Teacher as their leader. The northern sect, called the Preservation of True Nature Sect, was probably founded in the 13th century. It has its centre in Peking. Its goal is to strengthen one's vital force, and it depends on medicine and diet for prolonging life. Its priests renounce home life, adopt vegetarianism, and live in monasteries.

Besides practising astrology, geomancy, divination, and fortune-telling, the Taoist religion worships a great host of gods. There are gods of stars, mountains and rivers, natural objects, historical and fictitious persons, parts of the house, cities, literature, wealth, medicine, and so on. In addition, there are immortals who inhabit the 10 Heavenly Grottoes, 36 subsidiary Heavenly Grottoes, and 72 Blessed Places. This religion is extremely rich in ceremonies and rituals. Its roadside shrines, furnished with no more than a rock, and its magnificent temples, furnished with giant idols, dot the Chinese landscape. Its deities are patron gods of sailors, labourers, artisans, secret societies, and the underprivileged. Its priests are often physicians. Its temples have been the headquarters of boxing troupes and of political revolts. Since Taoism is the philosophy of weakness, the religion has been the religion of the humble and the lowly. To them it has given infinite comfort and protection, and from them it has received unbounded faith and affection. From Buddhism it has borrowed monasticism, the belief in Heaven and Hell, and masses for the dead, and has imitated Buddhism in its Trinity, Canon, and other points. The most significant loan is Kuan-yin (Seeing the Sound of Prayer). Taoism has turned this Buddhist saint into a female, the so-called Goddess of Mercy, a popular deity in the garden or in the home, a protector of women and bestower of children, with compassion and love for all. This deity is for the Chinese millions what the Virgin Mary is for non-Protestant Christians. A number of religious tracts, such as the *Yin-fu Scripture*, the *T'ai-shang kan-ying p'ien* ('Treatise on the Most Exalted One on Influence and Response'), and the *Yin-chih wen* ('Silent Way of Recompense'), are extremely popular and influential, and they have given the Chinese tremendous moral inspiration and guidance. In these short treatises, Taoist, Confucian, and Buddhist teachings are rolled into one.

The introduction of Buddhism

Taoism is essentially earthbound. Buddhism, on the other hand, is other-worldly. But it is, after all, the Middle Way, and as such it naturally lent itself to the syncretic tradition of China. Ultimately it was synthesized with the Chinese man-centred outlook, and in the process it transformed Chinese religion and thought.

Buddhism was known in China as early as 2 BC, when a student at the national university received instructions from a foreign envoy on Buddhist scriptures. In AD 65 an edict of the Emperor Ming (r. AD 58–75) mentions the Buddha and the Buddhist order. After the emperor had dreamed of a flying golden deity and had been told that it was the Buddha, he sent a mission to India about AD 68. The mission returned in AD 75 with an Indian monk, some scriptures, and some images. Thus Buddhism came into China by invitation, and the mission started the long Chinese tradition of going to the West to 'seek the Buddhist doctrine'—a tradition that lasted until the 8th century. Shortly after its official introduction, Buddhism became associated with the popular Yellow Emperor-Lao-tzu cult. The Buddhist practice of medicine and breathing-exercises was attractive to the Taoists. A bridge between a native and a foreign religion was therefore easily built.

This congenial atmosphere is reflected in the earliest Chinese Buddhist scripture, the *Scripture in Forty-two Chapters*, which was probably compiled in the 2nd century. Here Taoist ideas such as tranquillity, taking no action, and having no desires are expressed, and the word *tao* itself is used. As the religion spread and began to assert

its own identity, its basic doctrines of non-ego and renunciation of the home raised serious questions among the Chinese. Mou-tzu (2nd century) took great pains in his essay 'On the Removal of Doubt' to show that Buddhism and Taoism shared common ideals, such as taking no action, simplicity, and the nourishing of life, and that the Buddhist cultivation of virtue is a form of filial piety. Instead of making a confrontation, Mou-tzu chose to stress the similarities of the two ways of life. The translation of Buddhist scriptures now proceeded rapidly, and Buddhist thought started to grow in China. By the first quarter of the 3rd century two movements developed. One, that of concentration *(dhyāna)*, aimed at achieving calmness of mind and elimination of delusions, and the other, that of wisdom *(prajñā)*, aimed at obtaining the knowledge that things have no self-nature. As a result of these new developments, Buddhism began to attract Chinese intellectuals.

When the Chinese capital of Ch'ang-an fell to the foreign invaders from the north in AD 316, many monks fled to the south with government officials, wealthy people, and Confucian and Taoist scholars. Before the exodus, the Buddhists had begun to 'match' their concepts with those of the Taoists, using the Taoist term *pen-wu* (original non-being) for *tathatā* (thusness, ultimate reality), 'sage' for the Buddha, etc. Closer contact with fellow refugees heightened the process. At this time seven Buddhist schools of thought co-existed in limited Buddhist circles. Their fundamental issues were whether matter is empty and whether ultimate reality is being or non-being, and these were precisely the key problems of Neo-Taoism. Many Buddhist thinkers were specialists in Taoist philosophy. They also mingled with Confucianists and Taoists in the Pure Conversation movement, in which scholars engaged in carefree and witty conversations. Partly to escape from the turmoil of troubled times and partly in revolt against conventional standards, they shunned the vulgarity of politics and earthly values, and concentrated on the pure or light aspect of things, whether sex or poetry, with utter indifference to the distinctions of conventional right and wrong, wealth and poverty, and high and humble stations. This fellowship of intellectuals was paralleled by the close relation between the Buddhists and the rulers.

Unfortunately, contact produced friction. A number of contentious issues sprang up. One concerned the relation between religion and the state. When the question why monks did not prostrate themselves before the emperor arose, Hui-yüan (AD 334–417), one of the most renowned Chinese monk-scholars, was asked by the government in AD 402 to submit his opinion. In his famous treatise 'On Monks Not Paying Respect to the Sovereign', he argued that 'worldly society' and 'other-worldly society' perform different functions and follow different customs, that Buddhist teachings make a man more filial to his parents and more loyal to his ruler, and that bringing harmony by spreading the Buddhist doctrine matches any contribution a government can make. This encounter settled the question of the different spheres of life forever, and, theoretically at least, it also resulted in the separation of religion from the state.

Another important issue concerned the destructibility of the soul. The early Chinese Buddhists had misunder-

Emperor Wu founded in AD 502 the Liang, one of the most stable of the southern dynasties which arose after the fall of the Chin. A great patron of Buddhism, his beliefs led him three times to renounce his throne for holy orders. Here he is seen in a Buddhist temple. (8)

stood the original Buddhist idea of the ego to mean transmigration instead of its true meaning, according to which the self is the result of causation and is therefore without a nature of its own. But the belief in the soul transmigrating in cycles had no place in philosophical Taoism or Confucianism. In AD 507, Fan Chen (*fl.* 502) attacked the belief in his celebrated treatise 'On the Destructibility of the Soul'. He said that the soul perishes with the body, just as sharpness disappears with the knife. He also criticized the Buddhists for leaving home and for trying to lure people to Heaven and frighten people with Hell. Although the belief in transmigration has continued to this day among the ignorant masses, Fan Chen expressed once and for all the conviction of Chinese intellectuals.

While all this was going on in the south, Buddhism was also flourishing in the north. Here the foreign rulers did not have the benefit of a Confucian heritage and therefore turned to Buddhism for support. Government patronage was extensive. The rulers appointed many Buddhist monks as political, military, and diplomatic advisers; they supported the building of the world-renowned temples in Yün-kang and Lung-men caves, welcomed many Indian missionaries, and sponsored the translation p 110
(26,27) of Buddhist texts. Of all the missionaries the most famous was Kumārajiva (AD 344–431), who arrived in Ch'ang-an in AD 401. He was honoured as a National Teacher. A thousand monks attended his daily lectures. With the help of more than eight hundred assistants he translated a great number of Buddhist works into Chinese, thus giving rise to the Chinese Buddhist philosophical schools that were to thrive in the T'ang period.

Schools of Buddhism

Altogether ten Buddhist schools existed in China, some beginning in the 4th century and most flourishing under the T'ang dynasty. The Chü-she (Abhidharmakośa, Treasury of the Highest Dharma) school, which affirms the existence of all dharmas (elements of existence), the Ch'eng-shih (Satyasiddhi, Completion of Truth) school, which maintains that neither the self nor the dharmas

exist, the Lü (Vinaya, Discipline) school, which prescribes rules, and the Chen-yen (Mantra, True Words) school, which views the universe as the spiritual body of the Buddha manifested in both the static and the dynamic worlds, all were small and lasted for only a few centuries. The two main Indian schools of the Great Vehicle (Mahāyāna) in China, the Wei-shih and the Chung-lun, were more widespread, and they made greater imprints on Chinese thought; but they did not last much longer either, for their philosophy was too extreme and too one-sided to suit the Chinese syncretic temperament.

The Wei-shih (Consciousness-only) or Fa-hsiang (Dharma-character) school was founded in China by p 106–7
(20, 21) Hsüan-tsang (AD 596–664), who travelled in India for sixteen years and returned in AD 645 to translate seventy-five Buddhist works and to construct an idealistic system out of Indian doctrines. This school divides consciousness into eight parts and teaches that all dharmas and their causes are merely ideations. The Chung-lun (Mādhyamika, Middle Doctrine) or San-lun (Three Treatises) school was systematized by Chi-tsang (AD 549–623). It holds that neither being nor non-being exists and that all differentiations are to be dissolved in the True Middle or Emptiness *(Śūnyata)*. These two schools, like those before them, were essentially Indian philosophies transplanted to Chinese soil, and they never became acclimated. The remaining four, however, are Chinese in origin, they are true to the Chinese spirit of humanism, worldliness, and syncretism, and consequently they have remained the body and soul of Chinese Buddhism ever since. As the common saying goes, Chinese Buddhism is 'T'ien-t'ai and Hua-yen in doctrine and Ch'an and Pure Land in practice'.

The T'ien-t'ai school has its roots in 4th-century Chinese Buddhist thought, but it was Chih-i (AD 538–97) who founded the school in Mount T'ien-t'ai in Chekiang Province. The central doctrines of the school may be summed up in its three common sayings: 'the true nature of dharmas', 'the perfect harmony of the Three Levels of Truth', and 'the 3,000 worlds immanent in an instant of thought'. That the dharmas have no self-nature because they depend on causes for their production is the Truth of Emptiness. But since they *are* produced, they have dependent and transient existence, and this is the Transient Truth. Having no self-nature, and at the same time having transient existence, is the Truth of the Mean. These three levels include each other, so that one is three and three is one. In the realm of Transient Truth, that is, the phenomenal world, there are ten realms: Buddhas, Bodhisattvas (enlightened beings), Buddhas-for-themselves, direct disciples of the Buddha, heavenly beings, spirits, human beings, departed beings, beasts, and depraved men, each involving the others and thus constituting a hundred realms. Each of these in turn possesses the Ten Characters of Thusness: character, nature, substance, energy, activity, cause, condition, effect, retribution, and being ultimate from the beginning to the end, that is, each is 'thus-caused', etc. Each of these consists of living beings, of space, and of the fivefold aggregates of matter, sensation, thought, disposition, and consciousness. The result is 3,000 worlds, or the totality of manifested reality. Since each element is present in all others, the 3,000 worlds are immanent in a single instant of

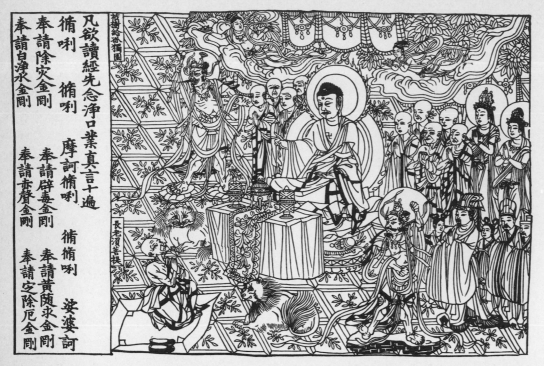

凡欲讀經先念淨口業真言十遍

備唎　備唎　摩訶備唎　備備唎　娑婆訶

奉請除災金剛　奉請辟毒金剛　奉請黃隨求金剛

奉請白淨水金剛　奉請赤聲金剛　奉請定除厄金剛

花樹給愁獨園

長老須菩提起

Frontispiece and beginning of text of the Diamond Sutra. This belongs to the group of Prajñāpāramitā scriptures, which were of fundamental importance to Mahāyāna Buddhism. It was translated in China by Kumārajīva, who was of Central Asian origin. The woodcut frontispiece of the scroll shows a group of Bodhisattvas, other deities and monks, with the Buddha preaching in their midst. (9)

thought. As the popular saying of the school runs, 'Every colour and every fragrance is none other than the Middle Way.' The special methods of the school, concentration and insight, are to understand Emptiness and temporariness, respectively.

The Hua-yen (Flowery Splendour) school may be said to begin with Tu-shun (AD 557–640), who lectured on the *Avataṁsaka* ('Flowery Splendour') *Sutra*, but the elaborate and well co-ordinated system was built up by Fa-tsang (AD 643–712). The fundamental concept of the school is Universal Causation of the Realm of Dharmas. According to its philosophy the universe consists of four realms: the Realm of Principle *(li)*, the Realm of Facts, the Realm of Facts and Principle Harmonized, and the Realm of All Facts Interwoven and Mutually Identified. Principle is Emptiness, static, the noumenon. Facts are specific characters, dynamic, constituting the phenomenal world. Interacting and interpenetrating, they form a Perfect Harmony. The doctrine is based on the theory of the Ten Gates of Mystery, according to which all things are interrelated and mutually inclusive. As Fa-tsang's treatise 'On the Golden Lion' illustrates, every part of the lion (phenomenon) embraces all other parts and the lion as a whole as well as the gold (noumenon), while the gold likewise involves the lion in its totality and all its parts. In this way, the one and the many are mutually compatible, mutually penetrated, and harmoniously merged. Thus each dharma is both one and all. The world is in reality a Perfect Harmony in all its flowery splendour. In this situation the Buddha is all, and all are basically Buddhas.

The Pure Land school is one of practice rather than philosophy. Nevertheless there are certain philosophical assumptions, namely the possibility of salvation by faith, the presence of Buddhahood in all, and the possibility of salvation for all. T'an-luan (AD 476–542) is regarded as the founder of the school, but its history is about 150 years older. Its chief text is the *Pure Land* (Sukhāvatīvyuha) *Scripture*. In its shorter version, which is called the *Amitābha* (Non-measurable Light) *Scripture* and which has been recited, copied, and distributed by millions of Chinese and Japanese for hundreds of years, every one is promised rebirth in the Pure Land so long as he recites the name of Amitābha Buddha as an indication of faith. To these millions it has been an inexhaustible fountain of comfort and hope. In the longer version the Buddha promises not only to give rebirth in the Pure Land to all but also to welcome each one personally. To help save them there are countless Bodhisattvas, i.e. enlightened beings who are qualified to become Buddhas but who deliberately defer their assumption of Buddhahood in order to remain in the world to help all beings to attain salvation. For this purpose they will endure all kinds of suffering, use all sorts of 'convenient means', and transfer their own merits to others.

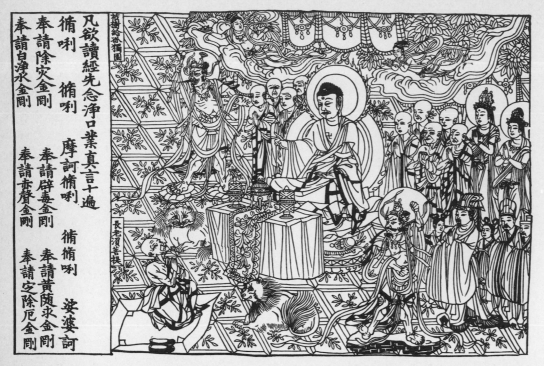 p 109 (25)

Of these Bodhisattvas the most shining one is Kuan-yin (Avalokiteśvara, One Who Hears the World's Sound [of prayer or recitation of his name]). With infinite compassion, Kuan-yin will protect, cherish, and save all. The Bodhisattva is so prominent that he occupies a special chapter in the *Pure Land Scripture*. His story is also dramatically told in the *Lotus Sutra,* indisputably the most popular and influential Buddhist scripture in East Asia. The Bodhisattva has also become the Taoist Goddess of Mercy, as already noted. Because the cult of faith has given solace and hope to all people—old and young, rich and poor, illiterate and educated—the Pure Land school has been the most widespread in China and Japan.

p 108 (23)

p 106 (19)

The name Ch'an is a transliteration of the Sanskrit *dhyāna*, meaning meditation. As we have pointed out, meditation was an old Chinese practice, especially in Taoism. When Indian meditation came in, the Chinese quickly adopted it and used it to control breathing, reduce desires, preserve nature. As Buddhism developed, it was more and more practised for its original Indian purpose, that is, to obtain Perfect Wisdom. Gradually it became a purely formalistic sitting in meditation, devoid of genuine spirit and serious purpose. The time was ripe for revolt.

Tradition says that the rebel was Hui-neng (AD 638–713), an illiterate fuel-wood peddler from Hsin-chou near Canton, who went to Hung-jen (AD 601–74) in Central China to seek Buddhahood. Hung-jen was the Fifth Patriarch of the Meditation School, which had taken for its First Patriarch Bodhidharma (fl. AD 460–534). He had come to China and preached the doctrine of achieving Enlightenment: the understanding that the True State or Nirvāna is total Emptiness devoid of any characteristic, duality, or differentiation and that the highest truth can be realized through uninterrupted concentration to the point of absence of thought. Hung-jen placed the emphasis on the mind itself. By his time the school had split the mind into the true mind, which has no thought or attachment, and the false mind, which does have. Hui-neng rebelled against the whole tradition.

According to the story, in a poetic contest to choose a successor to Hung-jen, Hui-neng defeated the Head Monk Shen-hsiu (AD 605–706) and was chosen to be the Sixth Patriarch. Whether or not this story is true, there is no doubt that he did give the famous sermon in AD 676 which is recorded in the *Platform Scripture of the Sixth Patriarch*. In this lecture he emphatically declared that all people possess the Buddha-nature, that one's nature is originally pure, and that the great wisdom by which one can reach the Other Shore (Buddhahood) is nothing but one's self-nature. Attachments are like clouds hiding the sun. All Buddhas, all dharmas, and all scriptures are immanent in it. Sitting in meditation, building temples or pagodas, practising charity, reading scriptures, reciting the name of Amitābha, and relying on any external means to be reborn in the Pure Land are futile, for the Pure Land is simply the straightforward mind itself. If one sees one's own nature, one will become a Buddha. The way to discover one's Buddha-nature is through calmness and wisdom, which reinforce each other or rather are identical. By calmness is not meant motionlessness, not thinking, or having nothing to do with dharmas, but an unperturbed mind free from erroneous thought, a mind that is not carried away by thought in the process of thought and not attached to dharmas while in the midst of them. When the mind is calm, there is meditation and one can then see one's originally pure nature and become enlightened immediately. Hence the standard sayings of the school: 'Directly point to the human mind, see one's nature, and become a Buddha', and 'Become a Buddha in this very body'. This is the doctrine of Sudden Enlightenment.

In AD 734 Hui-neng's pupil Shen-hui (AD 670–762) openly attacked Shen-hsiu's doctrine of sitting in meditation, or gradual enlightenment, which was then prevalent in the North. From then on Hui-neng's Southern School of Sudden Enlightenment overwhelmed Shen-hsiu's Northern School of Gradual Enlightenment. It is possible that the new movement was actually launched by Shen-hui and not by Hui-neng, about whom there are many unanswered questions. In any case, the Southern School of Ch'an represented a revolution in Chinese Buddhism, for it swept away all external authorities and institutions, it introduced an entirely new psychology, it restored the full self-sufficiency of man himself, and it dramatically intensified the doctrine of salvation for all and salvation

here and now. Taoist influence on Ch'an is obvious. Such Taoist teachings as the embracing of the One, tranquillity of mind, the nourishing of one's own nature, and the possibility for all to become sages, unquestionably prepared for Ch'an developments. Shen-hui used the Taoist term *tzu-jan* (being natural) and taught the Taoist doctrine of absence of thought.

To sharpen the mind the school later used many methods. In addition to lectures, it introduced in the 9th–11th centuries new techniques such as travel, not telling the whole story, enigmatic questions and answers, and even shouting and beating—all calculated to shake a person loose from his traditional ideas and beliefs, in order to enable his mind to become pure, clear, and sensitive enough to grasp truth instantly.

The Ch'an doctrine of sudden enlightenment has profoundly influenced Chinese poetry and landscape-painting by giving them the concept and technique of grasping reality in all its simplicity and wholeness directly and instantly. But this is only one example of Buddhist influence. The Buddhist doctrines of many universes, Buddhas and bodhisattvas, and heavens and hells have given the Chinese new dimensions of existence. Buddhism's cult of faith and its practices of reciting scriptures, reciting the name of the Buddha, making vows, and confessing have offered new ways to salvation. Its priesthood, its monasticism, its doctrine of celibacy, its renunciation of the home and marriage, and its custom of begging have added new institutions and new modes of life. Its teachings of compassion, salvation for all, transfer of merits to others, moral retribution according to karma (the influence of one's actions), rigid self-discipline, and renunciation of worldly goods have provided the Chinese with new ethical values. Its practice of setting creatures free vastly extended the traditional Chinese ethic.

p 108
(24)

The many rituals and festivals of Buddhism, including story-telling and other entertainments, have enriched Chinese folk life. Moreover, Buddhism has created new forms of music, architecture, sculpture, and painting in China. Its graceful pagodas and gorgeous temples have beautified the landscape, and many of its sculptures, frescoes, and paintings are now public and private treasures throughout the world. Its temples all over China have preserved forests, opened up scenic spots, and provided beautiful and quiet places for the Chinese people to enjoy. In literature and language, Buddhism has given China a new vocabulary, has devised a phonetic system, and has created such new literary styles as a concise, straightforward, and dignified prose, the story in combined prose and verse form, and the records of dialogues which the Confucianists quickly imitated. And, finally, it has had a far-reaching influence on Chinese philosophy.

p 111
(29)
p 110
(26,27)
p 111
(28)

But if Buddhism has transformed China, China has also transformed Buddhism. In one word, it has become Mahāyāna. Instead of aiming at becoming an arhat, one who is worthy of Nirvāna, as in Hīnayāna (Small Vehicle) or rather Theravāda (System of Elders), the new goal is the Bodhisattva. Instead of salvation for the self, the new vision is salvation for all. Hence the vehicle is great and not small. Moreover, salvation can be achieved in this world and 'in this very body' without renouncing or transcending the mundane world, and salvation can be achieved by oneself without depending on the clergy.

Thus the religion may be said to have been brought down on earth and its centre shifted from the monastery to society and the home. The One Buddha is manifested in 'Three Bodies' or 'Three Buddhas'. In organization, all sects overlapped and finally sectarianism disappeared. In philosophy the one-in-all and all-in-one theory has combined all doctrines into a broad syncretic movement. Some of these developments can be traced to Indian sources, but it was in China that they took root and came to full bloom. Given the Confucian and Taoist belief that all can be sages, that the world is one community, and that different roads lead to the same destination, these changes in Buddhism are virtually a foregone conclusion.

The Confucian reaction

The prevalence of Ch'an necessarily aroused an unfavourable reaction among the Confucianists. Han Yü (AD 768–824), the greatest Confucianist in the first millennium, attacked Buddhism for ignoring the virtues of humanity and righteousness, for neglecting human relations, for escaping from the family, the state, and the world, and for its inculcation of quietism and nihilism instead of action for the mutual support of life. In addition, Neo-Confucianists from the 11th century on have criticized the Buddhists for regarding the world as illusory and life as suffering. For them the Buddhists' belief in transmigration shows their failure to understand the natural process of life and death. The Buddhist doctrine of the mind is untenable because the Buddhists split it into two and try to look at the mind with the mind. To regard sex as unclean and marriage as a bondage is unsound and destroys the whole foundation of life and its continuity. To flee to the monastery is to confess inability to handle human affairs. To be a mendicant is to be a parasite, to seek life in Paradise is selfish, and to influence people with rewards in Heaven and punishments in Hell is immoral. Finally Buddhism is barbarian and unworthy of the way of Confucius and Mencius. The criticisms, though purely verbal and never violent, are in many cases quite unfair. Actually the vigour of this response is a measure

of the Buddhist challenge to Confucianism, a challenge so strong that Confucianism had to renew itself. The result has been Neo-Confucianism.

The Western name 'Neo-Confucianism' applies to the new Confucianism from the 11th century on. It involves many thinkers and a variety of tendencies of thought. Its main currents are two, the Ch'eng-Chu (Ch'eng I and Chu Hsi) School of Principle and the Lu-Wang (Lu Hsiang-shan and Wang Yang-ming) School of Mind, together called the School of Nature and Principle (*Hsing-li hsüeh*). As Chu Hsi reconstructed it, the whole philosophy rests on Chou Tun-i's (1017–73) cosmology, which begins with the Ultimate of Non-being and then proceeds from the Great Ultimate through the two material forces of *yin* and *yang* and the Five Agents to all things, with the Five Elements constituting their differentiations, and *yin* and *yang* constituting their reality. In this scheme the many are ultimately one, and the one is differentiated into the many. While the cosmology is derived from the Confucian Classic the *Book of Changes*, the influence of the Taoist concept of non-being and the Hua-yen Buddhist idea of the relation between the one and the many is obvious. Chang Tsai (1020–76) equated the Great Ultimate with the material forces of Yin and Yang.

P 99 (4

Heaven and man: philosophy 11th–16th centuries

It is strange that Ch'eng I (1033–1107) and his elder brother Ch'eng Hao (1032–85), who were students of Chou Tun-i and nephews of Chang Tsai, never mentioned the Great Ultimate. Instead they built their philosophy on the basis of principle. In fact they were the first philosophers to do so in Chinese history. According to Ch'eng I, particularly, for anything to exist, there must be its principle for being. The foundation of reality is therefore principle. It is everywhere and governs all things. It cannot be augmented or diminished. It is definite, self-evident, self-sufficient, correct, and good. It is the universal truth, the universal order, and the universal process of production and reproduction. It is in everything, even in a tree or a blade of grass. We must investi-

126

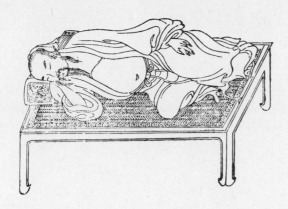

gate it to the utmost, as *The Great Learning* has taught us. This can be done by induction or deduction, by studying history or reading books, and by actually handling human affairs. Ch'eng Hao was no less rationalistic, but he tended to emphasize the state of mind. He saw the spirit of life in all things and was deeply impressed with the universal process of production and reproduction. In response to this and in dealing with things, he urges people to calm their nature so that their minds will not be disturbed or obstructed but will act spontaneously. The Ch'eng brothers also taught seriousness (*ching*, reverence), which means concentration on one thing. Their philosophy is summed up in Ch'eng I's saying, 'Self-cultivation requires seriousness; the pursuit of learning depends on the extension of knowledge.' This saying bears a striking resemblance to the Buddhist dual requirement of calmness and wisdom.

Chu Hsi's (1130–1200) philosophy is derived chiefly from Ch'eng I, but he has synthesized those of Chou, Chang, and the Ch'engs into a harmonious whole and has thus reconstructed or 'completed' Neo-Confucianism. His system is built on six pillars, namely, the Great Ultimate, principle, material force, the nature, investigation of things, and humanity. Before his time, the concept of the Great Ultimate was not important, but he needed it to explain the relation between universal principle and particular principles, the relation between principle and material force, and the possibility of production and reproduction. He therefore took from Chou Tun-i the concept of the Great Ultimate and made it the starting point of the entire Neo-Confucian philosophy. The Great Ultimate has no physical form and is at once the source and sum total of all principles, actual as well as potential. It is harmonious, whole, and unlimited in its capacity to produce new things. There is the Great Ultimate in the universe as a whole. There is also the Great Ultimate in each and every thing. In other words it is one and at the same time many.

The Great Ultimate involves both principle, which is 'above form', and material force, which is 'with form'.

Principle is the reason for the reality of things. It is universal, eternal, the essence of things, and beyond good and evil. Material force, on the other hand, is what makes the actualization of things possible. It is their physical substance. It is unequal in things and is changeable, and, as such, it provides occasions for both good and evil. In these matters of principle and material force, Chu Hsi follows Ch'eng I closely. Ch'eng I, however, never explained the relation between the two. Chu Hsi says that although logically principle is prior to material force, actually neither can be described in terms of time. They are two and yet one, principle being the law of material force, and material force being the embodiment of principle. Principle needs material force in order to have something to adhere to, he said. While principle is immanent in things, it does not mean that it cannot exist without them, for principle is prior to the existence of Heaven and earth. Yet principle is not abstract but concrete. It contains in itself the possibility of actualization, and actualization requires the 'concrete stuff' which is Yin and Yang.

To understand principle one has to investigate things in which principle inheres. In this doctrine, Chu Hsi adheres closely to Ch'eng I too. But whereas Ch'eng I advocates several methods, such as book-reading, Chu Hsi makes induction and deduction the chief means of inquiry. His approach is strictly rational and essentially scientific. He actually made a scientific discovery, that of the nature of fossils.

Though seemingly dualistic, principle and material force are never separate. They are always together because they are directed by the mind of the universe, which is the universe itself. In man this mind becomes, on the one hand, the moral mind, which is the principle of one's original nature and is always good, and, on the other hand, the human mind, which is the principle of original nature mixed with physical endowments and human desires and which involves both good and evil. But one can transform one's physical nature through moral efforts, as Chang Tsai had taught. Ultimately one can become identified with the mind of the universe. This is the highest reach of the Confucian virtue of humanity. For the Ch'eng brothers, the final objective of the man of humanity is to 'form one body with Heaven and Earth'. Chu Hsi describes humanity as 'the character of man's mind and the principle of love'. Here the two fundamental elements of Neo-Confucianism, nature and principle, and its highest ideal, humanity, are synthesized. In all these ways Chu Hsi 'completed' Neo-Confucianism, or at least the rationalistic wing of it, the School of Principle.

The other wing, the idealistic school or the School of Mind, began with Lu Hsiang-shan (Lu Chiu-yüan, 1139–93). In direct opposition to Chu Hsi, he considers principle as not in things but as identical with mind. It is one, all good, and self-sufficient. 'There is only one mind. My mind, my friend's mind, the minds of sages thousands of years ago, and the minds of sages thousands of years to come are all the same.' Mind fills the universe. Thus, 'the affairs of the universe are my own affairs, and my own affairs are affairs of the universe.' Mind cannot be divided into the moral mind and the human mind, nor is it the function of nature, as it is for Chu Hsi. It is principle itself. It cannot be distinguished from the material forces

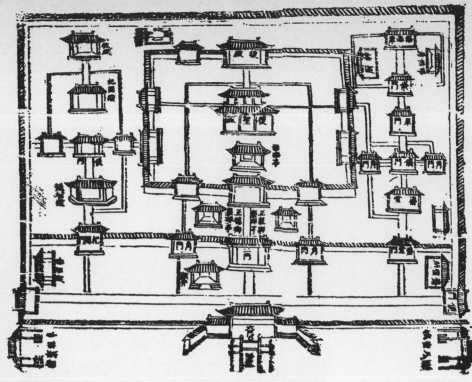

of Yin and Yang, as it is for Chu Hsi, for 'there is nothing outside the Way'. Since man possesses this original mind, 'all things are already complete in oneself', as Mencius had taught long ago. One's nature is originally good, and one possesses the innate knowledge of the good and the innate ability to do good. One's duty is to 'establish the noble part' of one's nature. With this and other oppositions between Chu Hsi and Lu Hsiang-shan, the divergency between the School of Principle and the School of Mind became definite and sharp.

Wang Yang-ming (Wang Shou-jen, 1472–1529) carried this difference to the point of irreconcilable conflict and pushed Chinese idealism to the highest point. He continued Lu's theme that principle is identical with the mind, but he emphasized its direction, namely the will. To him a thing or an affair is what the will is determined to make it. Filial piety, for example, is not real until one is determined to realize it in actual practice. Principle is therefore inherent in the mind. If it were not, filial piety would cease to be as soon as one's parents died. For this reason he strongly attacked Chu Hsi for going out to things to investigate the principles in them. The investigation of principle should not be an outward search; it should be an investigation of the mind. It should strive to eliminate what is incorrect in the mind so as to preserve the correctness of its original substance. In other words, 'To investigate things is to do good and remove evil.' Since the will is the key, instead of Chu Hsi's interpretation of the procedure in *The Great Learning* that investigation of things precedes sincerity of the will, Wang Yang-ming insists that the will must be sincere before one can investigate things.

In 1509 he came to the realization that knowledge and action are one. 'Knowledge is the beginning of action and action the completion of knowledge,' he said. No one really knows food unless he has tasted it, and no one really loves colour until he has actually seen it. The traditional emphasis on the correspondence between action and knowledge, and on the importance of each, is now raised to the level of unity, a level never reached before. In 1521 he began to teach the doctrine of the

extension of the innate knowledge of the good. This is not merely a combination of the idea of extension of knowledge in *The Great Learning* with that of innate knowledge in Mencius; it is a new concept that adds a new dimension to Chinese thought. Wang Yang-ming describes innate knowledge as 'the original substance of the mind'. It naturally knows the principle of filial piety— for example, when one sees one's parents—and it naturally extends it into action. In virtue of the humanity in the original substance of the mind, one will be compassionate and see oneself and other people and then all other things as being of one kind. One will become identified with others and will regard the world as one family and finally 'become one body with Heaven and Earth and the ten thousand things'. Thus Wang, travelling in the opposite direction from Chu Hsi, arrives at the same destination: the unity of Heaven and man.

p 98 (
p 99 (

Ch'eng-Chu's followers have attacked Wang as being a Ch'an Buddhist in Confucian disguise. His concepts of mind and intuitive understanding are certainly similar to those in Ch'an. He used some Ch'an terms and even some Ch'an techniques, such as asking shocking questions. But he emphasized 'always be doing something', which is a far cry from the quietism of Ch'an.

Whatever may have been their views about nature and principle, the Neo-Confucianists have raised traditional Confucian thought to the metaphysical level. The ancient ethical ideals of filial piety and brotherly respect have now a metaphysical basis. The Neo-Confucian methods of investigation, cultivation of seriousness, calmness and concentration, and transformation of physical nature are also new. Most important of all, an ancient ideal, that of the unity of Heaven and man, is now made the total objective. In this latter sense, Neo-Confucianism is highly religious.

Is Confucianism a religion?
Since it does not have a church or a clergy Confucianism is not an organized religion like the Taoist or the Buddhist religion. In Han apocryphal literature, Confucius was deified, but the belief lasted for hardly a century.

Temples dedicated to Confucius, to other great men, and to ancestors are not houses of gods; they are memorials and marks of honour. Confucian scholars are not priests; they are teachers. In fact, Confucius has always been revered as 'Great Perfection, Ultimate Sage, Ancient Teacher Confucius'. The Confucian Classics derived their authority from the moral principles that they teach and historical examples that they cite, and not from revelation. But Confucianism is unmistakably religious, as can be seen from its worship of Heaven, the honour that it pays to ancestors, its sacrificial rites in honour of great men, especially Confucius, its attitude towards *kuei-shen*, its sense of immortality, and its ideal of the unity of Heaven and man.

As has been pointed out, Confucius transformed the anthropomorphic Heaven of antiquity into the Heaven of the supreme spiritual and moral being. Our duty is to revere Heaven. A superior man stands in awe of Heaven, he said. Mencius taught us that the best way to serve Heaven is to actualize fully the potentialities of our originally good nature. There is the mandate of Heaven, but it is our duty to establish our own *ming* (fate, mandate, destiny). Do good, Mencius said, and 'wait for *ming* to take its course'. In the T'ang Age, Confucian scholars clearly distinguished the respective functions of Heaven and of man. There are things beyond man's control; but, contrary to the Han Age's belief that Nature could influence man, man is the master of his own house and is the maker of his own happiness or sorrow. Heaven is there, not to take over our moral responsibility, but for us to honour and worship. Traditionally, the emperor performed the periodic sacrifices as the representative of his people. Although the ceremony lapsed with the abolition of the monarchical system in 1912, the Confucian belief of Heaven as the source of life and of the Moral Law, though not as a man-like deity, has persisted.

The same moral emphasis characterizes the Confucian tradition of honouring ancestors. The keynote is reverence expressed in one's countenance and in the performance of ceremonies. This note was elaborated in Hsün-tzu, in the *Book of Rites* of the 3rd century BC or later, and in the *Classic of Filial Piety* of the Han Age. Ancestors are to be remembered and to be honoured. Traditionally, Confucianism has encouraged and sponsored the practices of burying parents according to prescribed rituals when they die, observing the three-year period of mourning for them, sacrificing before their tablets, and visiting their graves. These acts are so many demonstrations of filial piety. In the Han Age the doctrine of filial piety was almost made into a cult requiring absolute obedience to parents and constraining sons to continue the family line. Modern revolt has reduced, if not entirely eliminated, the custom of sacrifice before ancestral tablets and has weakened parental authority; but the basic feelings of gratitude and honour for parents has never diminished.

The honour has been extended to many great historical figures, most of all to Confucius. Temples have been built for them and sacrifices regularly performed. Again, the most important element is one's feeling. Confucius said that if he did not participate personally in a sacrifice, it would amount to not sacrificing at all. The *Doctrine of the Mean* stresses sincerity, which, it says, can influence

99 (6)

98 (3)
99 (5)

spiritual beings, so that they 'seem to be on the left and on the right'. Hsün-tzu went a step further and said that whether there are spiritual beings present or not is immaterial; what counts is one's sincerity. Many simpler people still believe in the existence of spiritual beings, and the Taoist religion has promoted such a belief, but enlightened Confucianists have always seen in *kuei-shen*, not ghosts, but spiritual forces operating behind all things in the universe. Survival after death is not thought of by Confucians as being a continuing existence in a spiritual realm. In Confucian eyes, the Taoist search for earthly immortality and the Buddhist hope for rebirth in Paradise is ignorant and even selfish. As Confucians see it, the best type of immortality is the immortality of virtue, of achievements, and of wise words. When virtue accomplished by wisdom reaches the highest degree, a human being becomes one with Heaven.

By the 17th century, Confucianism had dominated Chinese thought for five hundred years. By this time, Chinese thinkers were getting tired of empty speculations on nature and principle, and were resenting the political unorthodoxy and moral looseness of many of Wang Yang-ming's followers, some of whom declared that wealth, wine, and sex do not block the road to salvation. The introduction of science by Catholic Christian missionaries had aroused interest in the study of scientific subjects. The conquest of China by the Manchus in 1644 forced the Confucianists to rethink their philosophy.

The result was a general tendency to stress knowledge 'to put the world in order and for practical application'. Wang Fu-chih (1619–92) improved on Chang Tsai's materialistic philosophy, and several outstanding Ch'eng-Chu Neo-Confucianists concentrated on 'dwelling on seriousness and investigating principles [of practical affairs] to the utmost', thus diverting the attention from abstract speculation on the Great Ultimate to practical living and practical subjects. Yen Yüan (1635–1704) went so far as to reject book study altogether and to confine study to the practical subjects of ceremony, music, agriculture, and military science. In his school there were four halls, one each for history, literary matters, military science, and practical arts. Tai Chen (1723–77) strongly attacked the Sung concept of principle 'as if it were a thing'. Principle, he said, is merely the order of things such as eating and drinking. Feelings, 'if they do not err', are just as good as nature. In the field of scholarship, he demanded evidence, textual support, and concrete application. Empiricism and critical scholarship were the spirit of the day. In the late 19th century the Confucianists turned to the West, though only half way, for their slogan was 'Chinese learning for substance and Western learning for function'. That is to say that China was still deemed to be superior in such fundamental things as philosophy and religion, although it was now recognized that she had to learn from the West about mundane utilities such as railroads and arsenals. In the China of this age there was little creative thought.

The harmony of three religions

On the religious side the most important development, except for the introduction of modern Christianity, was the growth of the 'harmony of the three religions' and the spread of lay Buddhism. After a period of bitter controversies between Buddhists and Taoists on religious issues and between Buddhists and Confucianists on political and ethical issues in earlier centuries, the Chinese came to the conclusion that 'the three systems are one', or that 'the three teachings are harmonious', arguing that their different names and various terms mean the same things and that they are different roads to the same destination. We have seen how Buddhism and Taoism have cross-fertilized each other and how deeply Neo-Confucianism was influenced by Buddhism. At all times the force of synthesis was at work. By the 16th century this movement had become pervasive. It was vigorously promoted by scholars representing all three systems. Buddhist deities became Taoist gods and vice versa. Many 'temples for the Three Sages' were built. The masses frequented Confucian temples, Taoist shrines, and Buddhist temples without discrimination. Trade guilds and secret societies embraced all three religions. Towards the end of the 19th century, societies for three or more religions grew up in various parts of China. The old saying that the typical Chinese wears a Confucian crown, a Taoist robe, and Buddhist sandals has become trite.

It is significant that the spread of the lay movement in Buddhism was promoted by all three great priests of the 16th and 17th centuries: Chu-hung (Great Master Lien-ch'ih, 1535–1615), Te-ch'ing (Great Master Han-shan, 1546–1623), and Chi-hsü (Great Master Ou-i, 1599–1655). Emphasis was placed on daily practice at home, and the keynotes were piety and devotion. Of the many kinds of pious acts, setting creatures free was particularly stressed, societies for that purpose were organized, and the practice became widespread. A new class of lay Buddhists called 'Buddhists at home', including many Confucian and Taoist scholars, emerged. These lay Buddhists would worship the Buddha, fast or be vegetarians, and even don the Buddhist robe on certain occasions. The authority of the Buddhist clergy greatly weakened. Authority has passed from the clergy, the rulers, and the rich to the mass of the laity, in which the new movement has found its main support. For centuries the civil service examinations had been diverting most talented people away from the monasteries, and the quality and morale of the Buddhist monastic order had greatly deteriorated. As a result, more and more educated Chinese have become 'Buddhists at home' instead of entering a monastery. Thus the centre of Buddhism has shifted from the monastery to society and the home. These 'Buddhists at home' have also promoted the harmony of the three religions, as the Great Masters had promoted this before them.

The 20th century

Under the impact of the West, all Chinese philosophical and religious systems made strong efforts at modernization. The most significant was that of K'ang Yu-wei (1858–1927). He was the last outstanding Confucianist. He maintained that Confucius was a reformer and the founder of a religion. He envisaged a utopia which progresses from the Age of Chaos through the Age of Small Peace to the Age of Great Unity, when all distinctions between nations, families, and classes, and all other kinds of distinction, will be abolished. This, he said, was Confucius's goal. To bring about the second stage he engineered the abortive reform of 1898. After failure and years of exile, he dedicated his mind and energy to making Confucianism a state religion. He failed in this, too, because by the second decade of the 20th century the Chinese had become antagonistic not only towards a state religion but towards religion in general. The new idols were rationalism and scientism.

After the cultural revolution of 1917, the new intellectuals were importing the doctrines of Darwin, Dewey, Marx, and other Western thinkers wholesale. Abbot T'ai-hsü (1898–1947) attempted to harmonize Buddhist thought with Western rationalism and science. Chang Tung-sun (1886–1962) tried to build his own philosophical system, which he called 'revised Kantianism' and 'epistemological pluralism'. In Confucianism the efforts have been more creative and more influential, notably those of Hsiung Shih-li (1885–1968) and Fung Yu-lan (b. 1895). Hsiung derived his ideas from the *Book of Changes*, and looked upon the universe as an incessant process of 'closing', in which integration results in static matter, and 'opening', which is its own master and is the mind. Mind and matter are each both substance and manifestation, for they are two aspects of the same thing. He emphasized personal realization of truth, and he has exerted a tremendous influence on contemporary Chinese philosophers. At the same time, Fung was establishing what he called a 'new tradition', which means a continuation of the Ch'eng-Chu philosophy with the addition of new elements. His philosophy is based on the Ch'eng-Chu concepts of principle, material force, and the Substance of Tao. He conceives of the Substance of Tao as unceasing change in a universal operation resulting in the Great Whole, in which one is all and all is one. He has treated all these concepts as logical concepts, and this is his loan from Western philosophy. In 1950 he repudiated his own philosophy because, he confessed, he neglected the concrete and the particular. In 1962 he wrote a 'new version' of his *History of Chinese Philosophy* (1934), which had established him as the leading contemporary Chinese philosopher. The new version is written from the Marxist point of view, and yet Fung firmly holds on to the Confucian concept of humanity, which, he insists, is universal and abstract.

In 1959–62, many academic conferences were held in continental China, and many symposia were published on the philosophies of Confucius, Lao-tzu, Chuang-tzu, Mou-tzu, Wang Fu-chih, and others, but not on Ch'eng I, Chu Hsi, Lu Hsiang-shan, or Wang Yang-ming, to determine which elements in them should be maintained and which should be rejected. The criteria were the degree of their materialism and of their service for the masses. Opinions were by no means unanimous. The significant implication is that, even where Marxism is held to be the only correct philosophy, a synthesis of this with the Chinese heritage is possible. In Taiwan there has been a general revival of traditional religions and philosophies, with the harmony of the three religions being given a particularly prominent role. The main efforts, in Taiwan as on the mainland, are being devoted to rectifying man's mind and solving his problems. In both regions, Western ideas are extremely influential, and on some subjects they are dominant; but the age-old Chinese spirit of syncretism and humanism remains strong.

V THE EMPIRICAL TRADITION

Science and technology in China

S. NAKAYAMA

*Let us melt their [Western] materials
and cast them into the mould of the
traditional calendar.*

Hsu Kuang-ch'i

The Yin-Yang underlay all classical Chinese intellectual enquiry. It was a principle that explained all the phenomena in the universe – that is to say, in Western terminology, it was a metaphysical rather than a scientific concept, a method of comprehending what is known rather than a technique for discovering what is unknown. This in itself is significant. It is another facet of Confucian values, with their stress on orthodoxy, authority and precedent. The Confucian Classics were not in themselves relevant to science, but they encouraged habits of mind which determined how science would develop. While observation and the compilation of records accumulated on a scale often beyond anything achieved by the West, there were no corresponding advances in theoretical work. All data was fitted into the existing framework, and what would seem to a modern scientist to be the chief drawback of that framework – its all-inclusiveness, its immunity to proof or disproof – was to the classical Confucian its greatest merit.

Theory in the Chinese intellectual tradition was thus more akin to medieval theology than to science as it is now understood. The basic principles were given, and could not be questioned. To explain a new fact meant to interpret it according to the old principles. The Yin-Yang was ideally useful in this sort of undertaking, since it embraced all things at all times and all places. Logically, it began from the fact that every descriptive word has an opposite, so that every conceivable description can be formulated in terms of an interaction between opposites – light-dark, hot-cold, dry-wet, odd-even, male-female, etc. These opposites were seen as active forces, determining and creating the world as we experience it. Like all good metaphysical systems it produced a satisfying sensation of completeness. Nothing was left out; the whole universe was included, material and spiritual; the earth, men and gods were all within its compass. Thus it came to be endowed additionally with (again using Western terminology) a mystical significance. Representations of it, such as this board (opposite), where it is surrounded by the eight trigrams (see p. 175), had an almost talismanic power. The strength of that power is perhaps still not exhausted, even within the new ideology. Not without plausibility have parallels been drawn between the dialectic of Hegel (from which the dialectical materialism of Marx derives) and the cosmic dualism of the Yin-Yang. (1)

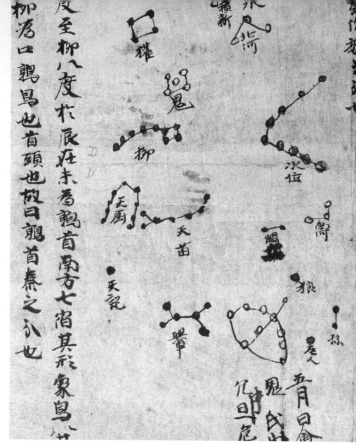

Teaching the Classics in Han China became the paradigm of scholarly activity. Endorsed by the government and incorporated into the examination system for civil servants, it effectively excluded the sort of open discussion from which a scientific method could evolve. Here the master sits on a raised platform on the left; his pupils form a half-circle round him. (2)

The star-maps of China were in advance of anything known to the West. This detail from a map of about AD 940 includes the constellation of Orion. Observation and recording were extremely exact, but from all this information no consistent cosmological theory ever grew. Astronomy was chiefly valued for its usefulness in astrology and for regulating the calendar. (3)

Knowledge of herbs was extensive, and ancient pharmacopoeias listed many hundreds of herbal preparations.

In this Ming dynasty painting a scholar is boiling herbs in a specially constructed apparatus. (4)

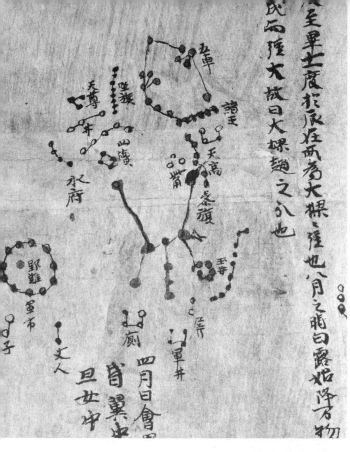

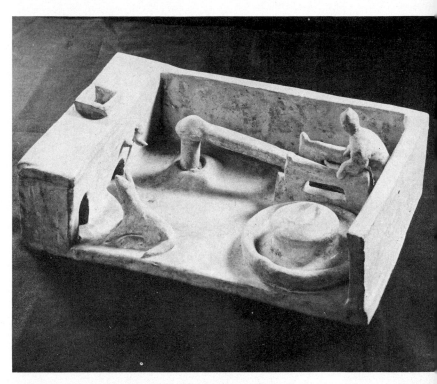

The machines of Han China were more elaborate than one expects. This pottery model from a tomb shows three examples. On the left, built into the wall, is a winnowing fan; all we see is the hopper, where the grain is fed in, a crank-handle for working the fan and two apertures for the corn and chaff. (Here what seems to be a large dog is sitting expectantly.) At the back a man works a foot-operated tilt-hammer for pounding grain. Next to him is a rotary mill; the grain is fed in through a hole in the upper stone which is rotated, depositing the flour in the circular trough. (5)

Chinese medicine created two techniques totally unknown in the West, acupuncture and moxibustion. The former is illustrated overleaf. Moxibustion, which is probably the operation being carried out in this Sung painting of a country doctor (right), consists of placing a cone of dried wormwood leaves (*Artemisia moxa*) over the affected part, burning it, and rubbing the ash into the resulting blister. (6)

Astronomy and games were combined in some of the complicated divinatory procedures of the Han age. The game of *liu-po* ('Six Scholars') was played on a board resembling a sundial, which gave the moves astrological significance. These were determined by the throwing of sticks and the pieces symbolized the four cardinal directions. After crossing a central belt (water or the Milky Way) they could be promoted to 'leading pieces'. (7)

Modesty forbade a Chinese lady of rank to submit to examination by a doctor, so these ivory and alabaster figurines came into use. She could point to the part that troubled her for the doctor to make his diagnosis. (8)

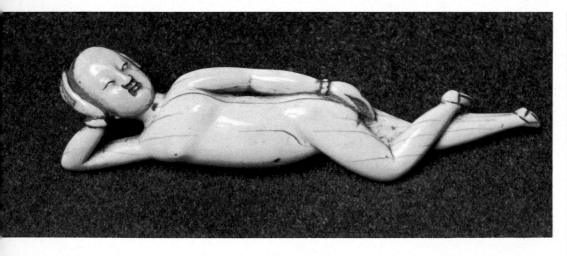

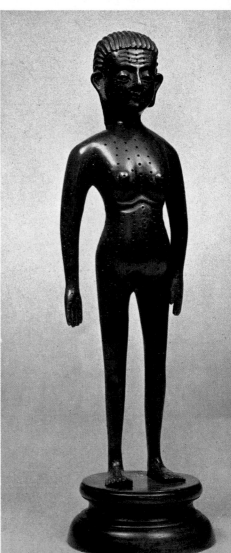

Acupuncture aimed to affect the *ch'i*, a sort of vital spirit which circulated through the bodily organs. This 18th-century bronze figure (right) shows the points where the insertion of needles would exert the most powerful effect. (9)

A village craftsman (right) of the Yuan dynasty constructs a barrel, using techniques that hardly changed over the centuries. Western scientists were aware of these craft techniques and often learned from them, but in China the traditional class-divisions kept them apart, to the detriment of scientific progress. (10)

Surgery made slow progress after the Han age, partly because the Confucian code stressed that every part of the body should be preserved. The treatment depicted here (below left) is part of legend. A great physician, Hua T'o, operated on the arm of Kuan Yü, wounded in battle. To take his mind off the agony the patient played *go* until it was all over. (11)

Detailed charts of the body showing the precise channels through which the *ch'i* circulated (below right) go back to very early times. The organs themselves were divided into the five *tsang* and the six *fu*. From such charts the most favourable combination of points for acupuncture could be worked out. (12)

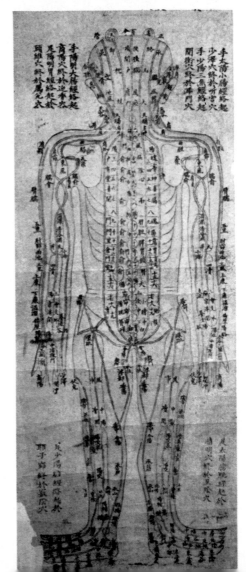

Water-control was an urgent concern of Chinese technology. Here, in the year AD 1006, gangs of workers build up a dyke that has burst its banks. (13)

The Jesuit observatory at Peking still retains some of its original instruments (left), including a globe and armillary sphere. (14)

The compass is a Chinese invention. This one, used for astrological and geomantic purposes, is of black lacquer on wood. (15)

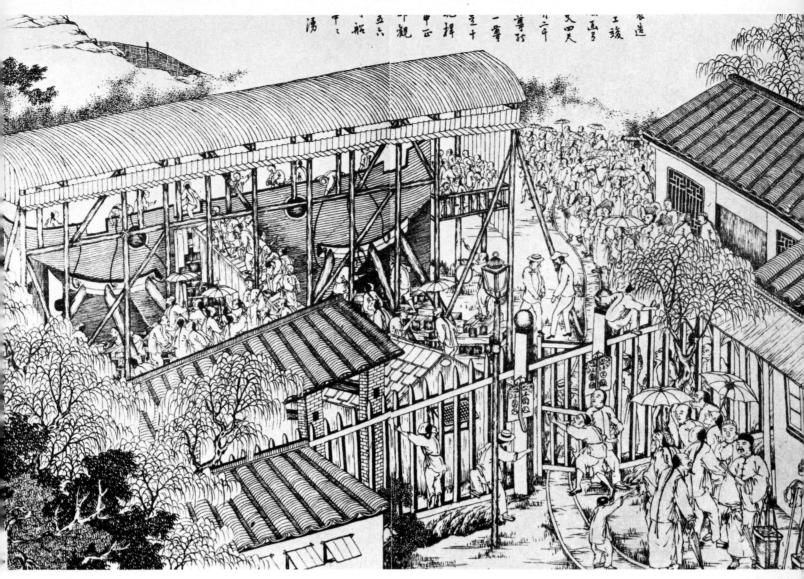

Western technology hit China after the Opium Wars and the opening up of the country to foreign business interests. In 1865 the government set up the Kiang-nan Arsenal at Shanghai. Most of its technical staff were by necessity European or American, but it was soon training Chinese engineers. Above: the launching of a warship in 1884. (16)

Railways came late to China. Right: one of the first trains, near Shanghai, in 1884. The peasants hated them because they disturbed the fields and sometimes the grave mounds of ancestors. The government feared – as did indeed come to pass – that foreign-controlled lines would be both an economic and a military threat to China. After 1898 Russian, Japanese, German and French lines sprang up within their respective spheres of influence. (17)

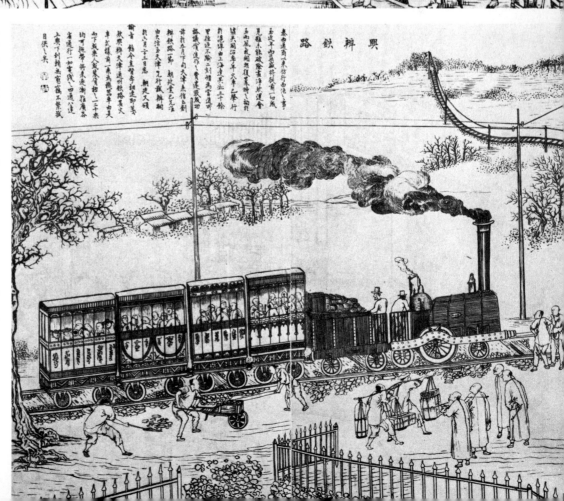

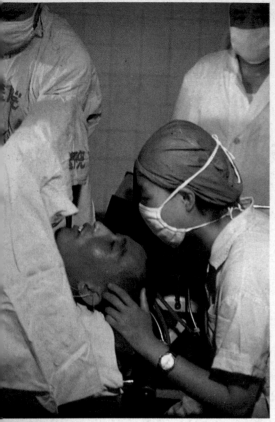

Acupuncture today has astonished Western doctors by its effectiveness in anaesthesia. Very thin needles are inserted into the lobe of the ear. These are then attached to an electrical manipulator which twirls them rapidly back and forth. The patient's awareness of pain is dulled, but he is still conscious and can co-operate with the surgeon. How this happens is still a mystery. The ancient *ch'i* theory seems to have no scientific basis, and we must look at hitherto unknown properties of the central nervous system. (18)

Science in the countryside: throughout the ages famine has been China's curse. Until the thirties of this century, a bad harvest meant the death of millions, and this happened so regularly that the rest of the world hardly took note of it. Under Communism the effort to increase food-production has been resolute and finally successful. It has been done partly by bringing new land into cultivation, partly by improving crops, partly by new methods of farming. Left: after studying and cross-breeding from 120 strains of rice, it was possible to evolve new strains to fit local conditions. Above: intensive fish-farming in the Pearl River delta in Kwangtung. The fish breed in the pools, while mulberries, fruit trees and sugar-cane are planted on the banks. The pool-ooze fertilizes the trees, the silkworm droppings and mulberry leaves feed the fish. By applying knowledge of marine biology, the same pond can be used to raise different varieties of fish which live at different depths. (19, 20)

S. NAKAYAMA

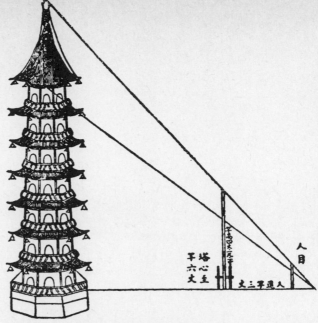

It is typical of the way science developed in China that advanced geometrical techniques should have been applied to practical problems without any unifying theory of geometry being evolved. This illustration from a 3rd century AD mathematical work shows how to measure the height of a pagoda by trigonometry. (1)

THE UNBROKEN CONTINUITY of Chinese culture, which has been stressed in all the previous chapters of this book, applies with equal force to the development of science. It makes a striking contrast in this respect with the history of science in the West, which has progressed by a series of revolutions originating in different areas and different cultures, and often provoked by confrontations between them.

Pre-Han: 'recording' versus 'debating'
If we take a world view of sciences and learning in their formative pre-Christian period, we shall observe two striking parallels between the histories of Western and of Chinese thought: one between Babylonian and Ancient China, and the other between classical Greece and China in the Warring States period (the 4th to the 3rd century BC). In the earlier of these two periods, intellectual activity in both regions mainly took the form of recording for purposes of astrology, whereas in the later this was succeeded by rational debate.

Astrology is essentially a recording activity. In fact, *t'ai shih ling*, the Chinese title for the official imperial historian, originally meant astrologer as well; his main duty was to record unusual occurrences in the heavens for making entries in the imperial chronicle. For the interpretation of such portents, past records provided the only criteria. When an unprecedented portent appeared, it must have created a crisis in the existing system of paradigms and have imperilled the 'time-tested' canonical interpretations; but, in actual practice, such crises were always resolved by modifications of the conventional directives. The recognition of a truly significant crisis was never permitted, and consequently no anomalous cases ever disturbed astrological theory. A mass of records of observations of portents simply accumulated continuously in the course of time.

This type of intellectual activity requires only a minimum of original thought. But it puts a premium on clerical accuracy and assiduousness; the employment of full-time manpower is needed in order to carry it out; and it requires the social framework of some stable institution. Hence, the tradition can be maintained best under governmental auspices. Government-sponsored learning, such as astrology, the compilation of chronicles, and instructions for court rituals, fitted in with the Chinese bureaucratic regime. As we have seen, this regime had an amazingly long run. It lasted from the Chou Age, in the last millennium BC, to the early years of the 20th century of the Christian era.

In the Warring States period, however, an entirely new mode of transmitting knowledge emerged. This was private education, pioneered by Confucius and Mou-tzu. This was an age of social and political turmoil. The previous social order was being jeopardized by the rise of political usurpers and by the development of commercial activity. Individualism was replacing clan solidarity, and private education now became accessible even to commoners.

The political turmoil of the Warring States period generated the 'debating' form of intellectual activity. The pre-Socratic Greek philosophers in the West had their Chinese counterparts in the intellectual blossoming of the 'Hundred Schools'. These scholars came mostly from the lower ranks of the ruling class. Politically ambitious men of this class now looked for openings as political or technical consultants in the service of influential princes or kings. They wandered from one feudal state to another, looking for a master who would be interested in using their knowledge and skill.

The Greek Sophists sold their art of persuasion at the street-corner to private citizens, whereas the customers of the Chinese 'debating' scholars were virtually limited to rulers or lords. A number of schools of ambitious 'Debaters', such as the Confucians, Moists, Legalists, Taoists, Natural Philosophers and others (see Chapter IV) competed with each other for listeners. Since the Confucian school's ideology was in close harmony with the

命官授時圖

A late Ch'ing illustration to the Book of Documents shows the legendary Hsi and Ho brothers receiving from the sage emperor Yao the imperial commission to organize the calendar and pay respect to the celestial bodies. (2)

existing feudal order and clan society, a rival school, headed by Mou-tzu, emerged. The Moist school attempted to integrate the axioms of optics, mechanics, and semantics. Its canon contains many germinal ideas. It offered a potential matrix for several authentic scientific disciplines such as logic, mathematics, and optics, if the climate had been favourable for this. In the Warring States period, technical specialists, craftsmen, and engineers were highly esteemed.

The two modes of intellectual activity, 'recording' and 'debating', have little in common with each other. 'Recording' accumulates a huge body of factual information, but falls easily into dull routine. 'Debating', by contrast, generates intellectual excitement and often leads to the discovery of something new, but it finds difficulty in settling down into an academic tradition of routine scientific study.

The intellectual paradigm of the Han Age

The term 'paradigm' is used in this chapter to mean 'a canonical corpus of classical literature which defines a style of learning, legitimizes the professional practice of an intellectual sect, and prescribes the course for the subsequent development of a standardized type of scholarship.' The acceptance of paradigms of scholarship —the Aristotelian in the West and the Confucian in China—was a necessary preliminary to the achievement

of a consensus among scholars about the legitimate programme and subject-matter of study. After this, the members of the community of scholars could proceed to work out their ideas on standard lines. The success of any particular discipline in any cultural region depends on the choice of the paradigm. This choice is decisive for the subsequent development of the academic programme, and therefore an examination of this bifurcation-point is of crucial importance for the comparative history of science.

Chinese history did not produce an intellectual giant comparable to Aristotle, who synthesized the antecedent controversies and presented them in a systematic, encyclopedic, and logical form. Confucian sayings are purely socio-ethical dicta. They offer no guidance for the way in which science is to develop. Confucius himself seems to have had no idea of the nature of academic disciplines. As we saw in Chapter IV, he was the 'charismatic' founder of an intellectual school (or a profession) whose function was mainly to give ethical significance to ritual observances and court ceremonies.

Among Confucius's followers, Mencius showed some sympathy with the Debater scholars of the 'Hundred Schools', but later, in the time of Hsün-tzu, a more academic attitude prevailed and Confucianism was codified into a set of canons.

In the Han Age the primary function of the Confucian school was the compilation and canonization of classics. The scope of the Confucian canons was now no longer confined to the court rituals of the early Confucians; they now borrowed all sorts of views that had been put forward in ancient classics, but they set these in the framework of their own Confucian style. The dominant tone is practical, this-worldly, and sober, a style of learning called the *ching-hsüeh* (the study of classics). This was the point at which the future course of Chinese learning was determined. The *ching-hsüeh* dominated the Chinese academic world from the Han Age until this century.

p 134–(2)

Why and how did Confucianism win its intellectual victory over the hundred competing schools? Because it was not a fair competition; the government interfered in the game.

In the process of establishing a centralized bureaucracy in the time of the Ch'in and Han dynasties, Confucianism prevailed over the Legalist philosophy that had been favoured by the Ch'in. The Han dynasty welcomed Confucianism as a buttress for the imperial regime, because Confucian doctrine stood for the restoration and preservation of social order. Since Confucian doctrine is neither specific nor provocative, it may be doubted whether the Confucian canons produced positive practical effects. They did, however, have a negative effect. They gave a quietus to the intellectual turmoil of the preceding period.

In the reign of the Emperor Wu (140–87 BC) of the earlier Han dynasty, Tung Chung-shu's policy of suppressing all schools of philosophy except Confucianism was put into effect. Confucianism now became the orthodox doctrine of the Chinese state. Consequently, ambitious careerists all flocked into the Confucian school. The consequence has been that in China, throughout her subsequent history, the academic tradition has been maintained chiefly by a special class of people who were

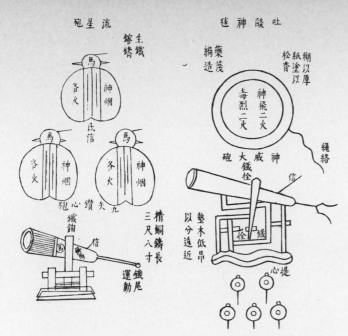

Gunpowder was invented by the Chinese. By the 13th century bombs, mines, grenades and cannons were part of the Chinese armoury. Weapons illustrated in a 17th century work include the 'divine-fire' ball (top right), the 'divine-frightening' cannon (bottom right), the 'meteor shooting-stars' cannon, (top left) and the 'nine-arrow heart-piercing' cannon (bottom left). (3)

'The Enemy-of-Ten-thousand-men is conveniently used to defend remotely located small cities, in which the cannons are either weak in firing power or too heavy and clumsy to be effective weapons. The sulphur and saltpetre in it are ignited to project incendiary flame and poisonous smoke in all directions, thus killing many men and horses instantly.' (4)

destined for administrative posts. The merchant class was excluded from the bureaucracy, and, at least nominally, it was given the lowest social status.

In China the canonization of classics was accompanied by a systematization of educational institutions. The study of the Confucian canons became the main part of the school curriculum. The Emperor Wu founded lectureships for Confucian studies and appointed salaried professors of classics. The primary aim of the educational programme was the recruitment of talented bureaucrats. The teaching profession was itself a part of the bureaucratic machinery, and there were frequent exchanges of personnel between administrative offices and educational institutions.

A bureaucracy always attaches importance to precedents, and the bureaucratic criterion of academic merit is a respect for the teachings of venerable classics rather than an adventurousness in opening up new intellectual horizons. The older the better. Thus the Chinese tradition of classical 'recording' activity—protected, as it were, by a well-established bureaucracy—enjoyed a much higher status than the Western doxographical tradition. Even in a scientific field, such as astronomy, respect for the classics prevailed. For instance, official astronomers gave full credit to the 'observational' records of the pre-Ch'in period and tried to 'save the ancient records' by modifying their own theories.

The Chinese preference for the specific and the tangible may have been a drawback to them in the field of theory, but was an advantage in technology. In many basic inventions, China was centuries ahead of the West. We need only mention the three most famous: paper, printing and gunpowder. The manufacture of paper from fibrous material in China goes back to at least the 2nd century BC. It did not reach the Islamic world until the 8th century, nor Christian Europe until the 13th. Block prints were made in Japan in AD 770. The first printed book is documented in China in AD 868. Movable type was used in the 11th century, but the enormous number of characters needed made it less useful to the Chinese than it subsequently became in Europe. Gunpowder was invented in China before the 10th century AD, and Chinese armies were using grenades and cannon by the 13th.

The character of Chinese science: astronomy, mathematics and medicine

Most of the major scientific classics, which eventually became standard texts for the Chinese scientific community, had been composed by the end of the Han Age. The most important of these are the *Chiu-chang suan-shu* (Nine chapters on the mathematical art) in arithmetic and mathematics; *Chou-pi suan-ching* (The arithmetical classics of the gnomon and the circular paths of heaven) in astronomy and cosmology; *Huang-ti nei-ching su-wen* (Pure questions, inner classic of the Yellow Emperor) and *Shang-han lun* (On fevers) in pathological and clinical medicine; and *Shen-nung pen-ts'ao ching* (Pharmacopoeia of the Heavenly Husbandman) in pharmacology. In the governmental organization, calendar-making, astrology, medicine, and mathematics were given a solid institutional basis.

There are two fundamental principles that, throughout Chinese history, have been applied to Chinese astrology, medicine, alchemy, and many other branches of Chinese intellectual activity. These two principles (already discussed in Chapter IV) are Yin-Yang and the 'Five Elements' (or 'Five Agents'). The Yin-Yang principle explains all phenomena in the universe in terms of a fundamental dichotomy between heaven and earth, male and female, and so on. The Five Elements principle was classificatory. Temporal phases and spatial orientations were functionally identified with five common substances: wood, fire, earth, metal, and water.

The date at which these principles were first formulated still eludes the historians, but the most probable date is the 4th century BC; they were certainly established during

19 (9)

p 134–5 (3)

p 134–5 (4)

p 133 (1)
p 175 (5)
p 101 (9)

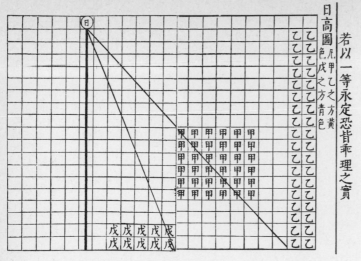

The 'Chou-pi suan-ching' is generally considered to be the oldest Chinese mathematical and astronomical classic. It was based on gnomon observations and this diagram from it shows calculations made when the sun (top left) is at its highest point. (5)

the Early Han dynasty (2nd to 1st century BC). From the start, both were closely associated with astronomical and cosmological speculations. They acquired the sacrosanct status of supreme metaphysical principles that no new discovery could refute. Even the report of the discovery of the sixth planet, Uranus, during the Ch'ing period never seriously shook the belief in the Five Elements theory, which required that there should be exactly five planets in the sky.

In the West the Aristotelian paradigm similarly burdened a later generation of scholars with an out-of-date synthesis which had to be overcome, and this eventually led to the great 17th-century scientific revolution. The Chinese paradigm failed to develop such a scientific synthesis. It was not sufficiently coherent to be overthrown by disproof. It formulated no general laws and attempted no rigorous demonstrations. Its spirit was empirical, but limited and practical. Chinese scientists showed apathy or even scepticism towards the belief in the existence of an invariable underlying regularity in Nature and towards any thorough-going 'general conceptual scheme' such as was implicit in the mechanistic philosophy of the West. For instance, inaccuracies in predictions of solar eclipses were attributed, not necessarily to imperfections in scientific technique, but as often as not to an inherent indeterminacy of celestial motions. 'Even the heavens occasionally go astray.'

Although basic cosmological ideas appeared in fragmentary form in the oldest classics, the first Chinese treatise on 'scientific' cosmology—scientific in the sense of being mathematical and entirely divorced from mythopoeic tradition—is found in the *Chou-pi suan-ching*, which is based on gnomon observations and the conception of heaven and earth as being parallel. This was opposed by another important cosmological school which—evidently under the influence of the development of armillary sphere observations—recognized the sphericity of the sky. Cosmological debate had been most active during the Han and Six Dynasties period. The controversy, however, died out. Astronomers lost their interest in it and occupied themselves solely with routine observations and calendrical calculations. In the T'ang Age the Chinese astronomers' attitude towards this particular speculative

pursuit was that 'Our business is exclusively calendrical calculations and observations, and our object is to give people the means of setting their dates right. Whether the cosmos is flat or spherical is no concern of the astronomers!' There were occasional cosmological debates among the Sung philosophers, but scientific cosmology was neglected by professional astronomers during the long time that elapsed before the Jesuits made their impact.

As observational astronomers, however, the Chinese were far superior to the West. At the very dawn of Chinese history, bone inscriptions refer to an eclipse of the moon in 1361 BC and of the sun in 1216 BC. By the time of the Warring States a catalogue of stars had been compiled containing 1,464 entries, each with its position carefully noted. So meticulous are the Chinese records that they are still proving useful to modern science. One of them tells how in AD 1054 a 'guest' star suddenly appeared at a particular point in the sky, so bright that it was visible by day for over three weeks. Only recently has it been recognized that this may have been the explosion of the Crab Nebula, now a patch of faintly glowing debris but an object of intense interest, since its precise 'age' is now known.

The purpose of these observations, however, was not any conceptual scheme or mechanistic model. When a Chinese official astronomer found out that the position of the moon was radically different from the place he predicted by calculation, the event should have naturally caused a crisis in his theory, but he had a convenient way out by labelling it as an 'irregular' phenomenon, saying 'the moon goes erratically'. For the Chinese, 'regularity' is one thing, and irregular and extraordinary happenings are simply others. While Platonic insistence on the search for and dogmatic belief in the existence of the hidden regularity in Nature often tended to exclude or at least limit their attention towards 'irregular' phenomena as casual and peripheral (such as appearances of comets, novae and haloes), the Chinese welcomed these and classified them. In contrast to the Western approach of seeking causal relationships in the physical universe, the major approach of Chinese science was classification, centred on natural history. The approach of the Chinese official astronomers was merely to describe the course of the celestial bodies in numerical terms. Their final aim was to reduce observations as accurately as possible to algebraic relations. Unlike Ptolemaic astronomy, Chinese astronomy showed no concern for the calculation of the dimensions of the universe; and for all purposes of measurement heaven was treated two-dimensionally. Considering the extent of the development of eclipse-predicting techniques, it is surprising to note that even the sphericity of the earth was not explicitly utilized in computations by Chinese astronomers until the Jesuits arrived.

Calendrical science enjoyed government sponsorship throughout its history, and had more prestige than other branches of science; it was China's most genuine contribution to exact science. Perhaps the most striking feature of the recastings of the civil calendar was their frequency. The Chinese calendar was revised more than forty times in two thousand years, and another fifty unsuccessful proposals are recorded.

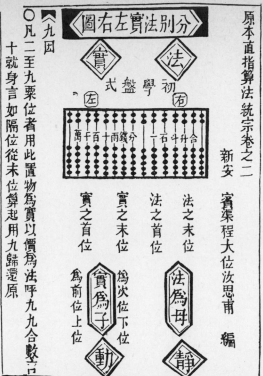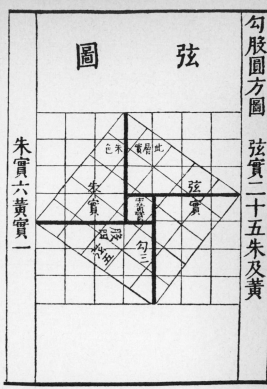

Right: a 16th century printed picture of the abacus. The abacus is a quick and sophisticated means of computation permitting the extraction of square and cube roots and is today still widely used in East Asia. (6)

Pythagoras' theorem was one of the few propositions where Chinese geometry coincided with Euclid. A form of proof is illustrated here in the 'Chou-pi suan-ching' (7)

The Chinese believed that a ruler received his mandate from Heaven; a new mandate meant a new disposition of celestial influences. In the early period, therefore, at the accession of a new ruler and, *a fortiori,* of a new dynasty, the new emperor was impelled to reform the official calendar in order to confirm the establishment of a new order which a new mandate implied. This notion was responsible for the subsequent course of development of Chinese calendrical science.

In the course of time, however, the political importance of calendar reform dwindled. Its restriction to the date of a change of dynasty was not strictly observed by the 5th century AD. In the time of the T'ang dynasty, the motive for calendar revision became simply to correct disagreements of the calendar with observed celestial phenomena, and reforms were carried out whenever a small error was found. This accounts for the frequency of revisions in later periods of Chinese history.

The Chinese calendar, from early times until its replacement by the Gregorian calendar in the 20th century, was a typical luni-solar calendar. Its compilers were not satisfied with providing a conventional scheme, in which the lunar months and solar years were adjusted to each other, merely for civil use; they also tried to include the anomalous motions of the sun and moon. Yet there was no separation of scientific astronomy from civil calendar-making. Astronomy was thus confined to the composition of a luni-solar system which stood or fell by the accuracy with which it could predict eclipses. The analysis of planetary motions was ancillary to the main problems of Chinese astronomy.

The *Chiu-chang suan-shu,* which is the most important of all mathematical Chinese classics, illustrates the point that Chinese mathematics is almost exclusively concerned with practical applications, or at least is highly application-conscious. There are no abstract and systematic proofs, i.e. no interest in mathematics for its own sake, and probably for this reason mathematics in China never achieved a high status among the sciences in the eyes of the bureaucracy and the scholar-literati. It tended

to be treated as a mere technique, with few philosophical overtones, for petty-officials to employ in such minor duties as mensuration, tax-collection, and book-keeping.

For calculating the Chinese had relied on mechanical tools. The early use of counting-rods and later use of the abacus encouraged the numerical solution of algebraic problems. Yet the Chinese could handle negative numbers by using rods of different colours—black and red—as early as the Han Age. Numerical quadratic and cubic equations, simultaneous linear equations, and the value of π, were all calculated more accurately in 3rd-century China than in the rest of the world, thanks to the use of the counting-rods. Dependence on tools, however, meant that the process of Chinese calculations vanished without leaving any record of the intermediate stages by which the answer had been reached. In ordinary mathematical texts, only the problems and the final answers were given. There was perhaps some relation between this custom and the absence of the idea of rigorous proof in Chinese mathematics. Calculation by writing was not practised in China until the introduction of Western mathematics after the arrival of the Jesuits.

Geometrical problems were treated only algebraically. Graphical treatment was employed as an auxiliary means for giving visual aid. No attempt was made to develop logical geometry of the Euclidean kind. There is not much to be said about trigonometry in the ancient Chinese mathematics, except that the Pythagorean theorem was studied enthusiastically in as early a work as the *Chou-pi suan-ching* in connection with astronomical measurements for which the gnomon was required.

Chinese physiological theory, as presented in the *Huang-ti nei-ching,* is deeply involved in the characteristic Chinese *Naturphilosophie.* According to the Chinese view of pathology, the cause of disease lies chiefly in the malfunctioning of the circulation of ch'i (a sort of pneuma). The ch'i in external forces, e.g. wind, coldness, hotness, humidity, penetrates into the body's internal organs and causes disease. Internally, the disturbance of the circulation of ch'i through the five tsang (the heart, liver, spleen,

P 136 (9)
P 137 (11)
P 140 (18)

145

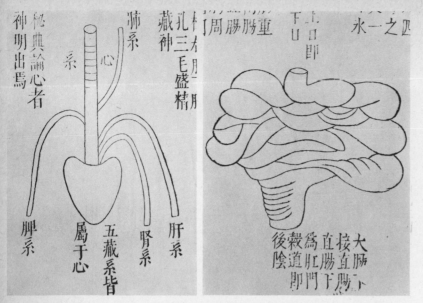

Dissection of dead bodies was probably carried out during the Han age, but thereafter little progress was made in anatomical knowledge. These illustrations from a late Ming encyclopaedia show the windpipe and heart (left) and the intestines. (8, 9)

lungs, and kidneys) and the six *fu* (the gall-bladder, stomach, large intestine, small intestine, bladder, and *san-chiao*, an imaginary organ) is also a cause of disease. The dissection of the human body was probably being practised to some extent before the Han Age. *Nei-ching* states that 'After death the body may be dissected and observations be made as to the size of the organs, the capacity of the intestines, the length of the arteries, the condition of the blood, and the amount of pneuma.' But surgery was never seriously practised.

In Chinese physiological and pathological theories, the brain never played a significant role. The brain was held to be merely a part of the marrow in the bones. Mental activity was attributed to the heart, which was regarded as being the prince of the body. The symptoms of disease can be detected readily by feeling the pulse, and hence sphygmic examination was considered to be as important in diagnosis as gross symptoms and case history. Climatic and topographical factors were taken into account, and the body was always treated as a whole. The uniquely Chinese form of therapy is perhaps acupuncture.

Natural history, chemistry, and alchemy were primarily ancillary to therapeutics. Presumably, the Chinese word *pen-ts'ao*, which is equivalent to 'pharmacology', originally meant the study of medicines for longevity or immortality. Later, it was applied to the study of *materia medica* in general. It included mineral drugs, but unlike their modern Western counterparts, Chinese physicians did not try to extract medicines from herbs. The primary goal of Chinese alchemy, too, was to find a recipe for immortality rather than to obtain authentic noble metal from base metal.

The Chinese academic tradition

The contrast between the two academic traditions, the Western rhetorical and the Chinese classical, becomes even more sharply pronounced when we look at the development of medieval academic institutions.

In earlier Chinese history, the higher posts in the Chinese bureaucracy were monopolized by powerful aristocratic families, but the reconsolidation of China into

a gigantic centralized state, first under the Sui (589–617) and then under the T'ang (618–906), required the recruitment of the best talent of the day under the direct control of the Emperor. The previous procedures of recommendation by patrons and of personal interviews for the recruitment of officials were now replaced by competitive civil service examinations. Educational institutions were only nominally independent; they were directed towards the education of prospective bureaucrats. All students now prepared for the state examination, and this provided a single prescribed avenue towards official success and at the same time served as an outlet for intellectual energy which might otherwise have taken a subversive course.

The civil service examinations have already been described in Chapter II. Persons of almost any economic or social background were eligible, at least in theory. Hence, the Chinese system of recruiting talent seems at first sight to be more effective and further advanced than even modern Western educational institutions. It was, however, completely controlled by the Government, which was thus able to stereotype all forms of learning. The examining body, which was composed of high officials, had complete authority over the examinees. The Government could use this machinery to inhibit original thought, by designating which interpretations of the classics were to be followed in the examinations. There was always a time-lag between the frontier of learning and its reflection at the level of examination questions. There can be no doubt that the civil service examination promoted the cultivation of learning, and popular respect for it, in China; but what matters is the style of learning that it prescribed.

In the T'ang Age, the state examinations and education were linked up with each other, and thus the official Confucian learning was perpetuated by giving it a firm footing in educational institutions. Other classics, such as the Buddhist and Taoist canons, were excluded from the standard school textbooks. If a Buddhist sutra was cited in a lecture, this was only for the purpose of criticism and eventual rejection.

Professionals and specialists were not in a happy position under the regime of bureaucrats who had had a general literary education. In pre-Han times, and even in the later years of the Six Dynasties (AD 420–580), it was still possible to attain a high position by virtue of specialized technical ability. However, the crystallization of educational institutions in China in the Sui and T'ang Age (the earliest known case of the kind) had some restrictive effects.

From the Sui Age onwards, Chinese educational institutions were given a consistent form and structure; and the Office of Mathematics *(suan-kuan)* was founded. An official position and rank was assigned to every technical function. The result was a reduction in mobility. According to an official regulation of the T'ang period, astronomical officials were not eligible for promotion to any position superior to that of Grand Astrologer. Naturally anyone who wished to rise higher was attracted to a career in conventional public administration.

This is not to say that the people were discouraged from learning mathematics and technical subjects. In the T'ang period, students of mathematics, like those who devoted themselves to law or calligraphy exclusively, were pre-

p 137
(12)

p 136 (9)
p 137
(11)
p 140
(18)

p 134–5
(4)

paring for careers, though as technicians rather than as administrators. But their number was small compared with the number of students of the Confucian curriculum, and the technicians seem to have been mostly children of minor officials and of commoners. The status even of a professor of mathematics was not high. Among the prominent figures who appear in Juan Yuan's *Ch'ou-jen chuan* (*Biographies of Mathematicians and Astronomers*), none are identified, for certain, as being either graduates of the Office of Mathematics or holders of the Master of Mathematics degree. Instead, many of them had a good background in the classics—some might be considered Confucian philosophers—and some were members of the elite who had passed the highest state examination in Confucian studies. On the other hand, it is likely that the majority of graduates of the Office of Mathematics ended their careers as petty officials. Thus, the Office of Mathematics did not necessarily promote the progress of Chinese mathematics, in spite of its having an educational function. It merely systematized the recruitment of minor officials.

Technical specialists in astrology, calendar-making, mathematics, medicine, and engineering were confined to careers in which they were subordinate to non-specialist administrators; but the centralized civil bureaucratic machinery did guarantee relatively uninterrupted (if unspectacular) support from dynasty to dynasty for a number of professional scientists and their assistants, and it thus promoted the continuity of the Chinese scientific tradition. Even at times of a cultural ebb, the institutions existed, at least in a routine form, and they maintained a minimum of tradition as part of the official duty of civil servants.

The relative status of various scientific institutions within the government is indicated by T'ang governmental regulations which give prominence to astronomical posts. Both astrology and calendar-making were important imperial functions, whereas the Government showed little respect for mathematics. Proficiency in technology and in chemistry was, to some extent, a disqualification for the attainment of public office; the compiler of a technological collection, *T'ien-kung k'ai-wu* (*The Exploitation of the Works of Nature,* 1637), declares cynically, in his preface, that 'the matters dealt with here have nothing to do with a successful career'.

A closer look at the way in which the examination system was operated reveals another characteristic of Chinese learning. The public examination was mainly a written one. It put a premium on memory and on the mastery of the classical literature, and this was regarded as a sacrosanct canon that was beyond criticism. It is remarkable to find written examinations appearing so early in China; this may be explained in part by the early abundance of paper. In the West, the written examination is unknown before 1702. The adoption of this system for civil examinations in Europe belongs to the 19th century, and it may have been inspired by the Chinese precedent.

The purpose of examinations was not to produce prospective research scholars; it was to select a small privileged body of officials. The examination was not, therefore, to any significant degree an occasion for the expression of original views; it was a bureaucratic procedure for identifying men of unimpeachable classical training and good memory. Since 'living for examinations' discouraged irrelevant reading, new growths tended to wither on the bough. Many aspects of the Chinese examination system tended to reinforce the Confucian bias against technical specialization. Although a successful candidate might have to assume administrative responsibility for flood control, weapons manufacture, and so on, 'unclassical' technical subjects were pointedly left out of the examination through which he won his entry into the bureaucratic establishment.

p 138
(13)

At this point it is pertinent to remind ourselves that the 'debating' form of intellectual activity had been maintained in the Western tradition. In the medieval West this was the primary notion of intellectual activity, partly because paper was late in making its appearance. The prevalence of disputation in medieval intellectual life led to a continued development of logical analysis, and also stimulated thought to enter anti-traditional channels. Some historians of Far Eastern science—for instance, Mikami Yoshio—are convinced that the failure to achieve logical consistency and capacity for generalization was what stunted the growth of Far Eastern mathematics and science.

The Chinese candidates for examination were certainly much more bookish than medieval university students in the West, where classical standards of literary form almost disappeared when everything depended exclusively on argument. The basic Chinese corpus of classical literature ran to an estimated 570,000 words, and all this had to be memorized for the examinations. The Chinese administrative class, whose members had spent a considerable time in preparing for the state examinations, cultivated highly sophisticated literary tastes and had free access to the stylistic resources of this long and continuous tradition. Literary sophistication remains tied to a single linguistic culture and appeals to individual taste, but logic is universal, and it can be mastered as easily by the barbarian as by the gentleman. This characteristic of universality was a prerequisite for the rise of modern science.

The historical context explains another characteristic difference between the Western and Chinese traditions. In China, from the Sui period onwards, printed books were widely diffused among the general public. As a result, amazingly compendious encyclopaedias and historical epitomes were published, for the purpose of saving the time and energy of prospective examinees. This enabled a provincial candidate to teach himself at home and to prepare for the examination solely by reading. In the West, on the other hand, oral communication and the copying of manuscripts were the only means of transmitting knowledge, for there were no printed books, and manuscripts were rare and precious. Medieval scholars travelled from town to town in search of learning. This provided intellectual stimulus; it facilitated the exchange of knowledge; and it served as an antidote to provincialism.

It is one of the ironies of history that the early accessibility of paper and printed books in China tended to stifle intellectual innovation. However, the same material media of intellectual communication, when they became accessible in modern Europe, were turned to account for the publication of scientific journals, which have been the chief vehicle for the advancement of science.

147

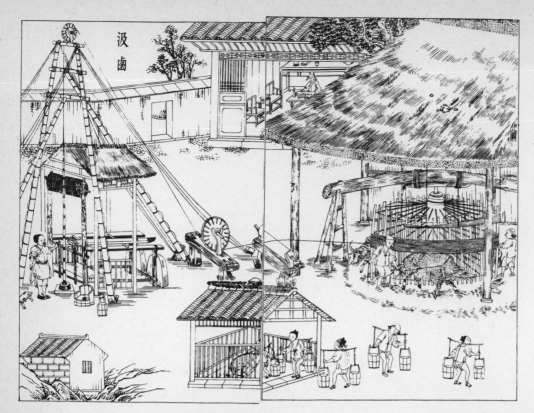

Raising brine from a salt well. In Yunnan and Szechwan, isolated from sources of sea salt, salt was obtained by drilling wells. The brine was brought up to the surface in a hollow bamboo stalk. At the bottom a valve was inserted permitting the brine to enter but not to leave. The bamboo is lowered into the well on a long rope and when filled with brine is raised by means of a pulley and a windlass turned by an ox-powered wheel. (10)

Alien currents and foreign influences

The Chinese civil service examination, and the official educational curriculum that went with it, met China's social and political requirements so well that they proved to be extremely stable. They could survive without needing to be supplemented by new foreign elements. This made it possible for them to elude confrontations with institutional and ideological novelties that would have forced them into making breaks of continuity. All the same, throughout history, Confucian orthodoxy was challenged by the rival creeds of Taoism and Buddhism, and these did have a disturbing effect on the established Confucian pattern of learning from time to time.

Wonder-workers and magicians must have found Taoist heterodoxy much more congenial to their taste than the established Confucian system. Genuine and well-founded science—for instance, calendrical science—was consistent with the established institutions and with the Confucian mode of thought. The mystical and even chimerical 'pseudo-sciences', such as the quest for immortality, that were also current in China have an aura of Taoism. In fact, alchemy can fairly be called a Taoist science. Revolutionary ideas might have been expected to emerge out of mystical thought rather than out of unimaginative routine. Taoism, however, seems to have suffered from having failed to become 'established'. The treasures amassed by Taoism's scientific endeavours have been buried in oblivion, and many of them are still dormant, awaiting disinterment by modern scholarship.

Pre-modern China was influenced to a major degree by two foreign cultures: the Buddhist and the Islamic.

Chinese Buddhist pilgrims who had studied in India brought home with them elements of Indian culture and science. However, we cannot detect very much positive influence of Buddhism on Chinese science, in spite of the fact that Buddhism was the most important and influential of the foreign cultures that ever impinged on China in the pre-modern age.

Buddhism laid stress on the importance of contemplation, and it dismissed the phenomenal world as an illusion. Physical theory and scientific systems were outside its scope. The Buddhists were concerned with science only as one of the marginal features of the Indian cultural tradition. They transmitted it merely as an incidental part of Buddhist theology.

I-Hsing is the only Buddhist monk who figures in the list of notable Chinese astronomers. The 'Nine Upholders' calendar, which was translated into Chinese in the T'ang Age, bears manifest marks of the influences of Hellenistic astronomy on the Indian calendar, but this Indo-Hellenistic influence did not make its way into the main current of the development of Chinese calendrical science.

Foreign influence is more potent in peripheral fields such as horoscopy and the introduction of the week cycle. But these importations were not purely Indian; they were a miscellany, culled from the whole area to the west of China. More Indian influence is discernible in the medical field. Many Indian medical treatises were translated into Chinese during the T'ang period.

Islamic culture must have exerted some influence on Chinese science and technology during the Sung period, but no systematic importation of Islamic culture was ever attempted. In the time of the Yuan (Mongol) dynasty, one effect of the Mongols' achievement of establishing a huge empire, uniting East and West, was an interchange and blending of techniques. The gunpowder and papermaking techniques of the Chinese are thought to have been transmitted to the West at this time, while Islamic military and irrigation engineers were invited to China. Islamic astronomers were employed at the Chinese court, and they competed with the indigenous Chinese school in the precision with which they predicted eclipses. However, these competing schools never merged, and the basic style of Chinese astronomy remained virtually independent of any appreciable foreign influence. This independence is exemplified in the work of Kuo Shou-ching.

Below: Plan of an irrigation survey from the Sung dynasty. The canal and fields are shown in a highly formalized way, but measurement on the ground was precise and accurate. The length of the canal is given as 59 kms. (11)

Right: Mathematical Treatise of the Jesuit, Jean Terenz. (12)

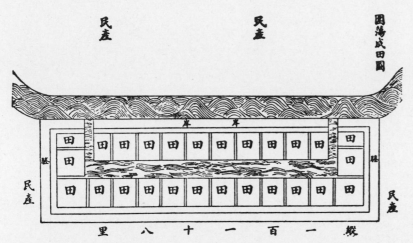

It is evident that the piecemeal infusion of knowledge, described above, could never have led to a conceptual revolution in Chinese science. Only a few material details, such as some out-of-the-way drugs and herbs, were easily transmitted. The basic paradigm of Chinese traditional science remained unaffected.

The arrival of the Jesuits

The Jesuits were in China from the 17th to the mid-18th century, and this was the period in which indigenous Chinese science was substantially affected by a foreign culture for the first time. The Jesuits in China generally took a flexible, and even conciliatory, attitude towards the established social order. Their strategy was to gain converts indirectly by impressing the Chinese social elite with their superior knowledge of astronomy. They hoped then to be able to enlist the elite for helping them to bring about wholesale conversions.

The Jesuits' efforts were rewarded by the making of some influential converts among the Chinese high officials. The Jesuits themselves obtained some key posts in the Imperial Bureau of Astronomy, and the official calendar, which hitherto had been based on traditional Chinese technique, was recast on the basis of Western astronomy from 1645 onwards.

In the pioneer generation of the Jesuits in China, Matteo Ricci had begun to introduce the Ptolemaic system of astronomy. The second generation introduced the essence of Tychonic astronomy and of pre-Cartesian mathematics. Copernicus was misrepresented. The Jesuits introduced him to the Chinese as the discoverer of an eleventh sphere and as a skilful observer. The Jesuits in China did not disclose the heliocentric theory before the middle of the 18th century.

What the Jesuits imparted and the Chinese adopted was all Tychonian. It included the geometrical method of estimating the values of parameters. But there was no change in the Chinese method of presenting and arranging calendrical treaties or in the real purpose of Chinese astronomy, which was the composition of a luni-solar calendar and precision in the prediction of eclipses. Hsu Kuang-ch'i, an eminent Chinese collaborator with Ricci, had said: 'Let us melt their [Western] materials and cast them into the mould of the traditional calendar.' Hsu Kuang-ch'i's successors acted in accordance with his precept.

Besides astronomy, many other elements of Western science and technology were welcomed in some quarters in China, especially during the reign of the Emperor K'ang-hsi (1662–1722), who was personally friendly to Jesuit activities. Euclidean geometry was taught at the Imperial court; a European anatomical chart was translated into Manchu and also into Chinese, but this remained unpublished. A survey of the whole area of the Empire was carried out—an undertaking that cost the French missionaries ten years' work. The art of making clocks, spectacles, telescopes, and other instruments was transmitted to the court and spread from there to the people.

From the Sung period onwards, printed books had been disseminated and economic productivity had been increasing. Partly as a result of these two developments, popular science and mathematics had been diffused to a considerable extent among the general public. All the same, in the Ming Age, when the Jesuits arrived in China, they reported that academic standards had declined and that scholars were finding it difficult to live up to the classical ideals of scholarship.

This was the moment at which China received the impact of Western science from the Jesuits. This impact did not lead to a complete subversion of the traditional Chinese style of science, but it did have the effect of reviving China's own scientific heritage. From the middle of the 18th century onwards, the rise of a school of classical scholarship in the field of Confucian studies was matched by a reconstruction of the Chinese scientific tradition. After the cessation of Jesuit activities in China halfway through the 18th century, Mei Wen-ting and his followers developed the thesis that the essential parts of Western mathematics had originated in ancient China.

It was not till the 19th century that the Chinese recognized the significance of the 17th-century scientific revolution in the West. This Chinese time-lag was mainly the Jesuits' fault. The Jesuits had frowned on the heliocentric theory and on modern science in general, and their negative attitude had hindered their Chinese pupils from penetrating to the heart of the new Western mechanistic philosophy. The Jesuits gave the Chinese only what was good for them in the Jesuits' opinion, but in any case the Chinese would have been antipathetic to the lack of moral sensitivity in the new Western attitude to life, if the Jesuits had been more frank in revealing it.

China had anticipated the West in many technological innovations, such as the invention of paper, printing, and gunpowder. The Chinese had created for themselves a better-founded educational system and a more efficient civilian-controlled bureaucracy than anything that the West had produced in these fields. China had accumulated a huge stock of empirical learning in the course of her age-long history. In spite of these advantages, Chinese science proved to be inferior to Western science during the period running from the 17th to the 19th century. What is the explanation? This is to be found in the distinctive characteristics of modern science, which are mathematization and the experimental method of investigating Nature. Many of the great figures in the 17th-century Western scientific revolution—for instance, Galileo—took an interest in physical facts and in handicrafts. They were not craftsmen themselves, so their vision was not limited by the short-term views and aims of practical men. They were able to approach the phenomena objectively and disinterestedly. They were men of letters, so they were much more competent to describe things scientifically than craftsmen were. Furthermore, they were equipped with the capacity for logical analysis. Consequently, they succeeded in constructing modern quantitative experimental science. But they were neither craftsmen nor men of letters of the traditional kind. They were an entirely new type of human being—the modern scientist. In contemporary China, on the other hand, learning and science continued to be based on literary study, and craftsmen continued to be almost entirely insulated from contact with men of letters.

p 137 (10)

Modern science in China

The second wave of Western influence hit China in the 19th century simultaneously with the economic and military invasion of China by the Western powers, and with the missionary activities of Protestants, such as Alexander Wylie. The Protestant missionaries' educational policy towards China resembled the policy of their Jesuit precursors, but the Protestants addressed themselves to commoners rather than to high officials, and

they brought with them the most up-to-date version of modern Western science. For instance, John Herschel's *Outline of Astronomy* was translated by Wylie with Chinese assistance in 1859. At the same time, some less conservative Chinese officials started to introduce the essence of Western military technology, and of the science on which this was based, by establishing translation bureaux and schools of modern engineering and military science. Their objective was to make China militarily a match for the Western powers. They emphasized the importance of surveying and of mathematics—two fields in which the superiority of the West had already been demonstrated by the Jesuits. On the other hand, modern medicine was left entirely in the hands of foreign missionaries.

p 139 (16)

So long as the time-honoured civil service examination system was still a going concern, such minor institutional novelties as the establishment of technological schools could not revolutionize the conventional Chinese pattern for a successful career or appeal to the hearts of a promising young generation. The examination system was maintained until 1905, but its abolition in that year stimulated the rising generation in China to look for a new source of intellectual nutriment in Western science. Many of them now made haste to study abroad. The government encouraged science students in particular, and sent them abroad at government expense.

The present Chinese word for science, *k'o-hsüeh*, has been borrowed from a new Japanese terminology that had been invented in the 1870s. The term literally means 'the learning of [one hundred] departments'. The 19th-century Japanese had perceived that the outstanding characteristics of modern Western intellectual activity was compartmentalization and specialization.

For the Chinese, science now came to play a still more radical role. It became a fashionable substitute for the old tradition of learning, which had been the Confucian paradigm. Since the second decade of the 20th century, the word 'science' has been used, like the word 'democracy', as a war-cry for overthrowing traditional Confucian ethics and institutions.

The present generation of senior scientists has been trained, for the most part, in the United States and in Europe (and to some extent in Japan). Under the regime of the Chinese People's Republic, many students belonging to the generation born in the 1930s were sent to the Soviet Union during the period of Russo-Chinese collaboration (1949–59). The subsequent ideological schism has impelled China, since 1960, to revert to in-breeding. She has been training her scientists at home. Today, China appears to be trying a new experiment. Apparently her objective is to replace the methods and the goals of modern Western science and technology by something new and more humane. This seems to be part of the programme of the Great Cultural Revolution. Speculation about the final outcome of this latest of Chinese revolutions is tempting but would be premature.

VI WORLDS AND LANGUAGE

The Chinese literary tradition

JAMES J. Y. LIU

Literature is a thing that concerns a thousand ages.

Tu Fu, *Casual Lines (ou-t'i)*

Universality of theme combined with artistry in expression has been a constant pattern in Chinese literature throughout its history. Poetry especially, written mostly by and for a cultured class, tended to embody the same established and accepted values, such as moral uprightness and enjoyment of Nature. Every scholar-official was expected to be able to produce verse, which was often linked to a particular occasion. It was compact, often associated with music, and highly polished.

From the 13th century onwards, the range of creative literature was extended two ways – through the drama and through the novel. Both incorporated verse, but each developed capabilities of its own. The subject-matter ranges from domestic life (love intrigues and *crimes passionnelles*) to historical, legendary, and mythological tales. In every case, poetic justice has to be observed, and

if the hero and heroine fail to find happiness in this world, they are sure to be vindicated in the next.

The illustration reproduced here shows a play being performed on a typical outdoor stage, which could be dismantled and put up again somewhere else. It is a Ch'ing copy of an original painting dating probably from the 12th or 13th century. The carpet marks the actual acting area; the actors outside it are off-stage. The two near the table are musicians. At the back is a dressing room. More elaborate theatres, with galleries, were built inside palaces and temples. The technique of performance was – and still is – symbolic, not naturalistic. Colours painted on the face denoted character – red for loyalty, white for evil, etc. – and sequences like climbing mountains and jumping into the sea were conveyed as stylized actions with minimal scenery. (1)

The beginnings of theatre can be traced back, *inter alia*, to acrobats and dancers who came from Central Asia in the 2nd century BC. A set of pottery figurines from the Han dynasty, recently discovered in Shantung province, shows such acrobats performing before a company of nobles. At the back is their orchestra of strings, wind and percussion. About 120 BC the Emperor Wu established the Music Department to compose music and words for ceremonies and entertainments, and to collect folk-songs from country areas. In time, songs and dances began to be linked together to tell a story – rather as Greek drama grew out of Dionysiac dances – leading eventually to fully formed drama, though still with a strong lyrical element. (2)

Romantic love is the basis of many popular plays produced in the Yüan (Mongol) period, 13th-14th centuries, when Chinese drama suddenly blossomed into a sophisticated literary art. In *The Romance of the Western Chamber* by Wang Shih-fu, the beautiful Ying-ying is loved by the student Chang. Her mother plans a grander match for her, but through the resourcefulness of her maid Hung-niang, the lovers are united. This 17th century painting shows the three together, in an interior richly furnished in the taste of that time. (3)

The Songs of Ch'u are attributed to the first great Chinese poet known by name, Ch'ü Yüan, who lived from about 340 to about 278 BC. Tradition makes him a loyal minister who was unjustly slandered and committed suicide. The *Nine Songs* attributed to him celebrate local deities and probably originated as shamanistic hymns. An exquisite manuscript with illustrations (right) was made in the 14th century. (4)

After dinner poetry was one of life's pleasures for the scholar-officials of China. Like their surroundings, their poetry was a well-adjusted combination of nature and art, often prompted by the social occasion, by wine, flowers or beautiful women. This painting is by the Sung Emperor Hui-tsung (1100–25). (5)

Poetry and nature became one, not only in spirit, but also visually. In China, where writing is itself a graphic art, poem and painting unite as a single image, like an engraved page by Blake. Above: listening to the Juan-hsien (Southern Sung, 13th century). Right: Ming landscape in the spirit of verses by Tu Fu (712–770), considered the greatest of Chinese poets. Far right: the Red Cliff, on the Yangtze, the scene of a famous battle in the 3rd century, and the subject of two famous Expositions and one equally famous lyric by Su Shih (1037–1101). Below: poetry contest at the Orchid Pavilion, held in AD 353; the painting is more than 1,000 years later. Wine cups drift down the stream on leaves. (6–9)

From the tales told in villages and towns grew the last great genre of Chinese literature – the novel. This detail (below) from the 12th-century scroll *Life along the river on the eve of the Ch'ing-ming Festival* (an inexhaustible source of information on daily life in Sung times) shows a bearded story-teller surrounded by enthralled listeners. The stories, often based on episodes in Chinese history, were arranged in long cycles. Popular among the people and often lacking in sophistication, they were disdained by scholars, and only began to be counted as literature at all in fairly recent times. (10)

'Water Margin' (right) is a prose romance which originated from oral stories told in the 13th century and evolved into a whole during the following four centuries. It tells of the adventures of a band of chivalrous outlaws who lived in the marshes in Shantung. Under their leader Sung Chiang, they defend the poor and the persecuted, often in conflict with the government but essentially loyal to the emperor. They are eventually pardoned and take part on the government's side in a war against other rebels. These illustrations show four scenes: Wu Sung avenges the death of his elder brother – Wu holds the head of his adulterous sister-in-law while her lover, Hsi-men Ch'ing, having fallen from the upstairs wineshop, lies dying on the ground. (11)

The bandits – continuing the story of the 'Water Margin' – led by Li K'uei (with axe) rescue Sung Chiang just as he and another hero are about to be executed; Magistrate Tsai flees on his horse. Then (centre) Li K'uei descends a well in a basket in order to save Ch'ai Chin. Finally, the heroes of Liangshan (top left), having been pardoned by the emperor, take part in a feast. (12–14)

'Journey to the West' (right), better known here as *Monkey*, is based on the monk Tripitaka's journey to India (described in Chapter IV) to collect Buddhist scriptures. Wu Ch'eng-en, in the 16th century, collated and added to earlier stories, some handed down orally, to make the version that we know. The result is a unique mixture of allegory, satire, and fantasy. Tripitaka is accompanied by three disciples – Monkey, Pigsy and Sandy. They encounter ghosts, demons and evil spirits, but triumph in the end through the help of Buddhist and Taoist gods. Here we see: Tripitaka and two companions captured by ogres – the other two are served up for lunch, while Tripitaka lies bound on the ground. In the next, Tripitaka and Monkey are confronted by six robbers whose names are the six senses. Next, Hui-an, a disciple of Bodhisattva Kuan-yin, accepts Sandy (in the water) into the faith. In the last drawing, Monkey revives the king of Cock-crow with the elixir he has procured from Heaven. (15–18)

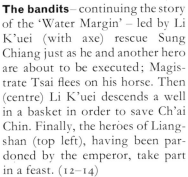

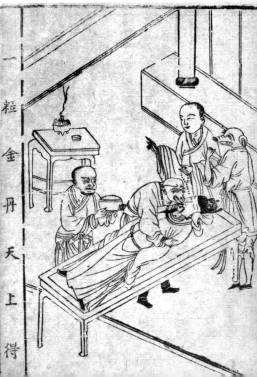

'The Romance of the Three Kingdoms' (above), which deals with the confused events of that period, was compiled by Lo Kuan-chung in the 14th century. It is an epic story with an endless succession of battles, sieges, stratagems and feats of heroism. Here a Wei general with his two sons rides into a valley where land-mines explode under them, but a supernatural rain-storm extinguishes the flames and allows them to escape. (19)

'The Dream of the Red Chamber' by Ts'ao Chan, styled Hsüeh-chin (c. 1716–63), is the greatest Chinese novel, following the fortunes of an upper-class family through a complete generation, especially the love affairs of its younger members. Largely autobiographical, it combines poetic sensibility and philosophical vision with psychological insight and realism. In this scene girls of the Chia family make riddles for the Lantern Festival. (20)

JAMES J. Y. LIU

The earliest Chinese poetry consisted of hymns and ceremonial songs sung at festivals and sacrifices. This design from a Chou dynasty bronze vessel shows such a scene. In the lower register women beat chimes suspended from the ceiling. (1)

CHINESE LITERATURE has had a history of over three thousand years, so that it is obviously impossible to deal with it adequately in a handful of pages. Even when we confine our attention to poetry, drama, and the novel as the main forms of creative literature, while excluding from consideration such other types of literature as historiography, philosophical writings, and informal essays, we still cannot hope, in the space of a single chapter, to follow the whole history of Chinese creative literature. What the present chapter will attempt to do, therefore, is to discuss some of its highlights.

The long history of Chinese creative literature may be described as a continuous and ever-renewed process of double exploration: an exploration of 'worlds' on the one hand, and of language on the other. By a 'world' in literature I mean a fusion of external reality and inner experience, and by 'exploration of worlds' is meant the writer's probing into the world he lives in (both natural and human) and into his own mind. 'Exploration of language' refers to the writer's constant efforts to embody the worlds he explores in new verbal structures and to exploit the inherent qualities of the language in which he writes, so that its potentialities as a medium of artistic expression may be fully realized.

If we accept this conception of literary history, it becomes apparent that attempts to divide the history of Chinese literature into periods based on dynastic successions or social changes are unsatisfactory and that the only thing to do, if we are to keep some sense of historical perspective, is to adopt a generic approach, taking the major genres of Chinese literature in the order in which they emerged and delineating the development of each. This approach does not lend itself to a rigidly chronological treatment and will involve some overlapping. Moreover, although most genres have survived to the present day, we cannot here trace the complete history of each, and must content ourselves with concentrating on the most important phases. Finally, since poetry in China has had a much longer history than drama and the novel, proportionately more space will be devoted to poetry. Translations of Chinese works are noted throughout the text, and full references will be found in the Bibliography.

The 'Book of Poetry', c. 1100–600 BC
Strictly speaking, The *Book of Poetry*, or *Shih-ching* (originally called simply *Shih*), is not a genre but an anthology,

the earliest one of Chinese poetry (trans. Waley, *Book of Songs*). However, since the poems that make it up do share certain characteristics, they may be said to constitute a genre. These poems, which number 305, fall into three groups.

The first group consists of hymns originally sung to the accompaniment of music and dance at sacrifices to gods and royal ancestral spirits. They include the earliest pieces in the anthology (*c.* 1100–950 BC) as well as some later works of a similar nature (*c.* 700–600 BC). These hymns express a sense of awe, but hardly reveal a supernatural world imagined in such vivid and concrete detail as we find, for instance, in the Homeric epics. Their language is archaic but straightforward, little adorned with imagery, and not very different from prose.

The second group (*c.* 800–750 BC) includes ceremonial odes and festive songs used at feudal courts. The external world reflected in them is an aristocratic one, in which banquets, hunting, and military campaigns play important parts. Some of them narrate dynastic legends and may be considered a kind of proto-epic, though they have never been developed into full epics. The language of these poems is somewhat livelier than that of the hymns, but still straightforward and unsophisticated.

The third group (*c.* 750–600 BC) comprises ballads and songs of popular origin from various feudal states, probably revised by court poets. They present considerable variety, ranging from social protests to unabashed love songs, and from epithalamiums to dirges. Most of them are concerned with the life of the common people: their joys and sorrows, their daily occupations in peace and war, their simple faith in life, and their instinctive sense of the dignity of man. This group is more advanced than the other two in artistry, displaying a fresher and more emotive diction, richer imagery, and more dexterous versification. The mode of expression is often oblique, making use of explicit or implicit comparison, and juxtaposition of logically unconnected but emotionally associated objects and ideas.

The musicians go in and play,
That after-blessings may be secured.
Your viands are passed round;
No one is discontented, all are happy;
They are drunk, they are sated.
Small and great all bow their heads:
'The Spirits,' they say, 'enjoyed their drink and food
And will give our lord a long life.
He will be very favoured and blessed,
And because nothing was left undone,
By son's sons and grandson's grandsons
Shall his line for ever be continued.'

The southern hills, they rise so sharp,
The storm wind blows so fierce.
Other people all prosper;
I alone can find no rest.

Book of Poetry

In spite of occasional complaints against social injustices and the hardships of life, the general tone of the *Book of Poetry* is one of quiet acceptance rather than bitter denunciation or bleak despair. With a few exceptions, the anonymous authors of these poems accept the existence of a supreme power known as Heaven or the Emperor Above, and of ancestral spirits. However, their eyes are focused not on Heaven but on this world. To them, Nature is not a manifestation of the transcendental but rather a backdrop against which is played the human drama of life and death, love and suffering. Yet there is a strong feeling of consonance with Nature, the rhythm of human life being perceived to correspond intimately with that of the natural world. Thus, the juxtaposition of human situations with natural phenomena, which has long been recognized as a major poetic device in the *Book of Poetry*, is also an indication of the early Chinese poets' sense of affinity with Nature.

Prosodically, the poems in the anthology are written mostly in four-syllabic lines, with occasional use of longer or shorter lines. Most of them are in two or more short stanzas. Except for a few of the earliest pieces, end-rhyme occurs regularly sometimes in fairly complicated schemes. Alliteration, internal rhyme, reduplication, and onomatopoeia also occur quite frequently. Structural features include parallelism and repetition.

Because of its association with Confucius, who was credited with its editorship and who praised its moral rectitude and emotional restraint, the *Book of Poetry* became the first work in the Confucian canon and was subjected to far-fetched allegorical interpretations and endless exegeses. It has exerted a profound influence on all subsequent Chinese poetry. However, its staple metre, the four-syllabic verse, ceased to be a vital poetic medium after the 5th century AD.

The 'Songs of Ch'u', c. 350 BC–AD 140

p 155 (4)

The term *Ch'u-tz'u*, or 'songs of Ch'u', refers, in a broad sense, to songs from the state of Ch'u, which flourished, in what was then considered the semi-barbarian south along the Yangtze and Huai rivers, from the 8th to the 4th century BC. In a narrower sense, it denotes an anthology, compiled in the 1st century BC and edited by a scholar in the 2nd century AD, of the poems attributed to the first great Chinese poet known by name, Ch'ü Yüan (*c.* 340–*c.* 278 BC), although it also contains some later imitations (trans. Hawkes, *Ch'u Tz'u*). It is in the latter sense that the term is used here.

Traditionally, Ch'ü Yüan is believed to have been a loyal minister of Ch'u, who suffered unjust banishment and finally committed suicide. His major work, *Li Sao* (often translated as 'Falling into Trouble', although 'Complaints' is a more likely meaning), is a long narrative poem in which the speaker repeatedly asserts his own virtues, deplores the conditions prevailing in his country, and protests his undying loyalty to his king (sometimes by assuming the *persona* of a discarded mistress). He then goes on a spiritual journey in search of a perfect mate, but his efforts to court various legendary princesses and goddesses fail, and the poem ends on a note of despair. Confucian scholars interpreted the whole poem as political allegory, and modern Chinese critics tend to praise Ch'ü Yüan for his patriotism, nobility of character, and concern for the people. To a more critical reader, the poem appears to involve several levels of meaning. Some sections are no doubt concerned with political morality, but others seem to be fantasies partly based on a shamanistic cult and partly born of subconscious desires. At the same time, the poem may be called a study in alienation: the poet feels cut off from his fellow men and rejected by the gods. Indeed, his sense of isolation in a hostile, corrupt, and uncomprehending world, his self-righteousness and self-pity, his yearning for love and his escape into the occult, are all strangely prophetic of certain attitudes current among the hippie generation. The poem displays great imaginative power and exuberance of language.

Other works attributed to Ch'ü Yüan include shamanistic songs which describe the shamans' longings for various deities in terms of erotic passion, incantations intended to lure disembodied souls back to the human world, self-laments, and one poem consisting of enigmatic questions about ancient mythology and legends.

The worlds of the *Songs of Ch'u* differ markedly from those of the *Book of Poetry*. The supernatural is much more prominent, and more vividly imagined and described, while the natural world is perceived in a more sensuous and animistic fashion. In contrast to the emotional restraint of the earlier anthology, the *Songs of Ch'u* are passionate, rising to ecstasy or sinking to despair; and instead of accepting life as it is, they often protest against Heaven and fate.

Many a heavy sigh I heaved in my despair,
Grieving that I was born in such an unlucky time.
I plucked soft lotus petals to wipe my welling tears
That fell down in rivers and wet my coat front.
I knelt on my outspread skirts and poured my plaints out,
And the righteousness within me was clearly manifest.
I yoked my team of jade dragons to a phoenix-figured car
And waited for the wind to come, to soar up on my journey.

Ch'u Tz'u

Likewise, the language of the *Songs of Ch'u*, in contrast to the simplicity and conciseness of the *Book of Poetry*, is expansive, highly charged, and richly evocative, making abundant use of imagery, symbolism, and mythology.

Even metrically, the *Songs of Ch'u* present striking contrasts to the *Book of Poetry*. Instead of four-syllabic lines grouped in short stanzas, we find much longer poems undivided into stanzas but made up of couplets, which afford greater opportunities for extended description or narrative and unbridled expression of emotion than do short stanzaic forms.

The Exposition, c. 250 BC–AD 1100

The word *fu* means, *inter alia*, 'display', and was used to designate one of the main modes of expression in the *Book of Poetry*, that of direct description. As a generic term—usually translated as rhymeprose, although it may be more literally translated as Exposition—it was first applied to some short moral exhortations in rhymed prose by the philosopher Hsün-tzu (*fl.* 255 BC). From this simple beginning, enriched by the vocabulary and style of the *Songs of Ch'u*, the Exposition developed into a highly artificial, formal, and elaborate kind of composition in a mixture of verse and prose. The best-known exponent of this genre, Ssu-ma Hsiang-ju (179–117 BC), wrote lengthy pieces on such subjects as royal hunting parks, in an erudite style which practically exhausted available epithets and synonyms. His descriptions of Nature often consist of a systematic and symmetrical cataloguing of rivers, mountains, flora, fauna, and so on, so that they make the impression of being somewhat monotonous and mechanical. Yet they have a deeper significance, for they reveal an underlying conception of an orderly cosmos.

For over two centuries after Ssu-ma, writers of Expositions continued to imitate his manner. Then poets like Ts'ao Chih (192–232), Lu Chi (261–363), and T'ao Ch'ien (372–427) extended the thematic scope of the Exposition, while rendering it more personal in nature and less formal in style. Lu Chi's *On Literature (Wen Fu)*, in particular, deserves mention as a remarkable *ars poetica* showing great insight into the creative process (trans. by S. H. Chen).

> *Writing is in itself a joy,*
> *Yet saints and sages have long since held it in awe.*
> *For it is Being, created by tasking the Great Void,*
> *And 'tis sound rung out of Profound Silence.*
> *In a sheet of paper is contained the Infinite,*
> *And, evolved from an inch-sized heart, an endless panorama.*
> Lu Chi

Still later, the Exposition became ever more ornate and more strictly parallel in style, in the hands of such writers as Yü Hsin (513–81), until it became a stereotyped kind of writing, practised only for the sake of passing imperial examinations. As a reaction against this, Ou-yang Hsiu (1007–72) and Su Shih (1037–1101) wrote Expositions that are really spontaneous, lyrical prose poems, thus giving the genre a new lease of life (trans. by A. C. Graham, in Birch, pp. 368–9, 381–4).

'Music Department' songs, c. 200 BC–AD 850

54 (2) The Music Department (*yüeh-fu*) was established by Emperor Wu of Han about 120 BC with two main purposes: first, to compose music and words for sacrificial hymns and songs for court entertainment; and, second, to collect folk songs from various parts of the country as well as to write words for imported tunes. The name of this office, *yüeh-fu*, then came to be used for the songs themselves. Previously, there had already been officials in charge of court music, and some surviving texts of hymns date back to about 200 BC. These may be said to belong to the formative phase of the genre. They are archaic in style and moralistic in sentiment. After the Music Department had been abolished by another emperor in 7 BC, court songs, naturally, continued to be written. The texts of some of these, together with those of folk songs, have been preserved, though not the music. Broadly speaking, the *yüeh-fu* reached its full maturity during the period from about 120 BC to about AD 200.

> *I am a prisoner in the hands of the enemy*
> *Enduring the shame of captivity.*
> *My bones stick out and my strength is gone*
> *Through not getting enough to eat.*
> *My brother is a Mandarin*
> *And his horses are fed on millet.*
> *Why can't he spare a little money*
> *To send and ransom me?*
>
> *Music Department*

Of the Music Department songs of this period, the hymns and songs for court entertainment are mostly imitative of earlier models and of little literary interest. The folk songs include ballads, love songs, laments, and didactic songs. Some of them bemoan the fate of soldiers, exiles, and orphans; others sing of faithful wives or lovers; still others express world-weariness and a wish for immortality (trans. Waley, *Chinese Poems*, pp. 49–56, and Frodsham, *Anthology*, pp. 1–8). Their attitude to life is down-to-earth and free from romantic illusions, yet they are by no means uniformly gloomy in tone, and can be humorous or whimsical. Their language is simple, direct, and often formulaic, with a charming naïveté of their own. Prosodically, they are in lines of unequal length, making frequent use of devices found in ballads the world over, such as repetition, exclamation, onomatopoeia, and meaningless syllables (comparable to 'tra la la' or 'hey nonny no').

Court songs and folk songs of later periods (*c.* 200–600) are also known as *yüeh-fu*. (Indeed, the term *yüeh-fu* has been loosely applied to much later poetic genres associated with music, such as the lyric (*tz'u*) and the type of song known as *ch'ü*. Even Shakespeare's plays were known as *Sha-shih yüeh-fu* or 'Mr Sha's *yüeh-fu* songs'.) Some religious songs and love songs of the 4th and 5th centuries are particularly delicate and fresh. At the same time, literary men of all periods wrote poems in the form of Music Department songs, even long after the music had been lost. Although these poems bear the titles of the old tunes, they are in fact independent poems largely dissociated from music. The same is true of the 'New *yüeh-fu*' that a group of poets led by Po Chü-i (772–846) wrote to denounce contemporary social and political evils. These are imitation ballads with an avowed didactic purpose, and though effective as social criticism in verse, they are as far removed from genuine Music Department ballads as Wordsworth's *Lyrical Ballads* are from genuine Border ballads.

163

Court entertainments during the Han dynasty consisted of music, dance, song and acrobatics. This tomb tile from Szechwan shows nobles in long robes, seated on mats, watching acrobats performing. It was from songs sung at such festivals, among others, that the Music Department poems were collected. (2)

Ancient Verse, c. AD 50–1200

Side by side with the Music Department songs flourished poems not written for music. These poems were written in various metres, the most important being the five-syllabic and the seven-syllabic. There were no set limits to the length of each poem, and no prescribed rhyme schemes. Later, after the rise of Modern Style Verse, the older and freer type of verse became known as Ancient Verse *(ku-shih)* or Ancient Style Verse *(ku-t'i-shih)*.

The five-syllabic verse probably first appeared about the middle of the 1st century AD. By about 200, it had become a well-established verse form, and during the next two and a half centuries it was used by some of the best poets that China has produced as their chief vehicle of expression. Only a few of them can be mentioned here. Ts'ao Chih, also known for his Expositions and songs in the Music Department style, has left some intensely personal poems in five-syllabic verse, often expressing frustration and sadness and written in a relatively plain style. Even more introspective and more deeply melancholic is the poetry of Juan Chi (210–63), who dwells not only on personal frustration but on the impermanency of all sublunary things. Although he sometimes indulges in the Taoist wish for immortality, he does not seem to believe in its attainability and is left inconsolable in his existential anguish. His poetry is full of striking imagery, at times obscured by allusions and symbolism, but generally powerful (trans. Frodsham).

> *I walked out through the Upper Eastern Gate,*
> *And gazed out northwards towards Shou-yang's peak.*
> *Down at its foot a recluse was gathering bracken,*
> *Up on its summit stood a grove of lucky trees.*

> *Where can I go out on this propitious morning?*
> *The hoar-frost glistens on the robe I wear.*
> *An icy wind makes the very mountains shiver,*
> *Black clouds come swagging darkly overhead.*
> *The crying geese have all gone winging southward.*
> *The shrike is sounding out its doleful cry.*
> *Now autumn's note has whelmed the world in white,*
> *My suffering has made me sick at heart.*
>
> Juan Chi: *Anthology*

In the works of some poets of the 4th and 5th centuries, we see a new attitude towards Nature. Instead of viewing Nature as the background of human life, or with fascination and awe, as earlier poets had done, these poets looked upon it as an object of philosophic contemplation and a source of spiritual solace. This new attitude towards Nature found its highest expression in the poetry of T'ao Ch'ien (trans. Hightower). Although he wrote in four-syllabic verse as well, his best poems are in five-syllabic verse. These poems extol the simple rustic life or express random thoughts that occurred after drinking. At first sight, his poetry may give the impression of being serene in mood and simple in language, but closer reading suggests that neither the serenity nor the simplicity is the result of primitive innocence. The serenity is achieved only after the resolution of inner conflicts, between Confucian this-worldliness and Taoist other-worldliness, between the need for affection and friendship and the aspiration to transcend human emotions and lose one's self in Nature. Likewise, the apparent simplicity of his style is not of an artless kind, but comes from a complete mastery of the language, which endows common words with a wealth of meaning through subtle implications, oblique allusions, and unexpected juxtapositions. T'ao Ch'ien remains the Chinese poet-recluse *par excellence*, although he is capable of writing in a heroic vein.

For some two centuries after T'ao, the five-syllabic verse showed tendencies towards ornamentation and strict parallelism, which eventually led to the formation of Modern Style Verse in the 7th century. However, in the same century the more archaic and robust style enjoyed a revival. Moreover, the seven-syllabic variety of Ancient Verse, which had first appeared in the 1st century but had not been widely used, became firmly established about the same time. The subsequent developments of these two kinds of Ancient Verse are hardly separable. Briefly, Ancient Verse reached new heights during the 8th and 9th centuries, and underwent further changes during the 11th and 12th centuries. Since practically all the great poets of these centuries also excelled in Modern Style Verse, it will be more convenient to discuss them in the next section. Suffice it to say here that after Modern Style Verse became popular, Ancient Style Verse remained a vigorous poetic medium. Being unlimited in length and comparatively free in prosody, it was particularly suited to narrative and discursive poetry.

Modern Style Verse, c. 650–1200

The tendency towards strict parallelism, together with conscious efforts to exploit the tonal qualities of the Chinese language during the 5th century, led to the formulation of various prosodic rules. Poetry which observed such rules was called Modern Style Verse *(chin-t'i-shih)* in contradistinction to Ancient Style Verse, and has continued to be so called, even though it is now no more modern than New College, Oxford, is new.

After a formative phase of about two hundred years, during which the rules of Modern Style Verse were not strictly followed, the new verse form fully matured towards the end of the 7th century. In the hands of the great masters of the 8th century, it reached unsurpassed levels of excellence.

Wang Wei (701–61), famous as poet, painter, and musician, is now chiefly known for his Nature poetry (trans. Chang Yin-nan and Walmsley), which embodies a Buddhist view of life, although in his earlier years he also wrote on courtly and heroic themes. His best and most representative poetry attains to a world in which man becomes equal with all living things and even inanimate objects, and the self is totally submerged in Nature. This poetry is marked by limpid imagery and a deceptive simplicity of style, which often conceals great skill in the choice of words and in syntactic and prosodic manipulations. His five-syllabic quatrains, in particular, are unequalled for their stark beauty and infinitely suggestive power.

> Men at ease, cassia flowers fall;
> Night silent, spring mountain empty.
> Moon rises, surprising mountain birds.
> Now and again they cry in the spring valley.
>
> Wang Wei: *Bird Cry Valley*

Whereas Wang approaches Nature in quiet contemplation, Li Po (701–62) shows a varied response to it, sometimes admiring its grandeur or its delicate charms, sometimes seeking to escape to it from his sorrows, or again seeing in it reflections of human suffering. His response to human life is also constantly changing: he may celebrate the joys of life, particularly wine, women, and song, with wild abandon, or he may lament the brevity of life with deep grief. He may glorify brave warriors, or depict the miseries of war. In his best-known poems he displays

像 白 太 李

A Ming representation of the T'ang poet Li Po. (3)

an untrammelled and restless spirit, but in his more sober and serious poems he dwells on history, expresses his frustrated ambitions, and then tries to console himself with the thought that all human efforts are futile. His poetry explores the highest realms the mind can reach, but is unconcerned with the humdrum business of everyday life. Artistically, his professed intention was to revive the great tradition of the *Book of Poetry* and restore poetry to its ancient noble simplicity after five centuries of decline, yet his own free spirit and exuberant imagination created styles undreamed of by his poetic ancestors. His most typical poetry is permeated by a driving force which shows itself in an irresistible rhythmic onrush and a quick flow of powerful imagery, but he is also capable of delicacy and fragile beauty. The most sublime of Chinese poets, Li Po is also the least imitable (trans. in Waley's *Li Po*).

> We launched our boat and sported on the stream, to the
>   sound of flageolet and drum.
> The little waves were like dragon-scales and the sedge-leaves
>   were pale green.
> When it was our mood we took girls with us and gave
>   ourselves to the moments that passed,
> Forgetting how soon they would be over—gone like willow-
>   down, like snow.
> Rouged faces, flushed with drink, looked well in the sunset.
> Clear water, a hundred feet deep, mirrored the faces of the
>   singers—
> Singing-girls delicate and graceful in the light of the young
>   moon.
> And the girls sang again and again to make the gauze
>   dresses dance,
> The clear wind blew the songs away into the sky,
> Music winged the air, twisting round the clouds as they
>   passed.
> Never again shall the joy of those days come back to us.
>
> Li Po: *Exile's Letter*

In contrast to Li Po's sublimity, Tu Fu (712–70) is universal. No Chinese poet has explored more widely or deeply the world of Nature and that of man, or with more empathy. Whether he is writing of the mighty Yangtze or a tiny dragonfly, a court audience or a war-torn village, the parting of a newly-wed couple or the meeting of old friends, historical heroes or contemporary events, he writes with minute observation and total identification with his subject. Deeply committed to life and humanity, Tu Fu is sometimes indignant or disillusioned, but he never gives up in disgust or seeks to escape permanently from this world. In the end, he accepts life with tragic dignity; yet he has a sense of humour, which enables him to see himself ironically even in adversity.

p 156–7 (7)

Just as Tu Fu's poetry is matchless for the range, profundity, and richness of its worlds, so it is unequalled for the variety and malleability of its language, which can be archaic or colloquial, solemn or flippant, concise or expansive, extravagant or austere, straightforward or oblique, according to the poetic world explored. Formally, he excels in both Ancient and Modern Styles. But his most distinctive poems are generally in the latter, distinguished by incredibly compact and complex structures, dense and kinetic imagery, subtle and varied auditory effects, elliptical and fluid syntax, precise allusions, and multiple meanings. More than anyone else, Tu Fu remoulded the Chinese language as a poetic medium (trans. Hawkes, *Primer*, and in Hung).

After Tu Fu, two opposite tendencies in poetry developed. Some poets strove, in different ways, after the extraordinary, while others aimed at the plain and commonplace. Among the former, we may mention three: Han Yü (768–824), Li Ho (790–816), and Li Shang-yin (813–58). Han evolved a gaunt and rugged style characterized by obsolete vocabulary, prosaic syntax, unusual rhythms, and far-fetched images comparable to 'metaphysical conceits' (trans. Graham). Li Ho describes macabre and phantasmagoric worlds in a language of strangely haunting beauty, full of daring and original images (trans. Frodsham, *Li Ho*). Li Shang-yin explores the private worlds of love, sorrow, fantasy, and death, and the public worlds of social and political realities, with uncommon intensity of emotion, sensitivity of perception, and boldness of imagination. His style varies, but at his most typical he uses highly ambiguous language, tight in structure and rich in sensuous imagery and recondite allusions (trans. in Liu, *Li Shang-yin*). As for those who sought plainness, Po Chü-i is a representative. His poetry is generally 'low-keyed', recording passing impressions of and reflections on life, rather than sounding the depths of feeling or thought, in a lucid and direct style (trans. in Waley, *Po Chü-i*).

> *I turn my gaze down the village byways and lanes;*
> *Of ten houses, eight or nine are poor.*
> *The north wind blows sharp as a sword;*
> *Their cotton rags hardly cover their bones.*
> *They can only burn a fire of bramble and straw;*
> *Sadly they sit, waiting all night for the dawn.*
> *I see now what misery is brought*
> *By hard winters to those who till the land.*
>
> Po Chü-i

The next major development in Ancient and Modern Style poetry took place in the 11th century, when some poets led by Ou-yang Hsiu reacted against their immediate predecessors, who had imitated Li Shang-yin's ornate style (trans. in Yoshikawa, pp. 49–52, 60–72). As a result, a more austere and intellectual kind of poetry became the vogue. The greatest poet of the century is Su Shih, whose works exhibit a cheerful stoicism, an ebullient wit, and a free, vigorous, and supple style, ranging from the erudite to the colloquial. However, it was his contemporary Huang T'ing-chien (1045–1105) who became the acknowledged founder of the Kiangsi school, which remained dominant for two centuries. The poetry of this school has a deliberately 'dry' flavour instead of facile sweetness, and an awkward grace achieved by such devices as tonal dissonance, syntactic convolutions, and unexpected phraseology (trans. in Yoshikawa, pp. 122–30).

A major poet who freed himself from the influence of the Kiangsi school and shaped his own style was Lu Yu (1125–1209). A prolific writer, he treats all kinds of themes, but his most remarkable poems are those expressing passionate patriotism or describing simple rural scenes. His style is spontaneous and free from mannerisms (trans. in Yoshikawa, pp. 145–59).

166

The lyric, c. 700–1300

The lyric *(tz'u)* refers to a type of verse originally written to existing music, in a great variety of metres involving lines of often unequal but always fixed length, as well as prescribed tone patterns and rhyme schemes. As early as the 6th century, a few poets had already started writing words to given tunes, but it was only in the early 8th century that a significant number of lyrics came to be written by anonymous writers to fit popular tunes, and still later, in the late 8th century, that literary men took up the lyric; even then it was not considered as serious as the other genres described above. Nevertheless, by the mid-9th century, the lyric had definitely become a mature genre.

The first important lyricist is Wen T'ing-yün (812–70), who wrote mostly about beautiful women and romantic love. His mode of expression is usually oblique, suggesting certain emotions through an accumulation of highly colourful images, which have a sort of 'pointillistic' effect. Treating similar themes but employing a more direct manner and less opulent imagery are the lyrics of Wei Chuang (836–910). Another major lyricist is Feng Yen-ssu (903–60), whose lyrics evoke elusive moods of groundless ennui and gentle melancholy in a delicate and refined style.

The scope of the lyric was extended by Li Yü (937–78), last ruler of the Southern T'ang, who expressed his grief, remorse and despair after the loss of his kingdom in short and simple lyrics, with a powerful emotional appeal.

During the first half of the 11th century, most lyricists still regarded the lyric as a genre suitable for only a limited range of themes and emotions: they used it to express sentimental love or nameless sorrow, to describe beautiful women or pleasant scenery, to capture nostalgic moods or enchanted moments, but not to convey serious thoughts. Outstanding among them are Yen Shu (991–1055) and Ou-yang Hsiu, both of whom wrote elegant lyrics which reflect an urbane environment and embody refined sensibilities.

Significant developments were introduced by Liu Yung (*fl.* 1034), who brought to the lyric a new emotional realism, a much more frequent use of colloquial language than previously seen, and many prosodic innovations.

It remained for Su Shih to free the lyric from its supposed limitations and elevate it to a new level as a serious poetic medium. To him, the lyric was no longer a song form but a literary form, suitable for any theme, from the sublime to the ridiculous. He could write about pretty girls or homesickness as well as any, but more characteristically he expressed his philosophical views on life and history, thus introducing a strong element of intellectuality, which had hitherto been almost totally lacking in lyrics. Further, he spiced many of his lyrics with wit and humour, again qualities seldom seen in earlier lyrics. Stylistically, he used both elegant and colloquial diction, and added a third type, the erudite, involving Classical prose syntax and particles, and learned allusions.

Whereas Su freed the lyric from its dependency on music, Chou Pang-yen (1056–1121) reintegrated the two, and whereas the former extended the scope of the lyric intellectually, the latter reverted to the narrower conception of the genre as primarily a vehicle for the expression of intimate personal emotions, especially love.

However, Chou's lyrics attained new heights of subtlety and sophistication as well as formal perfection.

Su and Chou started two rival schools of lyrics. Su's followers, notably Hsin Ch'i-chi (1140–1207), carried further the tendencies to philosophize and to be erudite. At best, their lyrics are powerful and noble expressions of heroic and patriotic sentiments or of philosophic views; at worst, they are pedantic pastiche. Chou's followers, such as Chiang K'uei (1155?–1230?), explored ever more rarefied realms of aesthetic experience and paid ever more attention to technical details, so that they produced lyrics of exquisite taste and intricate design, at the risk of falling into effete aestheticism and jejune formalism.

Non-dramatic songs, c. 1280–1600

When the lyric became too esoteric for ordinary people to appreciate, a new type of popular song arose, known as *ch'ü*. When used as integral parts of drama, such songs are called *hsi-ch'ü* or *chü-ch'ü* ('dramatic songs'); when occurring as independent songs or in suites *(t'ao)* not intended for dramatic performance, they are called *san-ch'ü*, literally 'scattered songs', which may be rendered 'non-dramatic songs'. These songs reached their zenith in the late 13th century, and continued to flourish till about the end of the 16th. Since most writers of non-dramatic songs also wrote drama, some of them will be mentioned below as dramatists. Here we shall only consider the distinctive qualities of non-dramatic songs as a genre, without discussing individual writers.

Metrically, non-dramatic songs are similar to lyrics, but they were written to a different repertoire of tunes. In non-dramatic songs, the length of lines varies even more than in lyrics, and additional words may be inserted, but tone patterns and rhyme schemes are strict. Stylistically, non-dramatic songs tend to be colloquial and lively, though some writers prefer an elegant style. Thematically, these songs enriched poetry by treating subjects hitherto considered too trivial or vulgar, such as a miser's reluctance to lend his horse to a friend, or a maidservant's furtive amorous activities. Naturally, the more traditional and serious themes are also found in non-dramatic songs, but their special contribution to Chinese poetry lies in comic or satirical presentations of everyday life, full of earthy humour, cheerful vitality, and racy slang.

The drama, c. 1280–1800

Traditional Chinese drama is a complex art form that integrates language, music, acting, dance, mime, and acrobatics. Various kinds of theatrical performance had existed for centuries, but full-fledged drama of high literary quality did not emerge till the late 13th century, when the Northern Drama, also called Mixed Plays *(tsa-chü)*, burst in full bloom. Like all other schools of Chinese drama, the Northern Drama is essentially non-representational, its primary purpose being to present a human experience through imaginary characters and situations, and not to provide a realistic imitation of life. Thus, plot (which is always taken from history, legend, or folklore but is never original) and characterization (which is conceived of in terms of conventional types rather than individuals) are of minor importance, whereas

A Sung woodcut of a puppet show. The extreme stylization of dress and make-up necessary in puppet shows for easy recognition of characters was a convention in all traditional Chinese theatre. (4)

interest focuses primarily on the songs that express the emotions of the protagonist of each play, and secondarily on the spoken dialogues and monologues that carry on the dramatic action. The songs often blend refined poetic diction with colloquialisms, and the spoken passages are mostly in colloquial speech. Each Northern Drama consists of four acts, with an optional 'peg' *(hsieh-tz'u,* which resembles the 'induction' in Elizabethan drama) at the beginning or between two acts. Generally, each act is dominated by a particular mood, and it is in the successive changes of mood rather than in the unfolding of the plot that the true structure of each play is to be sought.

In theme, the Northern Drama deals with historical and pseudo-historical episodes, religious conversions, domestic affairs, romantic loves, crimes and their detection, military heroes and chivalrous outlaws. The mode

53 (1)

167

Ming illustrations of scenes from Yuan dynasty Tsa-chü or Northern drama. The first is from a tragedy by Kuan Han- *ch'ing and shows the heroine, Tou O, about to be unjustly executed. The second depicts a popular historical theme in*

of presentation varies from the 'romantic' to the 'low mimetic' or even 'ironic' (in Northrop Frye's terminology). Tragedies are rare, and even in the few plays that may be considered tragedies, poetic justice always prevails at the end. The strength of this drama does not lie in offering original or profound philosophical insights into life, nor in creating memorable 'round' characters, but lies in presenting the imagined emotional experiences of different people in different circumstances.

The Northern Drama flourished for about a century. Its most eminent exponents are: Kuan Han-ch'ing (*c.* 1220–*c.* 1300), who wrote on all kinds of subjects but excelled in romantic comedies (trans. Yang Hsien-yi and Gladys Yang); Ma Chih-yüan (*c.* 1250–*c.* 1325), who had a penchant for expressing Taoist views on life in magnificent dramatic poetry and also wrote one of the few tragedies in Chinese, *Autumn in the Han Palace* (trans. by D. Keene in Birch, pp. 422–48); and Wang Te-hsin (better-known as Wang Shih-fu, early 14th century), who wrote the great love romance, *The Western Chamber (Hsi-hsiang chi)* in a cycle of five plays, depicting every phase of the pangs and joys of love (trans. Hsiung).

p 154 (3)

In the late 14th century, the Northern Drama declined, and the Southern Drama, which had actually come into being before the Northern but had not produced works of comparable literary excellence, enjoyed a revival. Then, having assimilated elements from the Northern Drama, it developed into the Dramatic Romance *(ch'uan-ch'i)*, which remained the dominant form of Chinese drama till the 19th century. Dramatic Romances are usually of immense length, running to dozens of scenes, with a prologue and sometimes an epilogue as well. Writers of Dramatic Romances treated themes similar to those found in the Northern Drama, with a noticeable preference for love stories, which almost always ended happily. There was a tendency towards ornate and elegant language, which, together with the enormous length of the plays, often resulted in a loss of dramatic power. However, the better Dramatic Romances show a much stronger sense of structure and a more individualized conception of characterization than the Northern Drama. Of the hundreds of Dramatic Romances written between about 1370 and 1800, we shall discuss only two.

The Peony Pavilion (Mu-tan T'ing) by T'ang Hsien-tsu (1550–1616) asserts the power of Love over all obstacles, even Death. The heroine dreams of making love with a young man, and dies of lovesickness. After her death,

168

生寫恨
調素琴書

drama, that of the T'ang Emperor Hsüan-tsung and his consort Yang Kuei-fei. The last one is a scene from a love romance. (5, 6, 7)

the same young man discovers her portrait, falls in love with her, and has an affair with her spirit. Eventually, her spirit is reunited with her disinterred body, and the two become truly married. This fantastic tale with a touch of the macabre is presented with great psychological truth and poetic beauty. Particularly remarkable is the dramatist's delineation of the repressed sexual longings of a well-brought-up girl in traditional China.

In *The Peach-blossom Fan (T'ao-hua shan)* by K'ung Shang-jen (1648–1718), the course of true love between a patriotic poet and a loyal courtesan intermingles with the momentous events preceding the fall of the Ming dynasty, and instead of being happily united at the end of the play, the hero and the heroine both renounce the world. The dramatist's profound sense of history, his consummate skill in dramatic structure, his vivid portrayal of the characters, and his superb poetic style all make this a masterpiece, worthy of comparison with Shakespeare's *Antony and Cleopatra*.

In general, the development of drama led to several important changes in modes of sensibility and of expression. First, it broadened the field of literature by exploring aspects of life largely ignored by poetry, such as crime and punishment, domestic strife, and litigation. Secondly

(and this is closely related to the first point), drama brought about a shift of interest from man as an existential being, the individual *vis-à-vis* the universe, to man as a social being, in his relations with other men. Thus, while poetry is usually concerned with the more intense kinds of experience and the nobler sentiments, drama is often concerned with the more superficial or sordid aspects of life and the darker sides of human nature. In Chinese poetry one rarely encounters villainy, but in Chinese drama villains abound. This leads to our third point: poetry generally maintains a serious tone, but drama, as mentioned before, sometimes employs the 'ironic' mode. Even in poems describing human suffering, man is not deprived of his dignity, and even in humorous poems, life is not seen as totally absurd and meaningless. In drama, by contrast, characters are sometimes shown as contemptible wretches, and life is sometimes seen as hopeless. Thus, despite its deceptive happy endings, Chinese drama often presents a far more pessimistic vision of life than Chinese poetry. Fourthly, whereas the world of a poem is a fusion of external reality with an individual consciousness, the world of a drama, though still conceived by a single intelligence, may be presented from several points of view. Moreover, the poetic world is revealed purely through the poem's verbal structure, while the dramatic world is revealed directly through the characters and situations and only indirectly through the verbal structure. Lastly, drama brought together various literary forms and styles; for, in addition to the indispensable songs, other types of poetry, as well as different kinds of prose, are incorporated in drama, which may therefore be considered a final synthesis of Chinese literary forms before the influence of Western literature came to be felt.

All these points, with the partial exception of the last, also apply to the novel, as will become evident in the next section. Furthermore, since the main medium of expression in the novel is colloquial prose, it presents an even greater contrast to poetry than does drama, which invariably contains verse. The differences between Chinese poetry on the one hand and Chinese drama and novel on the other are due partly to the inherent qualities of these genres and partly to Chinese conceptions of the nature of each of them.

The novel, c. 1300–1800

The Chinese term *hsiao-shuo* ('small talk') is applied to all kinds of prose fiction, but since to trace the history of Chinese fiction in its various forms would require too much space, we shall consider only a few major works commonly called 'novels', even though some of them actually bear more resemblance to medieval sagas or romances than modern novels. p 156–7 (10)

Romance of the Three Kingdoms (San-kuo-chih yen-yi) is a popularized chronicle compiled by Lo Kuan-chung (14th century), based partly on official history and partly on earlier storytellers' prompt-books (trans. Brewitt-Taylor). For many readers, its main interest lies in descriptions of military stratagems and political intrigues, but underlying such descriptions is a serious attempt to expound a view of history as an interplay between the will of Heaven and human endeavours. p 160 (19)

Water Margin (Shui-hu chuan) is a heroic romance which originated from oral stories told in the 13th p 158–9 (11–14)

unlike a modern novel. Despite its avowed didactic purpose, the work contains many pornographic passages which describe sexual debauchery with a mixture of fascinated horror and envious delight.

Dream of the Red Chamber (Hung-lou meng) by Ts'ao Chan (*c.* 1716–1763) is generally acknowledged to be the greatest Chinese novel and one of the greatest novels of the world (abridged trans. Wang). The hero is a sensitive, intelligent, and unconventional youth who, after having experienced unhappy love and witnessed the decline of his aristocratic family, leaves the hypocritical and corrupt society in which he has grown up to become a Buddhist monk. The author is incomparable among Chinese novelists for his tragic vision of life, his subtle psychological insights, his realistic descriptions of social manners and daily life, his advanced technique (such as the use of the interior monologue), his universal understanding of men and affairs, his encyclopaedic knowledge of arts, crafts, and pastimes, and his stylistic versatility.

p 160 (20)

Each of the novels mentioned above has its own imaginary world, though of course each world differs from the others in complexity, consistency, self-completeness, and relation to the 'real' world. The worlds of *Three Kingdoms* and *Water Margin* are relatively simple and predominantly masculine. Man is shown mainly as a social and political being, and attention centres on heroic deeds, battles of wits, struggles for power, and such supposedly male virtues as loyalty to one's friend or lord, justice, altruism, moral and physical courage, and sexual asceticism. *Journey to the West* and *Golden Vase Plum* are both concerned (though not exclusively) with man's animal instincts, the former allegorically and the latter realistically, the former seeing them in a comic light and the latter showing their fearful manifestations and consequences. The world of *Dream of the Red Chamber* is the most multi-dimensional, most self-contained, most consistently observed, and closest to being co-extensive with the actual world. It shows man in his social, intellectual, emotional, sensuous, and instinctive aspects, and it portrays men and women of all social standings and temperaments.

In their explorations of language, all the novelists contributed, in varying degrees, to the development of the colloquial language as an artistic medium. *Three Kingdoms* is only semi-colloquial, while *Water Margin, Journey to the West,* and *Golden Vase Plum* all employ pure colloquial language for narrative and dialogue, but often break into verse for descriptive purposes. Only *Dream of the Red Chamber* succeeds in describing people, dress, food, houses and gardens, in the colloquial language. Although it, too, contains all types of verse, they are not mere show pieces but are means of characterization or mood-painting.

Ultimately, Chinese literature (whether poetry, drama, or novel) is deeply humanistic and remarkable for its lack of cynicism. It is an affirmation of life, with all its glory and squalor; of the magnificent and indifferent universe in which man finds himself; and of man's own nature, with all its potentials for spiritual enlightenment and bestial depravity, its mortal fate and immortal aspirations. As a manifestation of the artistic capabilities of language, Chinese literature is surely one of the greatest achievements of the human mind.

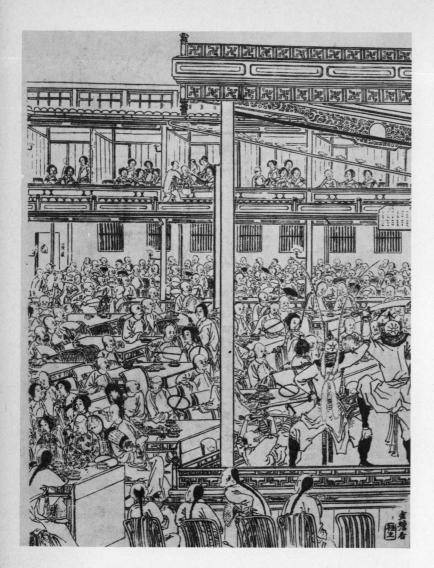

A theatre in Shanghai at the end of the 19th century. On the stage (right foreground) the actors are engaged in a display of swordsmanship. The audience takes refreshment during the performance, and tea is being sold to the occupants of one of the boxes. (8)

century, and underwent stages of compilation, expansion, and revision by several hands till it reached its fullest version in the early 17th century (trans. Jackson). It recounts the exploits of a band of chivalrous outlaws, their capitulation to the government, and their subsequent campaigns against other rebels.

p 158–9 (15–18)

Journey to the West (Hsi-yu-chi), generally attributed to Wu Ch'eng-en (*c.* 1506–82) though partly derived from earlier versions, is a unique mixture of religious allegory, social satire, and nonsensical humour, having as its ostensible subject the monk Tripitaka's journey to India to fetch Buddhist scriptures (abridged trans. Waley, *Monkey*).

Golden Vase Plum (Chin P'ing Mei, a pun on the names of three female characters) by an unidentified late 16th-century writer, is regarded by some as the first real Chinese novel, because it deals with the domestic life of the bourgeoisie instead of supernatural events or heroic deeds (trans. Egerton). However, its narrative is so interspersed with lyrics and songs that formally it is very

VII CHINESE CULTURE OVERSEAS

Korea, Japan, Vietnam and Tibet

ZENRYU TSUKAMOTO

The Highway of Ch'ang-an leads to every place in the world.

Proverb

The light of Chinese civilization shone out over the whole of East Asia – north to the nomad peoples (as we have seen in Chapter III); east to Korea and Japan; south to Vietnam; west to Tibet. In Tibet, for the first time, it encountered a culture as ancient as its own, that of India. Tibet is therefore the meeting place of two civilizations and her history a compound of influences.

The Janus-face of Tibet is symbolized in the person of one of her earliest kings (see pl. 3 overleaf) who married two princesses – one from China, the other from Nepal. Both brought with them their own form of Buddhist religion and their own form of script, with scholars to teach it. Thereafter Chinese influence tended to dominate culturally and socially, Indian in the sphere of religion. Tibetan Buddhism (Lamaism) is a bizarre mixture of Indian Buddhism, Hinduism and primitive demon-worship. 'Lama' means 'Superior one'; 'Dalai' means 'All-embracing'. The first Dalai Lama was the religious reformer Tsong-kha-pa (died 1419), who led a movement which penetrated to China and beyond. The cult of re-incarnation only arose later, when his third successor, who went to Mongolia in 1568, was reckoned to be a re-incarnation of his first disciple. The re-incarnation of his second disciple became the spiritual ruler of Outer Mongolia and of his third (the Tashi or Panchen Lama) of Tibet. It was not until the 17th century that the Dalai Lamas, as a result of Mongol and Manchu pressure, themselves took up residence in Lhasa, built the Potala palace and assumed temporal power. The Panchen Lama occupied another monastery to the west of Lhasa.

For the next two centuries Tibet was continuously subject to Chinese domination. During most of the Ch'ing period it was a Chinese protectorate and Indian influence faded. This 18th century '*tanka*', a temple painting on silk, is clearly Chinese in inspiration and in art-style. The second Panchen Lama (1485–1505) sits in three-quarter profile, not full-face as in Indian art. Wearing monastic robes and a yellow cap, he holds his right hand in the *vitarka* position. Above his throne a peach-tree blossoms. On his left is a monastery; above that the seated figure of Tsong-kha-pa; and above him the Panchen Lama is depicted a second time. At the bottom, centre, sits another Lama, reading, between a figure of the Dharmapala Sudevi and a wrathful deity wearing Mongolian armour and a butterfly-shaped headdress and carrying a lance. (1)

Lhasa is both the political and religious capital of Tibet. At its centre stands the Jokhang Temple (above), founded according to tradition in 652, at the very dawn of Tibetan history. It combined the functions of national shrine and administrative offices. But the golden pagoda roofs are unmistakable imports from China. (2)

Between his two wives King Srong-tsan Gam-po seems to symbolize the situation of Tibet between China and India. One was the daughter of the King of Nepal, the other (Wen-ch'eng) the daughter of T'ai-tsung, the second T'ang emperor. With her to Tibet came Chinese silks and Chinese documents. (3)

In the far south, Vietnam was drawn into the orbit of China as early as the Ch'in and Han dynasties. Here too, Indian and Chinese forms of Buddhism met, but there was never any real challenge. During most of Vietnam's history, the ruling class was Chinese or Chinese-educated, though the country was politically independent. In the early 19th century the ruling family (the Nguyen) acknowledged the suzerainty of China and the imperial palace at Hue (below) was modelled on that of Peking. This view shows the southern gate. (4)

Ideas from China: in this plate from Vietnam the centre is formed by the Yin-Yang sign (see Chapter IV), the rim by the eight trigrams – all the possible variants of a single line (corresponding to Yang) and two short ones (Yin) arranged in groups of three. They are used in the ancient Chinese classic of divination, the *I Ching* or *Book of Changes*. The present flag of South Korea has an almost identical pattern, but using only four of the eight trigrams. (5)

Tools from China: the long pole, *gánh*, used for carrying two baskets is a Chinese invention long ago adopted by the Vietnamese. Bottom: a village scribe writes a love poem in Chinese characters. Vietnamese is a separate language but belongs to the Chinese family. Under French colonial rule a Romanized script was introduced and Chinese characters are now only rarely used. (6, 7)

175

To Korea the Chinese of the Han dynasty came as conquerors, administrators and missionaries. In 109 BC the Emperor Wu attacked and annexed the far less advanced Korean state and for the next 400 years it was divided into four 'commanderies' and governed by China. In the wake of the officials many educated Chinese took up residence there and the whole peninsula was soon steeped in Chinese culture. The painted lacquer basket shown here (above) was found in a tomb at Lo-lang, one of the capitals of the Chinese administration. It was made at Szechwan and was probably brought to Korea as a gift. The lid is decorated with figures illustrating filial piety, a Confucian subject embodying a specifically Chinese ideology. (8)

On a dragon's back the Buddhist monk Gishō (below) returns from Ch'ang-an to Korea, bringing with him the teachings of the Kegon sect. This is one of the many miraculous stories connected with the spread of Buddhism in Korea and Japan. The dragon was in fact a beautiful Chinese girl called Zemmyō who had fallen in love with Gishō but upon learning his holy mission had pledged herself to help him. When he left on his return voyage she jumped into the sea, turned into a dragon and carried the whole ship safely to Korea. Gishō was a historical person who lived from 624 to 702 and was responsible for establishing Kegon Buddhism in Korea (see overleaf, pl. 12). This scroll painting dates from the 13th century, during a revival of the Kegon sect in Japan. (9)

Wealth and luxury flowed into Korea from Han China. This gold belt buckle was also found at Lo-lang and is roughly contemporary with the basket. It was inlaid with turquoises, of which only a few remain. Even before annexation Chinese had been the language of the educated classes. Confucianism and Taoism were widespread and Buddhism was already attracting adherents. (10)

For a thousand years, in spite of political vicissitudes, Korean civilization remained basically Chinese. In the 7th century the whole country was united by the Kingdom of Silla, to be followed in the 10th by that of Koryō. Under the long-lived Yi dynasty (1392–1910) Neo-Confucianism triumphed and foreign policy followed China's lead. Right: a Yi dynasty king of Korea, dressed in Chinese-style robes. (11)

Gishō's journey, one incident of which we saw on the previous page (pl. 9), ended on a mountain top in Silla where he founded a monastery (above) and began to propagate Kegon Buddhism. Kegon later became one of the six sects that flourished in Nara Japan (see Chapter IX). (12)

Buddha was received into Korea in the 4th century AD, and from there, a century or so later, into Japan. Korean Buddhism is therefore of crucial importance for later developments. The historical sequence is reflected in art. This 7th-century bronze Buddha from Korea (left) follows Chinese models and in its turn influenced subsequent Japanese religious art. (13)

An envoy to China (above right): when Chinese rule disintegrated in the 4th century AD Korea split into three kingdoms – Koguryō in the north, Silla in the east and Paekche in the west. This drawing of a man from Paekche is from a Sung copy of a 6th-century original. (14)

A mission from Japan (above far right) visited China in AD 753 to ask the Buddhist monk Chien-chen to come to Japan. In this scene the Japanese party has arrived at the gates of the monastery and is being welcomed by two monks. Chien-chen settled in Japan (where he was called Ganjin) and founded the Ritsu sect there (see Chapter IX). (15)

The art of Korea leant heavily upon Chinese prototypes but was more than mere imitation. During the Yi dynasty the two styles of Chinese painting, Northern and Southern, were successfully practised in Korea. This landscape (right), painted on silk by Yi In-man (1746–1825), looks back to the China of a hundred years earlier. (16)

Japan was culturally the daughter of China. From the first century AD onwards most of what was vital and progressive in Japan came from China, either directly or via Korea. After 538 Buddhism was taken up eagerly in Japan and became another powerful vehicle for Chinese influence. Among its most prominent supporters was Prince Shōtoku seen here (left) in a 7th-century drawing with his two sons. In 607 he founded the monastery of Hōryuji at Nara, which has survived basically intact until today. Its main feature is a five-storeyed pagoda (below left) – a Chinese, and specifically Buddhist, feature which never became completely integrated into the Japanese temple plan. (17, 18)

T'ang culture is paradoxically far better preserved in Japan than in China itself.

Opposite: a five-stringed musical instrument (*biwa*) made in the Nara period (AD 710–784) in sandalwood, tortoise shell and mother-of-pearl. On the plectrum-guard is an inlaid picture showing a musician riding a camel and playing a *biwa*. Such instruments were produced in T'ang China, but are known there today only through paintings and fragments.

Far right, above: warehouse of Shōsōin, Nara, built in AD 756 and still containing a unique collection of over 6,000 objects presented by the Emperor Shomu – ornaments, Buddhist cult objects, musical instruments, carpets, painted screens, textiles, games, weapons and manuscripts. The warehouse itself, of log-construction, is equally well-preserved.

Far right, below: detail from *Lady under a tree*, Nara period. This is part of a screen, also from Shōsōin. Both the style and the fashions (rouged lips and cheeks, green beauty spots) are completely T'ang though the artist was probably Japanese. (19–21)

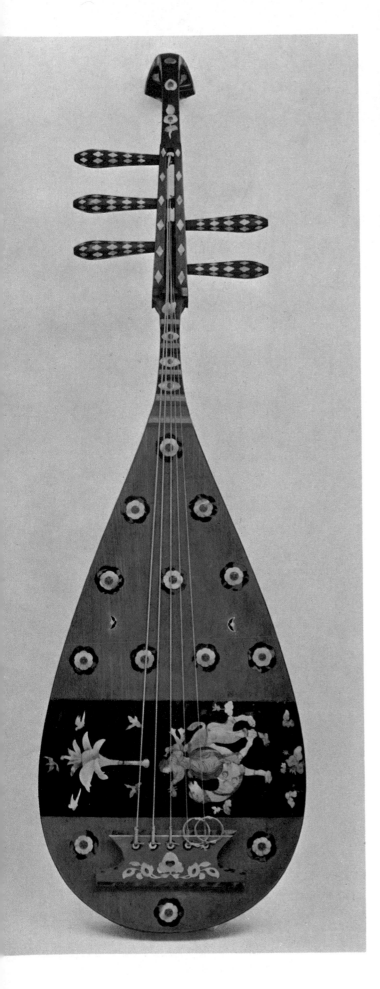

Ordeal by chequer-board. Between 630 and 894 nineteen Japanese embassies visited the T'ang court to study law, administration, Confucian and Buddhist doctrine and everything necessary for the scholar-gentleman. A certain inferiority complex was natural, and this comes through in the story of Kibi, a Japanese minister sent to Ch'ang-an in the 7th century. Jealous of his wisdom, the Chinese tried to humiliate him by a series of tests, including the exegesis of difficult Chinese texts and a contest at the game of *go*. It is this episode which is illustrated above. On the right Kibi, in the black robe, sits at the *go*-board facing the Chinese team, which is visibly despondent. One supporter looks under the board, suspecting that a *go*-piece is missing. Kibi has in fact swallowed it. On the left he has been given a purge and stands in his underwear while the Chinese examine his excrement; but by a magic trick he is able to keep the *go*-piece in his stomach. (22)

From India to China in the 7th century AD came the Buddhist priest Zenmui. His disciples took his doctrine to Japan where it flourished more fruitfully than ever and became the basis for the powerful Tendai sect. This painting of him (left) by a Japanese artist of the 12th century is alien to Japanese tradition and must be copied from a Chinese original. (23)

It was in Japan that many Buddhist sects from China reached their consummation, and are remembered today mainly in their Japanese form.

Right: Bodhidharma, the first Zen patriarch, known in Japan as Daruma. From the late T'ang period onwards the interchange between Zen monks of China and Japan was a two-way process. Through Zen, Chinese literary and artistic forms were introduced and developed, including that of ink and wash drawing, the technique used in this portrait.

Below left: Shingon, a tantric form of Buddhism, also came to Japan in the 8th century. Among its ceremonies is a baptismal rite which involves the use of a screen painted with landscape scenes. A detail from the oldest of such screens is reproduced here, showing an episode from the life of a hermit. Again, it is a Heian copy of a Chinese original. (24, 25)

The tea ceremony, one of the most characteristic items of Japanese traditional life, was introduced from China by Zen monks, who brought both the tea and the pottery. (26)

'Wo-nu, Prince of Han': the recent discovery of a golden seal in Kyūshū proves how early Chinese culture had penetrated into Japan. It was made in China in AD 57 and was probably given by the Emperor Kuang-wu to a Japanese envoy. The seal itself (above, enlarged) is in the shape of a curly-haired animal. The impression (left) is reproduced actual size. (27, 28)

Korea, Japan, Vietnam and Tibet

ZENRYU TSUKAMOTO

THE AREAS THAT we now know as Korea and Vietnam lay at the furthest limits of the Chinese Empire, as it had evolved during the Ch'in and Han dynasties. The establishment of Chinese 'commanderies' meant that Chinese officials were posted there, bringing with them in the course of time Chinese merchants and intellectuals. As Chinese culture was far more highly developed than any that had previously been known in these areas, it soon became dominant. Through Korea it also reached Japan, as has been proved by the discovery in northern Kyūshū of a gold seal inscribed *Han-wo-nu-wang* ('Wo-nu, Prince of Han').

The Chinese naturally saw their own civilization as supreme, and regarded the peoples of the outer marches as 'barbarians'. Such an attitude was reinforced, from the Han Age onwards, by the apotheosis of Confucianism and the consequent authority with which the Confucian Classics were endowed. It remained strong until the Republican revolution put an end to Manchu rule in China.

The Chinese were accordingly convinced that the Asian countries on their borders were in duty bound to render tribute and other forms of homage to their Emperor, who was the only Heaven-appointed ruler on earth, and to be joyfully submissive to his authority and grateful for the reflected glory of the vastly superior 'middle and flowering' civilization. They were similarly convinced that only the 'middle country' was directly governed by rulers whose authority, whose very lineage of rule (though not necessarily of blood), went back to the gods. These two ideas were being vigorously and uninterruptedly radiated outward to these same outlying regions.

Early in the 3rd century AD, even the Han empire, which had lasted more than four centuries, collapsed, and China was divided into three. Under these conditions the Chinese came increasingly under the pressure of the non-Chinese peoples whom they had so long despised as 'uncivilized', with the result that eventually they moved in large numbers from their former metropolises in the Yellow River (Huang-ho) basin into that of the Yangtze and still further south, leaving the north (as we have seen in Chapter II) to states now governed by non-Chinese. Thus the epoch immediately following was one of rivalry

between the states just mentioned and a succession of southern states, the latter governed by Chinese. Yet, even during this period of political division, which lasted four hundred years, the Chinese profited from the previous spread into the outlying areas of the authority of the unified Chinese Empire. There was consequently now an uninterrupted move of Chinese civilization into the border countries. On the other hand, this very period of division brought into China, by way of the 'Silk Road', a commercial highway across Central Asia that had been opened up in the Han Age, material evidences of the cultures of Greece, Rome, and Persia, with which the Chinese had virtually nothing in common. In addition to this, Buddhism, an Indian religion with a strong missionary impulse, began, from the late Han Age onwards, to advance along this same route.

Buddhism entered China, both north and south, not enshrined in the Indo-European languages that were native to it, but in Chinese translations. From Japan to the South Seas, it triumphed throughout the whole Chinese world. Thus, side by side with the learned and sophisticated ideas of Confucianism and Taoism *(tao chia)*, as well as the religious version of Taoism *(tao chiao)* that had developed on a base of traditional popular beliefs (see Chapter IV), came a strain from the Indo-European world, which enriched but also complicated it.

China was re-unified late in the 6th century, and she remained united throughout the next two dynastic eras, the Sui and the T'ang. During the T'ang Age, in particular, the power of the Chinese state was consolidated both internally and externally, and the flower of world civilization blossomed on Chinese soil with a brilliance that the ancient Ch'in and Han Age could not have rivalled. It was this civilization which was to spread to the Asian countries on China's borders and thus remake Asia, so to speak, in the image of the transformed Chinese culture. Even after the collapse of the T'ang, Chinese civilization still continued to exercise an extended influence, and a great one, over the Asian countries adjoining China's frontiers. In the present chapter, we shall describe the spread of Chinese civilization into Korea, Japan, Vietnam and Tibet. We shall focus our attention on the Sui-T'ang era, but we shall also take note, to a certain extent, of other periods, both earlier and later.

The Sui regime, as we have seen in Chapter II, was inaugurated in North China in 581, when the first Sui emperor went through the formality of accepting a throne ceded by the last monarch of the preceding dynasty, that of the Northern Chou, and thus became the ruler of the entire north. Next, in 590, he destroyed the state of Ch'en, which had held sway over the whole of South China, and thus he succeeded in bringing the whole country under a single rule. Unity under the auspices of the Sui lasted for less than thirty years, but the Sui regime did put an end to a long period of political division. The next dynasty, that of the T'ang, supplanted it as early as 618.

Under the Sui, the political power of the Empire spread into the outlying areas. Many border states recognized the Empire of Sui (and, later, of T'ang) as their suzerain. They sent both ambassadors and scholars to the imperial capital, and those emissaries sent the products of Chinese culture back to their own respective countries and

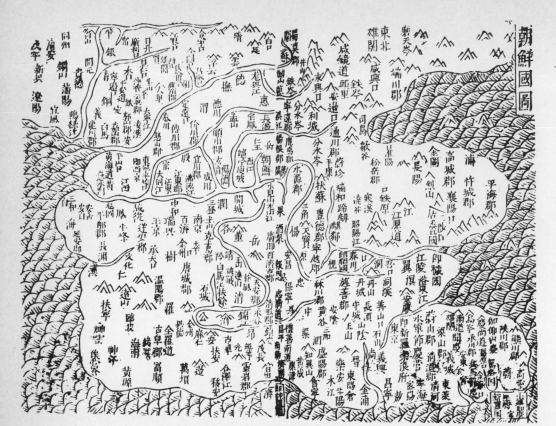

brought the products of their own countries into China proper, principally into the Ch'ang-an region, thus bringing about a cultural exchange. Inside China, the Sui court collected in the area of Ch'ang-an and Lo-yang the material products of the civilization of the whole country, north and south, and it exported the cultures of China as a whole to India and countries even further west, as well as to the lands on China's frontier, thus laying the groundwork for what was to be an international commingling and general union.

The T'ang dynasty, as early as the reign of its second occupant of the throne, T'ai-tsung (*r.* 627–649), specifically during the 'peace of Chen-kuan', reached a point at which the political power of the Chinese Empire was internally secure. There was external expansion as well, there was economic prosperity, and a way was opened for further cultural development. In the 7th and 8th centuries Ch'ang-an became a world metropolis.

One of the Sui dynasty's bequests that contributed greatly to the T'ang dynasty's achievement of ecumenical pre-eminence and to the advance of its culture was the network of communications that the Sui had created, connecting Ch'ang-an and Lo-yang with all other parts of China, particularly the north-south Grand Canal which ran northward from Yangchow. Not only did the Canal link the Yangtze with the Yellow River; it continued even further north, joining the wheat and millet country of the north to the rich rice country south of the Yangtze. It also facilitated the journey to Ch'ang-an for the Korean and Japanese envoys and scholars who had to cross the Sea of Japan, and the importation of material objects of foreign culture.

The Northern Chou dynasty, which had been the Sui dynasty's immediate predecessor in North China, had proscribed Buddhism and Taoism. The Sui had reversed this policy. They had not only tolerated Buddhism; they

had fostered it; and the fruits of this religious revival were inherited by the T'ang. The Buddhist element in the civilization of China in the T'ang Age assisted the radiation of Chinese influence into Korea, Japan, and Tibet, in spite of the increasing Confucian reaction against Buddhism, which eventually culminated in a persecution, in China itself.

Korea: conquest and acculturation

The political unification of China under the Ch'in and Han dynasties had an awe-inspiring effect on the Koreans. Early in the Han Age, during the reign of the Emperor Wu, the Korean state was attacked and annexed (109–108 BC) by China, and four Chinese commanderies were established there, all of them governed by officials appointed and dispatched to manage what was now regarded as being Han territory. This hastened the already rapid advance of the Han civilization into Korea. The four commanderies suffered vicissitudes, but their aggregate area expanded, and, under three successive dynasties, Han, Wei, and Tsin, Korea remained under Chinese rule till AD 313. During this period, the number of Chinese moving into Korea to take up permanent residence was large, and the transplantation of Chinese civilization proceeded notably into areas under the control of the Chinese Imperial Government, where there were resident Chinese officials, i.e. men of knowledge and culture. Material evidence of this process of sinification has been brought to light by archaeological excavations.

In the course of the 4th century, Chinese rule was liquidated in Korea, but this did not arrest the progress there of Chinese civilization. In the second half of the 4th century, Korea was divided into three kingdoms. The kingdom of Koguryŏ took possession of North Korea. In the south, the kingdom of Silla was established to the east and the kingdom of Paekche to the west.

p 176- (8)

p 176- (8,10)

The original base of the kingdom of Koguryŏ had been in what is now South Manchuria, where, as early as the era of the Warring States, the old North Chinese state of Yen had been constantly expanding its frontiers, particularly during the 4th and 3rd centuries BC. Many Chinese from Yen moved into the annexed districts of Manchuria, besides refugees from China proper, who were seeking relief from political insecurity. The unified state established by the Ch'in then extended its power to include Yen's Manchurian territory. Thus this area had been a recipient of Chinese civilization before the Han Age. This has been demonstrated by the retrieval of bronze implements, made in the Chinese style of the Spring-and-Autumn era (722–481 BC) and of the Warring States era (481–221 BC), in archaeological excavations of the ruins of Koguryŏ cities situated in Manchuria.

The state of Koguryŏ, after having been subjected at this early date to the influence of Chinese civilization, now moved into what is today North Korea and occupied two commanderies governed by Chinese residents, which were the centres of the penetration of Chinese civilization into Korea and of its spread there. Koguryŏ contrived to establish a capital in the centre of the Lo-lang commandery, in the area of what is now P'yong'yang. The sinification of Koguryŏ, however, was not interrupted, but rather intensified as a result of Koguryŏ's expansion into Korea.

176–7 (8,10)

In Koguryŏ, which since Han times had maintained its capital in the Lo-lang area, the Chinese written language was in use. It was also already in use in Silla and Paekche, and now these two countries, too, encouraged Confucian scholarship. They made the acquisition of it incumbent on all intellectuals and on all officials. Moreover, Confucianism was not the only Chinese import. The Chinese folk-beliefs which later furnished the basis for Taoism were also received into Korean society, where shamanistic beliefs were already widespread.

p 179 (14)

At the time of the division of Korea into three kingdoms, Chinese Buddhism was making its way into all three. (This was the period, in China, of the Tsin and of the division into North and South, a period in which Buddhism was flourishing in both parts of China.) From Koguryŏ, North Chinese Buddhism travelled southwards into Silla and Paekche. Since, however, Silla and Paekche established an oversea traffic route of their own to China, over which they sent tribute and ambassadors of good will to the Chinese kingdoms south of the Yangtze, the Buddhism of South China and its civilization also made its way into those two kingdoms. It was, generally speaking, in the 6th century that the Buddhism imported from China flourished in the Korean peninsula.

The spread, throughout the Korean peninsula, of Confucianism and Buddhism by means of the Chinese written word, and the spread of Chinese arts and crafts and other material expressions of Chinese civilization, worked together with the contemporary political situation in China to affect Japan. As a result of China's loss of territory in Korea, and of the division of the Chinese Empire itself into three kingdoms which were all at war with one another, there was a considerable movement of persons of Chinese stock from Korea into Japan, and, from the 6th century onwards, this led to the introduction into Japan of many facets of Chinese civilization.

In the course of the first half of the 7th century the kingdom of Silla united Korea politically by conquering the other two with the help of the T'ang. King Muryŏl of Silla then paid a personal visit to T'ang China. He was impressed by the grandeur of the Chinese civilization, he studied T'ang institutions, and he addressed himself vigorously to the task of importing T'ang civilization into Korea, in particular the Buddhist religion. Meanwhile, merchants from Silla, actively engaged in oversea trade with T'ang China, had created a string of Korean settlements along the Shantung coast. Silla's active oversea trade with T'ang China was of great help to Japan's trade with China as well; for, among the Koreans who had mastered the Chinese language, there were some who served as interpreters and guides for the Japanese, both lay and clerical, who had come to China to study.

The era of Korean unity under Silla coincides precisely with the T'ang era in China, and overlaps with the Nara era in Japan, an age in which the Japanese were fascinated by everything Chinese. Korea's political relations with Japan were tenuous, yet Korea's role in the conversion of Japan to T'ang culture was an important one.

Buddhism, enjoying the protection of the Silla government, flourished throughout Korea, not merely in and round the capital city of Kyŏngju. The gifted members of the Korean Saṃgha, like their Japanese contemporaries, had a passion for studying in T'ang China. T'ang monks also went from China to Korea at Silla's invitation, and some members of the Korean Saṃgha who had gone to China to study brought back with them not only the doctrines of Buddhism but also astronomical charts and other products of T'ang art and science.

p 176–7 (9)

The beginning of the Koryŏ dynasty (935–1392) in Korea coincides with the decline in China of the T'ang and with the ensuing chaotic age of the Five Dynasties. There was now no direct control from the Chinese court, yet the Koryŏ, which continued to regard China as Korea's suzerain, also continued to send tribute and to bring back into Korea the material products of Chinese civilization. With the re-establishment of peace and order in China under the Sung dynasty, Korea's contacts with China, including commercial contacts, became closer, and the flow of Sung civilization into Korea, aided by the Koreans, both lay and clerical, who went to China to study, continued unabated. Since the Koryŏ court and aristocracy were as devoutly Buddhist as those of the Silla, from whom they had inherited the faith, the Buddhist religion continued to be an important constituent of Korean culture under the new dynasty too. The Ch'an form of Buddhism continued without interruption to be exported from China to Korea (Sŏn). As a result of the contemporary Chinese practice of combining Ch'an contemplation with repeated invocations of Amida Buddha, the doctrines of Pure Land salvationism also made their way into Korea. The Buddhism imported from China into Korea was an old and well-established institution, but it eventually merged with Korean shamanism and other popular beliefs and thus turned into a genuinely popular religion.

Meanwhile the Buddhist civilization of China was losing some of its magnificence and grandeur. The new Buddhist culture created in Korea by the Koryŏ dynasty, a culture in which, once it had made the passage from

思縮前白曰壞寨使巳定舍館於城東將士欲各入城
摯家詣城東宿友規箄然之思縮箄大謀持白梃殺守
門者入府開庫取鎧仗友規箄智逃去思縮遂援城集
城中少年得四千餘人旬曰間戰守之具皆備景崇諷
鳳翔吏民表巳知軍府事朝廷惡之以王守恩為求典
節度使趙暉為鳳翔節度使以景崇為邠州為求典
復以孫方簡為義武節度使契丹將郎五蕃名郎五回
人之麻荅掠定州而道
初契丹北歸至定州以義武節度使孫方簡為大同節
度使方簡怨志不受命帥其黨三千人保狼山故寨契
丹攻之不克未幾遣使降漢漢主復其舊官使扞契丹

Two features of Chinese life exported to Korea: movable type (the first example, left, was a history of China printed in 1422) and the Civil Service examinations (above, in 1884). Here the successful candidates are borne in procession on horseback to the sound of music. (2, 3)

China, popularization and 'Koreanization' had gone to considerable lengths, had no more of the elegance or of the liberality that had been characteristic of Korean Buddhism under the three kingdoms or under the Silla. However, as a result of the rise of the Sung dynasty in China and of the developments in the art of printing that accompanied it (see Chapter V), the Confucian Classics were published repeatedly; and the art of printing benefited Buddhism too. When once the Northern Sung had produced an officially edited, printed edition of the Buddhist canonical corpus, there was a whole series of such editions, some public, some private, and the influence of this activity extended into Japan as well as into Korea.

Confucianism was temporarily submerged under Buddhism in the earlier part of the Koryŏ era, but the official patronage that was given in China to Neo-Confucianism under the Yüan (Mongol) dynasty made the fortune of Neo-Confucianism and led to the repression of Buddhism p 176–7 (11) in Korea too, after the Koryŏ dynasty had been supplanted there by the Yi (Chosŏn) dynasty, which was contemporary with the Ming and Ch'ing dynasties in China. The Yi dynasty based its domestic policy on Neo-Confucianism and its foreign policy on a recognition of China's suzerainty. Korean scholars continued to import and to study Chinese books dealing with all subjects, most notably with Confucian scholarship, and to associate with Chinese scholars. For these reasons, the Korean

aristocracy took to imitating the style of China's intellectuals. The supreme cultural achievement of this movement was the imitation of the two styles of Chinese painting, the Northern and the Southern, that had developed in China since Sung times. Under this inspiration, there developed in Korea a style that was a new departure from the minutely decorative Buddhist art that had been practised until then. The Korean artist now gave full expression to his feelings in depicting landscapes and human figures, and the earlier half of the Yi era was the golden age of Korean painting.

Japan: 'things from Cathay'

In the 1st and 2nd centuries of the Christian era, Japan had no strongly centralized state structure. Politically, she was in an underdeveloped condition, in which groups of people, led by local power-holders, lived by primitive agriculture, hunting, or fishing, using stone ware or simply fired earthenware. Already, however, tribute-bearing missions of good will were arriving in China from Japan, and Japanese rulers had the title of 'king' or 'prince' *(wang)* conferred on them, as the Chinese documents tell us. In northern Kyūshū, in fact, as already noted, there has been unearthed a seal reading 'Wo-nu, Prince of Han'. Conversely, there are accounts in old Japanese records of Chinese ships drifting to Japan and of the settlement of their occupants on Japanese soil. Archaeological discoveries testify that, over a period of several centuries spanning the beginning of the Christian era, material products of China's bronze culture, dating to the era of the Warring States, were making their way into Japan. Among these objects there were, without much doubt, some that came by way of Korea, but there must surely be some that came through direct contact with the mainland of China.

By the 3rd century, the Japanese court, which had established itself in Yamato, was working towards political unity at home, and by the 4th century it was already extending its power to the south of the Korean peninsula. In the 5th century, it was sending embassies to the southern Chinese courts of the Eastern Tsin, the (Liu) Sung, the (Southern) Ch'i, and the Liang, to request the conferment of the titles 'princes' and 'generals' from the Chinese court. In this way, the Chinese civilization, which had already come into Japan quite early by way of Korea, was now coming direct. In some cases it was conveyed by tribute-bearing missions on their way back home, in others by Chinese coming to settle in Japan. The rapid unification of Korea under the rule of the state of Koryŏ and the liquidation of Chinese administration in Korea brought to Japan, for permanent settlement, some Koreans, who were already culturally quite sinified, and some Chinese who had been resident in Korea. The Japanese court and the forward-looking aristocrats gave preferential treatment to these immigrants. They employed them as scribes or in the manufacture of textiles and other industrial products. There is literary and archaeological evidence that, in the era spanning the 2nd and 5th centuries, when the Japanese court, with its centre in Yamato, was growing and developing, Chinese civilization was making conquests among Japan's ruling classes.

The triumph of Buddhism in China under the Tsin, and during the period of political division into North and South, was reflected in a gradual movement of Buddhism into Japan as well, and in 538 the Korean kingdom of Paekche presented the Japanese court with a Buddhist icon and with one of the Buddhist scriptures in Chinese translation. This religion, with its civilized appurtenances, immediately won the hearts of the Japanese. In particular, the courtiers, the intellectuals, and powerful ministers of state committed themselves to the Buddhist faith and proceeded vigorously and enthusiastically to study and promote it. With this support from the Government, Buddhism was able to spread very rapidly. Among its

p 180 (17)

prominent supporters were Prince Shōtoku, a man steeped in Chinese scholarship, and the Soga clan, who were the real holders of political power. The Model Law (*kempō*), promulgated by the Prince in the capacity of regent, is based on a Buddhist faith superimposed on a knowledge of much of the Chinese classical tradition, Confucian and other. The commentaries, written in Chinese, on three Buddhist scriptures, the *Saddharma-puṇḍarīka*, the *Vimalakīrtinirdeśa*, and the *Śrīmālādevīsiṃhanāda*, all ascribed to the Prince, were probably made with the co-operation of Buddhist scholars, Chinese or Korean, drawing on Chinese commentaries dating back

p 180 (18)

to the Sui era and, even earlier, to the period of division

228–9 (7)

between North and South. Buddhist monasteries were also built, the most notable among them being the Hōkōji and the Hōryūji.

The date of the introduction of Buddhism into Japan was contemporary with the unification of China under the Sui and T'ang dynasties, when Korea was being intimidated by Chinese power and when Japan was being forced to abandon her long-standing presence in Korea. The perceptive Prince Shōtoku decided that the best foreign policy for Japan was to enter into direct relations with China and to raise Japan's cultural level to the height of China's by importing Chinese civilization, Buddhism in particular. The Prince acted on this decision by dispatching to China a state mission *(kenzuishi)*, as well as scholars both lay and clerical. The scholars pursued their studies at cosmopolitan Ch'ang-an, and here some of them absorbed China's metropolitan civilization for twenty or thirty years, in certain cases even longer, before going home again. Some of them became T'ang officials by passing the civil service examinations. There were some

p 182–3 (22)

who stayed in China for the rest of their lives. Nineteen Japanese embassies *(kentōshi)* were sent to the T'ang court, the first in 630, the last in 894, and, of these, sixteen completed the exacting voyage successfully. Thanks to the Japanese scholars in China, Japan's legal institutions were systematized on the Chinese model, tax schedules were drawn up, and a centralized state eventually took solid shape. Then a capital was constructed at Nara on the pattern of Ch'ang-an, complete with Buddhist monasteries, government offices, and aristocratic town houses, all on the T'ang model. The official life of the court was now highly refined. It, too, was modelled entirely on the T'ang prototype. The doctrinal scholarship brought back to Japan by the scholar-monks who had gone to China to pursue their studies was systematized in the form of the Six Schools of Nara. These were the first Buddhist

p 178 (12)

schools to exist on Japanese soil, and all six had flourished in Ch'ang-an under the T'ang.

From the Nara Age until the early Heian Age, the Japanese were fascinated by T'ang culture. Chinese poetry became fashionable. The verses of the T'ang poet Po Chü-i (Po Lo-t'ien) became as dear to the Japanese as to the Chinese themselves. The Confucian Classics, as well as Taoistic writings, were all studied. In a series beginning with the *Chronicles of Japan (Nihon shoki)* in the early 8th century and ending late in the 9th century, Japan's Six National Histories *(rikkokushi)* were compiled. They were all modelled on China's dynastic histories and were written in classical Chinese. The quantity of books, both Buddhist and secular, that made their way from China to Japan was enormous. Some of them have been preserved only in Japan. For the Japanese of the time, the ability to compose both prose and verse in classical Chinese was taken to be the highest intellectual achievement.

Of the material products of which Ch'ang-an could

p 181 (19–21)

boast at the height of her glory, many perished in China but have been preserved down to this day at the Shōsōin in Nara. The Japanese Buddhist temples and the Shōsōin are, in fact, not only distinguished museums of the T'ang civilization but actually its richest repositories.

At the end of the 8th century, the capital moved from Nara to what is now Kyoto. About this time, Saichō brought back from Mount T'ien-t'ai, south of the

p 182–3 (23)

Yangtze, the doctrines of the Chinese school of Buddhism named after the mountain (Tendai in Japanese), while

p 182–3 (25)

Kūkai brought back from Ch'ang-an a tantric form of

From the 7th to the 8th century, Japan was dominated by the T'ang culture of China. The poet Po Chü-i was as popular in Japan as in his native land. (4)

Buddhism known under the name Shingon (*chen-yen* in Chinese, equivalent to Sanskrit *mantra*). These two schools became central to the aristocratic culture of the Heian court. They were the 'Buddhism of the new era'. Both men brought back from their journeys to China, which they made within a few years of each other, an esoteric form of Buddhism, to the propagation of which they devoted themselves. The two new schools of Tendai and Shingon were associated in the minds of the Heian aristocracy with exorcism and with the banishment of sickness and, in the mind of the court, with prayers for rain and for plentiful harvests, for the banishment of natural calamities, and for the protection of the state. One consequence was the creation of a new art peculiar to esoteric Buddhism (such as images of furious-looking Vidyarajas).

Towards the end of the 9th century, when word spread in Japan that the T'ang was in decline, the official missions (*kentōshi*) were discontinued, and with that the dispatch of embassies and of state-supported scholars came to an end. However, Chinese merchant vessels still came to Kyūshū to trade, and Japanese monks still went to China to study. Indeed, throughout the turbulent era of the late T'ang Age and the Five Dynasties, and right on into the Northern Sung Age, there was a continuing importation of Chinese civilization into Japan, principally over the trade routes that connected Kyūshū with the China coast south of the Yangtze; and the Heian aristocrats, who were economically secure and were addicted to a life of pleasure and luxury, were well educated in Chinese literature and doted on what they called *karamono*, 'things from Cathay'.

At the Heian court after the discontinuation of the missions to Ch'ang-an, the Chinese civilization that had been imported so long and so plentifully was digested by a peculiarly Japanese process. Then, after the invention and diffusion of the *kana* syllabary, there was a transfer of interest in Japan from Chinese prose and verse to a vernacular literature. Thanks also to the development of a Japanese style in architecture and painting, an elegant Heian civilization developed. However, there was no falling-off of the tendency of the aristocracy, the scholars, and the Buddhist clergy to admire, and almost to worship, Chinese civilization as being the senior culture.

The decline of the Heian aristocracy and the beginning of martial rule in Japan corresponds to the period in the history of China that spans the end of the Southern Sung and the beginning of Mongol rule.

In China, the historical period extending from the late T'ang Age through the Sung Age into the Yüan Age was one in which the Ch'an school of Buddhism flourished more than any of the others. Even in Japan, when once the doctrines of Ch'an (Zen) had been brought over, the arrival of Ch'an monks from China and the departure of Japanese Zen monks for China became frequent, and this interchange produced a new wave of the importation of Chinese civilization into Japan. (These developments will be treated in more detail in Chapter IX.) The scope of this wave of Chinese influence was broad. It affected architecture, painting, the cultivation of Chinese letters, and the printing of Chinese books. Japan's Zen monks set themselves to shed the skin of Indian Buddhism and to hand on the study of a Ch'an that had now become a Chinese religion. They were therefore obliged to master Chinese prose and poetry. In particular, the Zen monks studying in China, quite apart from the mastery of literary Chinese, studied ink-and-water drawing, which had developed in conjunction with the Ch'an school and which was fashionable among educated Chinese, and they brought back with them the art of portraiture. The importation of tea into Japan by Zen monks was closely connected with the importation of pottery, and this led to the development in Japan of the tea ceremony and, in imitation of Chinese styles, of the manufacture of pottery as well. In the hundred years known as the Warring States period *(Sengoku)*, which followed the establishment of the first military government in 1467, Japanese culture was preserved by the literary scholarship of the so-called 'Five Mountains' (i.e., of the five leading Zen monasteries, *gozan bungaku*). This was focused on the training of these monks in Chinese culture.

In the second half of the 17th century, during the Tokugawa era, the Neo-Confucian doctrines of Chu Hsi, which had been gradually making their way into Japan thanks to her contacts with Ming China, became the official doctrine of the Government. As a consequence Neo-Confucianism spread from Edo into the feudal fiefs. The doctrine of Wang Yang-ming also made its way into Japan, where it found some students in the educated class. In recent times, Japan has achieved rapid progress by hastening to adopt the culture of Europe and America rather than by continuing to import Chinese civilization. But until the 18th century, it is true to say that she achieved most of her development through the vigorous and uninterrupted adoption of Chinese civilization.

p 182–
(24)
p 232–
(12–14)

p 182–
(26)

Vietnam: the refuge

74 (4)
Vietnam occupies the eastern part of the Indo-Chinese peninsula. It was known to the Chinese as *Yüeh-nan* (việtnam) or *An-nan* (annam). Since it is part of the same land-mass as the Kwangtung region of south-east China, and since it is also in a region which had maritime links with China, there are grounds for supposing that Chinese culture on a high level was making its way steadily into Vietnam from an early date. At any rate, the power of the unified (and unifying) Empire of the Ch'in extended southward as far as North Vietnam, and then, under the Han, the whole country became Chinese territory, organized in three commanderies, all of them governed by Chinese residents. When once this political development had taken place, the movement of Chinese immigrants into the area and the spread of Chinese civilization within it became rapid and intense.

It is true that the ancient Chinese civilization had originated in the Yellow River basin and had developed mainly in north China, and that the cultural development of the south was comparatively slow, and therefore the propagation of the Chinese civilization in Vietnam was not comparable to its steady and uninterrupted penetration of Korea. However, Vietnam, as well as Korea, was part of the East Asian continental land-mass; and, towards the end of the Han Age, i.e. at the end of the 2nd and at the beginning of the 3rd century, the collapse of the Han regime moved a number of Chinese intellectuals to migrate from the troubled areas into the comparative peace of northern Vietnam. They brought with them both Confucianism and Taoism, and it is thanks to them that, in Vietnam, the Chinese form of Buddhism too became an object of study, and of belief, alongside forms of Buddhism that had spread from India.

From the Age of the Three Kingdoms through the period of division between North and South, the court established to the south of the Yangtze by Chinese refugees rivalled the non-Chinese court in the North, and consequently Chinese civilization made rapid strides to the south of the Yangtze during this period. The ethnically Chinese government that had been established to the south of the river, and the educated and propertied class associated with it, gradually increased their contacts with Vietnam and with other countries opening on to the South Seas. This produced cultural exchanges. A majority of Vietnam's ruling and intellectual class consisted of Chinese, who were naturally at home in the Chinese language, spoken and written, and the natives strove to win social stature by adopting a Chinese way of life.

175 (6)
Consequently Vietnam was drawn into the Chinese cultural sphere, where the Chinese written word held sway, and there was a cultural development there on Chinese lines. In the T'ang Age the cumulative effect of the prolonged process of sinification raised Vietnam to a still higher level of Chinese civilization.

Among the Vietnamese who went to the T'ang capital to study, there were some who took the Chinese civil service examinations. Some even emerged from the examinations as *chin shih* (examinees qualified by passing one of the two most common types of civil service tests) to serve China in an official capacity. A Japanese resident scholar, known by the name Ch'ao Heng, won a high place in these examinations, and he was appointed to an

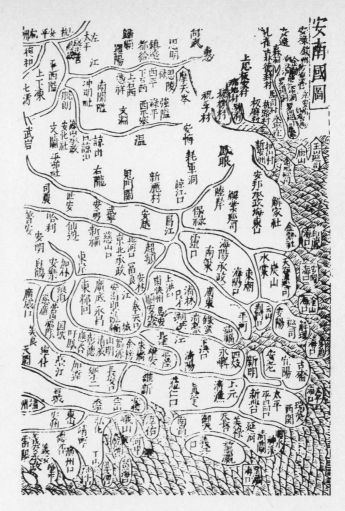

From the earliest times Vietnam (or Annam) belonged to the Chinese cultural sphere, and her ruling class was often in fact of Chinese origin. This map of the Mekong delta is from an encyclopaedia published in the early 17th century. (5)

official position by the T'ang Government, but, on his homeward voyage to Japan, his ship carried him adrift to the coast of Vietnam; and the T'ang Government then appointed him Protector-General of Annam.

The rise of the Chinese standard of living in the T'ang Age led to the importation of many things from Vietnam that were highly valued by the Chinese, such as tortoiseshell, pearl, coral, peacocks, rhinoceros-horn, and ivory. For these reasons, in addition to bureaucrats and intellectuals, merchants also went to Vietnam from China, and this trade stimulated cultural exchanges. These Chinese merchants won a foothold in Vietnam from which they would not be dislodged; and, in the society that they formed there, their traditional customs and beliefs, as well as the material apparatus of their traditional culture, continued to have currency. Through their efforts, shrines to Confucius and Kuan Yü, as well as halls in honour of Avalokiteśvara (Kuan-yin, quanâm), were built. The result was the spread of a syncretistic religion that included elements of Confucianism, Buddhism, and Taoism. Both during and after the period of direct Chinese rule, which extended from the Han Age into the T'ang Age, there were frequent changes of

1 The Bova or true King of Tonqueen.
2 The Literadoes in their China Habit.
3 The Captain of ye Life Guard riding upon
  an Elephant.
4 an Ordinary Captain on Horse back.
5. Soldiers of Extraordinary Stature.
6 The Umbrella's and Fans.

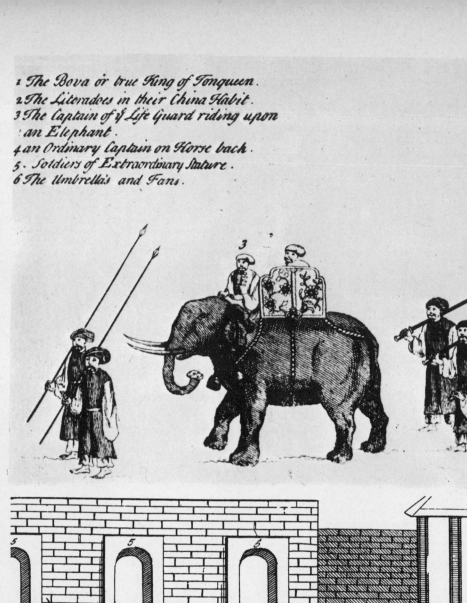

1. The King.
2. four Literadoes
3. two Literadoes under Umbrella's in the first Court
4 Officers that keep the watch in ye second Court
5. the severals rooms where ye Examiners sit
6. persons that are Tryed to be Chosen
7. the Guard of the first Court

192

This is when the Bova goes to Bless the Ground According to their Annual Superstition, Called Can-Ja, or Bova-dee-yan, which happens Usually in our ffeb:[ry]

An English travel book of 1732 provides valuable evidence for Vietnamese life of that period. Above: the king of Tongking—shaded by the umbrellas—takes part in a religious ceremony. The four men at the rear are scholars wearing Chinese dress. Left: Vietnamese sitting Chinese-style examinations. The candidates are immured in cells, watched by two invigilators. The king himself sits on a dais to the right. (6, 7)

government in Vietnam, but the majority of the rebels, including those who were rebelling against the central Chinese power with the aim of establishing an independent state, were themselves of Chinese ancestry, and the local governing class was imbued with Chinese civilization, which, in their hands, was long maintained and preserved.

74 (4)
In 1802, the ruling Nguyen (nguen) family conquered the whole territory and the leader designated himself 'emperor', but the Manchus 'enfeoffed' him as the 'king of Vietnam' and thus maintained China's status as the suzerain power and compelled the Vietnamese to abide 75 (7) by their tradition of friendly submission to China. In recent times, under French rule, the Chinese script was abandoned in favour of the Roman, a vigorous programme of Christian proselytization was pursued, and, in general, the acculturation of the Vietnamese people to the Western civilization progressed at great speed. Even so, the old-established power of the Chinese did not decline, and in 1936 a census conducted under French auspices gave the figure 326,000 for the number of the resident Chinese. The true figure was estimated to be 400,000.

Tibet: between two worlds

Tibet is adjoined on the east by two Chinese provinces, p 173 (1) Szechwan and Kansu. The Ti and the Ch'iang, two p 174 (2) peoples who were pastoral nomads in the Han Age, are said to be the ancestors of the present-day Tibetans. Tibet was unified politically early in the 7th century, at a date at which China, too, had only just been re-unified under the T'ang dynasty. T'ai-tsung, the second T'ang em- p 174 (3) peror, sought to conciliate the Tibetans by giving the Princess Wen-ch'eng to the Tibetan king in marriage. Queen Wen-ch'eng arranged for the importation into Tibet of Chinese silks and for the invitation of Chinese scholars, whose services were needed for dealing with documents written in the Chinese characters. Eventually Chinese Buddhism, too, made its way into Tibet, and some of the Buddhist scriptures that had been translated into Chinese were now translated from Chinese into Tibetan.

However, a Nepalese princess had also been brought to Tibet as a consort for the king, and her arrival was followed by an active propagation of an Indian form of Buddhism, introduced by way of Nepal, from Bengal. Then, in the 7th century, a Tibetan script was devised on the pattern of an Indian script; the Buddhist scriptures were translated into the Tibetan language in this script; and this gave an impetus to the reception, in Tibet, of Buddhism in its Indian instead of its Chinese form. Even so, the Tibetan king's Chinese marriage alliance brought with it some benefits for both Tibet and China. One result was the importation into Tibet of the material products of Chinese civilization at the time of the T'ang dynasty. A second result was the establishment of peaceful

193

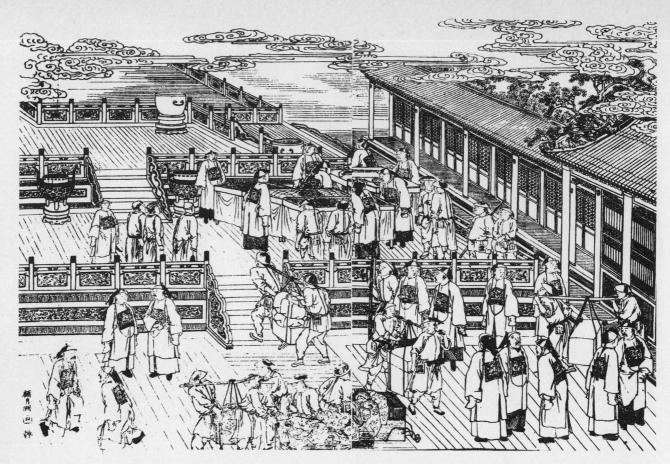

After a number of military interventions by the Chinese, Tibet was brought into the Ch'ing empire. But for long before this, the Tibetans had sent tribute missions to China. This late 19th-century illustration shows the arrival at the Imperial Palace in Peking of a Tibetan mission and their tribute goods. (8)

relations between Tibet and China. This contributed greatly to the development of Tibetan culture, and a statue of Princess Wen-ch'eng was worshipped in Tibet in recognition of her cultural services.

Early in the 8th century there was another marriage alliance between the T'ang dynasty and the royal family of Tibet, and, thanks to the arrival of this second Chinese bride, the Princess Chin-ch'eng, the importation into Tibet of the material products of Chinese civilization continued. But from the second half of the 7th century onwards the Tibetans became politically ambitious and

aggressive. They invaded and occupied the T'ang Empire's territory in what is now Sinkiang, and they then extended their military offensive to Ch'ing-hai, Szechwan, and Kansu as well. After the middle of the 8th century the Tibetans took advantage of the domestic crisis that had then overtaken the T'ang regime. A Tibetan army invaded Shensi and even occupied Ch'ang-an for a time. This military aggression had cultural effects on Tibet. The Chinese civilization of Kansu and Shensi, particularly the over-ripe 8th-century Chinese Buddhism, with its admixture of cultural elements from the west, was adopted by members of the Tibetan Saṃgha during the Tibetan occupation and was brought back to Tibet by them. Yet the mainstream of Tibetan Buddhism, like the Tibetan script, was still Indian, not Chinese, and consequently the Chinese Buddhism of the T'ang Age was never able to win in Tibet the hold that it won in Korea and Japan.

VIII FEUDAL JAPAN

Politics and society from the eighth century to 1868

CHARLES D. SHELDON

*Let me fall into the Buddhist hell; let
me be punished by the Shintō deities;
I have no will except to serve my liege
lord with utmost loyalty.*

Hagakure, an anonymous work of 1710
(in *Iwanami Bunko*, 2305-6, p. 114)

A chain of mountainous islands far from the land mass of Asia, Japan was clearly marked for a destiny different from China's. She was secure from invasion (even the Mongols, elsewhere irresistible, were beaten back), so that her history is to an almost unique degree self-contained. But at the same time her geography made centralized government difficult to achieve. The forces which in China operated to create it were absent in Japan: farming had to be small-scale; there was no need for river control or extensive canal works; nor for a standing army. China, during most of its history, submitted to an all-powerful emperor and his omnipresent civil service. But Japan, after a valiant attempt to create a similar bureaucratic state under the emperor, ultimately, after a process of centuries, became a complex of feudal fiefs. The emperor's political powers were delegated to a military authority, the Shogun, to whom the rulers of these fiefs owed allegiance, while enjoying varying degrees of autonomy in their own fiefs. In the Tokugawa period (1600–1868), a more bureaucratic form of government was gradually imposed, but local loyalties, born in the isolated valleys of rural Japan, remained strong.

In this artistic bird's-eye view by Kensai Joshin (1820), we are looking west from above the Pacific Coast, over the mountains of central Japan toward the Japan Sea and Korea in the far distance. As castles were the most conspicuous man-made features of the landscape of Tokugawa Japan, they are shown and identified by the names of the castle town. Besides these, the provinces, principal mountain peaks, islands and harbours are identified. The Shogun's castle at Edo (present Tokyo) can be seen, with its two keeps towering over the top of Edo Bay near the bottom right corner, and to the left of it, actually about seventy miles away, can be seen the white cone of Mount Fuji. Under the Tokugawa policy of enforced isolation, shipbuilding was limited almost entirely to small sailing boats for fishing and for the very active coastal shipping. They can be seen dotting the coastal waters. (1)

198

The foundation of Kyoto, then called Heian, in AD 794 gave a name to a period of almost four centuries of relatively stable government, initially modelled largely on that of T'ang China. Kyoto remained the imperial capital for over a thousand years, until 1868, but the earliest extant picture of it (left) is comparatively late, dating from about 1520. It provides an extremely detailed record, every shrine and temple, almost every house and shop, being depicted realistically. This section shows buildings of the palace, surrounded by humbler dwellings. It is the day of the Gion festival, in July. Right: an audience hall from the Heian period, rebuilt as an exact duplicate after a fire in 1855, as part of the Kyoto Imperial Palace. (2, 4)

Real power resided with the emperor for only a short time. By the middle of the 9th century it had been taken from him by the Fujiwara clan. The years 857–1160, much of the Heian period, are sometimes called the Fujiwara period. This detail from a scroll (below left) shows a principal founder of the family's political predominance, Fujiwara Yoshifusa (804–872), advising the emperor, who is seated on a cushion. The man who seems to be eavesdropping is probably a commander of the imperial bodyguard. (3)

Land was wealth and power throughout Japan's history until the mid-19th century. In the 7th century all land theoretically belonged to the state, periodic allotments being made to peasant families to spread labour efficiently on the land and assure a regular tax revenue for the imperial government. But in 743 reclaimed land – land converted into irrigated rice-fields (right) – became the private property of the reclaimer. Already, official positions were becoming hereditary, and the distinction between 'public' and 'private' land had begun to break down. (5)

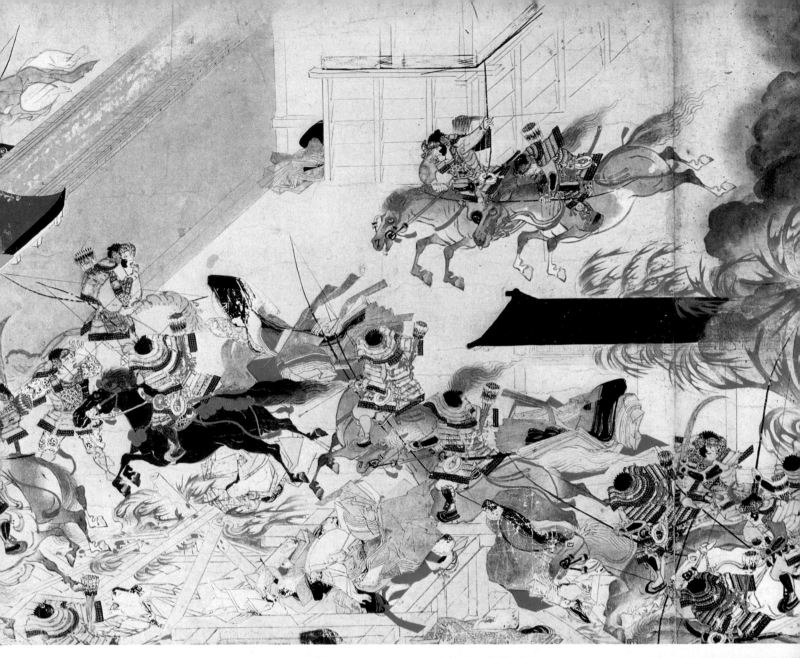

Civil war broke out in 1156 as the result of power rivalries within both the imperial and the Fujiwara families. A series of battles was fought in Heian itself. A famous scroll of the 13th century (above) shows the burning of the Sanjō Palace. The outcome was the rise to power of the Taira, then of the Minamoto clan. (6)

The military class, later called samurai, grew out of the troubled conditions of the 11th and 12th centuries. Local clans began to rely for protection on professional warriors. Left: a warrior's household about 1270, defended by ditches and fences. Right: a samurai commander in full battle array, dressed in flexible armour and carrying bow and arrow. The fan was used for signalling, to position and encourage subordinates. (7, 8)

The Shogunate was founded by Minamoto Yoritomo (above) soon after he defeated the Taira clan in 1185. The emperor, surrounded by Fujiwara administrators, could grant honours, but Yoritomo kept the reins of power. (9)

The emperors accepted the situation, though there were occasional attempts to restore their authority. In 1221 Go-Toba (above) rose against the Shogunal Regent but was quickly defeated and forced to go into exile. (10)

The invincible Mongols, having established their empire over China and most of Central Asia, invaded Japan in 1274 and again in 1281. On both occasions they established bridgeheads and were finally repulsed not by superior arms but by providential typhoons, hailed as *kamikaze* (divine winds) by the Japanese. In this painting (below) the Japanese warrior Suenaga boards a Mongol ship during the second invasion. (11)

The rewards of service to the Shogun included rights, often controlling rights, in estates taken from his enemies. These new landowners joined the Shogun's direct vassals, although legally the Shogun remained merely the emperor's delegate. Rights in land could be conferred by anyone holding them, including the emperor. This detail (above) from a 13th-century scroll shows a man reading to his family the document granting him rights in an estate. He is an artist, serving at the imperial court, and the estate is in Iyo province. (12)

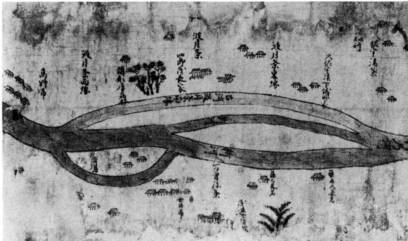

How such an estate would have looked is shown in this contemporary map. It is managed, and probably largely controlled, by a wealthy local family, and contains two markets near the river, the house of a metal-smith, and, somewhat more imposing, that of the land manager (*jitō*). (13)

203

In the fields and towns life went on, not for long disrupted by the tensions and struggles at the top. Left: the ceremony of rice-planting. The women in the centre have brought young shoots to be transplanted in underwater furrows. Near the top, local musicians and dancers celebrate the occasion. Above: a medieval market, the stall-keepers squatting under their roofs, on a market day. While three swordsmen threaten the monk Ippen, left centre, merchants are busy selling hats (at bottom), textiles (upper left), rice and fish (upper right), and pottery (centre right). (14, 15)

The armourer (above right), working on the floor above his shop, puts together one of the intricate suits of samurai armour. Light, flexible and strong, it consisted of hundreds of narrow, tough leather thongs, dyed with bright colours. They were tied together tightly and often incorporated steel strips. (16)

Fabric printers (right): the woman at the bottom dyes the cloth. Behind her a man prints it section by section with a hand-held block. In the foreground, a strip is being stretched to dry on tenterhooks. Above them strips of cloth hang up to dry. (17)

The cloistered emperor is a figure peculiar to Japan. As far back as 1086 emperors had retired into Buddhist monasteries. Above: the retired Emperor Hanazono, aged forty-four, in monastic dress, painted in 1338. His head is shaven, and he holds a Buddhist rosary. (18)

A new Shogunate was established by Ashikaga Takauji (above) in 1338, and lasted until 1573. Many of the Ashikaga Shoguns were able and resourceful men, but they found it increasingly difficult to control the local war-lords ruling virtually independent fiefs. (19)

War became almost endemic after 1467. This was the *sengoku* period, the Warring States, the age of the samurai. The local lords equipped themselves with superb castles, half fortress, half palace (above: Himeji, rebuilt and greatly enlarged in 1577). They would be defended by mounted samurai (right) each attended by retainers. (21, 22)

The arts of peace flourished paradoxically in this age of turmoil. Such typically Japanese achievements as landscape gardening, Nō drama, flower arrangement and the tea ceremony all originated at this time. Landscape painting reached a new sophistication with artists like Sesshū (left). (20)

From the competing war-lords of the late 16th century one man emerged triumphant: Tokugawa Ieyasu (above, in procession with his escort). By 1615 he had unified the country, created a government which balanced feudalism against centralism and achieved the peace which everyone desired. It was to last for 250 years. After Ieyasu's death in 1616, his son, the Shogun Ietada, strengthened his position by an imperial alliance. In June 1620 his daughter married the Emperor Gomino'o; part of the wedding procession is shown opposite. (23, 25)

With the new regime came a new capital – Edo (below), now called Tokyo, which within a few decades grew from a small fishing village to one of the world's great cities. The Sumida river, which intersects it, is crossed by several bridges, among them the Nihon Bashi (Bridge of Japan). In the background rises Mount Fuji. (24)

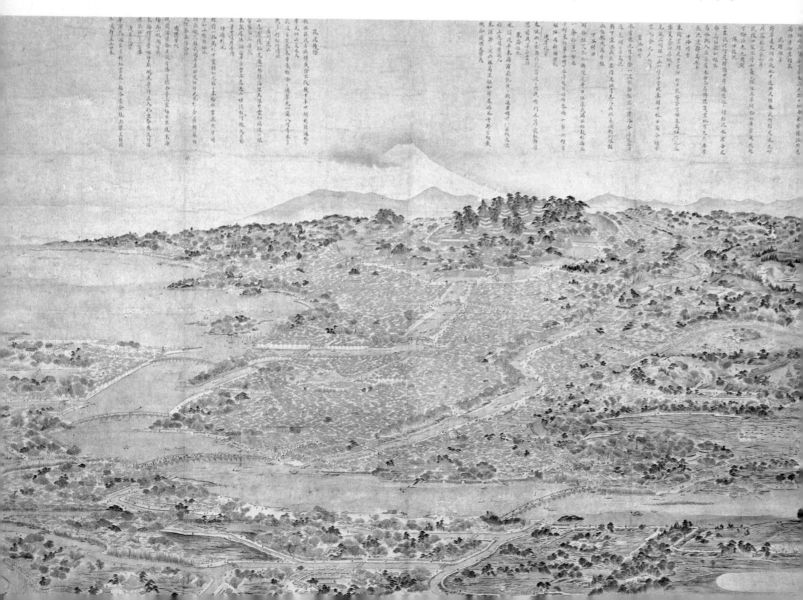

The power of the daimyō was limited in a variety of ingenious ways, the most effective being the *sankin kotai*. This required each daimyō to visit Edo at regular intervals and live there in ceremonial splendour and at ruinous expense. Here, on a 17th-century screen, is shown a daimyō's journey to or from the capital with about a thousand attendants. (26)

The samurai too (left) were eventually unable to maintain the elegant standard of living which their old code had demanded. (27)

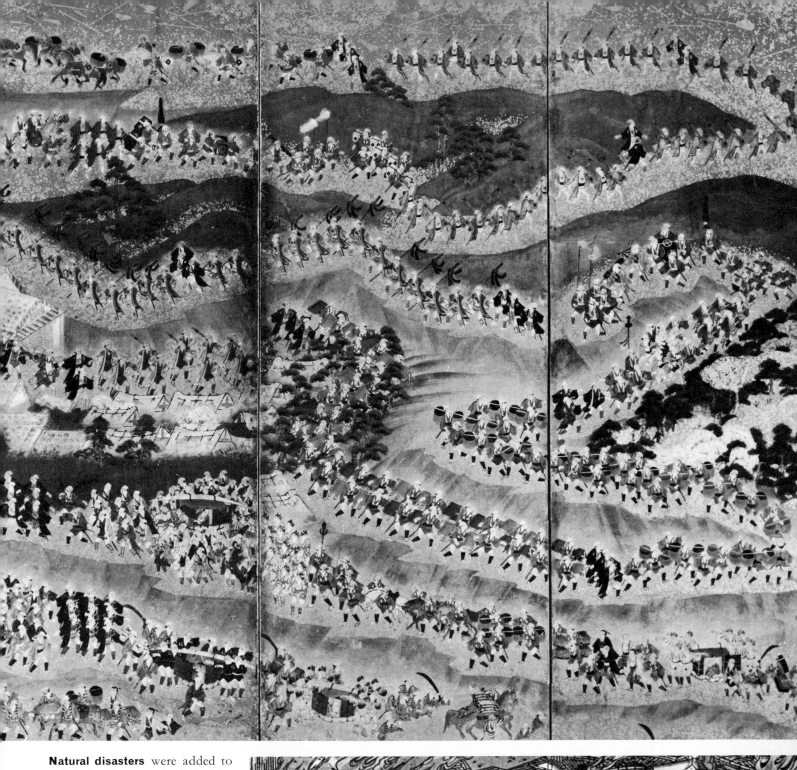

Natural disasters were added to political and economic difficulties as the Tokugawa period drew to its close. In the late 18th century harvests were bad. Many regions were on the verge of starvation, but the system was too rigid to allow new solutions. Then in 1855 two serious earthquakes struck Japan, killing thousands. Edo was set on fire and its flimsy wooden houses burnt like dry grass. Woodblock illustrations in occasional broadsheets of the time (right) gave vivid day to day impressions of the disaster. (28)

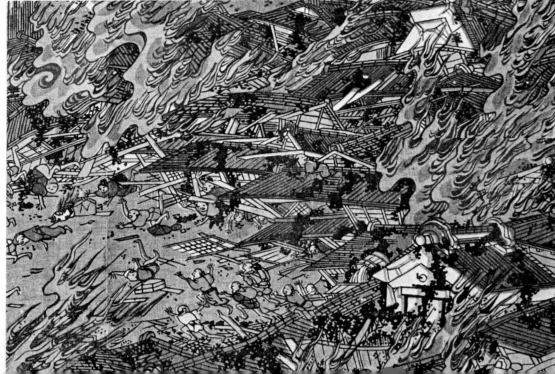

Agriculture remained the basic occupation of the people. Left: food is brought to workers in the fields. But the gradual shift from a barter to a money economy, and the growth of capitalism, brought about a widening gulf between rich and poor, with the poor peasants in the least privileged position. (29)

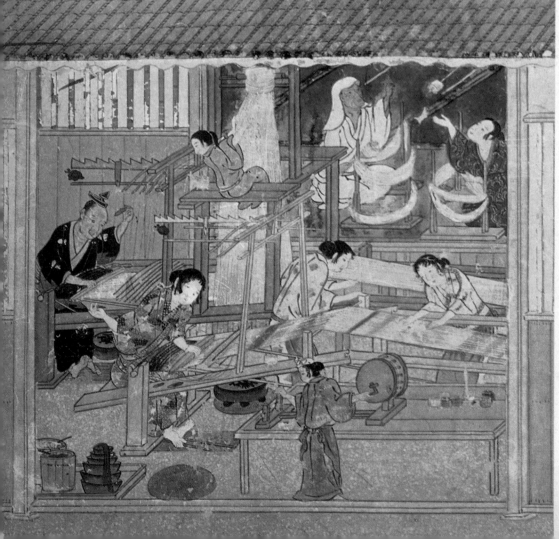

Industry, hitherto operating in small-scale units (left: a weaving shop with three looms), was now exploited by the new moneyed classes, making the old social ranks and values meaningless. The Shogunate, created to maintain the status quo, had no means of controlling the new world that was coming into existence. The opening up of Japan by the Americans in 1853 did not create but certainly intensified the problem, leading to the Meiji Restoration and the total re-organization of the state, to be described in Chapter XII. (30)

Politics and society from the eighth century
to 1868

CHARLES D. SHELDON

The crest of the Ashikaga family, who controlled the Shogunate from 1338 to 1573. Family crests, often incorporating flower and plant designs, were highly regarded in Japan as symbols of ancestral honour and prestige; many are still in use today. (1)

THE ORGANIZATION of a feudal system on a nationwide basis, in which a degree of regulation and standardization was imposed by a central authority, took place in England under Henry II (r. 1154–89), and in France under Philippe Auguste (r. 1180–1223). It is a curious fact of history that in Japan at the same time, entirely independently, another remarkable leader was doing essentially the same thing.

In 1185, Yoritomo of the Minamoto clan accomplished the final defeat of the rival Taira clan. His *go-kenin* (housemen, direct vassals) throughout much of Japan were linked to his military government (*bakufu*, or Shogunate) in Kamakura, a few miles south of present-day Tokyo, by bonds of loyalty strengthened first by a series of victories and then by grants of rights in land. With the elimination of his enemies, Yoritomo was in a position to exert an unchallenged military domination over the country.

It is no doubt convenient to mark the beginning of the feudal period in Japan by the date of 1185. It is also somewhat misleading, both because feudalism had been growing for many years before 1185, and because it was some four hundred years after 1185 before a truly national government, still a feudal one, was achieved. The growth of feudalism, at least from the early years of the Heian period (794–1185) from small beginnings in northeastern Honshū, where the local clans confronted hostile Ainu guerrilla fighters, continued through the Tokugawa period (1600–1868), when a higher degree of centralization, with a more impersonal bureaucratic system of government, was imposed within an essentially feudal framework.

We will not enter here into the controversy as to whether Japan, during the nearly seven centuries of her domination by a class of mounted warriors who came to be known as samurai, can properly be called feudal. Most authorities accept that the similarities to the feudalisms of western Europe are far more striking than the differences. It will be apparent from what has already been said that one of the differences was Japan's very slow institutional growth, in which changes of form continued for some seven centuries.

The debt to China

After the imposition of a Chinese-style imperial system of government modelled on the powerful Sui (589–618) and T'ang (618–907) dynasties, the very gradual decline, especially of the economic base, of the bureaucratic structure centred on the Emperor, stretching into the 16th century, is a striking feature of Japan's history. The lack of any military conquest, either internal or from the outside, meant that the reforms undertaken in the attempt to remodel Japan on Chinese lines could not be imposed simply by force. Owing to the delicate balance of power among the important *uji*, lineage groups, or clans, reforms had to be introduced gradually, and with caution so as not to interfere too much with vested interests.

In contrast to the great agricultural expanses of China, Japan's topography, with most agricultural communities in small valleys more or less isolated by mountains, had fostered a kind of clan localism. The strong tradition of local co-operative self-sufficiency, solidarity, and self-rule was an obstacle to the thoroughgoing centralization inspired by the Chinese example. Most Japanese historians characterize this early clan localism—with a degree of control exerted by regional groupings of territorial lords, the most important either related, or loosely allied, to the imperial clan—as 'proto-feudal'. The almost imperceptible slipping into feudalism after, and even during, the experience of a fairly effective centralized government under the emperor, can be seen as a sliding back into indigenous modes more adapted to the social and economic realities of Japan.

There was no need in Japan for the vast government projects for river control, large-scale canals, and other immense public works which had since early times necessitated strong central government in China, and had also led to widespread acceptance of it. Nor did Japan require a national army for defence against external enemies. The most immediate need was for a government

p 197 (1)

The rich fishing grounds off the coast of Japan have been an abundant source of protein and raw materials since prehistoric times. Left: fishermen surround and harpoon a whale. (2)

Right: plan of the Chōdōin or audience hall of the imperial palace at Heian (now Kyoto), c. AD 800. The Daigo-kuden or hall of state (on the right) is reached through the forecourt and main courtyard, containing twelve isolated halls, used on state occasions. (3)

sufficiently centralized to prevent the continuance of the endemic struggles for power among the powerful clans. In a more positive sense, the reforms were designed to strengthen the country in the way exemplified by the Korean kingdom of Silla, which had demonstrated the feasibility of becoming a successfully sinicized state, had expelled the Japanese from their colony in Korea, unifying the Korean peninsula, and had reached new heights of prosperity and culture. The reforms incorporated the more powerful clan chiefs into a new civil aristocracy surrounding the Emperor, and most of the less important chiefs were appointed to local government posts. Although ultimately deprived of much of their former economic, political, and military autonomy, they obtained compensating benefits which in the long run proved economically and socially advantageous, among them stability and peace. Moreover, the centralization of the country under the Emperor was the first step towards the studied borrowing and effective adaptation to Japanese needs of the superior Chinese civilization.

Historians commonly contrast the great success of the Japanese in the arts with their political failure to create a strong imperial-bureaucratic state like that of the T'ang which could maintain control against the centrifugal forces of feudalism. It is true that, in a surprisingly short time, Japanese were creating works of art no less great than those of the Chinese, and developing unique features of humanity and humour, as well as greater simplicity, which soon differentiated subsequent Japanese art from the usually more objective and monumental Chinese counterparts. It is also true that ideals and techniques of political and economic organization imported from a very different geographical, social, and intellectual environment proved to be far more difficult to transplant. But when one considers the obstacles that the Japanese centralizers and reformers faced, what is surprising is, not that their efforts ultimately failed, but that they achieved so much.

After the establishment in 710 of an imposing capital at Nara, and in 794 of the even more impressive capital city of Kyoto, then called Heian, Japan enjoyed some four centuries of generally peaceful, stable, and enlightened Emperor-centred government, which contrasted greatly with the pre-reform instability and weakness. With the benefit of hindsight, it is easy to criticize the Japanese for not having sufficiently adapted Chinese institutions and ideas to fit the different Japanese situation, and for having undermined some reforms by making compromises and exceptions which weakened their effects. But this is chiefly because we know that both the economic and the political reforms ultimately broke down. To judge by the general tone of much of the literature of Nara times, the period of most active borrowing, enthusiasm was not confined to the great advances in cultural life, but embraced the new order in general. However, the first literature which flowered in Japan was a literature of the court nobility, and this enthusiasm may not have been shared by the bulk of the population, mostly hard-working peasants whose livelihoods, very close to a bare subsistence, were not much improved.

p 198 (2,4)

Private versus public land

Until recent years, Japan's economy was overwhelmingly agricultural, and social power was based largely on landholding. As Sir George Sansom has put it, 'Land is the key to political history in Japan, at almost every point.' 'Through the heraldic battle cries and the lofty speeches of feudal warriors there can be heard the persistent murmur of Property! Property!' Perhaps the most important and fundamental aspect of the superimposition of a Chinese-style centralized government on Japan was the land allotment system, which was integrated with a new, uniform method of taxation consisting of taxes in kind (agricultural and handicraft products), money (much rarer), unpaid labour, and military conscription, and with a continuing effort to bring land under the Imperial (public) domain. The gradual replacement of this system by private proprietorships (shōen), involving multiple ownership and more and more exemptions from taxation,

214

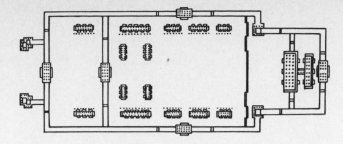

was a step towards feudalism. The second step was the growth of feudal fiefs defended by military, family-like groups who succeeded in cutting off taxes and rents due to the proprietors—mostly absentee officials, landlords, and protectors—and eventually in consolidating defensible units of land completely under their control.

The land allotment system adopted from China was perhaps the most complex government-managed system of land tenure in history. It represented as sweeping a reform, on paper, as the land reform carried out after 1945 during the period of the American occupation. No longer were lands and peasant cultivators to be considered as privately owned; they were to belong in principle to the central government, an impersonal state. This Chinese idea ran counter to deeply imbedded commitments to family or clan interests, and to the strongly entrenched hereditary principle, and was never really accepted in Japan. The new uniform system, with land surveys, censuses, allotment, and periodic reallotment of land to peasant families in accordance with the number of 'mouths' in the family prevented plots from being added to and kept as family property. But it was gradually applied to most of the rice lands of Japan as a rationalization of agriculture. It proved to be an efficient means of spreading technology and agricultural labour uniformly on the land. The extent of the application of the allotment system to Japan is still a subject of controversy, but recent field work has discovered widespread remnants of the equal-sized fields used in allotments from southern Kyūshū up to north of the Kantō plain.

The allotment system was applied initially to the extensive lands of the Imperial clan, and this served both for demonstration effect and as a means for training technicians and administrators. An opportunity came to expand the area of public domain when a succession dispute broke out after the death of the Emperor Tenchi in 671. The Emperor Temmu came to power as the result of a considerable military victory, and succeeded for the first time in converting lands of the upper nobility into public domain. This system reached the remoter parts of the country only much later; in Ōsumi and Satsuma, in Kyūshū, it was initiated a century and a half after the reforms had begun. Long before this time, however, the system had begun to break down elsewhere. From the beginning, 'garden lands', and lands set aside to provide income for the officialdom, were exempted from the usual taxation, and came to be regarded virtually as private property. Buddhist temples and Shintō shrines could own land which might be tax-exempt, and Emperors and court nobles were particularly lavish with gifts of lands to their religious retainers in their clan temples and shrines.

99 (5)

These were important precedents, but the practice of reclaiming land—that is, converting it to irrigated rice fields—probably had an even greater effect on the beginnings and the continued growth of private ownership. Land reclaimed by the government remained public land, but from early in the Nara period, privately reclaimed land became the property of the reclaimers for stated periods. In 724, rice land reclaimed from pond or marsh was declared to be the property of the reclaimers for three generations; from unirrigated fields to paddy, for one generation. But when the period of public ownership approached, owners would resort to exploitative methods, including neglect of irrigation systems, which could ruin the fields before they entered the public domain. In 743, privately reclaimed land became the reclaimers' permanent property, not subject to allotment and reallotment. Only the prospect of unhampered ownership could persuade people to undertake costly reclamation projects. The government seldom had funds for them, and government projects suffered from abuses, inefficiency, and high costs. The pressure of population and the need to employ peasants made it necessary to bring more land into cultivation. Keen competition to reclaim land ensued, and this increased the percentage of private lands and peasants who preferred to be tenants on private estates than to remain on public land. But the process was slow. Professor Hall has estimated that, as late as 1086, rice lands in Bizen consisted of roughly three-fourths public domain, only one-fourth private proprietorships. But with public office becoming hereditary, public domain in the next century was being treated very much like 'public *shōen*'. (*Government and Local Power in Japan, 500–1700*, pp. 123–4.) This means that multiple ownership, which did not at first exclude the central government, was extended to the public domain.

The reasons for the failure of the land allotment system are too numerous to detail here, but ultimately the personal rule of man replaced the impersonal law of the bureaucracy, and the system proved unsuitable to Japan, where the cultivator had such a deep attachment to the small plot which he and his family cultivated. The family, moreover, was thought of as being a continuum, residing in a particular village, on a particular piece of land, and the present generation's principal responsibility, to maintain and increase the family's landholdings, prosperity, and social standing, was not so much to itself as to the ancestors and to the generations to come.

Private versus public power

While land rights were finding their way into private hands, the formal machinery of government, although preserved in its entirety, was being bypassed by private institutions of the clans, including even the Imperial clan, and the great temples and shrines. Like the reigning Emperor himself, the central bureaucracy established by the reforms became more and more ceremonial, and remained a convenient source of honours and an organ to legitimize the emerging private centres of power which were at first economic, political, and judicial, but which became military and feudal as well.

During the middle and late Heian period, from about 857 to 1160, actual control of the government was in the hands of a series of heads of the powerful Fujiwara clan, and the Emperors reigned, but no longer ruled. During this 'Fujiwara period' the long process of naturalization

p 198 (3)

of the Chinese culture reached its culmination. The enthusiastic borrowing, which had become increasingly selective, came to an end, and official contacts with China were permitted to lapse after 838. Japanese classical culture reached a high point in the brilliant and sophisticated Heian court, producing such masterpieces as *The Tale of Genji* by the court lady known as Murasaki Shikibu. This poetic evocation of the refined court life of the early 11th century remains an embodiment of the Japanese aristocratic ideal in which people's lives were judged by the art in them, according to the strict canons of what Sansom has called 'the rule of taste'.

p 248 (8–10)

Historically, the Imperial clan never enjoyed complete political control, having always to rely for support upon important clans and, in the Nara period, on Buddhist institutions as well. The Fujiwara clan came spectacularly to the front of the political stage as the principal movers of the *coup d'état* of 645 which led to the Taika reforms. After this, Fujiwara leaders were prominent among the chief ministers and often married Fujiwara women into the Imperial clan. But for about two hundred years the Imperial clan succeeded in holding the balance of power. The effort of the court to escape the powerful Buddhist influence in Nara was supported by the Fujiwara clan, and the move to Heian, coupled with legal limitations on Buddhist establishments, served to eliminate this influence. The Fujiwara clan gained greatly from this, and continued to consolidate both its economic and its political power, relying on the right, which it acquired, and then monopolized, of supplying consorts to the Emperors. As grandfather or father-in-law to the Emperor, the principal Fujiwara leader could expect to control the Emperor before his coming of age, and to influence, if not dominate, him even after. In this the Fujiwara leaders had strong support from an ancient matrilineal element of family tradition. An aristocrat, who usually had two or three consorts, in addition to a principal wife, lived with none of them, but visited them in their own separate residences, which remained the property of these women or their parents. The children were under the care and responsibility of the maternal grandparents. Thus most Emperors were brought up by the Fujiwara family, in the family residence, and government business became very much of a Fujiwara family affair.

The transformation of the Fujiwara grandfather or father-in-law from loyal servant of the Emperor to his master in political affairs was a very personal matter, and it is not known precisely when it happened. But in 857 Fujiwara Yoshifusa became Grand Minister, and in the following year he became the first person outside the Imperial clan to take the title of regent. The next step was for his successor, Mototsune, to continue to act as regent even for adult Emperors, a position which he formalized in 880 by creating for himself the title of Kampaku.

p 198 (3)

Later in the Fujiwara period, Emperors found two ways of challenging the Fujiwara political monopoly, in an effort to regain something of the Imperial prerogatives. Both moves demonstrated the feeling that the loss of these prerogatives had been associated with the depletion of the public domain, which was the economic base for the Imperial structure.

The first move was the establishment in 1069 of a Records Office by the Emperor Go-Sanjō, whose mother was not a Fujiwara, in an attempt to halt the proliferation of privately held lands *(shōen)* by confiscating all those formed before 1045, and all others which lacked valid legal documents. This had scant success, since the Fujiwara chief simply replied that if there was anything wrong with the clan's documents, he would set it right. Largely as a result of this failure, the Imperial clan, for reasons of self-preservation, joined more actively in the competition for the acquisition of *shōen*.

The second move proved to be destructive of the Fujiwara monopoly of control both over the Emperor and over members of the Fujiwara clan itself, but to little purpose. This was the institution in 1086 of cloister government. The Emperor retired, freeing himself from the considerable burden of ceremonial observances, and entered Buddhist orders, taking along with him interests in *shōen* belonging to the Imperial clan. The cloistered ex-Emperor then proceeded to use his influence as father of the Emperor, attempting, with some success, to rule through him in the Fujiwara manner. In this he relied on the strengthening of the patriarchal clan tradition, and he acted as *de facto* head of the Imperial clan. With a strong economic base, he brought into his administration able members of other clans and of Fujiwara branch families who no longer relied on the Fujiwara clan chief for advancement. The result was a decline in Fujiwara power, prestige, and solidarity, and a confusion of authority, especially when, presently, there were actually two cloistered Emperors.

p 206

Warrior rulers: the Shoguns at Kamakura

When a succession dispute broke out in 1156, the cloistered Emperor was on one side, the reigning Emperor on the other, and there were Fujiwara members on both sides. The rival military clans, the Taira and Minamoto, were called in to settle the matter, and they fought in Heian a series of battles called the Hōgen and Heiji Insurrections, in 1156 and 1160, from which the Taira emerged temporarily as the military masters of the capital and, rather unexpectedly, of the organs of government as well. Typically, the Emperors, the cloistered Emperors, and the Fujiwara clan, with their administrative organs, were not swept away. They remained to play a largely economic and ceremonial role, but were overruled at will by the dictatorial Taira clan chief, Kiyomori, on any matter touching the Taira interests. This dual government continued, better balanced and more stable, under the firmer and more conciliatory military control of Yoritomo, head of the Minamoto clan.

p 200– (6)

p 202– (9)

The rise of the Taira and Minamoto clans, both offshoots of the Imperial clan, was a culmination of the development of a provincial military class in the last two centuries of the Fujiwara period, when central control over the country was slipping away. There was a steady growth of lawlessness, with the formation of robber and pirate bands, and the organizing of military groups by temples and shrines, by local officials and managers of *shōen*. Most of these local leaders were descendants of lesser pre-reform clan chiefs, but some—the more important ones—were descended from provincial branches of Imperial and court families. Beginning in the more

p 200– (7,8)

Agriculture has long been the basis of Japan's economy, with peasants living in small valley communities, sheltered and isolated by the mountains. The land allotment system, adopted from China in the 7th and 8th centuries, was ultimately unsuccessful, and was replaced once more by family ownership. Right: peasant huts, fields and a Shintō shrine nestling in a valley. (4)

remote provinces, these groups formed extended military clans with family or pseudo-family ties, but based much more on common geographical and economic interests than on lineage, and specializing in the military arts. Their prototypes had originated in the abandonment in 792 of peasant conscription, adopted from Chinese practice, which had proved both unnecessary for Japan and inefficient for repelling the Ainu aborigines of northeastern Japan. Instead, the task was delegated to a professional, permanent militia, organized by the pioneer families in the area who needed to protect their landholdings and desired to increase them. These local military clans transmitted to the rest of Japan, and to the samurai of later times, the techniques of the tough mounted knights of the border areas, skilled horsemen and archers, and deadly wielders of the incomparable, slightly curved Japanese two-handed sword. They also kept alive the simple and ancient absolute allegiance to lord and master and the contempt for death which was eventually elaborated, and given a Confucian framework, in the ideology of *bushidō*, the way of the warrior.

By settling in Kyoto and becoming in effect a new group of courtiers, the Taira clan under Kiyomori weakened its hold over the cliques in the provinces. Meanwhile, Minamoto remnants were mustering their strength in the Eastern provinces. Eventually they felt themselves strong enough for a counterblow, and there ensued a bitterly fought war on a large scale (1180–85). The Taira leaders were defeated, and either were killed or committed suicide to avoid capture (an early example of *seppuku*, or, more vulgarly, *harakiri*). The boy Emperor, the grandson of Kiyomori, died with his Taira relatives.

During the wars against the Taira, Yoritomo made a point of espousing the established legal rights of the temples and shrines which had suffered from the rapaciousness and needless destructiveness of the Taira forces. Also, he established a reputation for being able to control his subordinates. This, and his cautious approach to the court, helped to strengthen his support from threatened proprietary interests. For the unattached military families, his chief attraction was his continuing military successes. The systems of commendation and benefice, by which

private land rights had been protected from the Imperial tax collectors and allotment system by powerful temples and shrines, or by the court clans (for which they received an agreed share of the income from the land), was easily adapted to the new need for military protection.

Profiting from the mistakes of the Taira, Yoritomo built up a strong power based on the eastern provinces surrounding the great Kantō plain, historically the last, and most important, agricultural plain to be brought under cultivation. After the final defeat of the Taira, Yoritomo did not settle down in the Imperial city, but maintained his headquarters *(bakufu)* in Kamakura, near the estates of his family and partisans in the Kantō. Despite his early education in Kyoto and a knowledge of court culture which enabled him to bridge the warriors' and the court society, he was content to remain a military chieftain, assured of the support of his vassals, of whom he expected absolute loyalty, frugality, and simplicity.

Yoritomo was careful to see that his vassals were satisfied with their rewards in land rights, but he prevented their abuse of power by creating impartial courts to hear claims against them. While offering justice to outsiders, Yoritomo imposed a tough and often arbitrary discipline on his own followers. He was needlessly suspicious, cold and calculating when he felt that his interests were at stake, and quickly had all potential rivals put to death, including his dashing and popular younger brother Yoshitsune, who overshadowed Yoritomo himself as a military genius, but lacked his prudence and extreme caution. As a Japanese leader, Yoritomo has been admired for his achievements but never loved. Yoshitsune, in contrast, has become the tragic hero of the epic romances relating the dramatic rise and fall of the Taira and the Minamoto.

In 1192, seven years after his victory over the Taira, Yoritomo took for himself the title of Shogun, which became for the first time a lifelong and hereditary office, granted by the Emperor, whose civil government, along with the cloistered Emperors and Fujiwara administrators, he permitted to continue with a minimum of interference. He rewarded his housemen, not with posts in the civil government, but with more lucrative positions as

p 202–3 (12,13)

estate managers or stewards *(jitō)*, assigning them to lands confiscated from enemies, or simply appointing them to their own lands, thus confirming them in their holdings.

For some years before 1185, less and less tax commodities and rents had been reaching the capital. For the officials and landed interests concentrated in the capital area, Yoritomo's chief function, as well as justification, was to maintain order and guarantee that these payments were delivered. For this service, his men were given the right to levy a uniform portion of the rice crop in their areas of jurisdiction, to cover military expenses. Stewards *(jitō)* and the more important Protectors *(shugo)*, Yoritomo's direct vassals, were the agents through whom his control spread through the country. In 1185 Yoritomo induced the cloistered Emperor Go-Shirakawa to grant him Imperial permission to appoint these agents to all the provinces. Although not done immediately, and then only gradually, this was an invitation to extend the feudal system. But at the time, these military agents were seen as exercising a necessary function, and the Shogun's authority was recognized as being legally based on Imperial delegation. Yoritomo was careful to see that there was no direct contact between his vassals and the Kyoto court.

Among Yoritomo's vassals there were great differences of wealth and influence. Some could command large numbers of men; others presented themselves for duty alone, mounted and armed, perhaps with an attendant or two. But all had the right of audience with the Shogun. Around the Shogun in Kamakura were gathered the most powerful vassals, including the head of the Hōjō family, Yoritomo's father-in-law, who had acquired hereditary rights to the office of chief administrator. After Yoritomo's death in 1199, the Hōjō family emerged as regents, ruling on behalf of the Shogun. But until 1220 there was much factional strife in Kamakura, and the two Shoguns of the Minamoto line were assassinated, Yoriie

at the age of twenty-two, Sanetomo at the age of twenty-eight. The Hōjō regents first gave the Shogunal succession to members of the Fujiwara family (1220–44), then to Imperial princes (1245–1334).

In 1221, thinking to take advantage of a degree of disunity in Kamakura, the cloistered Emperor Go-Toba, who had already shown a good deal of independence, organized an armed rising against the Shogunate, gaining the adherence of some of the military houses, temples, and shrines in the area of the capital. This rising, called the Shōkyū Struggle, was quickly suppressed by Yoshitoki, the Hōjō regent, who deposed the boy Emperor, exiled Go-Toba and two other ex-Emperors, and confiscated large landholdings, with which he rewarded his loyal vassals. This greatly increased the Shogunate's control of land in the capital area, and correspondingly its political control over the court.

p 202–(10)

During the Kamakura period (1185–1333), there was relative peace and stability under the Shogunate's firm domination, especially after 1221, and there was a considerable economic growth in agriculture, handicraft industries, and domestic and foreign trade. A fusion of classical and provincial culture, as well as popular forms of Buddhism, began spreading to the provinces, to Kamakura, which became an important cultural and commercial centre, and to new military headquarters towns throughout the country, where Protectors *(shugo)* were building up their military and economic strength. The warriors' ideal of frugality and simplicity is seen in the art and architecture of the time, and a remarkable realism and strength, influenced by Zen Buddhism, appears in painting and especially in sculpture. Buddhist institutions, with their private armies, take on a feudal colour. Married Buddhist 'teachers' begin to replace unmarried monks and priests, temple headships become hereditary, and temples make money by protecting merchants and artisans, participating in foreign trade, and making loans.

p 204–(14–17)

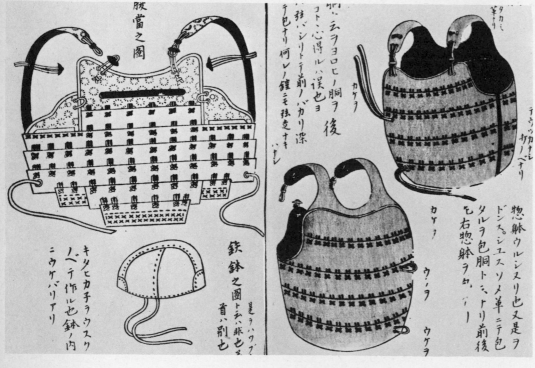

Japanese battles were characterized by duels between individuals. Armour such as this provided protection while being light and flexible. It was made from tiny scales of lacquered iron, or 'lamellae', laced together in rows with silk cords. (5)

218

The Confucian class system was adopted in Japan following the Chinese pattern. People were classed into four functional categories – ruling class, peasants, artisans and merchants – and it *was illegal to move from one to another. Above: artisans, makers of frozen bean-curd cakes, which were put out to freeze during a cold winter night, and then left to dry in the sun. (6)*

p 202–3 (11)

The unsuccessful attempts of the Mongols, with forced Chinese and Korean assistance, to invade Japan checked the expansion of the economy and increased the Shogunate's already grave financial troubles. The invasion attempts in 1274 and 1281 were repulsed by hard fighting and by providential typhoons, called *kamikaze*, divine winds, which scattered the enemy fleets and caused great loss of life, a fate similar to that of the Spanish Armada three centuries later. But for more than twenty years the Shogunate maintained a state of military preparedness. Only after the death of Khubilai in 1294 did the Japanese feel safe enough to relax their defence efforts. Meanwhile, agriculture was neglected, a deep depression followed, and the Shogunate had no means of rewarding the vassals who had fought so valiantly against the Mongols.

Despite the weakening of loyalties, leadership, and finances, the Shogunate survived the Mongol invasions by another fifty years, until yet another Imperial succession struggle, and another over-ambitious Emperor, provided a pretext for certain powerful vassals to turn against the Hōjō regents. Go-Daigo, having conceived an unfortunate plan to restore Imperial rule, began in 1321 to strengthen the ancient Imperial structure by abolishing cloister government, incorporating its activities and lands under his control. The adding of these lands to the vanishing public domain ironically speeded their eventual disappearance also. In 1331, Go-Daigo refused the Hōjō regent's order to abdicate in favour of a rival claimant and launched a revolt against Kamakura similar to Go-Toba's ill-fated attempt in 1221. Although the Shogunate had become very much weaker, feudal forces in the country had grown stronger, to such an extent that the idea of Imperial restoration proved anachronistic and unrealistic in the extreme. What Go-

Daigo began was a civil war between shifting feudal coalitions. This lasted until 1392, and it resulted in a vast redistribution of land and privileges, removing most of the court's wealth and prestige, and making it impossible to reconstitute an effective Shogunal control over the feudal lords.

In 1333, the Kamakura Shogunate was destroyed, and the Hōjō regent, with more than two hundred followers, committed suicide. Until 1336, Go-Daigo was busy re-creating some of the ancient offices, raising the old civil nobility above resentful military leaders. But the clock would not be turned back, and he could not change the nature of the feudal forces upon which he had to rely for support. In 1335 a conflict broke out between Ashikaga Takauji and Nitta Yoshisada, who between them had eliminated the old Shogunate, and Go-Daigo ill-advisedly took Nitta's side. Takauji captured Kyoto in 1336 and set up a new Emperor, while Go-Daigo escaped and set up his own court in Yoshino in the mountains south of Nara. Until 1392 there were rival Imperial courts. The feudal lords could choose between them. They gave their support mostly for reasons of self-interest, and the links which once tied the warriors to the Shogunate and to one another were broken once for all.

Kyoto: the Ashikaga Shogunate

Takauji had himself appointed Shogun in 1338, and the Ashikaga Shogunate, established in Kyoto, was to last, after a fashion, until 1573. But Japan now split up into local lord-vassal groups which the Shoguns attempted, with varying success, to control by alliances with the provincial Protectors. The high point in Ashikaga power was reached by the third Shogun, Yoshimitsu, who decided the succession dispute in 1392 by force of arms and

p 206 (19)

For some seven centuries, until the 19th century, women in feudal Japan were in a position of social and legal inferiority. Among the warriors, only sons, able to defend their property, could inherit. Above: a scene from the tragic story of the courtesan Giō (with fan), famous for her singing and dancing, who, after three years as mistress to a military dictator, was banished and replaced by a new favourite. (7)

treachery, accepted, as 'King of Japan', a status of tributary subordination to the Ming Emperor in order to benefit from official trade with China, and treated the Emperor ceremonially as an equal. After Yoshimitsu's death in 1408, Ashikaga strength waned. The Shoguns tried to enforce justice through the courts, but Japan was entering a new period of localized feudalism in which might became right.

By the end of the Kamakura period, rights in agricultural land were divided about equally between military and civil proprietors, the Kamakura courts having slowed down but not prevented the appropriation of land by vassals. The process was speeded up during the civil war, especially when Takauji increased the military tax—to be collected by his Protectors—to half the income of the non-military estates in their jurisdictions, in order to finance the civil war and to gain the Protectors' support. By 1467, at the beginning of the period of complete decentralization called *Sengoku* (the Warring States), a mere one-fourth to one-third of land rights were held by civil proprietors. During the following century, these were almost completely consolidated into fiefs by the feudal lords, who were now called daimyō. The Emperors were reduced to poverty. One Emperor sought to raise funds by selling examples of his fine calligraphy.

Since it was essential that one man should inherit a fief and be able to defend it, the feudal lord, or any fief holder, chose the most able man from among his sons, relations, or allies to succeed to the fief. This deprived women of what economic independence they might have enjoyed, and, in a society in which clan interests were traditionally put before individual or family interests, feudalism greatly extended this concept. Loyalty was of a very personal kind. It was transferable under stress, but the vassal was expected, if necessary, to sacrifice himself, and even his

wife and children, for his lord, and examples of this abound in the literature of the period.

The political instability from 1333 to 1600 was due basically to the fact that the Imperial bureaucratic system imposed from above was dying, and a natural growth from below—the vassalage system, with fiefs under the complete control of feudal lords, capped finally by a national military leader—had not yet taken the previous regime's place. But despite occasional warfare after 1392, and widespread warfare after 1467, this was a period of remarkably dynamic economic and cultural advance. The growth of increasingly larger economic units, the fiefs, meant a reorganization of economic life from the complex multiplicity of proprietary interests and often scattered lands making up the *shōen*, to a much simpler, direct feudal control which was effectively used to encourage agriculture, industry, and commerce. Markets flourished, money began to take the place of barter, and there was increased specialization of economic activities and the growth of a merchant class. Important ports and commercial towns grew up, of which Sakai, at the eastern end of the Inland Sea, became the most famous, achieving a large degree of independence as a fortified city in the 16th century. The growth of foreign trade, with manufactures and works of art appearing for the first time among the exports to China, was an indication of these economic changes, and the Japanese— pirates as well as legal traders—began playing a major role in East Asian, even South-east Asian, trade. Denial of trade on advantageous terms was apt to turn Japanese traders into pirates. One aspect of the *Sengoku* period was the ravaging of Korean and Chinese coastal districts by these greatly feared Japanese pirates. They ranged farther afield after about 1560, were effectively banned in 1588, and in the end were replaced by other traders (largely the Portuguese, who likewise seldom hesitated to use force in the name of free trade).

These closer and more continuous contacts with China stimulated cultural developments that kept pace with the expanding economy. Zen Buddhism continued to flourish, and Zen monks were important in commercial, as well as in cultural, contacts with China. Many of the artistic activities that we now associate with Japanese culture originated in this period, despite the growing political anarchy. Some examples are the tea ceremony, the pottery associated with it, the great landscape paintings by artists like Sesshū (1420–1506), flower arrangement, landscape gardening, and the Nō drama. All were influenced by Zen Buddhism, and were patronized by the Ashikaga Shoguns, and, increasingly, by the rising provincial lords. In the late 16th century, these competed in commissioning artists to decorate their colossal new castles and residences with highly colourful paintings in striking contrast with the restrained taste of the Ashikaga Shoguns.

In the period of endemic civil warfare after 1467, there was a speeding up of the feudal evolution. With local variations, this passed through four main phases. First, the Protectors, with dual roles as provincial military governors involved in Shogunal politics, often in Kyoto, and as daimyō of scattered fiefs usually delegated to subordinates, lost their control to vassals, mostly of Steward *(jitō)* origin, who were better organized and

p 202– (12)

p 202– (13)

p 204– (15)

p 206 (20) p 182– (26)

p 207
(21)

whose roots were far deeper in the local soil. Second, a large number of small independent daimyō, usually building small hilltop castles, competed for power. In the third phase, some of them, who had unusual military and organizational skills, brought large areas under their control, using the small fiefs as building blocks. They created efficient military organizations, ingeniously keeping their vassals dependent upon them, moving them about in the military command, building large castles and castle towns in which they concentrated a predominant power over any combination of vassals, and keeping hostages there to ensure their loyalty. They recruited

p 207
(22)

large bodies of foot soldiers, commanded by mounted samurai, from the peasantry, who acted as spearmen, spies, and incendiaries, and to whom were entrusted the muskets, introduced by the Portuguese, whose manufacture the daimyō encouraged. With these large fiefs as bases, they either subjected or were subjected by other powerful daimyō, or entered freely into alliances, each daimyō maintaining considerable independence. The imperial court and religious bodies were reduced to impotence, and temporarily self-governing religious and commercial towns and cities came under feudal control. By these means Oda Nobunaga, Toyotomi Hideyoshi, and finally Tokugawa Ieyasu, in turn, ruthlessly pursuing their own ends, succeeded in unifying the country under their leadership, achieving the peace which all desired. In the last phase, another, though only partial, replacement of daimyō occurred as some proved more adaptable than others to the needs of a peacetime bureaucratic government presided over by the Tokugawa Shoguns.

Japan's first encounter with Western civilization began in 1543 and lasted almost a century. The Portuguese, representative of the small but competitive, intrusive European trading states, brought chiefly Chinese goods, and introduced firearms and Christianity. The great Jesuit, Francis Xavier, arriving in 1549, found the Japanese 'the best people so far discovered'. Unlike the Chinese, who preferred the less troublesome Arab traders, the Japanese welcomed the Europeans. Virtually independent daimyō, competing for power, tolerated, or even embraced, Christianity to bring traders to their harbours. By 1614, out of approximately 18,000,000 Japanese, there were some 300,000 Christians, a percentage never since approached. Soon, however, suspicions were growing about Christianity as subversive of feudal loyalties and about the dangers of European imperialism, allied with local Christians and potentially hostile daimyō, and led to a radical reaction. An increasingly savage and effective persecution began, and thousands of steadfast converts suffered. All relations with Portugal and Spain were severed. This dramatic reversal of policy was possible because, from the newly attained national viewpoint, Japan's economy, like China's, was so little dependent upon trade that this was not worth maintaining at the price of further disruption. Japan settled down to enjoy two centuries of peace and a flourishing of the arts. A controlled, limited trade at Nagasaki with the Dutch, who promised not to bring in missionaries, maintained a small window on to a hostile outside world, a hostility increased by Hideyoshi's destructive but ill-fated invasions of Korea in 1592–93 and 1597–98.

The wholesale fish market at Nihon Bashi in Edo. With the increased use of money in the late feudal period, wholesale markets and commodity exchanges flourished. In addition, many retail markets were held, usually once or twice every ten-day week, in towns and ports throughout the country. (8)

The last Shogunate: 1597–98

The settling down of the country after the upheavals of war, and of rapid and disturbing economic and social changes, was not easy. Hideyoshi, himself of peasant origin and a remarkable example of the social mobility which had come to be regarded as social anarchy, took sweeping measures to restore stability. In 1583, he began a land survey to establish a uniform system of taxation and to create a subservient peasantry. This was the year in which Hideyoshi achieved mastery over most of Japan after a momentary return to feudal anarchy in 1582 when his lord, Nobunaga, was assassinated. In 1588, Hideyoshi's 'Sword Hunt' confiscated weapons held by peasants and soldier-monks, thus separating the professional soldiery, under feudal discipline, from the peasantry. These *ad hoc* measures, as well as relations with the daimyō, were built into a system by Tokugawa Ieyasu, who succeeded to the control of the country after Hideyoshi's death in 1598. Ieyasu's domination was complete after victories over groups of Hideyoshi's adherents in 1600 at Sekigahara and in 1615 at Osaka.

p 208
(23)
p 209
(25)

In 1603 Ieyasu became Shogun. He was determined to establish a firm and stable government which he could pass on to his heirs, and he was completely successful: the 'Great Peace' endured until 1868. Tokugawa government was unique in its ingenious balance between centralized and decentralized, feudal and bureaucratic forces, with the Shogunate in Edo (present Tokyo) as national authority, and the daimyō as regional administrators, largely independent economically, but politically less so. Taxation of the peasantry, which had risen during the wars, remained very heavy, ranging from 40 per cent to

p 208
(24)

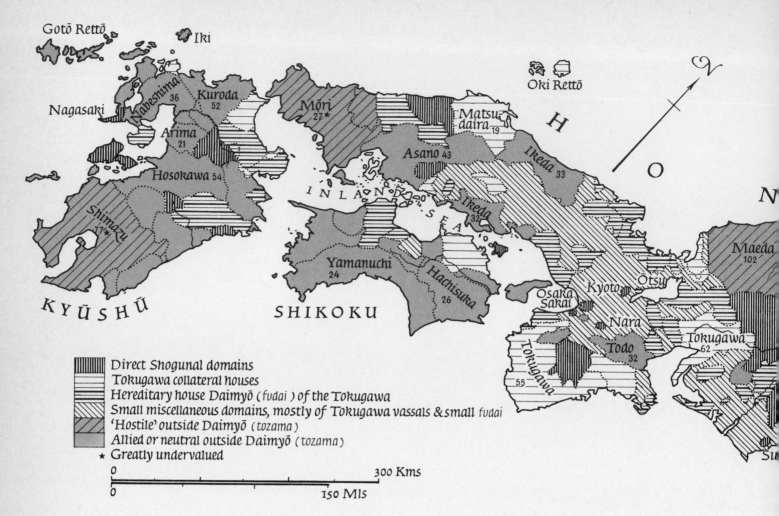

Tsushima

Gotō Rettō

Iki

Nagasaki

Nabeshima 36

Kuroda 52

Mōri 27★

Matsudaira 19

Oki Rettō

H

O

N

Arima 21

Asano 43

Ikeda 33

Hosokawa 54

INLAND SEA

Ikeda 32

Maeda 102

Shimazu 77★

Yamanuchi 24

Hachisuka 26

Kyoto Ōtsu

Osaka Sakai

Nara

Tokugawa 62

KYŪSHŪ

SHIKOKU

Tokugawa 55

Tokugawa

Todo 32

Su

|||| Direct Shogunal domains
Tokugawa collateral houses
Hereditary house Daimyō (fudai) of the Tokugawa
Small miscellaneous domains, mostly of Tokugawa vassals & small fudai
'Hostile' outside Daimyō (tozama)
Allied or neutral outside Daimyō (tozama)
★ Greatly undervalued

0   300 Kms

0   150 Mls

50 per cent of total production. The Shogun, who 'lived on his own', was, in effect, the most important daimyō. His own lands were extensive, increasing from a domain, gained in warfare, valued at two million *koku* (estimated annual yield, in units of 4.96 bushels of rice) to territories valued at 6.8 million *koku* in 1651, gained partly from daimyō who died without heirs and partly from confiscations for disciplinary purposes. Also, the Shogun reassigned more than seven million *koku* to reward his daimyō supporters during this period. His direct territories, which included the major cities and the most important mines, the sources of metal for coinage, supported about 23,000 retainers, some holding sub-fiefs, but most of them on stipends, who functioned in Shogunal military and bureaucratic posts.

The early Tokugawa leaders shifted the daimyō from domain to domain, raising and lowering their status, and giving close attention to strategic geographical dispositions, such as placing the domains of friendly daimyō next to doubtful ones. The feudal relations of the daimyō with the Shogun varied considerably. The closest were twenty-three collateral houses, of whom the most important three, descended from Ieyasu, could provide a Shogun should the main house have no heir. Their domains totalled 2·6 million *koku*. Next were the *fudai*, hereditary vassal daimyō of the Tokugawa house, who

staffed the most important Shogunal councils, and were considered completely reliable. Most had been raised to their position by Ieyasu, but some were created by Ieyasu's successors. They numbered 145 in the 18th century, and their domains, mostly small, totalled about 6·7 million *koku*. The greatest daimyō were the 'outside lords' *(tozama)*, whose rise as daimyō had paralleled Ieyasu's. They were treated more generously, but more cautiously, than the *fudai*. Their treatment depended upon whether they had been Tokugawa enemies (some of whose domains had been reduced in size by Hideyoshi or Ieyasu), neutral, or recent allies of Ieyasu in his last battles. There were 79 *tozama* in the 18th century, holding domains of 9·8 million *koku*.

The daimyō were required to maintain no more than one castle, to obtain approval for building or repairs, and to provide labour and materials for any engineering or building project that the Shogun required. Check-points were maintained on all roads to examine travellers. By custom, daimyō were expected, when required, to provide counsel or other special aid, military service (the *fudai* had to provide administrative service as well), and to administer their domains peacefully and well. Shogunal officials whose functions varied from spy to ombudsman kept the domains under constant scrutiny.

The key institution of Tokugawa feudal control, the

p 210–1
(26)

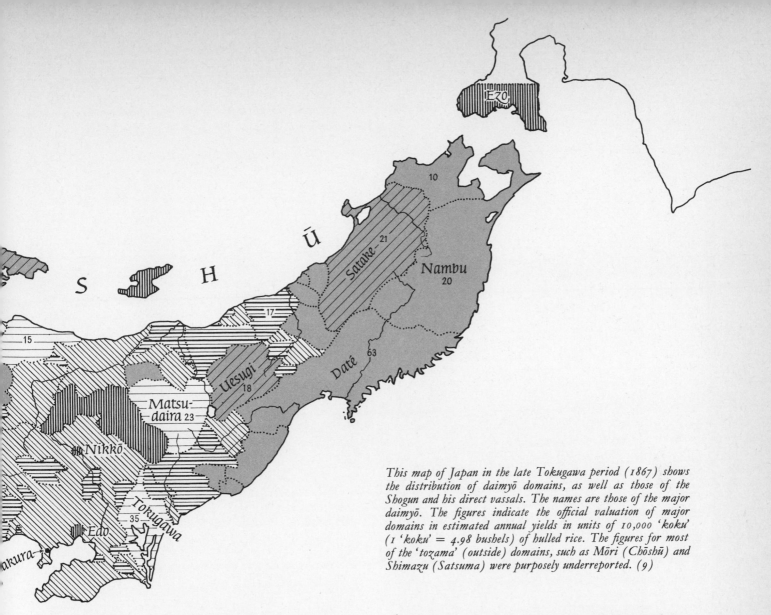

S   Ū   S   H   Ū

EZO

10

Satake 21

Nambu 20

17

15

Uesugi 18

Daté 63

Matsu-daira 23

Nikkō

Tokugawa 35

Edo

akura

This map of Japan in the late Tokugawa period (1867) shows the distribution of daimyō domains, as well as those of the Shogun and his direct vassals. The names are those of the major daimyō. The figures indicate the official valuation of major domains in estimated annual yields in units of 10,000 'koku' (1 'koku' = 4.98 bushels) of hulled rice. The figures for most of the 'tozama' (outside) domains, such as Mōri (Chōshū) and Shimazu (Satsuma) were purposely underreported. (9)

sankin kōtai, was the requirement of regular attendance of the feudal lords on the Shogun in Edo. They had to travel there with their retinues and remain for regular intervals, usually a year, spending the alternate year in their own domains. Since their families were required to live permanently in Edo, they had to build and maintain appropriately grand residences there, and their wives and children became hostages to guarantee the loyalty of the lords during their absences from Edo. It was an extremely effective device, in the atmosphere of suspicion engendered by the wars, for preventing insurrections of daimyō without military effort. It did much to knit the country into more of a national unity, and it had important economic consequences. The expenses entailed by the system soon came to account for about half the feudal lords' total expenditures, and had to be paid for in money which they had no right to coin. They were forced to convey a maximum quota of tax products to the national markets in the fast expanding cities, especially to Osaka, in order to earn this money. They were dependent in these operations on merchants whose numbers, importance, and prosperity rose rapidly.

The lands of religious institutions were reduced to a minimum, and temples and shrines were closely supervised. Ieyasu followed Hideyoshi in treating the Emperor and his courtiers with respect and some generosity,

setting aside lands for their support which reached a valuation of 187,000 *koku*; but he made certain that they should not meddle in the business of government, and he strictly controlled all access to the Imperial court.

In the late Ashikaga period, Confucianism was being rediscovered in Japan in attractive Neo-Confucian clothing. The attainment of peace presented the opportunity to apply these ideas, to provide a moral and philosophical justification for the power achieved by arms, to give education to the semi-literate samurai who were needed as administrators, and to make social cement for bringing harmony out of anarchy. For the ruling class, Confucianism virtually replaced Buddhism, and, despite its insistence on duties, loyalty, and conformity, it served to bring out the secular, pragmatic, positive side of the Japanese personality, though it did not necessarily purge the samurai of his military mentality and self-righteous arrogance.

The ancient Chinese idea of a four-class system was also seized upon. (In Japanese this was called *shinōkōshō*.) It was a physiocratic theory. People were classified into four main functional categories. These were, in order of importance: a small educated ruling class *(shi)*; peasants *(nō)*, who were the only real producers and the bulk of the population; artisans *(kō)*, who changed the form of things; and merchants *(shō)*, who merely moved things

223

A street scene of merchants trading in Buddhist rosaries. In the 17th century, the economy expanded greatly, and living standards rose, but the affluence of the merchants far outstripped that of the other classes. By the end of the century, the samurai, even the feudal lords, were deeply in debt to the merchants. (10)

about and held them available for purchase. A legal monopoly of function, including weapons for the samurai, and a criminal code were fixed according to class. The most important distinction was between commoners and samurai. A samurai could cut down a commoner with impunity to repay an insult, real or imagined, while a samurai might be condemned to suicide or banishment for an offence which, if committed by a commoner, would be considered minor. Sumptuary legislation according to class and social standing strove to impose frugality and to prohibit 'improper luxury and ostentation' in clothing, food, housing, etc. Movement from one class to another was illegal. 'The offspring of a toad is a toad; of a merchant, a merchant,' was a typical contemporary saying.

The 17th century was a period of energetic economic expansion. Population rose from about 18 million to about 26 million, but agricultural production and, much more, industrial production raced ahead of population growth, and the result was a considerable rise in the standard of living, in which even the peasants participated to some extent, and the samurai as well, chiefly by going into debt. The combined population of Kyoto and the two cities of Osaka and Edo had passed 1·5 million by the 18th century. With the spread of literacy among the affluent townsmen, a new popular literature, puppet theatre, and kabuki, and a new art, *ukiyoe* woodblock prints of the 'floating world', appeared, depicting for the first time the lives of common people. The Genroku period, 1688–1703, was the high point of this exuberant new culture. Sansom considers the period 'perhaps even the justification of feudal rule, for here was peace and plenty and a great flourishing of the arts—a happy society as human societies go.' (*The Western World and Japan*, p. 197.)

But both economic and demographic expansion slowed down in the early 18th century, and came to a virtual halt by the middle of it. One cause was the chaos in Shogunal and daimyō finances and severe retrenchment as the samurai class went deeply into debt to the merchants to sustain their accustomed levels of spending. Prices were rising; and the samurai were living on incomes from taxes based primarily on fluctuating rice production, which was difficult to increase. Moreover, the peasants were doing their best to shift to cash crops. To make matters worse, a series of natural disasters occurred later in the century and continued far into the 19th century. There was widespread starvation in some regions, and the Shogunate was unable to import food, even across neighbouring feudal boundaries. But the degree of the long-term depression into which the country was plunged has often been over-emphasized because our sources are mainly Confucian moralists who were deploring the fact that merchants were more prosperous than the ruling classes, that while others flourished, the peasants, who furnished the rice for their betters to eat, were on the verge of starvation, and that they were abandoning their fields, rioting and rebelling against local officials, wealthy peasants, or merchants, and resorting to infanticide to stave off starvation from their families. These miseries no doubt did exist, but on the other hand there is also much evidence of agricultural improvements.

p 210–
(27)

p 210–
(28)

p 212
(29)

The fact is that most members of the ruling class were intent on maintaining their positions in an ideally static society, and they did not know how to cope with the unprecedented money economy. This had developed earliest and fastest in the areas of the principal cities controlled by the Shogunate, where the 'cash nexus' was replacing feudal loyalties, and samurai, often with reduced stipends, were pawning their weapons, dismissing their retainers, and generally losing their fighting ability and spirit. The gap widened between those who succeeded in adjusting to the money economy, including peasant money lenders and small scale industrialists, and those who failed, while virtually every effort to turn back the clock, to penalize the merchants, to stop the price rises, and to control the economy simply made matters worse.

p 212
(30)

The Shogunate's problem was the greater and its failure the more spectacular. Certain of the daimyō were more successful in staving off bankruptcy, and in maintaining feudal discipline and morale among their samurai. The most prominent among them were Shimazu and Mōri, the daimyō of Satsuma and Chōshū, in Western Japan, who were well served by imaginative bureaucrats and who cherished a tradition of hostility towards the Shogun. They were to combine to bring down the old regime, in the name of the Emperor. This occurred only after the opening of the country in and after 1853; for this created problems that had never been anticipated during the building of a political structure that had been directed almost solely at potential domestic enemies. Some fourteen years—1853 to 1867—of floundering efforts to preserve its own establishment made it clear that the Shogunate, confined in the self-made prison of an outworn system, was incapable of organizing an adequate national response to the threat, and challenge, of the Western powers.

IX CULT AND CREED

Religion in Japan before the Meiji

CARMEN BLACKER

I do not know whether any being is present here, yet in holy dread my tears gush forth.

Composed by the Buddhist priest Saigjō
on visiting the Ise shrine, 12th century

Since I cannot think that reality is real, how can I think that dreams are dreams?

The priest Saigjō, 12th century

The dawn of Shintō is lost in prehistory, when the peoples who were to make up Japan's population were coming together in successive migrations from mainland Asia and from lands further south. By the 7th century AD, it had achieved something like a unified form, but our earliest records date only from the 8th and 9th centuries. Like most primitive religions, it was primarily a means of placating or influencing the supernatural powers which controlled weather, fertility and health. These powers were known as *kami* and an elaborate mythology eventually gathered round them. With the right rituals they could be persuaded to confer blessings or reveal the future. Until it came under the influence of Buddhism, Shintō seems to have been entirely unconcerned with ethical questions.

The earliest Shintō holy places were natural objects – trees, boulders, mountains or islands. One of the oldest identifiable sites, the Itsukushima Shrine, is on the island of Miyajima, near Hiroshima. The photograph opposite shows the *torii*, or gateway, which separates the sacred precinct from the outside world; here we are looking from the shrine across the water to the mainland. Within the gateway there are three areas, of increasing sanctity: first that used for public worship; then one which can be entered only by priests; and finally the innermost precinct, dwelling place of the three daughters of the god Susano-o-no-Mikoto.

During the course of its history Shintō has radically changed its character, taking over many important features from Buddhism. The original beliefs can be traced only in the earliest texts and in certain folk-practices that are still carried on in rural areas. Its revival in modern times has been a sophisticated, self-consciously nationalistic exercise, far removed from the archaic faith that the first inhabitants of Japan brought with them fifteen hundred years ago. (1)

Buddha and his Bodhisattvas were at first regarded by the Japanese as supernatural powers comparable to the Shintō deities they already knew. In the 7th century a state cult was set up, but this was still far from the authentic teachings of the Buddha, since its main functions were obsequies for the dead, exorcism of ghosts and the provision of worldly blessings. In some of the images made in Japan at this time, on the other hand, we do find that compassion and spiritual aspiration that is central to Buddhist doctrine. Right: Buddha and a Bodhisattva, both of the 7th century. (5, 6)

Shintō and Buddhism developed together from the 6th century onwards, with Buddhism affecting every aspect of Shintō, from its theology to its architecture. The oldest Shintō shrine in existence, at Izumo (above), is said to go back to the legendary palace of the god of healing and of agriculture, but such features as the roof-curve and the balconies reflect Buddhist inspiration. From Buddhism too came the practice of making sacred images. Left: the goddess Nakatsuhime (9th century), one of the ancestors of the Japanese race. (2, 3)

The thousand-armed statue of Senju Kannon made the Buddhist temple of Kokawa-dera a famous place of pilgrimage. In this scene (below) from a 12th-century manuscript it stands in a simple chapel, with villagers clustering round it. In later times Buddhist and Shintō shrines were often built next to each other. (4)

The first temples in Buddhist Japan were markedly Chinese in style. That of Hōryūji, near Nara, was founded in 609. Here the abstruse doctrines of the Hossō School would have been studied, but had little impact outside the monastic world. (7)

Travelling priests brought the message of Buddha to town and country, much as did the friars of medieval Europe. The most famous was Ippen (1239–89), a true mystic, who saw Buddha in every manifestation of Nature and who conveyed his doctrine by singing, dancing and story-telling, as well as in more orthodox ways. In this scene he is being carried on the shoulders of a disciple through the market at Kyoto, and causing a traffic jam by the crowd that collects around him. (8)

The mystic path was not an easy one, and many spiritual techniques were evolved as guides to enlightenment. Among the most revered texts was the *Lotus Sutra*, to make copies of which was considered an act of piety by Heian aristocrats. Below: part of a *Lotus Sutra* of the Late Heian period inscribed on a fan-shaped page together with a street scene in Kyoto which may be intended to link the faith more closely with everyday life. (9)

Amida Buddhism puts its trust in Amida, one of the manifestations of Buddha's godhead. This triptych (above) is nearly fifteen feet wide and shows Amida descending to earth to receive into his own paradise, the Pure Land of the West, the spirit of one who has died pronouncing the name of Buddha. Beneath him are two Bodhisattvas, one holding a lotus pedestal, while on either side are others playing various musical instruments. (10)

The old sects live on. These pilgrims (below) belong to the Nichiren sect and place their entire faith in the *Lotus Sutra*. The temple they are visiting is on Koyasan, founded in 816 as the centre of the Shingon sect. Mystical identification with the Buddha comes through *mudra* (ritual gestures), *mantras* (magical sounds) and meditation. Nichiren, in the 13th century, added an element of aggressive intolerance of other sects which perhaps accounts for some of its present-day popularity. (11)

Zen is a form of Buddhism, a technique for attaining spiritual enlightenment which has flourished particularly in Japan. Instead of relying on 'other strength', like the Amida Buddhists, the Zen disciple seeks to achieve his purpose by his own efforts. To this end he empties the mind of its ingrained rational prejudices by prolonged meditation (above), thereby opening it to the flash of 'sudden enlightenment' which cannot be expressed in words. Aids to such meditation are the *koans* (deliberately non-rational questions, like 'What is the sound of one hand clapping?'), the Zen garden of isolated rocks surrounded by raked sand (below left) and paintings which embody the non-rational. Below: a hanging scroll of about 1400 showing a man trying to catch a catfish with a gourd. Zen attained a position of dominance over other forms of Buddhism in the 14th century. (12–14)

The three faiths which make up Japan's religious history have undergone many transformations and revivals. **Buddhism** was for long compromised by being a state religion, its surrender to worldly values engendering the innumerable sects which strove to recover its true spirit. Above left: a hall of the Byōdōin Temple at Uji, built in 1053 and still much venerated. **Confucianism,** imported from China, provided the firm moral guidance which Buddhism did not stress and Shintō never achieved. Above right: an official handing an ancestral scroll, symbol of filial piety, to his son (17th century). The **Shintō Revival** in the 18th century was an attempt by scholars to purge the old cult of Buddhist accretions and restore the pure 'Japanese' religion. Below right: a baby being brought for initiation to a Shintō shrine, c. 1730. (15–17)

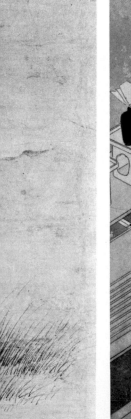

For the man in the street, as remote from the subtleties of the theologians as from the austerities of the mystics, both Shintō and Buddhism remain largely a system for ensuring happiness in this world and the next. The largest Shintō shrine in Kyoto, the Heian Shrine, was built as recently as 1895 and reconstructed less than forty years ago. One of the features of the great popular festivals is fortune-telling; if the news is unwelcome to the recipient he hangs the prediction on a twig and leaves it to flutter in the breeze. (18)

A god goes swimming. The island of Enoshima preserves an ancient ceremony in which a Shintō deity is taken out into the water, then brought ashore and paraded in his palanquin through the streets of the village. Here a priest waits to receive him by the sacred entrance made of bamboo fronds. (19)

CARMEN BLACKER

Members of the Shingon sect attend a secret ceremony com-memorating the death of a priest. The Shingon sect, introduced into Japan from China in the 9th century, is an esoteric branch of Buddhism with a strong emphasis on incantation, magic formulas, ceremonials and masses for the dead. (1)

27 (1)

ETHNOLOGISTS ARE BY NO MEANS AGREED as to the exact composition of the Japanese race, but they all acknow-ledge at least that it is a mixed one. Successive migrations in prehistoric times of peoples from the Altaic regions of the Asian continent, from South-east Asia, from Melane-sia and Korea, not to speak of the mysterious Ainu population, have all gone to produce a people of insolubly mixed origins. It follows that the religious cult practised by so heterogeneous a people is not likely to be a unified system. Early Shintō, though frequently described as 'native to Japan', as 'having been born with the Japanese people' and revealing their essential soul, is in fact a complex amalgam of different traditions brought by these various ethnic groups. The structure of its myths, its conceptions of deity, its views on the afterlife and the other world, all unmistakably betray its multiple origin.

But by the time it had assumed the form in which we first know it, that is to say by the 6th and 7th centuries AD, these different elements had already been welded into a religious system which possessed its own coherent struc-ture and its own internal logic and power.

Early Shintō

Our sources of information about this ancient religion fall into two distinct categories. First, we have certain literary works dating from the 8th and 9th centuries which tell us a good deal about the cult as it was practised in the region of the Yamato plain by the Imperial family and surrounding aristocratic clans. From the chronicles called *Kojiki* and *Nihon shoki*, committed to writing in the early 8th century but embodying material of much greater antiquity, we know the principal myths which underlay the ritual and worship of the cult, and can infer much else that has since vanished about its beliefs and practices. From a work of two centuries later known as the *Engishiki*, we have descriptions of the principal Shintō rituals and a valuable collection of *norito*, or Shintō prayers.

Secondly, for the remoter rural variations of the cult, we have a rich source of information in the surviving practices of what is known as *minkan-shinkō*, folk religion.

p 234
(19)

Here we may still find rituals, songs, and dances which have preserved, by oral tradition, a great deal that is genuinely ancient. This valuable and sadly neglected source of knowledge is likely soon to disappear under the impact of modern secularism. But the use made of it during the last fifty years by the great ethnologist Yanagita Kunio and his followers has been enough to transform our knowledge of the probable structure of the archaic religion.

What do these two sources tell us of the early Shintō religion? Let us look first at the sacred beings who were the objects of worship. They comprise chiefly the numina known as *kami*. Though one or two of the great *kami* mentioned in the *Kojiki* myths are given the rudiments of individuality, the great majority of them are shadowy, featureless beings, devoid alike of shape and personality. They are best understood as impersonal spiritual forces, conductors of power of a mysterious kind which is altogether beyond the ordinary competence of man. In their gift lay all the causes which affect human life but which are outside human control. The weather, the harvest, the incidence of sickness, fire, flood or accident, fertility and vitality—the causes of all these lay at the disposal of the *kami*. Whether a village, a family, or even the imperial house prospered or perished, therefore, depended on the good will of these beings.

The world they inhabited lay on a different plane or dimension from that of men—in the myths it is repre-sented as a high region called Takamagahara, elsewhere it is the tops of certain mountains—but communication between the two spheres was not difficult. Cajoled by the correct rites and music, the *kami* could usually be per-suaded to visit the human world and, during their sojourn, to bestow upon the village the boons and bene-fits of their power. On the mysteries of the immediate future—the rice harvest, summer storms and sicknesses,

p 228
(2)

winter privations, marriages and sons—they could be induced to deliver oracular utterances. Hidden causes of sickness or disaster they would also reveal, and if specially pleased might alter these connections in such a way as to benefit the village.

The *kami* possessed no form of their own. So far as we know, no images of them were ever made in the early cult, and later representations are entirely due to the influence of Buddhist iconography. They could manifest themselves in the human world only if a seat or vessel of appropriately inviting shape were provided for them. These vessels, known as *yorishiro*, were usually of a long, thin shape reminiscent of a lightning conductor. Trees and elongated stones were among the most common *yorishiro*; also wands, flags, swords, or dolls.

p 228 (3,4)

Best of all, however, were the human *yorishiro*, for these could provide the *kami* with a voice whereby he could transmit his utterances directly to the village. These mediums, who in the early cult seem usually to have been women, thus enabled the village to communicate at once with their tutelary *kami*, to question him, thank him for his favours, or plead with him for further boons.

The treatment which best propitiated the *kami* was care to make offerings of the correct kind—the *Engishiki* mentions cloth, horses, rice cakes, cooked fish—together with the recitation of magically efficacious sounds and prayers by men and women in a state of ceremonial purity. The behaviour which most offended and enraged them was neglect to make the due offerings, failure to visit the shrine, and above all the proximity of men who neglected the demands of ceremonial purity and fell into the state of pollution known as *tsumi*.

The principal causes of pollution recognized in early Shintō are set out in an important ritual preserved in the *Engishiki*, the Ōharai or Great Purification. They comprise a number of apparently miscellaneous acts and states. Wounding or being wounded, killing, leprosy, incest, snake bite, as well as certain crimes (such as breaking down the divisions between rice fields) calculated to threaten the livelihood of a primitive rice-growing community—all these made a man so offensive to the *kami* that he could not approach a shrine without fear of a *tatari*, or curse, which might blast the entire village. In common practice, however, the chief sources of *tsumi* have always been death and blood. The death of a relative, contact with any dead creature, proximity to a woman in childbirth or menstruation, so defiled a man that he could not visit a shrine until the pollution was removed by purifying rituals and a stated period of isolation.

It follows that we have here a cult still in the pre-moral stage of development. It is no conception of moral goodness that rejoices the *kami*, or of evil which offends them. It is a contamination of a physical kind which no man in the ordinary course of living can altogether avoid. Nor are the *kami* themselves seen as possessing any distinct moral nature. Their power is like that of fire or electricity. Whether they exert it for the good or evil of the human community depends largely on how they are treated, rather than on any innate moral propensities. The taboo against any kind of blood, on the other hand, at least preserved the cult from the impulsion towards living sacrifices such as we find practised in China throughout most of her religious history.

The vague term *kami* comprises a number of categories of numinous being which elsewhere in the world tend to be distinguished. The most ancient classification is the one found in the *Kojiki*, where the Amatsukami, or heavenly numina, are distinguished from the Kunitsukami, or earthly ones. But this distinction tells us not so much about the nature of the *kami* as about the status of those who worshipped them. The Amatsukami were the deities of the ruling class, the Imperial family, and its satellite clans, and the highest of them was the Sun goddess Amaterasu Ōmikami, who stands in the myths as the divine ancestor of the Imperial family. The Kunitsukami were the gods of the common populace, or possibly the deities worshipped in the countryside before the formation of the ruling class.

In the early form of the cult, most *kami* seem to have been of the tutelary kind known as *ujigami*, and were concerned with the welfare and protection of a particular group of people, a family or by extension a village. These *ujigami* originated sometimes in the deified ancestor of a family or in the founder of a village, and sometimes, as with the aristocratic clans of the Yamato plain, in a heavenly deity from the high region above the human world.

As the cult developed, however, the idea of the *kami* as bearers of mysterious power was extended into other spheres. *Kami* were seen to appear through the more enigmatic manifestations of nature. An unusually large tree, a peculiarly shaped boulder, a beautiful island or mountain, an animal of unaccountable habits – all these were recognized as vessels through which numinous power could be manifested.

The exercise of skill in certain occupations also came to be seen as the manifestation of numinous power. Weaving, fishing, hunting, and the forging of metals were recognized to be successfully performed only under the tutelage of the *kami* concerned with them. In the gift of the *kami*, too, were the mysterious processes of growth and fertility. The *sai-no-kami*, or phallic deities, represented not only procreative power but also the vigorous vitality that triumphs over disease and death. They are magical 'preventions' of the forces which threaten life, and are to be found today in such traditionally perilous spots as crossroads and bridgeheads.

Again, certain superior men were conceived to be *kami*, either during their lifetime or after their death. The Emperor, with all the numinous power of his office, was a *kami* while still alive. Others who proved their superiority to ordinary men by heroic abstentions, charity, or creative power, became *kami* after their death. But behind all these varied manifestations it is not difficult to discover the idea of a mysterious power which regulates the aspects of life beyond human control.

With its horror of the pollution of death, early Shintō had little comfort to offer with regard to the afterlife. From the myths of the *Kojiki* we gather that the dead were believed to go to a gloomy, polluted realm known as Yomi, situated somewhere below the middle world of men. The destination of a dead person thus in no way depended on moral conduct during his lifetime. Just and unjust alike were condemned to this shadowy country, escape from which came only with the introduction of Buddhism. In the central cult of the myths, therefore, a strict distinction was drawn between the *kami*, who inhabited a realm pure, sacred, and high, and the ordinary dead, who were condemned to a polluted underworld. Elsewhere, however, particularly in the districts where the dead were believed to go to mountains, a curious intermingling took place between the two kinds of supernatural being, which persists to this day.

Early Shintō thus bore many features which stamp it as archaic. It was pre-moral and pre-literate. Its sacred beings were invoked chiefly to promote worldly prosperity, to order for the benefit of the human community the forces of life beyond man's control. It seems to have had little grasp of the concept of spiritual salvation, and little comfort to offer against the terrors of death.

The coming of Buddhism

It is not surprising that Buddhism, a religion so remote

When Buddhism made its appearance in Japan in the 6th century Buddha and his attendant Bodhisattvas were soon adopted, not as images symbolizing a more sublime state of consciousness, but as potential bestowers of material blessings. Above: Amida Buddha watches over the fish catch. (3)

from such beliefs, should at first have been misunderstood when, in the 6th century, it made its appearance in Japan. The *kami* were spiritual powers, external to the human mind, capable of bestowing worldly benefits beyond the human grasp. The Buddha, on the other hand, had taught that mundane prosperity, the accumulation of what seem to be the blessings of this world, was in the long run of little account. The world as experienced in the ordinary human manner was invariably full of suffering. Only by a profound internal transformation of consciousness could one arrive at the illumination which comes from knowledge of the reality lying behind appearances, and in which alone bliss can be discovered.

When Buddhism was first introduced into Japan in the form of an image and copies of sutras sent by the king of one of the Korean kingdoms—the date is given in the *Nihon shoki* as AD 552—it was for some years regarded as no more than a new version of the native cult. The figures of the Buddha and his attendant Bodhisattvas were seen, not as images symbolizing a more sublime state of consciousness, but as potential bestowers of abundant harvests, male heirs and due monsoon rains, and as saviours from famine and pestilence. The Buddhist art of this period and the work of the saintly Prince Shōtoku both indicate that even at this early date there was some understanding of the compassion for suffering and the reverence for life which is so integral a part of Mahāyāna Buddhism. But more prominent seems to have been the state cult of Buddhism which was established in the course of the 7th century in Japan. Here Buddhism was called upon to fulfil two main functions, neither of which has anything to do with the original teaching of the Buddha, but both of which have survived to this day as the two principal duties which the average Japanese expects Buddhism to perform in his daily life.

p 228
(5,6)

237

Graves and shrines to the dead in 19th-century Japan. The ancient Shintō cult had provided no ritual means whereby the dead spirit could find rest and peace. Buddhism came to answer this urgent need and in spite of fairly obvious discrepancies between theology and practice, still does so. (4)

The first is the disposal of the dead and the pacification of ghosts. The ancient Shintō cult had provided no ritual means for the repose of the dead and no effective defence against the attacks of violent ghosts. It was Buddhism, therefore, which came to fulfil the urgent need for requiem masses whereby the dead spirit could find rest and peace. As early as the 6th century we find references in the chronicles to Buddhist rituals performed for the repose of dead members of the Imperial family and the aristocracy. That Buddhism should have continued to perform this function for 1400 years is strange when we remember that according to the early Buddhist doctrine in India such steps were irrelevant; the dead person was believed to be soon reborn in the state prescribed by his karma, the sum of his past actions. But the demand in Japan for some means to help the dead to final peace has always been so insistent that until today Buddhist temples have found one of their most lucrative functions to lie here. Some, indeed, subsist almost entirely on fees for funerals and other obsequies.

The second duty with which Buddhism was charged during the 7th century was to provide magical spells for the production of mundane benefits. The first Mahāyāna sutras to reach Japan—the Lotus Sutra, the Daihannya-kyō, and the Ninnōkyō—were used, not as guides towards an internal transformation, but as spells for rain,

p 230–1 (9)

for the emperor's recovery from sickness, for the birth of a male heir, for the arrest of an epidemic. Throughout the history of Japanese religion the same stress on benevolent productive magic has always persisted. The only Buddhist sects today to repudiate spells for worldly blessings are the Amidist sects and the Rinzai sect of Zen. For all the others, such spells are a principal source of wealth.

p 234 (18)

Thus the functions which Buddhism was destined always to fulfil for the average Japanese were defined within a century of its introduction. Side by side with these practices, however, there grew up in certain temples a literary tradition whereby teachings closer to the Buddha's original message were disseminated to a learned few.

In the course of the 7th century, and the 8th when the capital was founded at Nara, six schools based on Mahāyāna sutras were introduced and established in various temples in the vicinity. Without exception, they were too abstruse and metaphysical to be comprehensible by anyone outside the small groups of monks who were set to study their doctrines.

The Sanron or Mādhyamika school, introduced as early as 625 by a Korean monk, taught the Middle Path of the Eightfold Negation, wherein there was no production, no extinction, no annihilation, no permanence, no unity, no diversity, no coming, no going. The disciple must perceive the truth to be the Void. The Jōjitsu school, introduced about the same time, taught not only the Voidness of Elements, but also the Voidness of Self. The Hossō or Yogāchāra school, brought to Japan in 654 by Dōshō, a pupil of the celebrated Hsüan-tsang, taught the doctrine of *vijñapti-mātra*, that nothing exists beyond thought. The Kusha school, introduced in 658, was based on the Abhidharmakośa writings of Vasubandhu, wherein it was stated that once reality is seen in its myriad component parts, self too will be seen to be illusory, a mere aggregate of atoms. The Ritsu or Vinaya school, introduced by the saintly monk Ganjin in 753, prescribed the minute rules by which the lives of monks and nuns should be ordered. Finally, the Kegon school, reputedly introduced into Nara in 736 by an Indian monk called Bodhisena, was based on the Avataṁsaka Sutra which taught the sublime doctrine of a world in which there was no distinction between things, *jiji-muge-hokkai*.

p 228–(7)

p 179 (15)

p 178 (12)

Such metaphysical propositions, the product of minds which have reached advanced stages of enlightened consciousness, are not easily understood by those who have not. They have left no permanent imprint on Japanese Buddhism at all, except for the temples at Nara, some ceremonies of extreme antiquity and interest, and the great image in the Tōdaiji temple fashioned after the vision of the Buddha seen in the Kegon Sutra. On the lives of ordinary Japanese the Six Schools have made no impression.

Heian Buddhism

The oldest Buddhist schools still to survive as a meaningful religion in Japan are the two sects of esoteric Buddhism introduced from China during the 9th century, after the capital had been moved from Nara to Kyoto. The Tendai sect, based on the Chinese T'ien-t'ai school founded in

p 182– (23)

From the establishment of Buddhism as a state cult during the 7th century until today, one of its main functions has been to provide magical spells for the production of 'mundane benefits'. A steady stream of visitors to a Buddhist temple housing the Kannon or Goddess of Mercy in the 19th century arrives to ask for recovery from sickness, the birth of a male heir, etc. They make offerings, recite prayers and ensure that they are in a state of ceremonial purity. (5)

182-3 (25)

the 6th century by Chih-i, was brought to Japan in 805 by the eminent priest Saichō, known later as Dengyō Daishi. The Shingon sect, following the Chinese version of the right-handed Tantra, was introduced three years later by the even more remarkable priest Kūkai, who had studied the esoteric teachings for two years in China. Both these sects claim to transmit the real core of the Buddha's teaching—the experience of enlightenment and the path leading towards it. Both sects declare the essential nature of every man to be identical with that of the cosmic Buddha Vairochana. This perfect Buddha nature in man has been beclouded by the delusions of the phenomenal world, so that we fail to realize its presence within us. We can recover it by the complex discipline known as the *sammitsu*, the Three Secrets, a process of ritual imitation by which we can come to identify our actions, speech, and thought with those of the Buddha. Our actions we can identify by means of the ritual gestures known as *mudra*, our speech by *mantra*, or magical sounds, and our thoughts by certain modes of meditation such as gazing at the Sanskrit letter A. By these means we can achieve the state of *sokushin-jōbutsu*, becoming a Buddha in this very body. Both sects are described as esoteric in so far as their more profound mysteries were revealed only orally and in secret to those who had undergone the requisite initiations.

It is not surprising that such a complex spiritual discipline should have been undertaken only by a few priests of more than usual sanctity and inspiration. For the layman, the two sects provided what he had always demanded: spells, often potent-sounding corruptions of Sanskrit *mantra*, for warding off plague, fire, drought, and malevolent ghosts. In this form, Buddhism virtually for the first time began to reach the level of the ordinary Japanese, carried by wandering ascetics known as *hijiri*.

Doctrinally, the Tendai sect was more catholic than the Shingon. The only path taught by the Shingon was the esoteric one based on the teaching of the *sammitsu*. The Tendai offered a broader choice, including a form of walking meditation, based on the worship of the Buddha Amida, known as *jōgyō-zammai*, and another known as *shikan*, 'stopping and insight'. Unlike the Shingon sect, the Tendai gave supreme reverence to the *Lotus Sutra*, which it considered to expound the highest form of truth, and compared with which the other doctrines it embraced in its catholic fold were mere preliminary steps.

p 230 (9)

The truly Japanese forms of Buddhism which appeared during the 12th and 13th centuries ultimately derived, therefore, from the Tendai sect, the seed from which sprang the schools to which the majority of Japanese who call themselves Buddhist belong. Although Buddhism under the influence of these tantric sects was more widely disseminated than ever before, it was still predominantly an aristocratic and magical cult, catering for the needs of the elegant ruling class in the capital. Nor was the way to salvation which it offered an easy one. The disciplines leading to 'becoming a Buddha in this very body' were too complex for any but dedicated priests.

Medieval Buddhism

It was only at the beginning of the 13th century, in the Kamakura period, that Buddhism developed in such a way as to reach the ordinary man. The curious upsurge of new movements which occurred at this time marked an important stage in the development of Buddhism in Japan. For although these new sects differed from each other in ways which seem on first glance to be fundamental, yet they possess in common certain important traits which we now know to be characteristically Japanese.

In the first place, they all arose at a time of special misery and crisis. They may hence be regarded as a specific response to the anxieties of civil war, starvation, earthquake, pestilence, and maladministration. Secondly, they all arose at the inspiration of a charismatic figure, the Founder, who was later accorded reverence on a par with a Bodhisattva. And, thirdly, they preached salvation, in the sense of a complete change in man's state, rather than the local and temporary benefits which we have seen to be so characteristic of the earlier sects.

Beyond this common basis, the sects of the Kamakura period tend to fall into three distinct categories, each advocating a different path towards salvation.

p 230 (10) First we have the Amidist sects, the Jōdo and Shin, which worship the Buddha Amida. These are also known as the *tariki* schools, schools of 'other strength', because, like the prototype of the Amidist cult in China, they teach that there is nothing whatever that we ourselves can do to escape from the horrors of the ordinary human state, or of rebirth in a worse one. We must rely entirely on the superior power of Amida Buddha to enable us to be reborn in his own paradise, the Pure Land in the West. There, under idyllically perfect conditions, we can be sure of eventually attaining Nirvāṇa. We can rely on Amida's saving grace by simply repeating, with complete faith and purity of heart, the mystic invocation *Namu Amida Butsu*. We need then fear neither hell nor the realm of hungry ghosts nor any other limbo. Amida will come to meet us at our death and escort us to his paradise. In the present age our own efforts are negligible, for the world has entered the depraved period of *mappō*, the Latter Days of the Law, when, as predicted in the sutras, the Buddha's law loses its force. Our only hope of salvation lies in the grace of Amida to save all those who call on his name.

This doctrine thus envisages salvation as attainable only after death. The Pure Land, in which we pass our next incarnation, is strictly speaking only a stage on the way to final liberation, but for many Japanese its delights, vividly described in the Amidist sutras, are sufficient salvation in themselves.

The metaphysical tradition of Buddhism was mainly confined to the small groups of monks who devoted their time to studying Buddha's original message. Above: a priest, retired into a temple for study and contemplation, is disturbed by the soul of a dead girl in the form of a bird. (6)

There are several minor differences between the two Amidist sects, the most conspicuous of which, perhaps, is the teaching as to the number of times it is necessary to recite the sacred formula before one can be sure of achieving *ōjō*, or rebirth in paradise. Hōnen, the founder of the Jōdo sect, always insisted that it should be recited as many times as possible. Shinran, the founder of the Shin sect, declared that only one invocation, provided it was made with true faith, was enough to ensure a joyous rebirth. At first glance such a teaching may seem a travesty of Buddhist doctrine. It should be remembered, however, that the quality of faith which Shinran had in mind is by no means easy to achieve. It is a complete surrender of the self, attainable only by few.

A second path, complementary to that of the Amidist sects, is that of *jiriki*, self-help, a phrase usually used to describe the two sects of Zen which arose at this time. Far from totally surrendering his will in self-abnegating devotion to Amida, the Zen disciple is taught that through strenuous *zazen*, sitting and struggling with various meditational exercises designed to lead the mind to hitherto unsuspected depths, he can by his own efforts, guided by a qualified master, bring about in himself successively deepening experiences of illumination. It is here that we find the most profound and distinctive indication of Japanese spirituality. The Zen sect, with its unique and practical teaching towards 'sudden enlightenment', has deeply influenced much of Japanese art. p 232 (12–14 p 182– (24)

Of the two schools of Zen which took root in Japan, the Rinzai is the better known in the West owing to the writings of Dr D. T. Suzuki. Here we find the teachings of the Chinese school of Lin-chi transmitted to Japan with little admixture of native elements. The disciple must grapple with the meditational exercises known as *kōan*, problems without rational content designed to awaken the Buddha nature by stilling the mind, then rousing it to realize levels beyond the discriminating intellect. The *kōan* customarily used in Rinzai monasteries are all of Chinese origin, though the order in which they are presented to the disciple was devised by the great 18th-century Japanese Zen master, Hakuin. Most of the details of the meditational discipline, too, have come to Japan from China.

The Rinzai teaching was first introduced by the monk Eisai, who began preaching in Kyūshū at the end of the 12th century. He later founded temples in Kyoto and Kamakura by which the teaching was propagated. It found some of its most ardent disciples among the warrior class, which was rising to prominence at the time.

The Sōtō school of Zen was founded in Japan a few years later by the eminent priest Dōgen (1200–53). Although Chinese in origin, its development in Japan has been very different from the Rinzai school. It is today far wealthier, with twice as many temples and believers. The reason is not far to seek. It is that it has allowed its teachings to become so mingled with folk beliefs and practices that there is often little trace of anything that recognizably pertains to Zen. Its biggest temples are geared to the lucrative business of reciting spells for worldly blessings, and in the large Toyokawa Inari temple the presiding deity is Inari, the Shintō rice spirit in fox form. In its meditational practices, too, the Sōtō school differs interestingly from the Rinzai. *Kōan* of every kind

The Nishi Honganji in Kyoto is the main temple of the Shin-shu sect, a branch of the Buddhist 'Pure Land' Movement which because of its simple doctrines and egalitarian principles achieved immense popularity in Japan. (7)

are scorned, and instead a discipline known as *shikan-taza* is practised. The disciple does not attempt to concentrate his mind on any focal point, but simply sits in the faith that he is here and now a Buddha, observing objectively such thoughts as may pass through his mind. Whereas the Rinzai school relies almost exclusively on Chinese sources for its sutras and books of *kōan*, in the rituals of the Sōtō sect little is heard beyond the words of Dōgen, whose status has been raised, in the typically Japanese manner, virtually to that of a Bodhisattva. Indeed the voluminous writings of Dōgen are among the most profound and subtle in Japanese religious literature.

The third distinctive current of Buddhism which arose during the Kamakura period is represented by the Nichiren sect, and is best described as based on the *Lotus Sutra*. Nichiren was a turbulent priest who flourished during the disturbed period of the 13th century, and who vehemently declared that all Japan's ills, particularly the Mongol invasions, were due to divine retribution for her neglect of the true faith. This true faith was easily understood; it was the belief that the *Lotus Sutra* was the only scripture embodying truth and power, and that it should be worshipped by constant recitation of the mystic formula *Namu Myōhō Rengekyō*. Nichiren's vehement intolerance of all other forms of Buddhism and all other religions is curiously un-Buddhist and un-Japanese. Yet it is clear that it has had a compelling appeal, for the Nichiren sect has flourished since the 13th century and is today the best subscribed of all the older sects. It has had numerous offshoots, furthermore, which have split from the original sect on some minor point of doctrine but which still preserve the basic faith in the power and efficacy of the *Lotus Sutra*. The latest and most celebrated of these is Sōka Gakkai, which has pushed its intolerance to even more fanatical lengths.

The salvation preached by these *Lotus Sutra* sects is in interesting contrast to the other modes we have noticed. The Amidist sects promised salvation in the next world after death. The Zen school proclaimed that the Buddha nature lay unrecognized within us, but could be released

230–1
(9,11)

through meditation, so that we can attain full enlightenment in this life. The Nichiren sect vehemently denounced both these teachings and proclaimed instead a future terrestrial paradise, a millennium in which our descendants, once they have learnt to embrace the right faith, will enjoy perfect peace and bliss.

A new creed from the West

A word is needed here about what is known as Japan's 'Christian century'. This period extended from 1549, when St Francis Xavier arrived in Japan, to 1639, when the definitive edict of expulsion and proscription of all Christians was issued. Christian missionary work was at first the monopoly of the Portuguese Jesuits, a natural outcome of the Portuguese conquests in India and their successful commercial ventures further east to Malacca and Macao. Many of the Jesuit missionaries were men who were remarkable for courage, faith, and determination, yet to the last their efforts met with only limited success. In the first years of their mission no obstacles were placed in the way of their preaching, and several of the feudal lords in Kyūshū seem to have become genuine converts. In other cases it was more difficult to distinguish enthusiasm for Christianity from enthusiasm for the material goods—silk and gold—brought once a year from Macao by the Portuguese 'Great Ship', the visits of which were for some time made conditional on a kindly reception being given to the Jesuits. Later in the century the missionary ranks were swollen by a number of Spanish friars. All were kindly received by Nobunaga, the military ruler of most of the country during the mid-16th century, but this was largely because he detested Buddhism and saw in the missionaries a welcome ally against the common enemy. His successor Hideyoshi received them first with cordiality, but in 1587 he suddenly issued an edict expelling all missionaries. The real persecution, however, did not start until after 1614, when the first Tokugawa Shogun, Ieyasu, had come to power. The reason for his ruthless banishment of all foreign missionaries and proscription of all native Christians was largely the suspicion

p 208
(23)

241

The Neo-Confucian system of ethics provided detailed concepts regulating relations between ruler and vassal, father and son, husband and wife. The Onna Daigaku was one of a series of 'instruction books' for women written by a noted Confucian scholar Kaibara Ekken. This illustration from it shows women at needlework. (8)

that the missionaries were the forerunners of a political conquest by Spain, such as had befallen Manila. The story of the persecution is one of horrifying cruelty, culminating in the Shimabara Rebellion of 1637–38, when many thousands of native Japanese Christians were massacred. In the following year, 1639, the definitive edict of expulsion was issued. (See Chapter VIII)

The feudal period

p 232–3 (15)

The effects on Buddhism of the proscription of Christianity were twofold. During the 250 years of isolation from the outside world under the feudal rule of the Tokugawa Shoguns, the position of Buddhism was materially strengthened by the edict requiring all families to register at a Buddhist temple as *danka*, or supporters. But at the same time the growth and organization of the sects and their temples were subjected to a minute political control, which resulted before long in a sorry spiritual stagnation. Such religious enthusiasm as survived seems to have been directed towards the purely theoretical study of doctrine, at the expense of the cultivation of the spiritual wisdom which is the proper goal of Buddhism.

p 232–3 (16)

Far more potent than Buddhism during the Tokugawa period were the doctrines of Neo-Confucianism, particularly those of the Sung philosopher Chu Hsi. It was Neo-Confucianism which provided the first really vigorous system of social ethics that the Japanese had known. Early Shintō, as we have seen, provided no ethical rules at all. Nor had Buddhism in Japan ever provided a viable social ethic. Mahāyāna teaching emphasized compassion for suffering, respect for the sanctity of life, whether of man or beast, and prescriptions for a pure if solitary life. But it had failed to provide detailed precepts whereby the relations between ruler and vassal, father and son, husband and wife, and elder and younger should be regulated. Moral behaviour in Buddhism was in any case regarded as merely a preparatory and purificatory step towards the more important business of training and opening the mind through meditation.

The doctrines of Neo-Confucianism thus fulfilled a genuine need, and met it at the same time in a way that was very acceptable to the Tokugawa authorities. The philosophy underlying Chu Hsi's teaching—that the universe is a natural hierarchy and that, in consequence, human society is similarly vertical in structure, so that all men are naturally unequal—was a suitable creed for preserving the existing relations between rulers and ruled, and thus keeping the Tokugawas ruler securely in power.

p 232–(17)

The religious situation during the 18th and early 19th centuries was further complicated by a movement which became known as *fukko-Shintō*, the revival of Shintō. For centuries the cult that we have called 'early Shintō' had been virtually neglected by educated people. The early chronicles, poems, and rituals which transmitted the cult were no longer legible or comprehensible to scholars. The cult had become unrecognizably mingled with Buddhist elements, in forms such as Ryōbu-Shintō and Ichijitsu-Shintō, which had grown up since medieval times. The Shintō revival of the 18th century was an attempt by scholars to rediscover the Shintō cult in all its ancient purity, stripped of the foreign accretions which had debased and distorted it. At the same time they developed two powerful myths. The first was of a Japanese golden age in the past: a state of simple bliss and perfection which, they averred, had been the Japanese 'state of nature' before the corruption and innate viciousness of Chinese ideas had caused a fall from these idyllic conditions. The second was that the message of the ancient myths pointed towards the unique superiority of the Japanese race over all other peoples of the world. The special act of divine creation which had produced Japan, and the direct descent of the emperor from Amaterasu the sun goddess, were so many proofs that the Japanese were qualitatively different from other races and hence ineluctably destined to rule the world.

These compelling doctrines, neither of which, needless to say, was present in the ancient Shintō cult, were propounded by three notable scholars: Kamo Mabuchi (1697–1769), Motoori Norinaga (1730–1801), and Hirata Atsutane (1776–1843). All three produced monumental works of exegesis of the ancient texts. The *Kojiki*, which had long lain in a limbo of neglect and incomprehension, was resuscitated by Motoori; the poems of the *Manyōshū* were revived by Mabuchi; and it fell to Hirata to emphasize the two myths underlying the movement in a manner which, years later, was to produce momentous and terrible consequences.

By the mid-19th century the creed which functioned most powerfully as a 'religion' in Japan was the combination, known as Mitogaku, of Confucian ethical teachings with Shintō myth. These doctrines were not the loose amalgam that might have been expected; they were an organic whole, charged with explosive power. This became the creed underlying the movement to abolish the feudal system and to restore the emperor to the pristine and numinous power that he was mistakenly imagined to have enjoyed in ancient times.

X A LITERATURE OF COURT AND PEOPLE

Japanese poetry, drama and the novel before the Meiji

DONALD KEENE

Japanese poetry has for its seed the human heart.

Ki no Tsurayuki, Preface to the
Kokinshū, AD 905

Japan's literary heritage is one of the richest in the world, and probably psychologically more easily accessible to the Westerner than those of China or India. It began under peculiar difficulties. Until the 6th century AD it was purely an oral tradition. Only when Chinese characters were introduced at that time was an attempt made to record it in writing. But the Chinese and Japanese languages are totally unrelated. Forcing the Chinese characters, which were anyway not phonetic, to represent the sounds of Japanese resulted in a system of unparalleled complexity and difficulty. Yet Japanese literature never became a mere offshoot of Chinese, in spite of being subjected to continuous influence from it. The language of poetry was kept remarkably pure of loan-words, and the most typically Japanese literary forms – the diary, the novel, the *haiku*, the Nō and Kabuki drama – have owed almost nothing to Chinese models.

The earliest extant literature of Japan consists of myths and legends interspersed with poems. As early as 712 the *Kojiki* (Record of Ancient Matters) contained the first example of the classic verse form, the *tanka*, a poem of five lines with a set pattern of syllables. Some fifty years later came the greatest collection of Japanese poetry, the *Manyōshū* (Collection of Ten Thousand Leaves). It includes both *tanka* and *chōka* (long poems) and its subjects range from the death of emperors to the love affairs of peasants. These poems appealed to the whole population, sophisticated and unsophisticated alike.

By the beginning of the Heian period (794–1185) histories, religious works and other kinds of serious literature were mostly written in Chinese, but Japanese was still used for poetry describing moments of deeply felt emotion – love, the transience of life, the beauty of nature. The *tanka* especially reached a high pitch of artistry, the most important collection being the *Kokinshū* (Poems Old and New) of 905. The poetic diction established here lasted for a thousand years. Shown opposite is a section from the 'Collection of Thirty-Six Poets' made some time in the Late Heian period. The mood of the poem is matched by its physical appearance. The page has been made by pasting together pieces of differently coloured paper. On the white background a design of fruit and vine is imprinted from wood-blocks, with details added in silver paint. Over all this the poem itself is written in exquisite calligraphy.

The lower picture dates from the 13th century and comes from a set of scrolls containing portraits of poets and poetesses attributed to the celebrated painter Fujiwara Nobuzane. This one shows the poetess Ko-ōgimi. (1, 2)

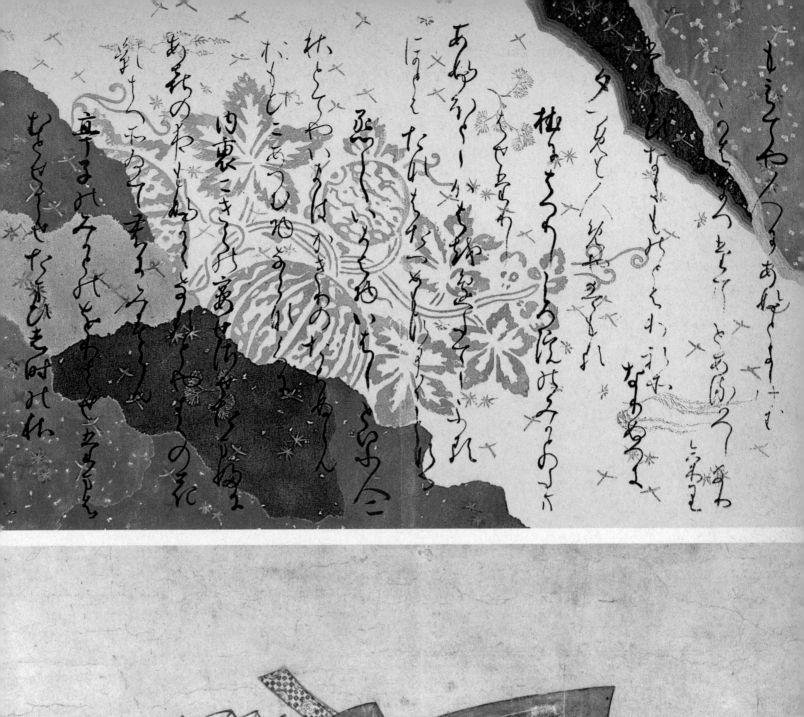

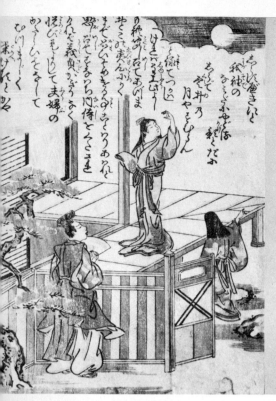

The etiquette of love saved Japanese poetry from being overwhelmed by Chinese. Women did not learn Chinese, and so the letters and poems that were exchanged between lovers – in contrast to works of serious scholarship – had perforce to be in Japanese. Partly for this reason and partly because they enjoyed social equality with men, women dominated Japanese literature during the Heian period. Above left: a double page from *Ladies' Literary Pursuits* showing a 14th-century poetess composing a poem about the moon, and being presented to her suitor by the Emperor Go-Daigo. Above right: a scene from the 10th-century collection of stories, *Ise Monogatari*, most of which concern the adventures of Ariwara no Narihira (825–880), famous equally as a poet and a lover. Here he has eloped with a court lady; her brother has overtaken them in a field and separates them by threatening to burn the grass. Below: the delivery of love-letters, from a 17th-century painted screen. The lady has been identified as a beautiful widow of the Tokugawa clan, the man as a samurai. (3–5)

'The falling of the leaves on an Autumn evening' was one of the occasions listed by Ki no Tsurayuki in the 10th century as likely to inspire the poet. Throughout Japanese history the seasons remained perennially popular in both art and poetry. City dwellers made special excursions to watch the cherry trees blossoming or the maples turning red. Mount Takao (above), northwest of Kyoto, was a favourite spot. (6)

'The moon . . . seems tonight to come out of the waves' wrote Ki no Tsurayuki in his *Tosa Diary* (left, from a 19th-century edition), an account of his homeward journey to Kyoto from the province of Tosa in AD 935. The diary proved a particularly congenial form of writing to the Japanese, and soon led from fact to fiction, turning into a loosely constructed series of tales, the *monogatari*. (7)

247

The novel as a mature literary form made its appearance in the 10th century, its masterpiece being *The Tale of Genji* by Lady Murasaki Shikibu. The greater part is devoted to the life of Prince Genji, the ideal courtier and lover. Men and women are here portrayed with a depth and sensitivity that no previous writer had approached. Left: Lady Murasaki composing the story, sitting on a balcony open to the moon and the scent of the spring blossoms. According to tradition, in order to write the story she retired to a Buddhist temple overlooking Lake Biwa. Far left: an incident from *The Tale of Genji*, from a 17th-century painting. The novel has been celebrated for the last thousand years. Below left: a print by Torii Kiyonobu (1664–1729) showing a street bookseller in the early 18th century. The topmost of her pile of books is *The Tale of Genji*. Beneath that are books on music; the inscription on the box underneath is an advertisement. She holds a writing brush in one hand and a guide to letter-writing in the other. (8–10)

The drama traces its origin back to 14th-century adaptations of even earlier mimes. Buddhism prescribed the chief subject-matter – the sin of attachment to material things, forcing the dead to revisit the world and relive the passions of their former existence. The Nō-play reached its perfection in the 15th century and thereafter has hardly changed, a classical, conservative, highly stylized art form, relying on gesture, dance and song rather than on realistic acting. Costumes (right, first half of the 17th century) are of the utmost splendour. The stage (below) is a wooden platform, entered from the left by a bridge, the *hashigakari*. Scenery is minimal and the musicians remain at the back throughout. (11, 12)

'The floating world', the world of the 'gay quarters' of Edo, came to typify the glittering culture of 17th-century Japan. In the rigidly authoritarian Tokugawa society, the gay quarters were oases of relaxation, pleasure and wit; literature and art increasingly revolved around them. Above left: a typical 17th-century woodcut showing the private apartments of courtesans. (13)

Drama for puppets (left) offered a way out from the strict formality of the Nō-plays. It became extremely popular among the ordinary people, and with the playwright Chikamitsu Monzaemon reached the status of a true art – lively, tender, poetic and occasionally humorous. Here three puppets (glove-puppets, not manipulated from above) are raised above the screen that hides the puppeteers from the audience. (14)

The conflict between duty and feelings was the source of many popular tales and plays. *Chūshingura* tells the true story of how a gentleman of rank, Enya Hangan, was provoked into striking, while in the Palace, the Governor of Kamakura, Kōno Moronao – a mortal offence in the Tokugawa code. He was ordered to commit suicide and did so. Forty-seven of his loyal retainers, however, swore to avenge him. In this scene (above) they murder Moronao while the spirit of Enya Hangan looks on. Then they too, sentenced by the law, killed themselves. (15)

The haiku distils the essence of an experience into seventeen syllables. Right: a disciple of Bashō's, with his poem:

'How the waters
Of the lake have swollen
With the summer rains' (16)

Ghosts, prodigies and medieval warfare (right) mingle with didactic philosophy in Takizawa Bakin's fantastic novel, *Hakkenden* (Biography of Eight Dogs), of the early 19th century. (17)

The people's theatre, as distinct from the archaic Nō-drama which appealed chiefly to the aristocracy, was the Kabuki. Kabuki began in the early 17th century. At first women appeared on the stage but this was soon banned and in later times some of the most famous Kabuki actors were those who played female parts. Its stage (left) differed from that of Nō mainly in its 'flower-path', a long ramp stretching through the audience, along which the characters can slowly progress. Acting is still stylized but much more lively than in Nō. In this scene two brothers are plotting revenge. (18)

Theatre Street, Edo. By 1800 Kabuki was immensely popular and whole districts were given over to theatres. This woodcut of the early 19th century shows posters and brightly-coloured scenes from plays, lining and overhanging the street.

The opening up of Japan after 1853 meant a revolution in Japanese literature, as in Japanese life. Western forms (e.g. the novel and the film) were eagerly taken up and today rival the West on their own terms. Nevertheless, Nō and Kabuki have survived and have even increased their audiences. (19)

DONALD KEENE

JAPANESE LITERATURE has a history about as long as that of English literature, and includes a rich variety of poetry, prose, and drama. If certain genres, such as satire or literary biography, never developed, others (like the diary and travel account) achieved an importance not found elsewhere. There has never been a 'dark age' barren of literature, but changing social or political conditions have fostered different varieties of writing.

For long periods Japanese literature was under Chinese influence. The introduction of Chinese characters in the 6th century AD – the only script known at the time to the Japanese – inevitably led to a study of Chinese books, and in the 7th century a few educated Japanese began using Chinese for official or religious documents, rather in the way that Bede, about the same time, used Latin for his theological and historical works. There are striking similarities in the ways in which the Japanese borrowed from Chinese and the English from Latin when they needed new words, especially of an intellectual or abstract nature, but there are important differences too. Anglo-Saxon and Latin, though quite dissimilar, are both Indo-European languages, but, as has been explained in Chapter 1, Chinese and Japanese are totally unrelated. Again, there is no particular difficulty about writing Anglo-Saxon in roman letters, but to write the polysyllabic Japanese with Chinese characters that were intended to represent monosyllables involved inordinate complications, and resulted in what is perhaps the most intricate writing system in the world. Finally, the Chinese and Japanese languages are so different phonetically that words borrowed from Chinese, even when rendered in Japanese approximations, tended always to stand out as foreignisms.

Chinese civilization attracted the Japanese enormously, and a knowledge of the famous works of Chinese poetry and prose came to be expected of all educated men. At the same time, there was a contradictory insistence on the purity of the Japanese language used in literary writings. Virtually all words of Chinese derivation were barred from poetry and prose during the 10th and 11th centuries, the greatest period of Japanese literature. Even when, towards the end of the 12th century, Chinese loan-words had become common in speech and were

tolerated in prose, they were excluded from *tanka* poetry (considered to be the most important branch of literature), and this continued to be the case until late in the 19th century.

The Japanese have often been accused of a proclivity for imitation, but it is to be marvelled at that they so effectively guarded their cultural heritage even during periods when Chinese influence was strongest. In any case, the charge of imitation cannot be taken seriously by anyone familiar with Japanese literature. The characteristic verse forms (the *tanka*, linked verse, and the *haiku*) are unlike those of any other country; the different varieties of drama (Nō, Bunraku, and Kabuki) developed without foreign influence; and Japan boasts the oldest novels written anywhere, apart from the Graeco-Roman world. Nevertheless, the readiness of the Japanese to borrow abroad, in contrast to India and China, which rarely looked beyond their own borders, again and again resulted in new literary activity. The theories of poetry expounded by Chinese critics of the age of the Sung dynasty inspired the Japanese to write a different kind of *tanka*, just as Western literary theories, introduced in the 19th century, resulted in a new kind of novel. But the borrowings were always selective, and the Japanese freely modified whatever they borrowed to suit their own tastes.

The dawn of poetry: before 794

The oldest document referring to Japan is the account written by a Chinese traveller which is included in the *Wei History*, compiled in the 3rd century AD. The few terms he recorded in Chinese transcription indicate that the language spoken by the natives he encountered was unquestionably Japanese. We may gather, too, that the religious ceremonies he witnessed were accompanied by songs, and that tales of the past and legends were recited. However, the date of the oldest surviving Japanese book, the *Kojiki (Record of Ancient Matters)*, is only 712. Undoubtedly it contains materials of a much more distant past, perhaps even earlier than the 3rd century, but we cannot distinguish them.

The preface to the *Kojiki* states that the text was written down from the oral narration of one Hieda no

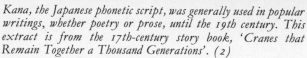

Kana, the Japanese phonetic script, was generally used in popular writings, whether poetry or prose, until the 19th century. This extract is from the 17th-century story book, 'Cranes that Remain Together a Thousand Generations'. (2)

Theatre in all its forms has traditionally been a popular pastime and social occasion among all classes in Japan. Performances of Kabuki often lasted all day; here part of the audience relaxes between acts in an early 19th-century theatre. (3)

Are, a man who could repeat anything he had once heard. It also mentions earlier records, including a chronology of the imperial family and legends of the gods, which were no longer extant. The main intent of the *Kojiki*, though nowhere so stated, seems to have been a justification of the claims of the imperial family to rule Japan. It is divided into two parts. The first, containing the legends of the 'age of the gods', is of some literary interest; the second describes, often in bleak chronological sequence, events concerning the emperors, beginning with the legendary Jimmu, whose 'coronation' was arbitrarily dated 660 BC.

The text of the *Kojiki* includes a number of poems attributed to gods, emperors, and other personages. With rare exceptions they are so crude as to be hardly recognizable as poetry, but occasionally they suggest the first stirrings of literary awareness. The prose looks like an exceedingly barbarous Chinese, but the great scholar Motoori Norinaga (1730–1801) spent thirty years of his life establishing how to read the text throughout as pure Japanese.

Eight years after the completion of the *Kojiki*, the *Nihon shoki* (Chronicles of Japan, 720) was presented to the court. It is curious that a new national history should have been needed so soon after the first one. Perhaps the court felt that Japan must be provided with a history in proper Chinese which could be displayed to Chinese or Korean visitors as proof that Japan had a long and glorious past. The compilers embellished their accounts of the successive reigns by putting into the mouths of Japanese emperors speeches taken word-for-word from Chinese histories, even conforming to continental traditions to the extent of making one emperor (about whom the *Kojiki* is silent) a monster who delights in perverse wickedness.

Some songs in the *Kojiki* and *Nihon shoki* reveal an incipient literary sensibility, but nothing in either work prepares us for the magnificence of the *Manyōshū*, the greatest collection of Japanese poetry. The establishment in 710 of the first permanent capital, Nara, ushered in an age of spectacular advances in the arts of civilization, largely under Chinese influence. This in-

fluence is present in the *Manyōshū*, not only in the relatively few poems derived from Chinese models but in the vastly heightened artistry. The *Manyōshū* may originally have been compiled to demonstrate that Japan had not only a long history but also a rich store of poetry, the mark of a civilized nation.

The title *Manyōshū* means literally 'Collection of Ten Thousand Leaves', leaves meaning poems. The number 10,000 was, of course, not intended literally; the collection in fact numbers some 4,500 poems by about 450 poets. Compilation was completed about 777. It is generally assumed that the poet Ōtomo no Yakamochi (718?–785) was the editor, because the honorifics we should expect are not applied to his name. The collection includes poems written between the mid-7th century and 759, and is arranged in twenty books.

The *Manyōshū* differs markedly from subsequent, officially sponsored anthologies in the variety of the poetic forms, the subject-matter, and the authorship. Although the five-line *tanka* is overwhelmingly the predominant form, accounting for about 4,200 of the poems, it is the *chōka* (long poems), only 260 in all, that impart grandeur to the *Manyōshū*. In addition, there are some fifty poems in other forms. The subject-matter ranges from elegies on the deaths of emperors to the songs of rustic sweethearts, and includes many themes that the later poets would not have considered appropriate. Most *Manyōshū* poets were noblemen who served at the court, but there are poems also by soldiers on the frontier, farmers, and fishermen. These departures from what was to become the standard format of the court anthologies – a collection of *tanka* written by aristocrats on themes approved of by the arbiters of poetic taste – all contribute to the *Manyōshū*'s unique importance.

The supreme poet of the *Manyōshū* (and perhaps of all Japanese literature) was Kakinomoto no Hitomaro. Little biographical information survives, but there is reason to believe that he died in the epidemic of 707 while in his fifties. Hitomaro, a kind of poet laureate, accompanied the emperor or empress on their travels and commemorated them in poetry. Even during his lifetime his greatness was recognized; the courtiers knew his poems by heart, and farmers made them into folk songs. After his death his reputation continued to grow, as we know from the many imitations of his work.

Hitomaro's poetry is marked by the powerful sincerity of its expression. This 'sincerity' should not suggest that he artlessly narrated his emotions; Hitomaro was a master of poetic techniques, whether in the use of imagery or in the choice of syntax. Nevertheless, the unmistakable note of conviction even when, in his capacity as poet laureate, Hitomaro described the grief occasioned by the death of a prince he had never known, gives his poetry an intensity rarely again attained. The later poets were not necessarily insincere when they penned their exquisitely turned *tanka* on the scattering of the cherry blossoms or the blowing of the autumn wind, but their themes lent themselves to conventional melancholy or even to gallantry; Hitomaro's poetry is appropriate to the solemn occasion of addressing a dead prince and assuring him that his glory will never be forgotten.

The *chōka* survived only as long as poets could approximate Hitomaro's emotional intensity and stylistic skill. Because the Japanese language lacks a stress accent and rhyme is so easy as to be meaningless, a poem that lacked poetic tension at once dropped into prose. It was not too difficult to maintain the tension through the five lines of a *tanka*, but Hitomaro and two or three other *Manyōshū* poets, notably Ōtomo no Yakamochi and Yamanoe no Okura, alone combined a genius for amplitude with the more typical Japanese skill at suggestion. Perfection of tone, language, and sentiment, rather than grandeur, was to become the ideal of later poets. Many subjects could not be treated within the brief compass of a *tanka*; narrative poems or poems with a philosophic content disappeared after the *Manyōshū*. But the *tanka* poets, like sonneteers in the West, gladly accepted the restrictions they had imposed on themselves, and they arrived eventually at a perfect congruence between what they wished to express and what the *tanka* easily allowed.

Amplitude in poetry was also hampered by a weakness of construction apparent in most extended Japanese

The poems of Kakinomoto no Hitomaro, the 'poet laureate' of his day, were popular among both courtiers and peasants. He was the supreme poet of the 8th-century 'Manyōshū' or 'Collection of Ten Thousand Leaves', probably the greatest collection of Japanese poetry. (4)

literary works. The Japanese did not conceive of a work in terms of proportion; their emphasis was placed on the smoothness of transition from one passage to the next.

A 'feminine' preference for suggestion and intuitive perception, and a more 'masculine' directness of utterance and concern over society, can both be found in the *Manyōshū*. Sometimes a poet wrote in both idioms, but a polarization eventually developed by the end of the 8th century: the masculine style was channelled into the composition of poetry and prose in Chinese, but women p 245 (2) (or men when writing to women) expressed themselves p 246 (3) in the feminine *tanka*. The decision of the men not to use Japanese when writing their serious compositions meant that the literature of the Heian period would be dominated by women, perhaps the only time that women have enjoyed this literary supremacy.

Nature, love and artifice: the Heian period

The literature of the early Heian period – the first half of the 9th century – was written mainly in Chinese. Several anthologies of poetry prove how skilfully the Japanese had learned to write Chinese, and there is also stylistically distinguished prose, especially the religious writings of the priest Kūkai (774–835), the founder in Japan of the Shingon Sect. So great was the adulation of Chinese culture at this time that there was a real danger that the Japanese language might cease to be used for literary purposes. Probably it was the elaborate etiquette p 246 (5) of courtship that saved Japanese poetry. Lovers were expected to exchange poetry as part of the elegant formalities of becoming intimate, but since it was not considered ladylike for a woman to learn Chinese, the men had to address poems to women in Japanese.

The most famous of the *tanka* poets of the day was Ariwara no Narihira (825–80), the paragon of Heian p 246 (4) lovers. His poetry is melancholy rather than passionate, and curiously lacking in masculine assurance, but evidently this was the most winning tone for wooing a Heian lady. By this time the *chōka* had become almost obsolete. Already in the *Manyōshū* we can see how the *chōka* was beginning to give way to the *tanka*. Yamabe no Akahito wrote competent *chōka*, but his fame rests chiefly on the 'envoys', the *tanka* that were appended to them. These *tanka* so effectively suggest the content of the long poems they follow as to make them seem unnecessarily wordy. When the Heian poets wrote *chōka*, it was not because they had too much to say for a *tanka*; it was merely a literary gesture, vapid in content.

One important cultural development helped to shape the literature of the Heian period, the invention of the *kana*, the Japanese syllabary. *Kana* replaced the cumbersome and confusing methods of writing Japanese employed in the *Kojiki* and *Manyōshū* with a simple and accurate phonetic transcription. Presumably the *kana* was invented by someone familiar with Sanskrit – tradition ascribes it to Kūkai – but the time and circumstances are unknown.

The first important literary works to be composed in the new writing were the poems included in the *Kokinshū* (*Collection of Poems Old and New*, 905), an anthology consisting of 1,111 poems arranged in twenty books. The preface by the editor, Ki no Tsurayuki (859?–945), announced the ideals of Japanese poetry in terms that became definitive not only for Heian writers but for the poets of a thousand years later. 'Japanese poetry', he wrote, 'has for its seed the human heart', an enunciation of his belief that the *tanka* must arise from the emotions rather than from the intellect. The specific occasions he considered likely to inspire poets included: 'When they look at the scattered blossoms of a spring morning; when they listen of an autumn evening to the falling of the leaves; . . . when they are startled into thoughts on the brevity of life by seeing the dew on the grass or foam on the water.' Such subjects could indeed inspire beautiful poetry, but the range of expression, hardly going beyond a gentle melancholy, was certainly limited by comparison with the *Manyōshū*.

p 247 (6)

The *Kokinshū* poets are sometimes blamed for having injected into Japanese poetry an artificiality that vitiated the simple nobility of the *Manyōshū*. Word-plays are easily contrived in Japanese because of the many homonyms, and the *Kokinshū* poets often employed them, not only as a display of virtuosity but because word-plays were a means of enriching the content of the thirty-one syllables of a *tanka*. More objectionable are the quibbling ('is it a mountain or is it a cloud?') and the poetic conceits. But it was not the fault of the *Kokinshū* poets if later men so idolized their work as to make it the absolute standard against which all poetry had to be measured.

The *Kokinshū* established a poetic diction obeyed by most *tanka* poets for a thousand years. It also determined the prevailing moods and thematic content of subsequent poetry. Like the *Manyōshū* it was divided into twenty books, but the contents were classified: six books of seasonal verse were followed by books of congratulatory verse, poems about parting, travel, love (five books), mourning, and miscellaneous subjects. The importance of seasonal and love poetry, accounting for more than half the total number of books, indicates what the Heian courtiers considered to be the main functions of poetry. The emphasis on the seasons, especially as witnessed in the capital, gave rise to the cult of cherry blossoms and reddening maple leaves that would inspire innumerable poems. Love became the chief subject of the *tanka*, contrary to Chinese poetic usage, but the joys of courtship were seldom described; instead, the prevailing emotions expressed by the poems on love were the uncertainty before meeting the beloved, the anguish of parting, the hopeless realization that an affair has ended. The reluctance to treat the central area of experience, in favour of beginnings and ends, deprived Japanese poetry of some of the strength of Western love poetry; but, given the shortness of the *tanka* and its prevailingly 'feminine' mood, the *Kokinshū* poets chose wisely. It should not be supposed, however, that the *Kokinshū* poems are pallid, if beautifully fashioned, verse; the poems of Narihira, Tsurayuki, and such women as Ono no Komachi (9th century) and Ise (877?–939) have depth and sometimes blazing emotional intensity. But the easiest parts of the *Kokinshū* for later poets to imitate were inevitably the least impressive, the poems composed on set occasions with prescribed themes; they show superb technique but little emotional intensity or individuality.

p 246 (5)
p 247 (6)

Ki no Tsurayuki, the compiler of the *Kokinshū*, is famed also for *Tosa Nikki* (*Tosa Diary*, 935), an account

p 247 (7)

of his homeward journey to the capital from the province of Tosa. Tsurayuki wrote in Japanese, though men normally kept their diaries in Chinese; in order to escape reproach for this unmanly style, he pretended that the diary was written by a woman in his entourage. Events of the journey and poems composed on various occasions make up the bulk of the work, which is given a peculiarly moving quality by repeated, half-spoken references to Tsurayuki's daughter who had died in Tosa and whose absence deprived the return to the capital of its joy.

Tosa Nikki is the earliest surviving example of an important genre of Japanese literature, the diary. Diaries have been kept by people in almost every country, of course, but normally they do not rank high among literary works. The Japanese found the diary a particularly congenial form, perhaps because the difficulties they experienced when constructing an extended work were alleviated by the day-to-day continuity of a diary, or by the successive events of a journey. The poetry, included as part of the record of happenings, gave the diary a subjective, 'feminine' quality. The literary diary easily passed from fact to fiction, especially when the events described were recorded long after they occurred. The diary in fact influenced the development of the *monogatari* (tale), the characteristic Heian form of narrative fiction.

Ki no Tsurayuki pretended he was a woman writing a diary; subsequent Heian diaries in the Japanese language were in fact almost all by women. *Kagerō Nikki* (*The Gossamer Years*) describes the life between 954 and 974 of the author, the second wife of the prime minister. The first volume covers the period 954 to 970 in the manner of an autobiographical novel written in the form of dated recollections; even the author confesses that fiction may have crept into her account. The remaining two volumes cover only five years, and many entries were apparently made in true diary fashion, on the days indicated. The writer (known as 'the mother of Michitsuna') relates, with many touches of self-pity, her unhappy life with her husband. She evidently assumed that readers would sympathize, and often we do, but her self-centred grievances are not endearing. She shows no interest in the thoughts or wishes of others. Her obsession with her own woes is displayed to worst advantage in a passage where she gloats over the death of a rival's child. Yet her journal is extraordinarily moving, precisely because the author, by confining herself to universally intelligible emotions, makes us forget the vast differences separating Heian Japan from our world.

Two varieties of fiction were being written at about the same time as the *Kagerō Nikki*. The first, the 'poem tale', originated in the prefaces explaining the circumstances under which a poem was composed. The *tanka* is so brief and elusive that often the full meaning escapes the reader without such information. *Ise Monogatari* (*The Tales of Ise*), a collection of 125 episodes ranging in length from a few sentences to several pages each, consists mainly of the narration of events that occasioned poems by Ariwara no Narihira. The romantic nature of these episodes and the beauty of the style have won for *Ise Monogatari* exceptional popularity through the centuries, though the work is neither well sustained nor deeply moving.

p 246

The 'Tales of Ise', a series of 125 episodes, each centred on one or more romantic poems, was written in the 10th century. In this copy illustrated by Hishikawa Moronobu in the 17th century a boy and girl are shown looking over the parapet of a well. (5)

The second variety of fiction was the fairy tale. At the beginning of the 9th century a collection of Buddhist miracle stories, *Nihon Reiiki (Account of Miracles in Japan)*, was compiled in Chinese by the priest Keikai. Fantastic elements remained prominent in later religious or folk tales. *Taketori Monogatari (The Bamboo Cutter's Tale)*, probably written late in the 10th century, is a fairy tale containing elements found in the stories of many countries. It tells of a childless old man who finds a tiny girl in a bamboo stalk. She quickly grows into a beautiful woman, and is given the name Kaguya-hime, 'the shining princess'. Many suitors are attracted, but she refuses to marry any man unless he proves himself by carrying out an impossibly difficult task of her choosing. Each of five suitors throws his energies and fortune into his assigned task, but all fail, to the evident relief of Kaguya-hime. She next unwittingly attracts the Emperor's attention. Unable to treat him in the same high-handed manner, she dissolves into a ball of light. In the end she leaves the earth to return to her old home on the moon. The fantastic elements of *Taketori Monogatari* prevent us from taking it seriously, but the story is organized far more effectively than *Ise Monogatari*, and its humour is endearing.

Ise Monogatari and *Taketori Monogatari* represent the two streams of fiction that were combined in the mature *monogatari*; but before it could achieve literary distinction still another element was needed, the introspection of *Kagerō Nikki* and the other 'feminine' writings. Murasaki Shikibu (978–1016?), whose own diary is a fine example of the genre, achieved the miraculous fusion of the different varieties of Japanese prose in *Genji Monogatari (The Tale of Genji)*, the supreme work of Japanese literature. *Genji Monogatari* has been studied with immense devotion almost since its creation, and innumerable theories have been advanced concerning the motives, circumstances, and techniques of

p 248
(8–10)

composition, but Murasaki Shikibu's marvellous understanding of the human heart will always leave the reader lost in admiration. The judgment on her work that is the most persuasive, even today, was made by Motoori Norinaga, who said that its central theme was *mono no aware* – an almost untranslatable term meaning something like 'a sensitivity to things' or 'an awareness of things'. Unlike earlier Japanese fiction, *Genji Monogatari* is concerned not so much with plot as with the portrayal of sensitive and lifelike people. In this respect it may suggest a modern novel, though careful readers will be aware of the distinctly non-modern religious and social beliefs that shaped the Heian world.

The novel consists of fifty-four chapters. The first two-thirds describe the peerless Prince Genji; the remainder are devoted to the world after his death. Genji is the ideal Heian courtier – an accomplished poet, painter, dancer, musician, and even football player. But his supreme accomplishment was in the art most prized by Heian society, love-making. For the Heian courtiers, love, like any other art, required much practice before mastery was achieved. *Genji Monogatari* describes many affairs, from the first tentative poems sent by Genji to some woman he knew only by name, to the bitter-sweet moments of parting after a single night or many years together. Genji's involvements are numerous, but he is no Don Giovanni seeking only to extend the list in Leporello's catalogue. He is an infinitely varied lover, and his mistresses range from the grandest noblewomen to insignificant creatures terrified by so magnificent a suitor. The reader can only feel that it would have been a criminal waste if, having fallen in love with one woman, Genji had never looked further afield.

Genji is wholly convincing, yet we realize that no person so flawlessly accomplished ever existed, and no society could have attained the aesthetic and emotional elegance of his world. Our doubts are confirmed if we read Murasaki's diary, or the third of the novel in which the action takes place after Genji's death. The world of the two princes Niou and Kaoru, Genji's successors, is still beautiful, but the Buddhist expressions of disenchantment with the world, so often on Genji's lips, now carry conviction. Niou's affairs are cheapened by a shallowness that brings him conquests rather than love; Kaoru's are vitiated by his incapacity to savour happiness. Niou and Kaoru, opposites though they are, are fragmentations of Genji, representing his romantic ardour and sensitivity. Later generations found it easier to identify themselves with Niou and Kaoru than with the incomparable Genji.

One other masterpiece of the same period must be mentioned, *Makura no Sōshi (The Pillow Book of Sei Shōnagon)*, a collection of essays and impressions by a court lady. Japanese critics have often contrasted the *aware* of *Genji Monogatari* and the *okashi* of *Makura no Sōshi*. *Aware* meant the perception of the tragic implications of a moment or gesture; *okashi*, the comic overtones of perhaps the same moment or gesture. The lover's departure at dawn evoked the wistful descriptions of Murasaki Shikibu but also the wit of Sei Shōnagon, who noted with uncanny precision the fumbling, ineffectual movements of the lover and the unpoetic irritation he aroused in the lady. Murasaki

Shikibu's *aware* is present throughout Japanese literature, for it fits the pattern of sensitivity expected of all under the spell of the aristocratic culture, but Sei Shōnagon's wit belonged to a particular moment of history. If George Meredith was correct in maintaining that wit is possible only in a society where men and women meet on equal terms, the Heian court alone provided the necessary conditions; in later times the position of women was so subservient that the give-and-take of wit was out of the question.

Drama and romance: 1185–1600

The Heian court society did not collapse in a year or even a century. Long after its political power had been seized by military leaders and its economic basis seriously weakened, the court retained an unshakable prestige. The military men regularly turned from warfare to composing poetry, as proof that they were cultured, and the court poets became their mentors. But after the removal of the seat of government from Kyoto to Kamakura at the end of the 12th century, the nobles could no longer describe their lives in terms of the *Genji Monogatari*. The position of the court ladies especially suffered; it is sad to note, after their brilliant literary activities during the Heian period, that scarcely a woman writer of distinction appeared between the 14th and 19th centuries. The poets suggested their alienation from society by preferring other-worldly themes, finding a meaning for life beyond the realm of daily experience.

The symbolic poetry of *Shin Kokinshū* (*New Collection of Poems Old and New*, 1205) represents perhaps the supreme achievement within the *tanka* form. The poets, unlike those of the *Kokinshū* three centuries earlier, had lost interest in quibbling and similar intellectual exercises; the fall of the cherry blossoms often became a symbol of death. Fujiwara Shunzei (1114–1204), his son Teika (1162–1241), and the priest Saigyō were especially successful in evoking the lonely beauty of the monochrome which, by its very lack of colour, suggested more than the brilliantly tinted paintings of an earlier age. Teika expressed this perfectly, finding in the bleak loneliness of a scene a beauty not present in the conventionally admired sights of nature:

1 *miwataseba*	1 In this wide landscape
2 *hana mo momiji mo*	2 I see no cherry blossoms
3 *nakarikeri*	3 And no crimson leaves:
4 *ura no tomaya no*	5 Evening in autumn over
5 *aki no yūgure*	4 A straw-thatched hut by the bay.

The characteristic prose form of the period was the war tale. The warfare described occurred in the 12th century in a series of struggles that culminated in the triumph of the Minamoto clan over the Taira clan. Though the Japanese have the reputation of being a martial people, these tales reveal little pleasure in the deeds of war; instead, a sense of loneliness and a Buddhist conviction that this world is meaningless pervade their pages.

The masterpiece among the war tales is *Heike Monogatari (The Tale of the Heike)*. Originally, it appears, this was the chronicle of the rise and fall of the Taira (Heike) family, written by a court noble about 1225. Before long, this tale was being recited by entertainers who accompanied themselves on the *biwa*, a kind of lute. The dissemination of the tale by many performers, each of whom might embroider on favourite sections, resulted in an enormous variety of texts, but the main themes are common to all and reflect the sombre tone of the medieval era. *Heike Monogatari* opens with a celebrated statement: 'The sound of the bell of the Gion Temple echoes the impermanence of all things.' The work ends with the bell tolling at the Jakkō-in, the tiny convent where the former empress, the mother of the drowned boy-emperor, lives out her remaining years in the tattered habit of a nun. The memorable scenes of *Heike Monogatari* continued to move audiences for centuries, and plays describing its heroes still dominate the traditional theatre. The work is episodic, and sometimes the narration is interrupted by fussy details, but at its best it suggests with almost painful vividness the illusory nature of glory.

Hōjōki (*An Account of My Hut*, 1212) by Kamo no Chōmei (1153–1216) is like a cry from the heart of medieval darkness. The author, after enumerating the disasters he has witnessed that have made him realize the folly of possessions or pride in worldly achievement, describes the quiet beauty of life in a hermitage. Yet, even as he writes words of comfort for others who, like himself, are aware of the terror of life in this world, he realizes that attachment to the hermitage, though it is only a hut with hardly an object in it, is a sin: attachment to *anything* is a hindrance in the path of deliverance.

The Nō plays of the 14th and 15th centuries are largely concerned with this sin of attachment. An inability to forget their lives in this world prevents the dead from gaining release, and forces them to return again and again as ghosts to relieve the passion or violence of their former existences. Only prayer and renunciation can bring about deliverance. These plays, especially those by Zeami (1363–1443), are magnificently poetic, but possess almost no interest of a conventionally dramatic nature. There is little conflict of character, plot development, or individuality in the personages, and hardly any movement except for the stylized dances which are their climaxes. At their best, as in the supreme masterpiece *Matsukaze*, they suggest a world invisible to the eye but evoked by the actors through the beauty of movements and speech.

p 249 (11,12)

Underlying the literature of this period were aesthetic principles that owed much to Zen Buddhism. *Tsurezuregusa (Essays in Idleness)* by Yoshida Kenkō (1258–1350) crystallized the tastes of the time and influenced many generations to come. The inevitable transience of beauty, the importance of beginnings and ends (as opposed to the climactic moments), the pleasure in the broken or imperfect, were typical aesthetic views voiced by Kenkō, and all were in consonance with the symbolism favoured by poets and painters of his day.

Works in the traditional forms, including court romances, continued to be written by the nobility, at least until the warfare at the end of the 15th century destroyed the city of Kyoto and with it much of the old culture. The nobles were forced to flee the capital, dispersing their learning throughout the country, while men of humble birth, taking advantage of the breakdown of the old order, were rising to literary eminence.

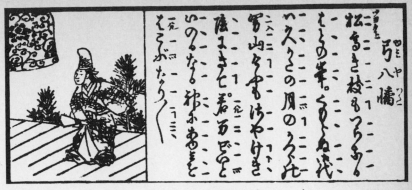

In Nō drama the actors and chorus chant their lines to the accompaniment of rhythmic instrumental music and the scripts are in verse or highly stylized prose. The chanting notation is inserted into a passage from the famous Nō play 'Yumi Yawata'. (7)

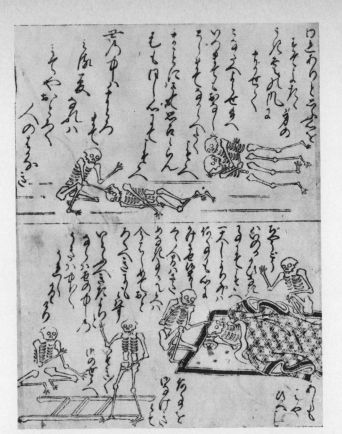

Sōgi (1421–1508), the outstanding poet of linked verse (*renga*), became an arbiter of poetic taste who was no less respected than the great Teika, though his base birth would in earlier times have made association with the nobility inconceivable.

Linked verse originated in a practice, dating back even to the *Kojiki*, of two men composing a single *tanka*, the first supplying three lines, the second the concluding two lines. It was not until a third 'link' was added, breaking the original *tanka* form, that linked verse emerged as a distinctive genre. By the 14th century, composing linked verse had become a popular pastime. The court poets, seeing the artistic possibilities of what had been little more than a game, drew up 'codes' that established linked verse as a full-fledged art. These codes made possible the masterpieces of the 15th century, but their insistence on formalities inhibited vigour and freshness. The linked verse composed by Sōgi and his associates, notably *Minase Sangin* (*Three Poets at Minase*, 1488) are unique in their shifting lyrical impulses, moving freely from link to link like successive moments of a landscape seen from a boat, avoiding any illusion that the whole was conceived in a single mind.

The 16th century was one of warfare, and the prose literature reflects the uncertainties of the time. The stories are often marred by fantastic elements, but they are interesting because of their fusion of folklore with the literary techniques of the older fiction, and because they describe Buddhist priests, merchants, bandits, and others living in a society frequently turned topsy-turvy by disorders. Even if many promising stories are vitiated by absurdities, they tell us, intermittently at least, what life was like in an age of chaos.

'The floating world': 1600–1865

The historical background of this period has been described in Chapter VIII. Restoration of peace, and the unification of the country after the Battle of Sekigahara in

Left: 14th- and 15th-century literature inspired by Buddhism was much concerned with the sin of attachment to possessions and pride in worldly achievement. 'Gaikotsu' (Skeletons) by the priest Ikkyū describes the vanity of worldly appearances, comparing them to the skin that only briefly hides the bones. (6)

1600, ushered in a period of 250 years of uninterrupted stability and order, fostered by the regime of the Tokugawa family, whose government in Edo (the modern Tokyo) was conducted on military lines. The state philosophy of the regime was the Chu Hsi school of Confucianism. Many ethical attitudes that are typical of the Japanese – their reliance on rigid concepts of obligation, filial piety, loyalty, and the like – stemmed from this Confucianism, which paradoxically also promoted the growth of the gay quarters and other places of amusement, as necessary evils in a well-managed society. The gay quarters became the subject of much literature and drama because they were the only places in Tokugawa society that were not subject to the oppressive Confucian morality. The rake who exhausts the pleasures of all the gay quarters of Japan, or the hard-pressed merchant who is torn between love for a prostitute and duty towards his wife, became the heroes of comedy and tragedy. The arts, especially the *ukiyoe* prints, gave publicity to the courtesans and actors, the denizens of the 'floating world'.

p 250 (13)

Genroku, the name of the era 1688–1703, is considered to have been the most brilliant period of Tokugawa culture. The favoured kinds of writing were all Japanese in origin, and were hardly touched by outside influence because the government's policy of seclusion had cut Japan off from the rest of the world. The Japanese, thrown back upon their own resources, produced a literature with a highly distinctive flavour, but it tended to become private and particular when fertilizing influences from China dried up. In the latter part of the Tokugawa period the greatest ingenuity was devoted to devising surprising twists to familiar plots, but in the Genroku era everything was new.

One source of Genroku literature was *haikai no renga*, the comic variety of linked verse. This originated in the 16th century as a reaction against the excessive formalization of linked verse itself, and became a popular literary

'Suddenly she noticed him. Speechless with embarrassment, she clasped her hands imploringly. But he only leered all the more . . .' – an illustration from the first novel of Saikaku (1642–93), 'The Man Who Spent his Life at Love-making'. Saikaku delighted his public with his comic portrayals of merchant families and tales of the gay quarters of Osaka. (8)

p 251
(16)

diversion. The opening verse *(hokku)* of this humorous poetry developed into the *haiku* of Bashō and his school, and the linked-verse techniques also helped to form the style of Ihara Saikaku (1642–93), the first important Japanese novelist for almost five hundred years. Saikaku first won fame by his ability to compose extended linked-verse sequences all by himself, reaching the amazing total of 23,400 verses in a single day in 1684. Obviously the quality of these verses, composed at the rate of several a minute, cannot have been high, but Saikaku's fertility of invention compels admiration.

Saikaku's first novel, *Kōshoku Ichidai Otoko* (*The Man Who Spent His Life at Love-making*, 1682), is the tale of Yonosuke, whose amorous exploits begin precociously in his seventh year, and who is last seen fifty years later as he sails off on a ship loaded with aphrodisiacs for an island populated exclusively by women. The manner and incidents hardly suggest that this novel was based on the *Genji Monogatari*, but parallels in the text and even the number of chapters indicate that Saikaku was consciously attempting to write about a Genroku Genji. Yonosuke displays none of the sensitivity of Genji, but in a mechanical, uninvolved manner he amasses a staggering total of amorous conquests.

The name Yonosuke was short for Ukiyonosuke, *ukiyo* being a key term in Genroku culture. Originally it meant 'the sad world', a Buddhist phrase, but by a pun it came to mean 'the floating world', the world of uncertainties. Uncertainty has generally been a source of worry and grief, but in Genroku Japan it stood for the fascination of an endlessly changing, unpredictable world. To be abreast of 'the floating world' meant to share in the latest fashions and slang, and to delight in the momentary, rather than in the eternal, truths of the Nō plays or the medieval poetry.

Saikaku's masterpiece, *Kōshoku Gonin Onna* (*Five Women Who Loved Love*, 1686), is filled with sharp observations of the foibles of his society. If we do not take his characters very seriously, neither did Saikaku; he seems to be watching them through the reverse end of a telescope, maintaining his objectivity and detached humour. He certainly did not dislike his characters, but even when they meet tragic ends they seem somehow comic when viewed from his great distance.

Saikaku is often contrasted with the playwright Chikamatsu Monzaemon (1653–1725), Saikaku being labelled a realist and Chikamatsu a romantic. Certainly Saikaku's portraits of prostitutes are completely unsentimental, while Chikamatsu insists that even a common prostitute is capable of the deepest affections. His heroines gladly commit suicide with the men they love, in preference to being 'ransomed' from their brothels by a despised suitor. It is cynically assumed, therefore, that Saikaku was writing the truth, and that Chikamatsu glossed over unpleasant realities in the interests of pathos;

In the Tokugawa period puppet performances gained in popularity and almost achieved the status of drama. At first puppets were small enough to be operated by manipulators who remained out of sight, but these were gradually replaced by large wooden puppets. The puppets seen here in production were often about two-thirds life-size and made to act in close imitation of real actors. (9)

Portrait of the playwright Chikamatsu, published shortly after his death in 1725. In his historical dramas and contemporary domestic plays Chikamatsu paid great attention to the structure of his plot, dialogue and characterization contributing a new richness to the Japanese theatre. (10)

more probably, each man modified reality to suit his needs. Hard-boiled prostitutes were probably no more typical of the gay quarters than Chikamatsu's self-sacrificing victims of misfortune, but Saikaku, a comic writer, could not make his characters too pathetic.

250–1
(14)
Chikamatsu wrote mainly for the puppet theatre (later known as Bunraku), a form of drama that originated early in the Tokugawa period. He apparently chose to write for puppets, rather than actors, because the latter considered plays to be no more than vehicles for their talents. The puppets performed the texts as written, but they imposed a special requirement of exaggeration, which was necessary if wooden figures were to seem to be alive and human. Chikamatsu's texts were a compromise between what he wished to express and what his audiences would accept. His plays contain flights of poetry that soared above the heads of the spectators, but also crudities that lessen their literary value, included to please the badly educated commoners who attended the theatre.

Chikamatsu's plays consisted of histories (*jidaimono*) that were based at least vaguely on the deeds of famous personages, and domestic tragedies (*sewamono*) that portrayed the lives of merchants or low-ranking samurai. Modern critics unanimously prefer the domestic tragedies; they are better constructed, more realistic, and closer to European drama. Chikamatsu's audiences, however, enjoyed the bombast and violent actions of the histories. His most popular play, *Kokusenya Kassen* (*The Battles of Coxinga*, 1715), is filled with extravagant and improbable doings, but it exploits the potentialities of a puppet theatre better, say, than a masterpiece like *Shinjū Ten no Amihima* (*The Love Suicides at Amihima*, 1720), which can be performed by Kabuki actors as successfully as by puppets.

Chikamatsu's works are often discussed in terms of the conflict between *giri* (obligation) and *ninjō* (human feelings). The characters are constantly worrying about their obligations to their family or to society as a whole, but when pressed to the wall they are likely to give way entirely to the emotions, abandoning any attempt at a rational solution. The rash actions of Chikamatsu's heroes accord poorly with the Confucian ideals, but he was sure that audiences would sympathize because these

The most popular of Chikamatsu's works was 'The Battles of Coxinga' which ran for seventeen consecutive months when it was first produced. In this contemporary play-book illustration, the swashbuckling hero Coxinga, a famous Chinese-Japanese adventurer, can be seen in the top illustration with his newly won followers. Below are the battles of the four seasons from which Coxinga was to emerge victorious. (11)

heroes were emotionally pure. It was by virtue of the intensity of his emotions that even a clerk in a paper shop could achieve the stature of a tragic hero. Aristotle might have denied that a man of so humble a calling could figure as the hero of a tragedy, but Chikamatsu believed that tragedy took no account of social status.

Japanese drama after Chikamatsu tended to be a mixture of historical and domestic elements, often interlarded with comic relief. The most popular play, *Chūshingura* by Takeda Izumo and others, is a superb example of how the faults of the puppet theatre could be surmounted by a foolproof story, the vengeance wreaked by the forty-seven loyal retainers. p 251
(15)

Saikaku and Chikamatsu, though different in style and outlook, both clearly belonged to the Genroku world. The third great writer of the period, the *haiku* poet Matsuo Bashō (1644–94), seems aloof from the age, a throwback to the hermit-priests who took no interest in the floating world. Bashō's detachment has been exaggerated; for all his devotion to the poets of the past, he always insisted on freshness. He once advised a pupil, 'Do not follow in the footsteps of the men of old. Seek what they sought.' Nevertheless, Bashō's patient craftsmanship sets him apart from most writers of the Genroku era. He wrote little more than a thousand *haiku* in his lifetime, less than many poets have produced in a single year. Although he turned out impromptu verses on occasion, his memorable *haiku* were the result of many recastings. His insistence on perfection caused him to spend five years on writing his most celebrated work, the p 251
(16)

The greatest of haiku poets was Bashō (1644–94), a former samurai who established himself at Edo as a professional master of the haiku – seventeen syllables 'at once eternal and momentary'. (12)

travel diary *Oku no Hosomichi (The Narrow Road of Oku,* 1694), a mere thirty pages in most editions.

In Bashō's hands, the *haiku* developed from the flashing perceptions typical of Saikaku into a distillation of the world into seventeen syllables. Bashō's most famous dictum was that the *haiku* must be at once eternal and momentary. If it is not eternal, it will be ephemeral, but if it is eternal in the hackneyed manner of the late *tanka,* it will have nothing to say to men of this time. The *haiku* describes a particular moment, but this moment acquires its interest from the background of timelessness. A *haiku* often consists of two components: an unchanging element, whether the expanse of the sea or the silence of the mountains, and a momentary occurrence that interrupts the eternal. A *haiku* composed on his *Oku no Hosomichi* journey exemplifies this:

shizukasa ya	How still it is!
iwa ni shimiiru	Stabbing into the rocks,
semi no koe	The locusts' voices.

The stillness is the eternal component, interrupted by the momentary trills of the locusts, so sharp that they seem to stab into the rocks. Only after the interruption are we aware of the otherwise imperceptible silence. The season, an essential element of a *haiku,* is disclosed by mention of the locust, an insect of late summer. The time of day is evening, when the locusts trill. The landscape is dominated by rocky crags. Even the sounds of the words contribute to the effect: five of the seven vowels in the second line are *i,* suggesting the locusts' trill.

The two elements of a *haiku* must be fused by the reader. A *haiku* fails if it merely describes a scene or makes a statement. The greater the tension between the two elements – the eternal and the momentary – the more

successful the *haiku.* The *haiku* poets, aware of this, sometimes tried too hard and included elements whose relationship was excessively obscure. Just as a *haiku* fails if it places no distance between the two elements, and thus denies the reader the pleasure of a moment of creative intuition, it will fail also if the elements are too far apart for the reader to bridge. Bashō, rejecting obscurity, insisted in his last period on 'lightness' *(karumi)* as the touchstone of a true *haiku.*

Bashō had many disciples, some still admired, but the next *haiku* poet of first magnitude was Yosa Buson (1716–83). Buson's *haiku,* like his paintings, have warmth and evocative power, but they lack Bashō's depth. He often used the *haiku* to relate a story with a few superbly selected details:

mi ni shimu ya	How it chills my flesh!
bōsai no kushi	The comb my dead wife used,
neya ni fumu	Stepped on, in our bedroom.

By the early 19th century, Tokugawa culture seemed to have exhausted itself. The novels had largely degenerated into frivolous tales about the gay quarters that were purchased as much for their illustrations as for their content; the theatre had turned increasingly to the morbid and grotesque; a *haiku* was often no more than an artful perception. Literature, like the late *ukiyoe* prints, tended to be elegantly composed, but to be interested more in the display of technique than in revealing deep human emotions.

Some writers reacted to these frivolous works by choosing the opposite extremes. Takizawa Bakin (1767–1847), for example, combined the war tales of medieval Japan with Confucian philosophy to write his immensely long and desperately didactic novel *Hakkenden* p 251 *(Biography of Eight Dogs,* 1814–41). His avowed purpose (17) was to use literature as an instrument for 'encouraging virtue and chastising vice', but his novels were probably read mainly for their fantastic plots, involving prodigies and ghosts, rather than for their Confucian wisdom.

The late Tokugawa poets, like Kobayashi Issa (1763–1828) in the *haiku* and Tachibana Akemi (1812–68) in the *tanka,* showed their impatience with worn-out conventions by treating the humble, ordinary events of life, and Rai Sanyō (1730–1832) wrote poetry in Chinese to express his concern over political and social questions. But neither poets nor prose writers could come seriously to grips with the problems of the age.

In the 16th century, Portuguese and Spanish missionaries had won many converts to Catholicism, but the Japanese gained little knowledge of European literature as a result. *Aesop's Fables,* and possibly a part of the *Odyssey,* were introduced and even exerted some influence on Japanese writing, but the lasting effects were slight. The arrival of Commodore Perry's fleet in 1853 initiated developments that eventually brought about the ending of the closed society of Tokugawa Japan and the Meiji Restoration of 1868. The European penetration of Japanese life after this was to affect all forms of writing so profoundly as to create an almost totally different literature.

XI EUROPE GOES EAST

The first impact of the West on China and Japan

PAUL A. COHEN

They understand to a certain degree the distinction between superior and inferior, but I do not know whether they have a proper system of ceremonial etiquette. They eat with their fingers instead of with chopsticks. They show their feelings without any self-control.

Chinese interpreter speaking of the Portuguese, 1543

When the first Portuguese carracks dropped anchor in Chinese waters in 1514 a new era began in the history of East Asia. So much we can say now, with the benefit of hindsight. At the time it was a minor incident, attracting little notice at the Ming court at Peking. That court, indeed, had the means to send as large an expedition to Europe as Europe sent to China. What it lacked was the motivation. China was self-sufficient, satisfied, incurious. Europe was restless and avid for new knowledge; it needed the silks and spices of Asia; very soon the tireless members of the Society of Jesus, the Jesuits, would come to claim the whole world for Christianity.

During the Middle Ages there had been isolated journeys by Europeans to the East. Marco Polo's is the most famous. Portugal was the first European country to make contact by sea at a national level. Encouraged by her position on the edge of Europe's seaboard and by the vast opportunities to be gained by expansion, the Portuguese built up a navy that had few rivals in Europe and none outside. Their ocean-going vessels, the 'Great

Ships' of Chinese and Japanese historians, were carracks with high sterns (often, as opposite, with four decks) and weighing up to 16,000 tons. Bartolomeu Dias rounded the Cape of Good Hope in 1488. Vasco da Gama reached India in 1498. Alfonso d'Albuquerque established bases in Malaya and Java in 1511. In 1514 Portuguese ships entered the estuary of the Hsi river below Canton.

These first visitors did nothing to correct the view current in China that Europeans were barbarians. Hardly better than marauders, they built a fort on Lintin Island, ignored Chinese laws and bought children as slaves. Although an official embassy arrived in 1517 and visited Peking, relations continued to deteriorate. There were fights at sea between Chinese and Portuguese ships, and in 1522 the Portuguese were expelled. It was several decades before they were able to set up a permanent base at Macao. By then European missionaries had also begun to arrive in East Asia, and China soon found herself not only buying and selling with the barbarians, but listening to them, and even learning from them. (1)

A Chinese 'Age of Exploration' seemed to be beginning in 1405, fifty years before the great voyages of the West. Between that year and 1433 seven Ming expeditions under Cheng Ho (above) visited India, Persia, Arabia and in two cases the east coast of Africa. They were far larger than any similar enterprises organized from Europe, with up to 62 ships and 28,000 men, and are known in some detail from the accounts written by three men who served as interpreters. The ships, usually three-masted, were 500–600 feet in length and held between 400 and 500 people each. Chinese sailors had the compass before Europeans and could also navigate by the stars. Although they carried goods for trading (porcelain, fabrics of silk, satin and cotton, gold, silver and spices) the purpose of the emperor's expedition was mainly, as the *Dynastic History* says, 'to show his military strength to foreign countries'. Religion was certainly not a motive; Confucianism had no missionary impulse, and Cheng Ho actually took Buddhist and Moslem priests to make foreign contacts easier. Below: two 'credential tablets' issued by the Emperor Yung Lo to Cheng Ho in 1407. They were found in India. After 1433 no more voyages were undertaken and China turned her back upon the rest of the world. (2, 4, 5)

From Russia overland caravans travelled the long road across Siberia. During the mid-17th century Cossack forts were set up on the Amur river, challenging Chinese rule in the north both by terrorizing the population and by persuading some of the local chieftains to change their

Christian revelation reached China through the Jesuits, who were broad-minded enough both to conform to Chinese manners in dress and behaviour and to recognize the values of Confucianism. The three figures below are the patient and resourceful Jesuit pioneer Matteo Ricci, with Adam Schall and Ferdinand Verbiest, both of whom aided the emperor with their astronomical knowledge and talents for diplomacy. Schall wears the mandarin's White Crane plaque on his chest. At the bottom is Ricci's most famous convert, Hsu Kuang-ch'i. Hsu, who took the name of Paul at baptism and, like Ricci, saw no inconsistency between Christianity and Confucian observances, is pictured with his granddaughter. Between them is the back and front of an inscribed cross designed to condense Christian theology into a few Chinese characters. (6)

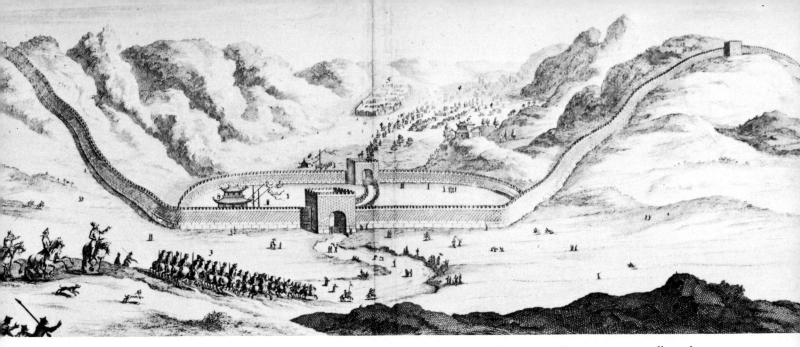

allegiance. In the 1680s the Manchus sent out armies to eject them, and in 1689 a treaty was signed at Nerchinsk on the Shilka river, a tributary of the Amur. On the Chinese side, Jesuit priests acted as interpreters and advisers. The limits of Russian advance were fixed.

Every three years a Russian trading caravan was allowed to enter China and go as far as Peking, a concession not extended to any other European country. This engraving (above) shows the first such mission passing through a gate in the Great Wall. (3)

Confucian enlightenment filtered back to the West through missionaries and travellers, and was eagerly taken up by the *philosophes* and *encyclopédistes*. Below: '*Confucius, le plus célèbre philosophe de la Chine*' from a work of 1735. The artist places him in a European-style library, though with a touch of *chinoiserie* added. Right: the Imperial Spring Ploughing Ceremony – the emperor scattering the first seeds in the furrow. This was the paternalist monarchy of China as seen by a French poet of 1779. The Jesuits were partly responsible for this idealized portrait of a rationally ordered state founded on the principles of the natural law. Philosophers like Leibniz, Poivre, Hume and Voltaire, whose enthusiasm outstripped their knowledge, saw China as a Utopia which had solved many of the problems facing their own society. (7, 8)

Under Ch'ien-lung (below, a portrait by the Jesuit painter Castiglione) the missionary influence waned. Official hostility was increased by the papal 'Rites' decision of 1742 forbidding Chinese Christians to participate in Confucian ceremonies. The Jesuits had earlier lost imperial support by involving themselves in court politics. Ch'ien-lung's reign (1736–95) saw a stepping up of active persecution until by 1800 there were probably only about 200,000 Christians in China. (10)

The Portuguese outpost of Macao has lasted from its foundation in 1557 until today. The town lies on a small peninsula about 2½ miles long by 1 mile broad, south of Canton. On its east side runs the Great Quay, Praya Grande, seen (left) in an early 19th-century watercolour, with the fort of S. Pedro in the foreground, then the palatial Governor's Residence and the hilly southern end of the peninsula in the distance. The Jesuit church of St Paul (right) was built between 1594 and 1602 but in 1835 it was destroyed by fire and only the façade remains. (9, 11)

A British mission arrived in Peking in 1793 led by Lord Macartney. Its purpose was to negotiate trading terms bu the emperor, Ch'ien-lung, could conceive it only as an offering of tribute by the King of England, whose 'respectful submission' he commended. Macartney tried to impress the imperial court by his train of 90 wagons, 200 horses and 3,000 coolies carrying expensive presents, and clearly to some extent he succeeded, judging by this tapestry (below) depicting 'the arrival of the Ambassador Ma-Kha-Erh-Ni bringing tribute from the King of the Red-haired People of England'. It is doubtful, however, whether the artist actually saw them. His Englishmen were copied from earlier pictures of Elizabethans and his globe and armillary sphere from Dutch instruments – made far too big. Ch'ien-lung dismissed the English with the statement that 'our celestial empires already possesses all things in prolific abundance'. (12)

The Dutch replaced the Portuguese as the leaders of the spice trade in the 17th century. In Japan, as we shall see, they attained an outright monopoly. In China they were less successful and their ships were often in conflict with those of the Ming government or its supporters (above). In 1624 they were driven out of an island they had attempted to fortify between Taiwan and the coast, but by siding with the Manchus in 1663 they improved their position and a certain amount of trade was permitted. Left: a delegation from the Dutch mercantile capital of Batavia arrives at Peking in 1668. At the gate of the Imperial Palace the Dutch visitors sit on a carpet. Their gifts are laid out on a table to the right. (13, 14)

Commercial empires which increasingly took on the responsibilities of government were created by the two East India Companies of the Netherlands and Great Britain. The Dutch were based on Indonesia, the British on India. Both strained every effort to unlock the supposedly vast markets of China. Dutch vessels (left) were well known all over East Asia. In 1645 a Dutch embassy visited Canton (above) and was received by Chinese dignitaries, sitting under a canopy in the centre, outside the walls. (15, 16)

The popularity of China tea created a problem for the British East India Company. The only commodity for which there was a comparable demand in China was opium from India. But the importation of opium into China was illegal. In 1837 the Chinese government launched a fresh campaign to suppress the trade. An imperial commissioner, Lin Tsc-hsu, was sent to Canton, where he vigorously searched out and arrested importers and distributors, forcing the foreign merchants to surrender their stocks and publicly destroying them (right). Friction mounted. After several violent incidents Britain prepared an expeditionary force. Peking conceded defeat, and the Treaty of Nanking, signed (below) on 29 August 1842, ended the first so-called Opium War. It was the beginning of the system of treaty ports, extraterritoriality, unequal treaties and commercial privileges which was to burden China for the next hundred years. (17, 18)

Outside the walls of Canton was, until the Opium War of 1840–42, the only place in China where foreign traders were allowed to establish their factories. All dealings had to be with a small number of specially licensed Chinese merchants. The foreigners were strictly confined to their own district, called the 'Thirteen Factories', shown here about 1800. European vessels mingle with Chinese junks. On shore, national flags proclaim the various trading posts, though by this time the British were dominating all their competitors. The Chinese government was well content to limit access in this way to a port at the furthest

possible remove from Peking. Below: an incident in the Opium War. The *Nemesis*, an iron-clad paddle-steamer belonging to the East India Company, bombards Chinese ships near Chuenpi, January 1841. The battle, which effectively put paid to China's sea-power, led to a provisional agreement which was later rejected by both governments. Later in the year the British invaded the mainland and established garrisons all along the south China coast. In the spring of the next year they seized Shanghai and were threatening Nanking when peace was concluded. (19, 20)

In Japan too first contact was made by the Portuguese, and the first real impact was that of Jesuit evangelism. St Francis Xavier arrived in 1549 and received a friendly reception. Japan was in many ways more open to foreign ideas than China. The Jesuit missions attracted ready converts. Right: an early 17th century panel illustrating the Mysteries of the Rosary. St Ignatius and St Francis Xavier appear in the foreground and scenes from the lives of Christ and the Virgin fill the sides. Below: the Portuguese 'Great Ship' which called once a year from Macao, portrayed here on a Japanese 17th century screen. (21, 22)

Missionary and merchant came hand in hand to the shores of Japan – were sometimes, indeed, combined in the same person. Part of the Jesuits' success sprang from the fact that they were so closely tied to commercial interests. Here a Portuguese party has landed from a 'Great Ship' and is being received by a local daimyō. For fifty years the Jesuits could show an almost unbroken record of success. The number of converts in Japan even exceeded that of China, in spite of Japan's much smaller population. (23)

'The Temple of the Southern Barbarians', as the Japanese called the Jesuit church at Kyoto (below), was built in 1576. The Jesuits took particular pains to conform to the national style – in architecture as in other matters. (24)

Oda Nobunaga (below), the first of the great unifiers of the 16th century, deliberately favoured the Christian missions as a counterweight to the Buddhists. He was also genuinely impressed by Jesuit attainments. (25)

The tide turned when Christianity seemed to be growing so fast that it might undermine not only Buddhism but the state itself. Several of the daimyō had been converted and Nobunaga's successor, Hideyoshi, feared that they might combine against the central government. In 1587 he decreed the banishment of the Jesuits. Ieyasu (below) and his successors acted more firmly. Between 1606 and 1630 a campaign of increasing ruthlessness was waged to suppress Christianity. After the 'Great Martyrdom' of 1622 (see overleaf) the Christian community gathered its strength for one last desperate rebellion, which erupted in 1637 at Shimabara, near Nagasaki. The flag (above right) which flew over the doomed town reads 'Praised be the Blessed Sacrament'. Right: the attack on Hara Castle, which marked the end of the rebellion. (26–28)

MARTYRES LII
IN IAPON UX SEPT
MDCXXII

The 'Great Martyrdom' of 10 September 1622, commemorated in the Gesù, Rome, by a Japanese Jesuit artist, was only one of many mass executions carried out with horrifying cruelty. 'I saw fifty-five of them martyred at one time', wrote an English merchant. 'Among them were little children of five or six years, burned alive in the arms of their mothers.' In the painting (above) the victims are enclosed by a fence. One group in the foreground are being beheaded and their heads placed on spikes. Those at the back are about to be burned. (29)

Japan closed her doors to foreigners. The British left in 1623, the Spaniards a year later. In 1639 the Portuguese were expelled and the Christian communities virtually exterminated. The Japanese themselves were forbidden to go abroad and even to build ships big enough to take them. Only from one port, Nagasaki, and by special licence, the 'vermilion seal', could a Japanese vessel (left) ever make contact with the outside world. (30)

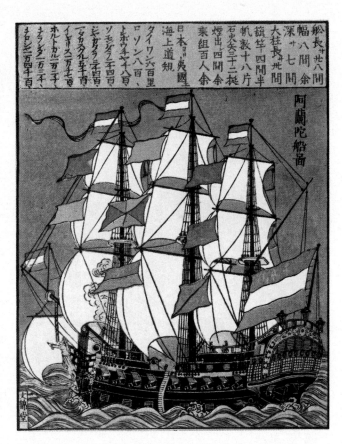

松長廿北八間
幅八間余
深廿七間余
大柱長七間半
帆桁長四間半
帆数十八片
石火矢三十二挺
煙出一四間余
乗組百人余
日本ヨリ英國
海上道規
タイワン六百里
ロソン八百
トモウギヤ百
ソモダ千四百
ジャガタラ字四百
一タカスクル五十五百
ホルトカル一万十
イギリス三万七千
オランダ一万三千、
チロン二万四千百

阿蘭陀船圖

There was one exception to the ban on foreigners. A
Dutch factory was allowed to remain at Nagasaki,
though hemmed in by many restrictions. As Protestants
the Dutch were considered less dangerous than the
Catholic Portuguese. They had in fact supplied the
government with cannon during the attack on Hara
Castle. Their ships were the only tangible signs of Western civilization that the Japanese saw between 1640 and
1853, and for that reason seem to have been objects of
fascinated interest (above). (31)

The Dutch at Nagasaki were confined to an artificial
island called Deshima, the crescent-shaped area in the
foreground of the view below, connected to the mainland
by a single bridge. Personal relations between Dutch and
Japanese were kept to a minimum, but intellectual contact proved less easy to break off. (32)

於肥州彼杵郡

Through the 'window' of Deshima Japan was able to see, as from a great distance, what was taking place in the rest of the world. Dutch books on scientific and technical subjects came increasingly to be read, translated and copied. This map, printed in Kyoto in 1671, not only shows the outlines of the continents with reasonable accuracy but also incorporates such typically Dutch features as the representatives of the different races in the grid on the left. By the 18th century translations were being made of Dutch works on medicine, anatomy, astronomy, physics and many other subjects. But still there was no political relaxation. Inside Deshima the Dutch merchants, deprived of their families, lived lives of monotonous social quarantine. The lower picture (left) shows the island in the 18th century, with its well-built warehouses and quays. In the upper picture Japanese customs officials sit in their office near the landing-stage, while upstairs to the left a party of Dutchmen has gathered for a meeting. By the early 19th century, purely through the medium of 'Dutch studies', Japan was better informed about the West than any other Asian country – certainly far better than China in spite of China's greater opportunities. Progressive Japanese thinkers were already talking in terms of modernizing their country many years before Commodore Perry in 1853 confronted them with the decision inescapably. (33–35)

278

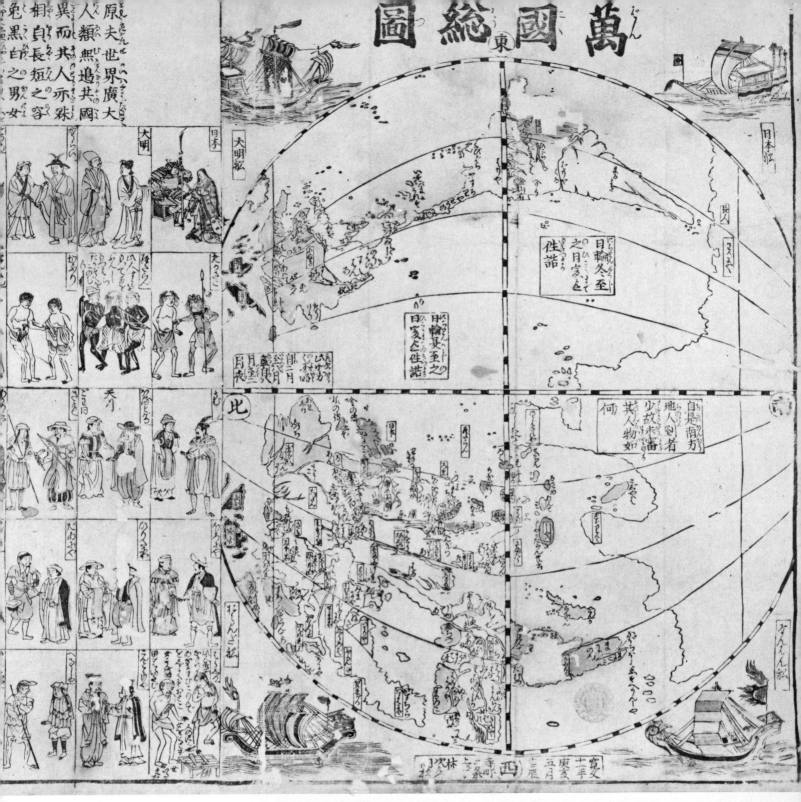

萬國總圖

Perry's visit was a calculated move by the United States government to open up Japan to American shipping. Entering Edo Bay (right, in a Japanese colour print) with two steam frigates, the Commodore obliged the authorities to deal with him and accept a letter from his President to the Emperor of Japan. The following year, 1854, he returned with a larger force. The Shogun, having consulted his most powerful daimyō, signed a treaty conceding limited trading rights. (36)

This 'barbarian invasion' by America aroused fierce resentment among the conservative ranks of Japan. It was likened to the attempted invasion by the Mongols in the 13th century and a similar fate was wishfully predicted for it in popular prints (above). Perry's ultimatum, shortly followed by parallel demands from Britain, the Netherlands and Russia, revealed the deep split in Japanese society between the isolationists and those who wanted to see Japan take her place in the modern world. (37)

Within twenty years of Perry's landing the modernizers had won. The abolition of the Shogunate and the Meiji Restoration of 1868, described in detail in Chapter XII, marked the beginning of a new age, in which an outward-looking Japan would transform herself first into an industrial and then into an imperialist power. In December 1871 the first Japanese foreign mission left Yokohama for the United States and Europe (left). Led by Iwakura, Kido and Okubo, three leaders of the Meiji reforms, it included also fifty-four students to study the West at first hand. The mission failed, however, in its primary purpose of persuading the foreign governments to modify the unequal treaties signed before 1868. (38)

The first impact of the West on China and Japan

PAUL A. COHEN

Woodcut of a three-masted ship used by Cheng Ho. Many of the sea-going junks used by his great maritime expeditions were of considerable size, sometimes over 600 feet in length, and built with four decks and watertight compartments. (1)

HISTORIANS often sin in reading more into the past than is warranted. We look at an event, like the arrival of the first European ships in Asian waters, and we burden it with future meaning. Straining our gaze, we make out on the distant horizon the fire and smoke of the Opium Wars. The Portuguese carrack becomes, in our minds, the opening wedge in a process of maritime expansion that, before spending itself, will force the entry of Asia into the modern world. An event is transformed into a fateful symbol. Modern times have begun.

This is a dramatic perspective. In so far as it defines the contours of a major historical phenomenon, it is also a useful one. It does not, however, suffice. Unlike a plant, the final form of which is largely determined at the seed-stage, history is the product of an on-going process of causation. The 19th century was not foretold in the events of the 16th; nor can the 16th century be understood by reference exclusively to the 19th. It is essential, therefore, that the grand perspective on modern European expansionism be balanced by separate examination of the discrete phases of this process. When we do this with the early Western impact on East Asia, we discover a number of things that might otherwise fail to show up: first, that the effects of the West's presence on China and Japan were radically different; second, that between the 16th and the 19th centuries, the West itself underwent vast changes; and, third, that concurrent with the exertion of Western influence on East Asia, there was a very substantial Chinese impact on the West. These are some of the themes to be explored in the present chapter.

Before getting to them, though, there are some broader questions that need to be raised. Why is it that modern world history has been shaped by the expansion of Europeans instead of some other people? Was Europe the only civilization, *c.* 1500, that had the skills and the wherewithal to send traders, missionaries, and soldiers of fortune from one end of the globe to the other? Or was it simply the only civilization that wanted to?

The Chinese self-image

In answering these questions, it is instructive to look at another example of early overseas expansion, one that was almost contemporaneous with the exploratory voyages sent out by Prince Henry the Navigator. In 1405

a huge fleet – 62 ships carrying 28,000 men – sailed from China to India at the command of the Ming Emperor. Other expeditions followed, two of them reaching the east coast of Africa before returning. Then, after the seventh such expedition (1431–33), the voyages suddenly ceased. China did not go on to become a great sea power. There was no 'Age of Exploration and Discovery' to spark the heroic fantasies of Chinese schoolboys. The very memory of the Ming expeditions was effaced by time.

From this remarkable episode it is clear that Europe, in early modern times, was not alone in possessing the requisite technology for worldwide expansion by sea. China had it too. What the Chinese lacked, and the Europeans had in abundance, was motivation. The motives behind the Chinese voyages seem to have been narrowly political, aimed at the enhancement of dynastic prestige and the incorporation of new states into the Chinese tributary system. Certainly, there was no Confucian mission to convert the world. Nor was there any dynastic interest in developing foreign commerce, though some participants in the expeditions did engage in trade on their own. Among the leaders of the expeditions were eunuchs, traditionally despised by Confucian scholar-officials. The unseemly concern for foreign exotica and tremendous extravagance of the voyages constituted further grounds for Confucian opposition. The costs were in fact prodigious, and modern scholars generally agree that the strain placed on the imperial treasury was the most important reason for terminating the whole venture. This is true. But it is equally important to recognize that, in terms of the Chinese tradition of overland expansion, the Ming expeditions were an aberration to begin with, less mysterious in their conclusion than in their commencement.

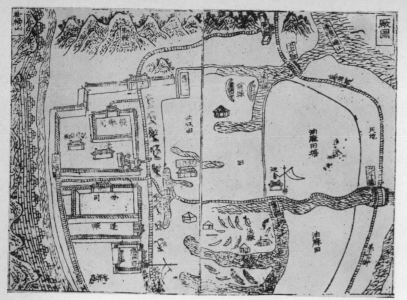

Cheng Ho's ships were built and fitted out at the imperial ship-yards a few miles up the Yangtze river from Nanking. This plan shows administrative offices on the left and the slipways and docks of two shipyards on the right. Below: the compass, from an imperial encyclopaedia. Chinese development of techniques of navigation over many generations lay behind Cheng Ho's voyages. (2, 3)

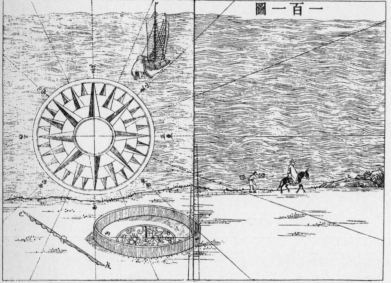

The contrast with Europe was sharp on this point. Smaller by far than China and much less self-sufficient economically, the young nation-states of post-feudal Europe had a large stake in the expansion of foreign commerce. This was true not only of Europe's merchants, but also of her princes, whose usual impecuni-ousness (by Chinese standards) was greatly augmented, in an age of growing national rivalry, by mounting military costs.

Rivalry and competition served as a stimulus to Christian missionary activity as well. Christianity, like other universalistic religions (Islam, Buddhism), had always been prone to expansion – witness the conversions of Rome and northern Europe, the Crusades, and the abortive Catholic effort in China under the Mongols. After the Reformation, however, the proselytizing zeal of the Church reached unprecedented heights, as the hope grew that some of the ground lost to Protestantism in Europe might be recovered elsewhere in the world.

One other reason, intangible but important, why it was European rather than Chinese civilization that embarked on a course of worldwide expansion in the 15th and 16th centuries derives from a peculiar feature of Europe's cultural psychology. Myron P. Gilmore remarks that:

'although the western world was . . . assured of its possession of Christian revelation, it was never completely convinced that its own institutions were the most perfect embodiment of that revelation. . . . The vision of a mythical "better place", a Utopia that existed somewhere else, fitfully haunted the mind of Latin Christendom and was a spur to curiosity. . . . What was shared . . . by no other society of the "pre–Da Gaman belt" was the complex of traditions, doubts and hopes that seemed to promise the existence of a center of civilization outside and beyond the horizon with which the Christian world might eventually hope to be in contact.'

Thus were Europeans driven from the recesses of their culture to seek out new worlds which – there was always that slender filament of hope – just might be more perfect than the old. For Chinese, however, the possibility of perfection already existed in the here and now. Absolutists to the core, there was no question in their minds of a hierarchy of civilizations, some better than others. China *was* civilization. Nor was it thinkable for Chinese to contemplate a journey elsewhere in space, in search of a more perfect world, for there was only one world and China sat at its centre. China's experience was limited to tribal peoples with little civilized development and to settled societies (such as Korea, Japan, and Vietnam), whose civilizations had been deeply influenced by China's own. Historical experience thus validated the lofty Chinese self-image.

Nor, indeed, was it an image at odds with reality. Marco Polo's account of his travels was classified by medieval bibliographers under 'romance'. Yet, when Europeans returned to China in the 16th century they found, to their surprise, that the main outlines of Polo's story were true. With a population probably approaching 150,000,000, China was far and away the most populous country in the world, as she had been since Roman times. In collective terms she was also the richest.

Interpreters on the voyages kept records of the physical features, products, people and customs of the lands they visited. One page from an illustrated record of strange countries features a zebra. (4)

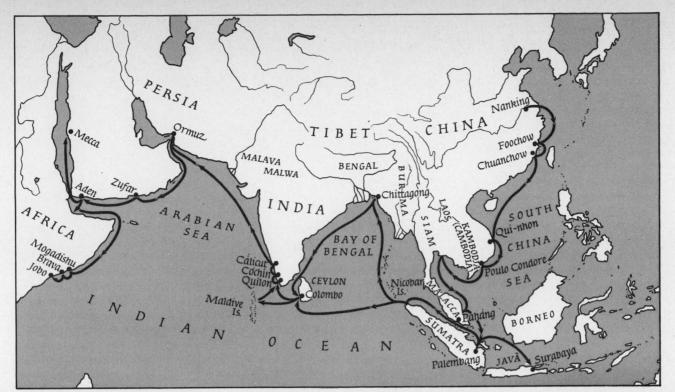

Map showing the sea routes of the great Ming expeditions under Cheng Ho. The first fleet sailed in 1405–07 with sixty-two vessels carrying 28,000 men and reached India. Later voyages went to the Persian Gulf, Aden and the east coast of Africa. (5)

The Chinese could be equally proud of their genius in the field of technology, as we have seen in Chapter v. Although they were now being overtaken in this sphere by Europe, it is one of the crowning ironies of history that some of the most important technological foundations for European modernization were first invented by Chinese. Printing, gunpowder, and the magnet, Francis Bacon declared in 1620, 'have changed the whole face and state of things throughout the world, the first in literature, the second in warfare, the third in navigation; whence have followed innumerable changes; insomuch that no empire, no sect, no star, seems to have exerted greater power and influence in human affairs than these mechanical discoveries.'

China's material achievements were matched by her rich intellectual heritage and by political institutions and traditions that were, in many respects, unique. In the 16th century, the Chinese intellectual world was presided over by Confucianism, though Buddhism and Taoism remained influential at the popular level. Confucianism, as we have already seen in many different contexts, provided the personal ethic for China's educated classes, as well as the guiding philosophy for her governmental system. This system, in its major outlines, had been in existence since the 3rd century BC. With all its shortcomings, it was an impressive human achievement, and Mendoza's contemporary assessment – 'this mightie kingdome is one of the best ruled and gouerned of any that is at this time knowen in all the world' – was richly deserved.

Matteo Ricci, Christian Confucian

Such was the China encountered by 16th-century Europeans. Although the encounter was initiated by the West, the challenge at this point was at least as arresting on the Chinese side – a fact which the best of the early missionaries appreciated and took full account of in their work.

In no case was this more true than in that of the brilliant Jesuit pioneer Matteo Ricci (1552–1610). Representative of a new breed of European missionaries, Ricci was rigorously trained in theology, steeped in the humanistic learning of the Italian Renaissance, and prepared to respond with warmth and respect to the achievements of non-European cultures. Upon arriving in Portuguese Macao in 1582, he immediately embarked on a course of study in Chinese language and civilization. The following year, he and a colleague became the first Catholics in over two centuries to be given official permission to carry on missionary work in the Empire.

p 266 (6)

The mission strategy gradually evolved by Ricci was notable less for its originality than for its sensitivity and realism. It was guided by two essential principles: first, that wherever possible, Christianity and Christian missionary work should be adapted to the native culture; and, second, that every effort should be made to gain the friendship and protection of the higher strata of society. The father of this approach was Alessandro Valignano, the director of Jesuit missionary operations in East Asia. Valignano, however, was mainly based in Japan, and it was left to Ricci to apply the strategy to the concrete conditions of China.

Ricci proceeded by trial and error. Thus, after discovering that the Buddhist clergy was generally held in contempt by the powerful scholar-official class, he exchanged the monk's robes that had been his initial choice of dress for those of the Confucian literatus. In time Ricci also mastered the fabled intricacies of Confucian etiquette and social intercourse. He was meticulous in returning the visits paid him by Chinese scholars and officials. He learned when and how to lubricate his Chinese relationships with gifts. Utilizing his prodigious powers of memory, he even became adept at seasoning his conversation with quotations from the Confucian Classics – something guaranteed to fortify any Euro-

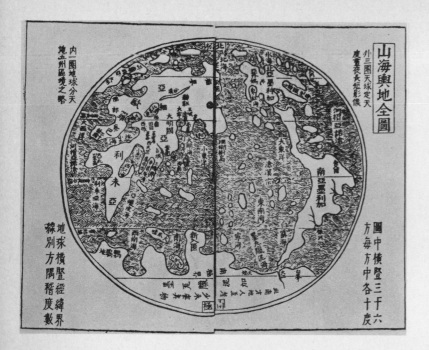

Jesuit science comes to China. Above: the second edition of Matteo Ricci's world map, placing China prominently near the centre. Right: the first page of a Portuguese-Chinese dictionary compiled by Ricci and his fellow Jesuit Ruggieri. (6, 7)

pean's reputation as a gentleman-scholar or, as the Chinese put it, a 'Western Confucian' *(Hsi-ju)*.

The true strength of Ricci's approach, however, lay less in his adoption of the Chinese scholar's dress and style, as important as these were, than in the genuine respect accorded by him to Confucian teaching. While critical of Sung Confucianism and positively scornful of Buddhism and Taoism, he judged the thought of Confucius himself to be mainly ethical in content and quite in accord with the canons of reason. Primitive Confucianism thus could be viewed as complementary to Christianity, rather than antithetical to it. And, in his Chinese writings, Ricci was not at all averse to citing passages from Confucius to show where the teachings of Christ harmonized with those of China's sage.

Ricci's assent to the participation of Chinese converts in ancestor worship and other Confucian rites reflected the same spirit of generosity and conciliation. Where some of his contemporaries, and practically all of his successors of the 19th century, viewed Confucianism as a mortal enemy, to be destroyed root and branch if Christianity were to make any headway in China, Ricci was more inclined to see Confucianism as an errant friend, in need of Christian correction and enrichment, but not replacement. Chinese culture, in his view, did not have to be destroyed in order to be Christianized.

An equally telling point of contrast between Ricci and 19th-century missionaries may be seen in their attitudes towards the introduction of Western scientific knowledge. As part of his general effort to appeal to the rational in prospective Chinese friends and converts, Ricci made a habit of presenting as gifts clocks, prisms, copies of a

world map he had devised, and other items of scientific or technical interest. He also composed a number of treatises in Chinese elucidating the principles of Western mathematics and astronomy. Ricci's only purpose in all this, however, was to smooth the way for Chinese acceptance of Christianity. One will look in vain for any indication that he believed China *needed* Western science in order to survive. The modern scientific revolution was just getting started in his day, and the age of railroads and steamships lay far off in the future. It was still possible, therefore, for Ricci to see in China a culture which, though very different from his own, was equally advanced.

At his death in 1610, Ricci's success was to be measured not in numbers of converts but in the foothold which, through patience, tact, and infinite resourcefulness, he had succeeded in securing for Christianity in the Empire. Permission had been won to inaugurate a Jesuit residence in Peking. Close friendships had been formed with countless Chinese officials. And, if the roll of converts was not very long (something over two thousand in Ricci's lifetime), it included names of such lustre – Hsu Kuang-ch'i (1562–1633) was the greatest – that this may aptly be described as the heroic age of Chinese Catholicism.

Politics versus religion

Ricci's successors continued his two-pronged strategy of adaptation to Chinese culture and conversion from the top down. But where Ricci had concentrated on forming close bureaucratic connections, later Jesuits actually became members of the Chinese bureaucracy and served the throne directly. The new relationship was founded mainly on the superior astronomical knowledge of the missionaries, which enabled them to devise more accurate calendars than Chinese astronomers. In a ritual-oriented, agrarian society like China's, calendrical accuracy was deemed to be of the utmost importance, and in the late Ming Adam Schall and other Jesuits were invited to join the government's Calendrical Department. Schall, around this time, also advised the court on military matters and supervised the casting of cannon for use against the threatening Manchu forces to the north. With the Manchu conquest in 1644, however, the Jesuits readily transferred their loyalties to the new Ch'ing dynasty, and it was not long before they acquired even greater power than under the Ming. Schall soon became the first of a succession of Jesuits to be appointed director of the Bureau of Astronomy. Jesuit missionaries were instrumental in the negotiations leading to the Sino-Russian Treaty of Nerchinsk (1689). Schall and the Flemish priest Ferdinand Verbiest developed close personal relationships with the Emperors Shun-chih (r. 1644–61) and K'ang-hsi (r. 1662–1722), respectively. So great, indeed, was K'ang-hsi's faith in his Jesuit friends that he permitted them at one point to treat him for an attack of malarial fever.

By making themselves useful to the throne in a multitude of ways, the Jesuits acquired much prestige and influence. But they also courted danger. Power brought enemies as well as friends. And as the proscription edict of 1724 dramatically showed, a moment of imperial wrath could do much to undo a century's patient labour.

The immediate occasion for this edict, which reversed the edict of toleration that the missionaries had finally won from K'ang-hsi in 1692, was the succession struggle that ensued on K'ang-hsi's death. In this struggle the Jesuits had the misfortune to back the wrong contender, and when the Emperor Yung-cheng (r. 1723–36) ascended the throne, he naturally turned against them.

Irritation with the missionaries had been mounting for other reasons as well. The Society of Jesus had long since been joined in China by other Catholic orders, and in time irreconcilable differences had emerged within the missionary community. Dominicans and Franciscans were, as a rule, less tolerant than the Jesuits and more inclined to work directly with the masses. Beneath these missiological differences, moreover, there were deep-seated nationalistic rivalries, the Jesuits tending to be natives of northern Europe, the low countries, and Italy, while the friars hailed mostly from Portugal and Spain.

Although there were many issues dividing the missionaries, the most important by far was the controversy over the rites performed by Chinese to their ancestors, Confucius, and Heaven. These rites, especially the ancestral observances, were of paramount importance in Chinese culture, and the decision as to whether or not they could be performed by converts would materially affect Christianity's chances of success. Consistent with their general policy of accommodation, the Jesuits for the most part condoned the rites, judging them to be merely civic or political in character, while the members of the other orders tended to regard the rites as idolatrous, and so, from a Christian standpoint, unacceptable.

Eventually, the issue was joined at the summit, when the Jesuits secured from K'ang-hsi an edict supporting their position, and the Pope, under the influence of the Jesuits' adversaries, promptly took the opposite stand. The Rites Controversy, as it came to be known, was settled once and for all by a papal bull of 1742 forbidding Christian participation in 'the Rites and Ceremonies of China'. By this time, however, the issue had become academic, since the propagation of Christianity in the Empire had already been declared unlawful.

Although the Chinese were particularly wary of the political threat discerned in Christianity, they challenged the religion on intellectual grounds as well. If God were really as good and as powerful as the Catholics claimed, asked the more sceptical, how could He permit Adam and Eve to commit a sin so contaminating that it was transmitted to all subsequent generations? If even man, in his weakness and impotence, could to some extent guard against evil, should not an all-powerful God have been capable of rooting out evil altogether?

When intellectual scepticism was aggravated by personal jealousy and vindictiveness, persecution might easily result, as the early Ch'ing encounter between Yang Kuang-hsien and Adam Schall made plain. Yang, a Moslem scholar-astronomer, responding with outrage to the power given a foreigner, launched a violent crusade against Schall, his calendar, and his religion. The Spanish conquest of the Philippines lent credibility to his charge that the Europeans represented a political threat, and Schall was brought to trial and condemned. Although it was not long before the tables were turned on Yang, as the Jesuits once more proved the superiority of their calendrical calculations, among Chinese detractors of Christianity the name Yang Kuang-hsien continued to be revered, and in the 19th century his writings went through one printing after another.

p 268
(10)

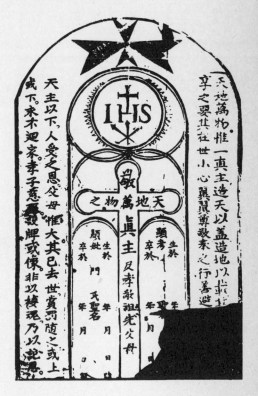

This tablet shows how Chinese Christian converts harmonized their new religious beliefs with their old ancestral commitments. The text within the cross says: 'Worship the true Lord, creator of heaven, earth and all things, and show filial piety towards ancestors and parents.' (8)

285

Persecution of Christianity was only sporadic and local in the 17th century. But in the 1720s, as we have seen, it became imperial policy. Chinese Christians were now commanded to renounce their faith; missionaries, except for those Jesuits still attached to the Bureau of Astronomy, were requested to leave China; and Catholic properties were confiscated and converted to secular use. For the next 120 years, although a handful of missionaries continued to work incognito in the interior, Christianity was officially designated as a heterodox cult, making it seem little different in Chinese eyes from the dreaded secret societies that periodically threatened dynastic stability.

It has been estimated that the Chinese Catholic population reached a high point of about 300,000 early in the 18th century. A hundred years later, in 1800, the total had probably dropped to somewhere between 200,000 and 250,000, where it remained until the eve of the Opium War. This decrease in the absolute size of the Catholic community scarcely tells the whole story, however. For even in the absence of such a reduction, the Chinese population explosion of the 18th and early 19th centuries would have meant a halving of the ratio of Christians to the total population by 1800 and a still further percentage reduction by 1840.

Two-way enlightenment

The failure of the early missionaries to Christianize China had its counterpart in their failure to affect Chinese culture significantly through the introduction of Western secular knowledge. Points were scored, to be sure: Schall's and Verbiest's cannon technology, the new calendrical knowledge and astronomical instruments of the Jesuits, the use of longitudinal and latitudinal markings in map-making, Western perspective drawing and oil painting, Ricci's translation of Euclid, and a smattering of writings on trigonometry, geography, human physiology, music, and other subjects. The trouble was that the new knowledge led nowhere. For every Chinese who came under the spell of Western learning, there were tens of thousands who remained wholly impervious to it. The central concerns of the Confucian scholar were no more touched by Euclidean geometry or Aristotelian philosophy than they were by the miniature Versailles erected on the grounds of the Manchu Summer Palace by the Jesuit court painter Castiglione.

Not only were all emanations of Western culture consigned indiscriminately to the realm of exotica, but the general level of Chinese knowledge about the West remained appallingly low. More than two hundred years after Ricci's death, a new edition of the Kwangtung provincial gazetteer stated authoritatively that Portugal was situated near Malacca, England was a Dutch dependency, and France (believed to have been originally a Buddhist country) was the same as Portugal. The editor of this work, Juan Yuan, was one of China's foremost scholars, and its subject, Kwangtung, had enjoyed more extensive contact with the West than any other Chinese province.

p 266 (6)

p 267 (7,8)
Jesuit missionaries, as has often been observed, were far more successful in conveying information on China

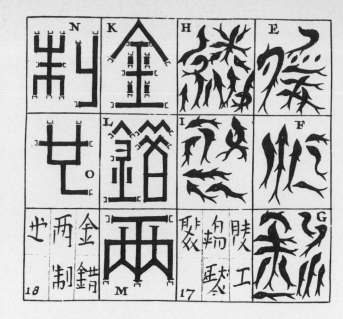

to their compatriots in Europe. As knowledge of the Rites Controversy spread, the Jesuits were obliged to defend their accommodationist approach by painting Chinese culture in the brightest colours. The picture that emerged – of a rationally ordered state and society, organized around the precepts of natural law, ruled by philosopher-kings, free of religious bigotry and clerical interference – held an enormous attraction for the men of the Enlightenment, and interest in China soared. The mathematician-philosopher Leibniz suggested, only half-playfully, that 'Chinese missionaries should be sent to us to teach us the aim and practice of natural theology, as we send missionaries to them to instruct them in revealed theology'. To the French philosopher Poivre, writing in 1769, China offered 'an enchanting picture of what the whole world might become, if the laws of that empire were to become the laws of all nations'. David Hume, in what for Hume was highest praise, spoke of the Chinese literati as 'the only regular body of Deists in the universe'. And Voltaire, the greatest Sinophile of all, applauded the Chinese for having 'perfected moral science . . . the first of the sciences'.

So great, indeed, was Europe's enthralment with China that, in the view of one scholar, literate Westerners probably knew more about that country in the 18th century than they do in the 20th. Knowledge and influence are, however, two distinct things. While it is true that, here and there, we may discern a thin ray of direct Chinese influence on the thought world of 18th-century Europe – the economic theories of the Physiocrats come to mind – by and large the role played by China was more subtle. China did not create any of the great issues that stirred the men of the Enlightenment. Yet she seemed to speak to many of them. She could serve as a weapon, a stimulus, a source of reassurance, even a guide, but she could not alter the course of European intellectual development. The great substantive contributions made by China to Europe's modernization lay not in the realm of thought but in that of technology. And it was precisely here that her influence was most anonymous.

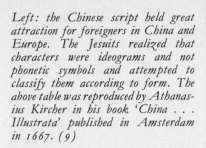

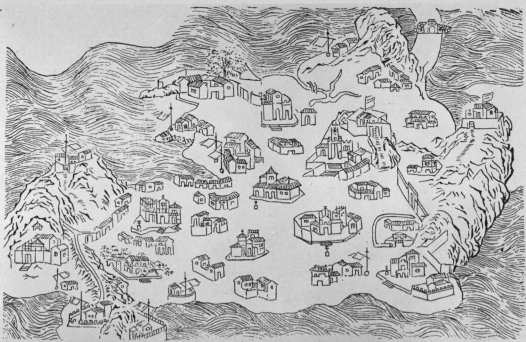

265 (1)

Left: the Chinese script held great attraction for foreigners in China and Europe. The Jesuits realized that characters were ideograms and not phonetic symbols and attempted to classify them according to form. The above table was reproduced by Athanasius Kircher in his book 'China . . . Illustrata' published in Amsterdam in 1667. (9)

Right: a view of Macao, several decades after the Chinese had permitted the Portuguese to establish a permanent base there. Entirely cut off from the mainland by a wall across the neck of the peninsula, it was to become one of the most flourishing entrepots of the Far East (10)

The missionaries of commerce

The commercial dimension of the early modern encounter between China and the West differed fundamentally fom the religious-intellectual dimension. The basic difference, from which all others stemmed, was the fact that foreign traders engaged China along her coastal periphery, where politically and militarily she was weakest and socially and culturally she was least resistant to change. Change, in fact, had already begun by the time the first Portuguese carracks arrived off the south China coast in the early 16th century. In parts of south-eastern China, agriculture was being commercialized on a significant scale for the first time. The Chinese junk trade with South-east Asia, which had started centuries earlier, was still growing. Not least important, on the coastal fringes of China a new social alliance was in the making, composed of merchants, junkmen, corsairs, and a variety of other shady types, and oriented more towards the outer world of commerce than towards the heartland of Chinese culture. When Peking referred to these people as 'Chinese traitors' *(Han-chien)*, it was not all hyperbole, for the new maritime civilization with which they were linked would eventually become powerful enough to shatter China's cultural insularity and radically alter her relationship to the world.

The Portuguese sailed to Asia initially in search of spices, which brought huge profits on the Lisbon market. It was only after getting there that they discovered the existence of an equally profitable intra-Asian carrying trade. Determined to capture a portion of this trade, the Portuguese at first tried to bully their way in. When that proved disastrous, they moved up and down the China coast, setting up fly-by-night marts on offshore islands, pillaging, and in general making a prime nuisance of themselves, until the Chinese authorities, for reasons still unknown, permitted them to establish a more permanent base on the Kwangtung coast, not far from Canton. This was in 1557. Before many years had passed, p 269 (9,11) the new port, which the Portuguese called Macao, had become one of the most flourishing entrepots in the Far East.

The main basis for Macao's rapid growth was the lucrative trade in silks and metals between China and Japan. Traditionally this trade had been monopolized by Chinese junkmen. But, in the pirate-infested seas of the 16th century, the well-armed Portuguese carrack made an attractive alternative carrier, and it was not long before Macao began to receive a regular part of the silk trade, holding on to it until well into the 17th century.

For a time, Portugal's only European rival in the Orient was Spain, which had secured a base in the Philippines shortly after the middle of the 16th century. Although direct Spanish trade with China never amounted to much, Manila (founded in 1571) eventually became the Macao of a prosperous, if somewhat circumscribed, commerce between China and Spanish America. One interesting feature of the American trade was its influence on the Chinese money system. For the silk carried by Fukienese junks to Manila and thence by Spanish galleons to Acapulco brought in exchange a steady flow of silver coins. And these 'Mexican dollars', as they were called, became by the 18th century the leading silver currency in the coastal cities of China.

An important by-product of early Sino-American contacts was the introduction of new crops such as maize, tobacco, peanuts, and sweet potatoes. The exact routes taken by these crops from America to China varied, some coming overland through Burma and India, others by sea. The new foods, above all the sweet potato, soon became essential ingredients in the diets of many of China's poor, and contributed substantially to the increase in population that occurred from the late 17th century on.

Although Macao has survived under Portuguese rule to the present day and the annual voyages of the Manila galleons to Mexico did not cease until 1815, the dawn of the 17th century ushered in a new era in European trade with Asia. The hallmarks of this new era were, first, the ascendancy of the Protestant nations, Holland and England, as the dominant trading powers, and, second, a fundamental change in the character of the trade itself. Ever since Roman times Western trade with China had

287

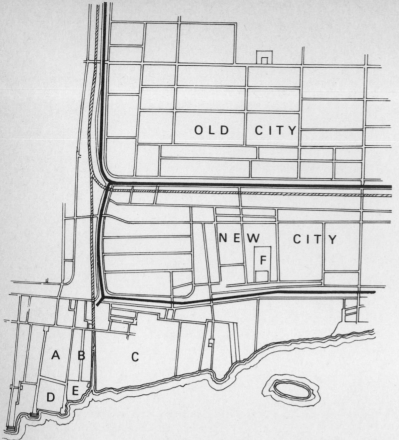

'Factory' was the term used for the offices of European traders. Before the first Opium War these were confined to an area outside the walls of Canton (the thick black line). A, the older foreign factories. B, the new English factories. C, houses of Chinese merchants licensed to trade with foreigners. D, E, public gardens flying the American and British flags. F, the governor general's house. (11)

great bulk of British trade was henceforth concentrated. The 18th century witnessed the evolution of an elaborate institutional matrix for the regulation of Anglo-Chinese trade (and traders). It also witnessed, within the framework of this 'Canton system', a revolutionary change in the trade itself.

The cause of the change was the British public's growing penchant for tea-drinking. Little more than a century after its introduction in 1657, tea was consuming a full 5 per cent of the average London working-class family's daily budget. The impact of this mass market on the China trade, hitherto dominated by luxury items and specie, was stupendous. By the end of the 18th century, tea accounted for 81 per cent of all exports from Canton, 20 million pounds of the commodity being marketed in England each year. Between 1719–25 and 1828–33, the tonnage of European ships trading at Canton increased 23 times, almost entirely as a result of the commerce in tea. So large did this commerce become that the tax on tea imports eventually supplied the English exchequer with 10 per cent of its annual revenues.

This enormous expansion of Sino-Western trade produced problems that ultimately were too large for the old Canton framework to handle. The basic problem in the 18th century was the absence of a significant Chinese market for any foreign commodity. For a long time, therefore, exports of tea and silk had to be paid for with specie, and it was not until the end of the century that the imbalance began to be corrected through the import into China, first of Indian raw cotton, and then of Indian opium. The opium trade grew so rapidly that by the 1830s it had become the largest commerce in the world in any single item. This was a boon to the Chinese and foreign interests directly involved. But it wrecked the Canton system and so aggravated Anglo-Chinese relations that war became unavoidable.

p 271
(17,18)
p 272
(20)

The two characteristics of the opium commerce that caused it to play such a destructive role were its profitability and its illegality. The first characteristic attracted to Canton growing numbers of private British and American traders, thereby undermining and eventually destroying the monopolistic arrangements that were the Canton system's heart and soul. The second characteristic, expressed in the Chinese government's frequent bans on opium importation, eventually drove the drug traffic from Canton, freeing it of the restrictions that had so long encumbered Sino-Western trade and transforming it into a massive coast-long smuggling operation.

Opium, as is often pointed out, was only the occasion for a confrontation that was rich in diplomatic, legal, cultural, and economic implications, and would, it is almost certain, have taken place anyway sooner or later. The root cause of the confrontation was the contradiction between European expansion and Chinese self-sufficiency. The tea trade was 'huge' only in terms of its impact on the English market; its capacity to affect the Chinese market was relatively small. Even after the Opium War, recent studies argue, the impact of foreign trade on the Chinese economy as a whole remained, for many decades, negligible. Much more important was its political and cultural impact, as expressed in the unwillingness of Westerners to accommodate themselves to time-honoured Chinese patterns and their insistence,

been principally in items of low bulk and high value, such as silks and porcelains. Now this luxury trade was, for the first time, superseded by another, in precious metals, gold being exported from China in exchange for silver bullion from Europe.

p 270
(13,14)
p 271
(15,16)

During the first three-quarters of the 17th century, Holland had the lead over England. The Dutch succeeded gradually in wresting control of the overseas trade in spices from Portugal. Also, after the expulsion of the Portuguese from Japan in 1639, the Dutch became the only Europeans permitted to carry on trade with that country. Holland was less successful, however, in her efforts to establish regular commercial intercourse with China, and by the time she did, she found the China trade dominated by her chief rival, Britain.

English trade was carried on under the aegis of the British East India Company, a joint-stock corporation organized in 1600 with monopolistic rights to Asian commerce. After repeated efforts failed to break Holland's grip on the spice trade, the Company turned its attention increasingly to the huge potential markets of India and China.

During most of the 17th century, British trade with China was slow and erratic. The periodic sealing off of the entire coast for security reasons during the early decades of Manchu rule did not help matters. Nor did the continued iron grip maintained by Macao over the trade in and out of Canton. The British finally broke this grip, however, in 1699, and it was here, at Canton, that the

p 272
(19)

which was worse, that all of the adjusting be done by China.

Although it was not until a generation after the Opium War that the Chinese themselves began dimly to perceive it, in retrospect it is evident that this kind of challenge, backed as it was by superior power, called into question the very capacity of Chinese civilization to survive. Not because the challenge penetrated China's inner fibre – her geographical and cultural, as well as her economic, heartland remained remarkably impervious until very recent times – but because many of China's most distinctive traits as a civilization, in particular her view of herself as the political and cultural epicentre of the world, were a direct consequence of her long development in relative isolation from other major civilizations. And this condition, it became increasingly clear as the 19th century unfolded, had now been permanently revoked by history.

Japan: 'The Christian Century'

Japan, having grown up in China's cultural shadow, never faced this problem. Her culture diverged, in important respects, from China's, and the Japanese were proud of the differences. But behind the pride there was always the consciousness that civilization could exist elsewhere. To describe the Japanese, as is sometimes done, as a 'nation of borrowers' is to dwell crudely on one aspect of Japanese cultural development to the exclusion of all the rest. Borrowing did, however, constitute a significant part of Japan's historical experience. And if there were no other factors differentiating Japan from China, this one factor alone would have made a sizable difference in the reception accorded to Western civilization.

There were, of course, other factors. When the first Portuguese traders arrived off the Japanese coast (apparently in 1543), they encountered a country which, both in territorial extent (smaller than France) and in population size (20 million), was minuscule in comparison with China. It was also organized along radically different lines. The authority of the central government, represented at the time by the Ashikaga Shoguns, had fallen to an unprecedentedly low level, and effective power was lodged in autonomous feudal realms, each of which was ruled by a daimyō (feudal lord) and his samurai (warrior) retainers. This was the period of high feudalism in Japanese history. The spirit of rivalry among the daimyō was intense, and warfare was endemic.

p 274 (25)
p 275 (26)
In the second half of the 16th century, however, order was gradually restored and central rule re-established by three successive military leaders of outstanding ability: Oda Nobunaga, Toyotomi Hideyoshi, and Tokugawa Ieyasu. The turn of the century brought a new Shogunate, the Tokugawa, which instituted a highly centralized form of feudal rule, leaving the daimyō more or less autonomous within their fiefs but otherwise under closest supervision from the centre. Peace and stability now became the order of the day, and by 1650 the contrast with the Japan of a century earlier was complete.

Thus, the European missionaries and traders who ventured to Japan in early modern times, unlike their compatriots in China, confronted a situation in which change was taking place at a rapid pace. China in the 17th century shifted dynasties, but Japan, for all practical purposes, changed her form of government. Such extreme change had a correspondingly extreme effect on the capacity of Westerners to influence Japanese culture.

p 273 (21)
At the outset this capacity proved nothing short of remarkable. Christian missionary activity in Japan was started in 1549 by the Spanish Jesuit known to history as St Francis Xavier (1506–52). A few months after his arrival Xavier recorded his first impressions of the country and its inhabitants:

'. . . the people whom we have met so far, are the best who have as yet been discovered, and it seems to me that we shall never find among heathens another race to equal the Japanese. They are a people of very good manners . . . and prize honour above all else in the world . . . they highly regard arms and trust much therein . . . never yet did I see a people so honest in not thieving. . . . They like to hear things propounded according to reason; and granted that there are sins and vices among them, when one reasons with them pointing out that what they do is evil, they are convinced by this reasoning.'

Xavier's premature death prevented him from seeing his high hopes for the Japanese bear fruit. By 1582, little more than a generation after his arrival, the number of converts totalled an astonishing 150,000 (as compared with two thousand Chinese Christians made during the first thirty years of Jesuit activity in China). Such was the degree of the Church's success that there was even talk of England's defection to Protestantism being offset by the complete conversion of the Japanese islands.

As the Jesuit mission in Japan matured, the man who was most instrumental in shaping its strategy was the Italian Alessandro Valignano (1539–1606). Arriving in 1579 and spending approximately half of the remaining twenty-five years of his life in Japan, Valignano followed closely in Xavier's footsteps. He placed the Japanese, as a race, on an absolute par with Europeans and insisted that European missionaries conform, as far as possible, to the social customs and life-style of their adoptive home.

p 274 (24)
Newcomers from Europe were required to spend about a year and a half in intensive language work and to make a careful study of Japanese etiquette. Jesuits were permitted to take part in popular festivities, such as gift-giving at New Year's time. Also, they lived in native-style houses and adopted the dress and status of Zen priests, then the most powerful, intelligent, and respected members of the Buddhist clergy in Japan.

The other aspect of Jesuit strategy, as in China, was the courting of the highly placed elements in Japanese society. This involved, first, making friends and converts of the daimyō and samurai, in the belief that the lower social classes would follow their superiors' lead, and, second, seizing every opportunity to gain the favour and protection of the powerful military chieftains who were then in the process of unifying the country. Initially, this dual approach brought high dividends. The daimyō of Kyūshū, the island where the largest number of converts were concentrated, often befriended the missionaries and sometimes embraced their religion. One Christian daimyō, in 1579, entrusted the Jesuits with the government of Nagasaki, after this town had become the main port of call for Portuguese traders. Others sent embassies to Rome to mark their devotion and zeal. On occasion, Christian daimyō even compelled the people living in their fiefs to adopt the foreign religion.

For a time, the Jesuits were also successful in gaining the favour of Japan's unifiers. Oda Nobunaga respected them for their iron discipline and high attainments, and welcomed their antipathy to a Buddhist Church whose power he himself was bent on crushing. Even Hideyoshi and Tokugawa Ieyasu, although becoming increasingly hostile to the Christian community, were reluctant to press their attacks all the way, as long as the Jesuits remained useful to them.

In China the Jesuits had made themselves useful through their superior knowledge of calendrical science; p 274 (23) in Japan it was through their intimate connection with the lucrative Portuguese-carried silk trade, a trade that was not merely tolerated but actively desired by Japan's leaders. The classic description of this improbable relationship between God and Mammon is provided by C. R. Boxer:

p 273 (22) 'It was in the Great Ship that the Jesuits came to Japan; it was mainly from their share in the sale of its cargoes that they supported their promising mission field; it was the wish for the Great Ship which induced otherwise hostile or indifferent daimyō to welcome them to their fiefs and to permit the conversion of their retainers; it was the fear that the Great Ship would no longer come, if the Jesuits were driven away, which repeatedly caused Hideyoshi and Ieyasu to hold their hands when they were on the point of expelling the missionaries.'

Under these advantageous conditions, the Church in Japan flourished. There were 300,000 Japanese Christians by 1600, and by 1615 possibly as many as half a million. Although in absolute terms the Japanese Christian community was not very much larger than the Chinese (at its peak), in percentage terms it was a dozen times bigger. How is this striking contrast to be accounted for?

Certainly economic inducements and forced conversions played an important part, though just how important remains to be determined. This was especially true in the period before 1600, when the daimyō, not yet under the strict control of the Tokugawa house, were still free to do pretty much as they wished. Economic and political factors were only part of the story, however. Just as important, in the long run, was the relatively greater openness of the Japanese to foreign cultural influences: witness the craze for European knick-knacks and the upper-class fad of dressing up in Portuguese costume – something the Chinese would have found beyond comprehension.

This general receptivity to foreign influence was reinforced by the specific circumstances surrounding the late 16th-century encounter. For one thing, Christianity was presented in such a way that it seemed to many Japanese to be similar to Buddhism and therefore not altogether foreign. It was further favoured by not having to confront, as in China, a powerful state-sponsored orthodoxy. (Not until well into the Tokugawa period was a comparable orthodoxy instituted in Japan.)

Again, the values of 16th-century Europe, where honour and the martial virtues were still much cherished, seemed far more familiar to the Japanese warrior than to the Chinese literatus. As a result of these special circumstances, the ideal of accommodation, though espoused with equal fervour by Jesuits in China and in Japan, could come much closer to being realized in Japan. Much of the Japanese Church's strength derived from this fact.

One other circumstance that deserves mention in this connection is the far greater investment in personnel made by the Church in Japan. In 1614 there were 116 Jesuits working in the country, as compared with 59 in China in 1701 (when Christianity was at the height of its influence there). China's population in the early 18th century, however, was seven or eight times larger than Japan's in 1614. When the missionaries of other orders are added to these figures, the disparity in absolute missionary totals narrows somewhat (156 in Japan in 1614, 127 in China in 1701), but it remains very substantial in per capita terms. Relatively speaking, then, the missionary enterprise in Japan was a much larger operation than its Chinese counterpart.

Counter-reaction

The high visibility of the Japanese Church, coupled with its rapid growth in strength and influence, eventually produced a devastating counter-reaction. Bans against the missionaries were issued by both Hideyoshi and Ieyasu, and in 1597 Hideyoshi had nine missionaries p 275 (26) and seventeen Japanese Christians crucified. It was not, however, until 1614, towards the close of Ieyasu's reign, that the proscription of Christianity began to be enforced with severity. Many missionaries now left the country and those who chose not to were tortured and put to death by Ieyasu's successors. The same terrible fate awaited more than three thousand Japanese Christi- p 276 (29) ans who refused to renounce their faith; and many thousands more were slaughtered in the Shimabara p 275 (27,28) revolt, the great Christian peasant rebellion that erupted near Nagasaki in 1637–38. This marked the end of Japan's 'Christian century'. Less than a hundred years after Xavier's arrival, the missionary movement had been annihilated and an indigenous Church that had once been the glory of Asian Christianity had been reduced to complete impotence.

Why? One reason for the Church's demise in Japan has already been suggested: it had become too powerful. Had Japan remained in the fragmented condition in which Europeans initially found her, the growing power of the Church would very likely not have been a handicap. But as unification proceeded, Japan's new leaders perceived, in the existence of an autonomous community of Christians with strong local and foreign attachments, a dangerous threat to their rule. The transcendent loyalty of the Christian to his God was potentially subversive of a feudal system in which vassals were supposed to be unconditionally loyal to their lords. Also there were fears, which events seemed to substantiate, that the Christian community presented a foreign political menace. In 1592 the first Dominicans and Franciscans arrived from Manila, armed with their abrasive proselytizing methods and strong anti-Portuguese outlook. The customary in-fighting that commenced between Portuguese Jesuits and Spanish friars soon gave rise to rumours of Spanish conquistadorial designs. And shortly before his death, Hideyoshi, aware of what had happened in the Philippines, instituted the first severe persecution of the Japanese Church.

Why, if the political motives of the Church were truly feared, was it allowed to grow even after the promulgation of the original bans? The answer seems to lie principally in the Jesuits' connection with foreign trade. As long as Japan's rulers believed the missionaries to be indispensable to the continuation of this trade, they were reluctant to take final action against them. In the early years of the 17th century, however, the missionaries lost their first line of defence, as it became progressively clear that Japan could have foreign trade without foreign religion. The initial source of this discovery was an English pilot, Will Adams, who, after being stranded off the Japanese coast in 1600, won Tokugawa Ieyasu's confidence by building European-style ships for him and advising him on commercial matters. Adams's information was confirmed with the arrival in 1609 of a Dutch trading vessel, followed four years later by an English ship. The Dutch and English traders had no connection with missionary activities, and when it became known that they intended to establish trading missions at Hirado (an island off the Kyūshū coast), Ieyasu finally decided to move against the Church.

The expulsion of all foreign missionaries from Japan turned out to be the forerunner of an isolationist policy that in time embraced foreign traders as well. This reversal in the Japanese government's attitude towards foreign trade was brought about by a number of factors. One was the growing vigour of Japan's domestic commerce and manufacture, in spite of the Tokugawa Shoguns' general tendency to favour the agrarian sector of the economy. Foreign trade, in such circumstances, seemed less necessary than before, and also less desirable. Its undesirability was enhanced by the fear of a security-conscious Shogunate that foreign traders would supply arms to the daimyō of the Kyūshū coastal area, whose loyalty remained perennially suspect, and its more general fear that trade might funnel foreign cultural influences into Japan, thereby disturbing the brittle stability of the Tokugawa social order.

p 277
(30)

The policy of quarantining Japan against foreign contact evolved by stages. The voluntary exit in 1623 of the British, who did not find the Japanese trade especially profitable, was followed a year later by the expulsion of the Spaniards and the banning of further intercourse with Manila. Additional restrictions on foreign trade were imposed between 1633 and 1639. Since the contaminating effects of foreign culture could be carried by native as well as European traders, all Japanese were prohibited from leaving the country, and those who were already abroad were banned from returning on pain of death. A flourishing Japanese overseas commerce was thereby nipped in the bud; and, with the severance of trade relations with Portugal in 1639, as a result of that country's alleged complicity in the Shimabara uprising, the sealing off of the islands became all but complete. Japan had come full circle. Initially much more enthusiastic than China in her reception of Western trade

and religion, she now had rejected both with a fury and determination that could only be the envy of the Chinese court.

The circle was closed, however, only by the extreme vigour of the Japanese response. In real terms, there was no circle. For in the hundred years since the first Europeans had appeared off her shores, Japan had become a very different country. To what extent, we may logically ask, was the difference a consequence of foreign contact? How much influence had Europe exerted on Japan's cultural and historical development? The argument can be made that, although the impact of Christianity was far more dramatic, the marks left by a century of European contact on Japan's secular culture were longer lasting. The Japanese language was enriched by many Portuguese words, some of which, such as *pan* (for bread) and *tabako* (for tobacco), became permanent additions. New food products (such as potatoes) were introduced from the Americas and, in the fine arts, the Jesuits taught the Japanese the techniques of oil painting and copper-plate engraving. It was in the military field, however, that Europe's impact was greatest. Within a generation of the arrival of the first Portuguese ships, Japan was manufacturing her own firearms for the first time. Firearms soon became a major factor in Japanese warfare, and along with improved methods of castle construction, which may also have been brought in by the Portuguese, they added measurably to the military strength of the daimyō.

More important than any specific cultural influence was the effect that Europe had on Japan's relationship to the outside world. Here again we are presented with much sharper contrasts than in the Chinese case. For a time, in the 16th and early 17th centuries, there were ample indications that Japan was headed towards full participation in the newly evolving maritime civilization. Her leaders welcomed foreign trade. Her own merchants had, over the years, built up a tremendous commerce, especially with South-east Asia. Her economy, in general, was more deeply affected by overseas trade than China's.

Then, with the unfolding of the 17th century, this whole trend was dramatically reversed, as Japan's leaders deliberately aborted the promise of an expanding foreign commerce and beat a hasty retreat from their country's growing involvement with the external world. Although there is much room for controversy as to the precise effects of isolation on the ensuing two centuries of Japanese development, it is generally agreed that these effects were considerable. The expansion of European power and civilization, to which the policy of seclusion was principally a response, must therefore be credited with an important, if somewhat negative and indeterminate, share in the shaping of early modern Japanese history.

'Dutch studies'

But there was a positive aspect, too, to Europe's influence on Tokugawa Japan. The expulsion of the Portuguese left Holland and China as the only nations whose traders were still permitted to reside in the country. The Dutch, who had proved their indifference to (Catholic) Christianity by providing the government forces with artillery support during the Shimabara revolt, were transferred

A deputation from the Dutch East India Company leaves Nagasaki for its annual audience with the Shogun at Edo in 1690. The members of the procession include a Dutch and Japanese cook and their equipment (1, 2), two guides (3), luggage master (4), the Dutch envoy's horse (5), a Chinese soldier (6), medicine and treasure chests (7, 8) and the envoy in his litter which was carried by four men in relays and his three servants (9). These were followed by interpreters, secretaries, and servants and friends of the Dutch party who have come out from Nagasaki to see them off. (12)

p 277–9
(31–35)

in 1641 to an artificial island in the harbour of Nagasaki (Deshima), where they could be closely watched by the Japanese authorities and their contacts with the native population minimized. Through this small opening, the Japanese were able to catch an occasional glimpse of what was going on in the West, and some samurai were so intrigued with what they discovered that in time a diminutive 'Dutch studies' (*rangaku*) movement came into being.

Japanese study of Dutch began in the second half of the 17th century, and by 1670 there were interpreters at Nagasaki who could read as well as speak the language. It was not, however, until the administration of the Shogun Yoshimune (r. 1716–45) that Western learning acquired a modicum of respectability. Himself greatly interested in Western science, Yoshimune decreed in 1720 that previously banned Chinese-language works by Jesuit scholars, if they did not expound Christian doctrine, might be placed in circulation once again. Twenty years later he took the much more affirmative step of ordering two prominent scholars to learn Dutch, so that a start could be made in the translation of Western scientific literature.

The study of Western learning now moved forward with great speed. Translations were made of Dutch works on anatomy, astronomy, physics, and a variety of other subjects. Dictionaries and grammars were produced. The year 1789 saw the opening in Edo (Tokyo) of the first Dutch-language school, and shortly after the turn of the century the Shogunate established a special office for the translation of Dutch books. Although most of the interest was directed towards Western science (especially medicine), a few scholars ventured much further afield in their explorations. Shiba Kōkan (1738–1818), in addition to introducing Copernicanism to Japan, became an accomplished practitioner of Western painting. Honda Toshiaki (1744–1821), perhaps the greatest and certainly one of the most radical of the *rangaku* scholars, was deeply concerned over the foreign military threat and wanted Japan to become an imperial power like England. Measuring all things by their utility, Honda favoured Japan's adoption of Western alphabetic writing in place of the cumbersome Chinese characters.

As a result of the Dutch studies movement, the Japanese by the end of the 18th century were, according to Donald Keene, 'better acquainted with European civilization than the people of any other non-Western country'. The main effect of this new knowledge, as also of the revival of native Japanese learning (the sponsors of which were, to some extent, influenced by the *rangaku* scholars), was to challenge, subtly but unmistakably, Neo-Confucianism's hold on the Tokugawa intellectual world. The Shogunate's efforts, in the early decades of the 19th century, to strengthen Confucianism and to restrict Western studies showed, as clearly as anything could, the degree to which Confucianism had been thrown on the defensive. As Japanese, in increasing numbers, awakened to the insight that China was not the sole source of civilization, or Confucianism the fountainhead of all wisdom, a new spirit of relativism took shape. Gradually, imperceptibly, the Japanese view of themselves, of their relationship to China, and of their place in the larger world began to change. Japan was 'opening' herself, and by the time the Perry expedition arrived in 1853, her intellectual preparation for entry into the modern world was already well under way.

p 278
(36)
p 279
(37,38)

The spread of Western learning in Japan during the hundred years preceding her official 'opening' in 1853 seems all the more remarkable when compared to the reception accorded to the West in China in the century leading up to the Opium War. China's access to the West during this period was infinitely greater. Yet her capacity to assimilate Western secular culture proved even smaller than her capacity earlier to absorb Western religion. There was no Honda Toshiaki in 18th-century China, no 'English studies' movement to jar the foundations of Chinese Confucianism. Indeed, the Chinese literatus, on the eve of the Opium conflict, probably knew less about Western civilization than his forbears had a hundred and fifty years earlier. China, self-contained and self-absorbed, was thus much less prepared than Japan for the onslaught of the 19th-century West. Despite Japan's greater physical seclusion, China was the more genuinely isolated of the two countries. For hers was a cultural isolation, and it was in the field of culture that the primary adjustments to modernity had to be made.

XII A NEW ROLE FOR JAPAN

The Meiji Revolution and its sequel

Y. TORIUMI

Knowledge shall be sought throughout the world, so as to strengthen the foundation of imperial rule.

The fifth of the 'Five Articles Oath' issued
by the Meiji emperor in 1868

The return of the Emperor to active power after many centuries of subservience to the Shogun marked the birth of modern Japan. It was a curiously paradoxical move. In order to meet the challenge of the West, represented by the intrusion of the American fleet in 1853 and the subsequent treaties with the USA, Britain, France and Russia, Japan seemed to be turning back to an institution even older than the Shogunate.

After 1853, with great suddenness, Japan found herself obliged to compete with the West in military affairs, science and technology. The promotion of men with a knowledge of such disciplines disturbed the old Tokugawa social system, and demand mounted for change at the political level as well. Ending the Shogunate entailed putting something else in its place, and the only acknowledged national authority was the Emperor. An appeal to him over the Shogun's head preserved constitutional legality – it was a 'restoration', not a revolution – and for a time united both those who wanted a complete new start and those (especially the samurai class) whose only

programme was 'Honour the Emperor! Drive out the foreign barbarian!' In November 1867 the last Shogun voluntarily resigned his authority to the Emperor, though it took another year of fighting with the Tokugawa clan to make this resignation effective. On 26 November 1868 the young Emperor Meiji, who had ascended the throne only the previous year, left his traditional capital of Kyoto and entered Edo (Tokyo), the seat of Shogunate power (opposite).

The Shogunate had been a feudal system depending on the loyalty of virtually autonomous daimyō. Now the Shogun had gone, but the daimyō remained. Could the new regime impose a centralized system of government control upon this deeply entrenched tradition? One of the most surprising revelations about the Meiji Restoration was that it could – partly by buying off the samurai retainers. In 1871 the daimyō principalities were abolished and replaced by 'prefectures' administered by officials. Japan, under the fiction of returning to her ancestral past, had become a modern state. (1)

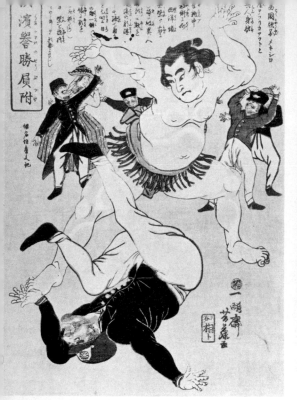

'Drive out the foreign barbarian!' A woodcut of the early 1860s puts the samurai point of view: the traditional Japanese wrestler overcomes his Western barbarian adversary. Such an attitude helped to promote a 'Back to the Emperor' movement but stood in the way of further change. (2)

When the samurai saw that the restoration meant the end of their privileged position, some accepted the situation (e.g. by going into business) but others staged a last resistance. In 1877 a group in Satsuma revolted. In an eight-month war the proud warrior caste was defeated by the new conscript army. (3)

The Shogunate fought back. Its chief opponents were the *hans* (feudal domains) of Chōshū and Satsuma, both of whom aspired to the leadership of the imperial party. Against the Chōshū, especially, the Shogun waged a

bitter campaign with the best Western-type weapons available (below). But they maintained their independence, twice defied the Shogun's armies and assumed leading positions in the subsequent Meiji regime. (4)

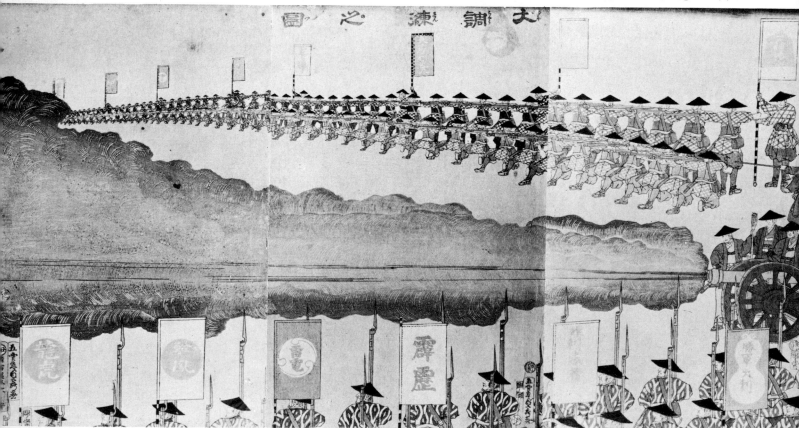

The last Shogun was Keiki (above), who took office in January 1867. Aware that reforms were needed, he began to reorganize the government and the army, but was overtaken by events. Two proposals for sharing power with the daimyō came to nothing. Finally, with the union of the Satsuma and Chōshū *hans*, the imperial party was able to seize power, but some pro-Shogunate diehards kept up resistance until 1869. (5)

The restored emperor – aged only fifteen in 1868 – was in fact a constitutional monarch on the European pattern. Behind a façade of traditional ceremonies and honorary titles, power rested with men who as a ruling class, were new to Japan – young samurai of humble birth, not tied to feudal tradition and determined to make Japan free of the West by Western methods. In November 1890 a new constitution was inaugurated, partially modelled on that of Germany. It established an Imperial Diet (below) made up of a House of Peers and a House of Representatives, and a range of government departments answerable directly to the emperor. (6)

The Meiji reforms constituted a full-scale social revolution. Land taxes were standardized and made uniform, and farmers were given legal recognition of ownership. The young emperor took an active interest in agriculture. Here (left) he visits farmers harvesting the crop. (7)

Education became compulsory in 1872, though it took time to make this a reality. The majority of children did not start attending until the 1880s and at first received only sixteen months schooling, later extended to four and then to six years. (9)

The new army (left) which replaced the samurai class was conscripted from the people as a whole. Trained by Western advisers, they adopted Western uniforms and quickly mastered the techniques of modern armaments. (8)

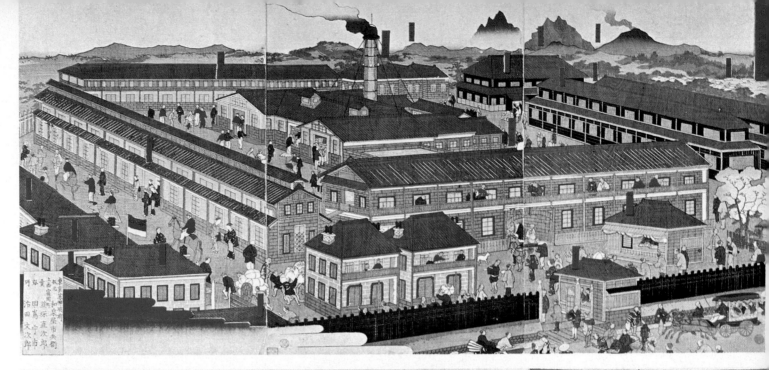

Instant Industrial Revolution was the Meiji recipe for progress. At first nationalization seemed the answer, but in the 1880s it was decided to give private enterprise its chance, expansion being fostered by government subsidies. The most rapid advances were made by the cotton industry. Between 1891 and 1901 output increased 4½ times, about a third of it being exported. Above: exterior and interior of the Tomioka silk reeling factory in the 1870s, the first to apply mass-production techniques employing women. (11, 12)

The first railway in Japan, between Tokyo and Yokohama, opened in 1872 (left). It was only nineteen miles long, but splendidly equipped with stations and locomotives. Soon it was carrying two million passengers a year. (10)

299

Change came too fast for some classes of society, and was the more bewildering the less it was understood. There were peasant risings in 1873, easily suppressed by government troops. More serious was the continued unrest of the old samurai class. Trouble had been held in check by paying pensions to daimyō retainers. In 1867 these were suspended and armed revolt (left) flared up in Kyūshū and Satsuma. (13)

Banking – the capitalist enterprise *par excellence* – had grown up in feudal Japan to cater for the peculiar financial requirements of the daimyō and their retinues. Now, with the appearance of new markets and new trading systems, its business suddenly boomed. The house of Mitsui began as a *sake* brewery, went into the cloth business and after 1868 developed into the most powerful banking firm in Japan. Their head office (below) was among Tokyo's most imposing buildings in the 1870s. (14)

Heavy industry took longer to evolve. The Yawata Iron Works, a government enterprise, opened in 1901 (right). It contained Japan's first blast furnaces and made possible the production at home of many items which formerly had to be bought from abroad. (15)

'Foreign countries are the common enemy of our empire', said Iwakura Tomoni in 1869. It was an attitude (partly inherited from the days of isolation, partly the result of rivalries that came later) that was to characterize Japanese policy – or at least a strong body of policy-making opinion – until the end of World War II. The army (below right, at a birthday parade in 1905) was virtually a European army on Asian soil. It was becoming clear that Japanese equality with the West would involve the acquisition of a Western-style empire. (16)

聯合軍北京包撃
日軍朝陽門
占領之圖

The road to imperialism began in the 1870s, when Japan started to see herself in the role of a leader committed to 'the development of Asia' on Western lines. In 1875 she forcibly 'opened' Korea, as Perry had opened Japan. China eventually (1894) intervened but was beaten by Japan's new navy. Further expansion into Manchuria was frustrated by the Western powers, but during the Boxer uprising Japan took part in the international expedition to relieve the legations. This colour print (left) of Japanese troops entering Peking in 1900 is a clear enough indication of her ambitions, ambitions to be fulfilled thirty-seven years later. (17)

Against Russia Japan was drawn into war through their clash of interests over Manchuria and Korea. Japan acted fast, beating the Russian army at Mukden and surprising their fleet at Port Arthur (below). As a last resort the Tsar sent his Baltic fleet half way round the world only to be decisively defeated off Tsushima. (18)

Against the world: during the twenties the moderates in Japan lost power, until the country was in fact being ruled by the army. In 1931 she took over Manchuria, and in 1937 invaded China itself. World War II gave the Japanese leaders their great opportunity. In December 1941, in an astonishing and brilliantly planned campaign, they eliminated the American fleet at Pearl Harbor and conquered all the former East Asian colonies. To the peoples of these countries Japan proclaimed herself a deliverer, calling what was in fact an empire 'the Great East Asian Co-prosperity Sphere'. To the Allies she was a monstrous octopus (right) reaching out across the Pacific. An Italian postcard (below right) shows, against a background of Axis flags, the samurai of old, straddling the ocean and dealing death to the navies of the West. (19, 20)

Defeat in war was a disaster without precedent in Japanese history, and the psychological shock was made all the more numbing by the physical horror of the atom bomb. Hiroshima (left) has become the ultimate symbol of mass destruction. Other Japanese cities, including Tokyo, had suffered almost as much damage by conventional bombing. Surrender in 1945 was followed by seven years of military occupation – a third 'impact' of the West, possibly as decisive for the future as the other two. (21)

Recovery took less time than even the most hopeful expectations. By 1955 production exceeded pre-war levels. In another decade Japan was one of the world's great industrial nations – an achievement bought at the price of new problems in the shape of overcrowding and pollution. Below left: the Yawata Steel Works in 1970. (22)

Booming industries have given Japan a high standard of living and a new appetite for durable consumer goods. Two areas where she has overtaken almost every competitor are shipbuilding and electrical equipment. Right: painting a giant oil-tanker before launching at the Mitsubishi shipyard, Nagasaki; and assembling transistor radios at the Sony works, Atsugi. (23, 24)

Riot police struggle against student demonstrators in Tokyo (below) – a sign of tension within the well ordered structure of Japanese society. The younger generation is conscious of a lack of moral purpose. Bizarre new religions have arisen to fill the spiritual vacuum. (25)

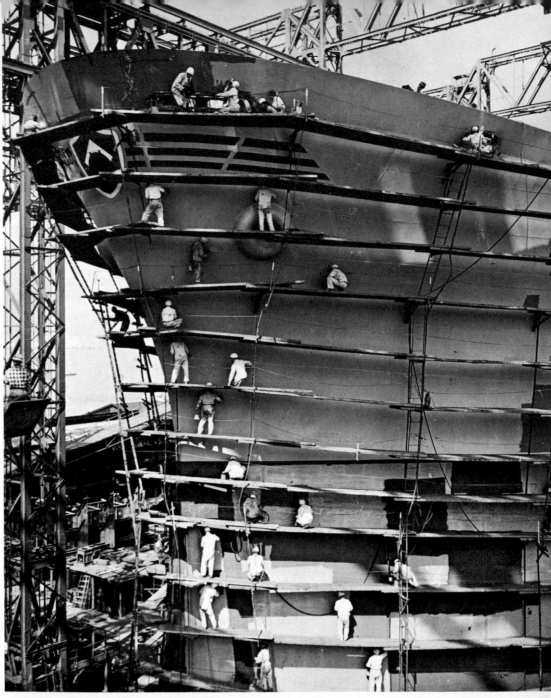

Has Japan's future been fixed by her decision to throw in her lot with the West? Did the 'Tower of the Sun' (left) at the Osaka Exhibition in 1970 – an event which set the seal on her eminence in world commerce – symbolize merely energy and optimism, or was there a trace of anxiety also? Certainly, Japan's problems are those of Europe and America, posed possibly in an even more acute form. Poverty has been overcome, the economic gap between town and country eliminated. Yet Utopia has not been achieved. To many, material prosperity seems to have outrun human capacity to use it creatively. Japanese cities sprout skyscrapers (below: the Shinjuku district of Tokyo), but as well as benefits they bring social disorientation, ugliness and misery.

This is not the first time in Japan's history that her traditional way of life and code of values have disintegrated. What is to come will, no doubt, as in the past, be very largely a combination of elements from outside. It will also, no doubt, as in the past, be distinctively Japanese. (26, 27)

Y. TORIUMI

Shop signs in Nihon Bashi, Tokyo, a woodcut by Hiroshige. The opening of Japanese ports to foreign trade benefited the more active business classes but led to a shortage of consumer goods at home—both results resented by the samurai. (1)

FROM THE EARLY 17TH CENTURY to the mid-19th, as we saw in Chapter VIII, while the Western powers were engaged in 'destruction and construction', Japan enjoyed a long period of peace. For more than two hundred years, she lived without falling into any major civil war or external conflict.

This peace was secured by the fulfilment of two principal conditions. In the first place, the Tokugawa Shogunate, by using ingenious means to control the daimyō, or feudal fief-holding barons, had established a fairly high degree of centralism under the Shogunate-daimyō system and had eliminated practically all other political powers important enough to rival the Shogunate. In the second place, Japan was an insular country lying to the east of continental Eurasia, and she was largely secluded from foreign contacts under a national policy of exclusionism. Consequently she was subject to only a minimum of political and economic influence from other countries.

In the latter half of the Tokugawa period, factors that were to shake the stability of the Shogunate-daimyō system began to develop within the system itself. These domestic developments, however, did not lead directly to the Meiji Revolution. What brought the internal conflict to an explosion point, and set in motion a vast process of radical political change, was a crisis in external relations due to a 'Western impact'. The destruction of the *ancien régime* and the construction of a modern state in Japan came as a result of an effort to survive by meeting the impact of the West effectively.

The opening of Japan

At a time when Japan was finding it increasingly difficult to maintain her traditional policy of exclusionism, Commodore Perry arrived in 1853 with a letter from the President of the United States calling for trade with Japan. His four warships anchored off Uraga, a harbour town not far from Edo (Tokyo).

p 278 (36)

Five years before Perry's arrival, the United States had vastly extended its frontage on the Pacific coast by taking California from Mexico. Desiring further to open a trans-Pacific trade-route, and looking for proper transit ports, the United States was bent on constraining Japan to open her ports to external trade. In contrast to representatives of other Western Governments who had hitherto visited Japan on similar missions, Perry had a mind to resort to arms if Japan refused to open her doors.

The demand for the opening of ports from the mouth of this 'plenipotentiary in command of a large fleet, speaking words of peace, but looking dangerous' (Alcock), made the Japanese feel that 'the worst crisis in history' had come. The Shogunate felt unable to act on its own judgment as it had always done in the past. It now broke all precedent by referring Perry's demand to a council of daimyō and asking for their advice. It also made a report to the Imperial court in Kyoto. Although many of the daimyō spoke in favour of continuing to observe the 'ancestral law' of exclusionism, it was evident that the military strength of Japan, after more than two hundred years of Tokugawa peace, compared poorly with that of the Western powers. In 1854 Perry reappeared, and strongly pressed the Shogunate for a reply. The Shogunate reluctantly yielded, and the Treaty of Kanagawa was concluded. Four years later the Shogunate signed treaties of amity and commerce, providing for freedom to trade, with the United States, Holland, Russia, Britain and France. The exclusion system, which had been in force for more than two hundred years, thus came to an end, and Japan opened her doors to the Western world.

The opening of the ports under foreign pressure naturally created an acute feeling of external crisis in the minds of the samurai class and other intelligent men. Their predominant concern now was how to defend their national independence against the tremendous impact of the West. The awareness of the crisis prompted the Shogunate and such major local daimyō governments as Satsuma, Chōshū, Tosa, Hizen, Echizen, and Mito to start actively importing Western military science, and to strengthen their defences by manufacturing modern weapons, building warships, and constructing forts. Science was encouraged, and scientific research institutions were set up. Men who possessed the new knowledge were recruited and were put in important positions, regardless of their social class. Even under the policy of exclusionism some Japanese intellectuals had managed to learn something of advanced Western science and technology through the half-open port of Nagasaki, and their knowledge now began to be useful. It is noteworthy that, through such reforms, many capable samurai of low birth found their way to high positions in the Shogunate and in the local daimyō governments. These men helped to carry out still further reforms.

Nevertheless, this complete reversal of the traditional policy of exclusionism sharply increased political tension at home because the change had been made, not by Japan's own free will, but reluctantly under the military pressure of the Western powers. The authority of the Shogunate was seriously shaken, and it rapidly lost its capacity to perform its historic function of serving as the focus of the country's political unity. The opposition radicals were no longer content with demands for intra-Shogunate reform; they began to aim at overthrowing the Shogunate itself.

p 295 (1) The anti-Shogunate movement was carried forward under the slogan 'Sonnō Jōi!', or 'Support the Emperor (Mikado); drive out the foreign barbarians!' The Japanese emperor in the Tokugawa period was a curious institution. The Shogunate dealt with state affairs almost exclusively on its own judgment; the emperor was kept under surveillance by Shogunate officials; and he was insulated from practical politics. Nevertheless, he was still the national symbol of authority, and, as political conflict intensified throughout the country, many anti-Shogunate activists took the line that the Tycoon (the Shogun) was not effectively carrying out his mission of ruling the country, and they began to seek political reform by appealing directly to the Emperor over the Tycoon's head. As a result, the Imperial court rapidly regained a say in politics, and calls for 'supporting the Emperor' led to a radical anti-Shogunate movement.

Moreover, since this intensification of political conflict had been brought about by a crisis in external relations, the stand of 'supporting the Emperor' was necessarily coupled with the aim of 'driving out the foreign p 296 (2) barbarians'. It is no wonder that the common samurai – who were ignorant, after more than two centuries of isolationism, of what had been happening abroad – should have instinctively adopted an anti-foreign attitude. They regarded the Westerners as 'foreign barbarians', and they were wary of the major change that was bound to result from opening Japan's doors to the Western world. Another reason, which was more practical, for opposing the opening of ports was the experience that, as foreign trade began to expand, shortages of consumer goods occurred at home and that commodity prices rose.

The Meiji Revolution

In 1860–63, a radical 'Sonnō Jōi' movement developed in Chōshū. Meanwhile, the Western powers were becoming exasperated by repeated physical attacks on their nationals and by artillery attacks on their vessels.

They decided to take retaliatory action. In 1863 a British fleet bombarded Kagoshima, the capital of Satsuma. In the following year, a joint British-American-French-Dutch fleet attacked a fort at Shimonoscki (Chōshū), and temporarily occupied it.

In 1867 the office of Tycoon was assumed by Tokugawa (Hitotsubashi) Yoshinobu. He attempted to restore the strength of the Shogunate by taking advantage of French aid, and he launched a number of reforms aimed at uniting the nation under his control. But it was now too late to save the Tokugawa regime.

Meanwhile, one group of anti-Shogunate forces, led by p 296 Satsuma and Chōshū, planned to organize a military expedition in the name of the young Emperor Meiji, p 295 who had ascended the throne in 1867, to destroy the Tokugawa regime. But another anti-Shogunate group, led by Tosa, attempted to ward off a head-on armed collision between the rebels and the Shogunate by proposing that the Tycoon should peacefully resign his powers to the Emperor and that a conference of daimyō governments, including that of the Tokugawa government, should be convened to save the situation. Apparently in response to Tosa's proposals, Tycoon Yoshinobu in November 1867 suddenly offered to hand over his authority to the Emperor. It seems unlikely that the Tycoon really intended to abdicate at that time.

However, the Imperial 'Restoration' was actually followed by a complete purge of pro-Shogunate court nobles, and the imperial court formally decided to abolish the Shogunate. Subsequently, a new regime, including anti-Shogunate daimyō retainers, was organized, and one of the first steps that it took was to confiscate the Tokugawa House's estates. Pitched battles were fought between the forces of the new government and those of the Shogunate at Toba and Fushimi, two suburbs of Kyoto, and this led to a major domestic conflict known as the Boshin Civil War. At Toba and Fushimi the Shogunate forces had suffered heavy defeats, and most of the daimyō, who had been neutral, now declared in favour of the new regime. Soon the Tycoon capitulated, and the forces of the new government occupied Edo without meeting with much resistance. This definitive victory of the new government reunited the nation after the temporary division of political power between the Shogunate and the imperial court. Meanwhile, the new government officially notified its establishment to the foreign diplomatic corps, and informed them that the Emperor was the chief of state. It was made clear that Japan would remain open and friendly to the rest of the world.

The most urgent task of the revolutionary government was to set up a centralized system of national control under which Japan would be able to grow into a rich and strong country comparable with the Western powers.

Initially, the new government was a coalition regime consisting of a mixed group of leaders including court nobles, daimyō, and daimyō retainers. It had hardly any armed forces of its own, and its future was therefore uncertain. The various daimyō continued to hold their hereditary territories, and remained the effective heads of what were virtually autonomous local regimes with administrative, financial, and military organizations of their own. As part of its ideology for a new Japan, the

A Meiji banknote. After the Restoration the government embarked on a series of monetary, banking and tax reforms, adopted the yen as the standard unit and substituted tax payments in cash for payments in kind. In the early days banknotes were usually printed in Germany or America. (2)

government spoke frequently of 'direct rule by the Emperor' and 'respect for public opinion'. The former concept was a logical consequence of the fact that the revolution had been carried out as a 'Restoration'. To make it universally known to the public that the Emperor was the true sovereign of the new Japan, and to spread loyalist thought throughout the country, a massive propaganda campaign was launched. In this way the Emperor's role of serving as the symbol of the nation was effectively turned to account. The slogan proclaiming 'respect for public opinion' derived from the concept of 'government through public discussion' that had been developed towards the end of the Tokugawa Shogunate. It reflected the new government's need to broaden the basis of its power by securing the support of the local daimyō regimes and of the people at large, and it was the first item in the 'Five Articles of the Imperial Oath' that had been promulgated during the Boshin Civil War to define the basic policy of the revolutionary government.

In 1871 the daimyō principalities were abolished, and were replaced by new 'prefectures' administered by officials who were under the Central Government's control. This was the most miraculous event in the whole history of the Meiji Revolution. The abolition of the daimyō principalities was carried out without provoking much resistance and without any bloodshed. One important reason for this success may have been that many of the smaller daimyō principalities had been in serious financial difficulties as a result of successive disturbances, and they were on the point of breaking down. In this connection, it should be noted that the central government promised to take over the obligation of the daimyō regimes to pay the salaries of their samurai employees. Whatever the reason, this coup put an end to the Shogunate-daimyō system that had lasted for nearly three hundred years, and it gave birth to a centralized system of rule headed by the Emperor.

In this political setting, a series of reforms designed to liquidate the *ancien régime* and to strengthen the foundation of the new Japan as a modern state were quickly carried out by the Government when once daimyō regimes had been abolished.

98 (7)
In the field of finance, a land-tax reform law promulgated in 1873 standardized the method of collecting land taxes (paid in rice), which had varied from one province to another under the Shogunate-daimyō system of administration. The introduction of uniform tax rates, and of tax payments in cash rather than in kind, put the

Government's finances on a solid basis, and the title of tax-paying farmers to their land was legally recognized. In 1876, the Government suspended salary payments to the former samurai, which had been a heavy burden on its finances, after paying each of them a lump sum in public bonds. The feudal class of daimyō retainers was thus dissolved completely, not only in name but also in reality.

In the military field, conscription was brought into force in 1872 to replace the old system of recruiting soldiers exclusively from the samurai class. A national army on a popular basis was thus brought into being. p 298 (8)

In the cultural field, the education law of 1872 introduced compulsory education and a public school system. p 298 (9)

In addition, the Government lifted the previous ban on Christianity; it prohibited the wearing of swords by former samurai; it officially recognized each citizen's freedom to marry, regardless of social class, and his freedom to choose his residence and his occupation; it adopted the solar calendar; it built railroads and telegraph lines. These reforms, which were to have far-reaching effects on the life of the people at large, had been carried out for the most part by the end of the 1870s. p 298–9 (10)

The Government was so eager to push on with the reforms that it sometimes tended to disregard the requirements of private life in its excessive preoccupation with the national interest. Moreover, the Government needed a great deal of money to implement these reforms, and its main source of regular income was the land tax levied on the farmers. The result was that the farmers' tax burden continued to be very heavy. Modernization also brought with it sweeping changes in traditional way of life on the farm. In consequence, there were frequent peasant revolts. p 300 (13)

Another social group that strongly resisted the reforms was the *shizoku* (former samurai), who had been robbed of their old class privileges one after another with the progress of the revolution. In 1877 a group of former samurai in Satsuma revolted under the leadership of Saigo Takamori, the most respected leader of the revolution. This led to a major domestic conflict called the Seinan War, which became a bigger affair than the Boshin Civil War. After eight months of fighting, the confrontation ended in a victory for the Government forces. It is of great significance that the Government's new army, largely consisting of commoner conscripts, defeated the proud samurai of Satsuma. The Seinan War destroyed a local centre of power at Satsuma which had p 296 (3) been almost independent of the Central Government since the beginning of the revolution, and the Government now secured a firm hold over the entire country. The process of political centralization was now largely completed both in name and in reality.

As may be seen from the foregoing survey, Japan took the first step towards 'modernization' when she carried through the Meiji Revolution and secured national independence by effectively countering the Western impact. For Japan, 'modernization' meant 'Westernizing' herself by importing and transplanting new ideas, systems, and skills from the West. Her objective was to become a rich, strong country that would be able to hold its own against the Western powers in the world community. While many other Asian countries suffered heavy inroads of Western influence or fell under colonial rule, Japan alone met the Western impact successfully, and in competition with the Western powers she even grew into an 'empire' with colonies of her own.

The Meiji Revolution set Japan's feet on a road which led her in a completely different direction from the course along which so many of her Asian neighbours were driven. Why was this important change accomplished successfully in Japan in a relatively short time – and this with little bloodshed and with no chaotic confusion? It may be instructive to approach this question from the two angles of external and internal conditions.

One of the external conditions that was favourable to Japan was that the West's impact on her was milder than its impact on India and China. There had, of course, been the attack on Shimonoseki by the four-nation joint fleet, the bombardment of Kagoshima by the British, the occupation of Tsushima by the Russians, and other cases of direct military action taken by Western powers against Japan in the last days of the Tokugawa Shogunate. But these incidents were smaller in scale than the kind of military action that was taken against India and China by the Western powers, and the West's demands were not insuperably difficult to meet. One explanation of this may be that the anti-foreign activities in Japan were less radical. But another important reason must have been that the Western powers were generally less interested in Japan than in India and in China. This is true of Britain, in particular. The triumph of the policy of free trade in Britain in the late 1840s now restrained her from embarking on further military adventures of the kind in which she had indulged at China's expense in the Opium Wars.

As for internal conditions, Japan in the days of the Tokugawa Shogunate already had a fairly high degree of national unity. Under the Shogunate-daimyō system, the Shogunate came near to being the national government. It was a considerably centralized institution. There was also a nationwide commercial economy with substantial markets in Edo, Osaka, and elsewhere. Moreover, this insular country was inhabited almost exclusively by a single people speaking a single language, and it was free from those religious divisions which have often proved a major hindrance to unity in other countries. This degree of national unity was hardly to be found elsewhere in Asia in the 19th century. In the earlier days of the Tokugawa Shogunate, when the

nation had little contact with the rest of the world, these conditions were merely latent. But, when faced with a crisis produced by the Western impact, this homogeneous nation reacted with a keen (often too keen) awareness of the threat, and this sensitivity was particularly strong in the ruling samurai class. The consciousness of a national crisis was undoubtedly the main stimulus for the Meiji Revolution. The same mental attitude made it possible for the various domestic forces to unite under their common national symbol, the Emperor, in the common cause of preserving national independence. Even when political strife intensified between the anti-Shogunate and pro-Shogunate camps, neither of them attempted to utilize foreign military strength to destroy the other – apparently because they were both aware that, fundamentally, their interests were identical.

It should be noted, also, that the Japanese had never entertained the belief, so conspicuous in Chinese thought, that their country was the centre of the world. Hence they had always been eager to learn from foreign (especially Chinese) culture, in order to enrich their own. In carrying out the Meiji Revolution, they did not fall into a blind cult of things Western; they found how to use them in order to make up for their own weaknesses. They could do this because they had traditionally been receptive to imported culture.

These internal and external conditions must have worked together to carry the Meiji Revolution to its successful conclusion.

Towards a 'Westernized empire'

'Turn our country into a Westernized empire. Turn our people into a Westernized people. Make of Japan a new Westernized empire in the East.' This is a passage from a statement discussing the necessity for treaty revision that was written by Foreign Minister Inoue Kaoru in 1887. The Japanese Government and a majority of the Japanese people since the Meiji Revolution have been animated by a common aspiration to make of Japan a powerful country comparable to the Western countries. But in what respects was there actually a difference between Japan and the Western countries? And what had Japan to do in order to become a 'Westernized empire'? In the last days of the Tokugawa Shogunate, most Japanese intellectuals believed that the difference in national power between Japan and the West meant the difference in military power and in the relevant technology. This belief was shared by the leaders of the Meiji Revolution, who concentrated their efforts on building up Japan's military power under the slogan 'Fukoku Kyohei', i.e. 'Enriching the country and strengthening its arms'. These same leaders, however, also took a broader view. They realized that military strength was not the most important constituent of national power. They recognized that one essential factor was the kind of institution which would make it possible to exploit to the full the people's spontaneous effort to support their own country. They also recognized the need to accumulate national wealth by developing modern industries.

An event which probably did much to promote this broad-minded and far-sighted outlook was a tour of

Europe and America by a mission led by Iwakura Tomomi in 1871–73. The members of this mission brought back home with them a strong conviction that the only means by which Japan could hold her own in such a severely competitive international society was by adopting as much as possible from the Western nations as soon as possible, so as to build a Westernized empire. Having become convinced of this, they were also convinced that Japan could not afford to wait until the people became fully ripe for developing the 'modernization' of Japan spontaneously. The urgent task would be for the Government to impose 'modernization' on the people by providing strong political leadership.

There is no doubt that this conviction prompted them, upon their return to Japan in 1873, unanimously to oppose agitation for the invasion of Korea and to advocate domestic reforms. Ōkubo Toshimichi, who was the most capable statesman within the Government at the time, cited two reasons why Britain had attained a degree of prosperity which Japan could not rival, notwithstanding the comparability of the two countries in the size of their territories and populations and in their geographical locations. Britain's first asset was the British people's determination to build up their nation as an independent power and the British Government's commitment to safeguard the people's rights. Britain's second asset was her industrial growth, which had been fostered by her economic policy. The recognition of these truths gave Japan two basic objectives of nation-building that were pursued until about the middle of the Meiji period: a gradual transition from despotic monarchy to constitutional government, and the promotion of policies designed to encourage industry.

These basic national objectives were not, of course, pursued by the Government only. The transition from despotism to limited monarchy, in particular, was the most important and most contentious issue between the Government and the anti-Government factions in the first half of the Meiji period. The Government had not as yet finished the working out of its blueprint for nation-building. Indeed, the modern institutions that were introduced down to about 1880 give the impression of being random transplantations from the Western countries. In the military field, the army was modified first on a French and then on a German pattern, while the navy followed British precedents. In the field of education at the pre-university level, Japan imitated France first and America later. In the economic field, America was Japan's teacher in the banking system, France in the technique of silk-reeling, and Britain in cotton-spinning. Most Western powers, with the exception of Russia, were taken by Japan as models in some enterprise or other. The Government, too, was engaged in a series of experiments by trial and error.

The Liberty and Popular Rights movement was strongly influenced by British parliamentarianism and party politics and by the ideas of the French Revolution. In its confrontation with this movement, the Government favoured the Constitution of the Second German Reich, with its emphasis on the authority of the imperial crown. It saw in this a suitable model for a constitutional regime in Japan. In October 1881, an Imperial Rescript was issued which provided for the establishment of

a National Diet in 1890. This step established the Government's ascendancy over the Popular Rights party and laid the foundations on which the Japanese Constitution was actually built.

Itō Hirobumi and others who visited Europe in 1882 devoted themselves to the study of the constitutions of Germany and Austria. After his return to Japan, Itō took the lead in instituting the Cabinet system, the local administration system, and other political institutions. In February 1889 the Constitution of the Empire of Great Japan was proclaimed, and in November 1890 the first Imperial Diet was convened. The so-called Meiji Constitution borrowed a great deal from the Prussian Constitution of 1850, but the way in which it was operated counted for more than the letter of the Constitution itself. According to the provisions of the Constitution, the Emperor was invested with sovereign power and possessed extensive prerogatives, including the command and organization of the armed forces, the appointment and dismissal of government officials, the declaration of war and the making of peace, the conclusion of treaties, the convening and dissolving of the Imperial Diet, the approval of laws, and the promulgation of Imperial Rescripts. The Cabinet, the House of Peers, the House of Representatives, the Privy Council, the General Staff Office, the Naval General Staff, and other state institutions were each linked to the Emperor independently, with no direct relations among themselves. Theoretically, therefore, their actions could be unified and integrated only under the leadership of the Emperor.

However, the Emperor was not an absolute monarch who could exercise his prerogatives at his own discretion. Actually, a small number of *genrō*, or elder statesmen, who had carried out the Meiji Revolution and had built up the Empire with their own hands, performed the Emperor's functions collectively as his proxies. It was the *genrō* who provided for a harmonious integration of the mutually independent institutions of the state. Direct Imperial rule was the picture that was presented to the people, but the Emperor's entourage apparently thought it expedient that the Emperor should behave like the Queen of Britain rather than like the Emperor of Germany. In short, Japan under the Meiji Constitution was governed 'in the name of the Emperor' rather than 'by the Emperor'.

The establishment of the new state institutions raises the question of the training of the government officials who had become responsible for formulating public policies. Most of the high-ranking officials in the early years of Meiji were natives of Satsuma, Choshu, Tosa, and Hizen. This element of clannish structure in the Meiji Government rapidly faded away at the end of the period. The reason is that the University of Tokyo, which is Japan's earliest modern institution of higher learning, began to play an important role in educating Japan's high-ranking officials by the later 1880s. (In 1897 only 4 out of 125 officials of various ministries ranking higher than bureau director were graduates of the University of Tokyo; fifteen years later, the ratio was 93 out of 158.) Anyone could gain entry into the establishment if he graduated from this training ground of bureaucrats – even if he were of humble origin. This has been a major characteristic of modern Japanese bureau-

p 297 (5)

p 297 (6)

300–1
(14)

cracy. Many of the bureaucrats who were graduates of the University of Tokyo belonged by origin to the middle or lower classes. This is significant because it explains the rapid disintegration of a traditional hierarchic order of society and its replacement by a high degree of social mobility.

The progress of industrialization was another task that had to be undertaken by the Meiji leaders in their nation-building endeavours. Early in the Meiji period, the Government nationalized the factories that had been built by the Shogunate and by various daimyō governments in the last days of the Shogunate, and they invested huge funds in importing machinery and equipment from the Western countries and in establishing 'model factories' under the guidance of foreign engineers and technicians. In the 1880s, however, the majority of these factories, except those of a purely military character, were transferred to private ownership in order to encourage the development of modern industries in the private sector. The Government also fostered private enterprises by subsidizing them. Consequently, from the end of the 1880s, a number of new private enterprises came into being in rapid succession, and the result was a rapid growth of modern industries. Of the p 299 (11,12) newly risen industries, the cotton-spinning industry achieved the most explosive development, especially after Japan's victory in the war with China (1894–95). In the ten-year period 1891–1901, the output of this industry increased four and a half times. Not only did the new Japanese cotton goods satisfy the domestic demand, but by 1901 some 30 per cent of the total product was being exported. Japanese cotton-products soon monopolized the Korean market and came into competition with British products on the Chinese market.

Mechanization was also in progress in the 1890s in the silk-reeling industry, one of the traditional industries of Japan, with the result that it grew into a major export industry, with the United States as its main market.

Thus, by the year 1900 or thereabouts, Japan had carried out an industrial revolution in the field of the textile industries. Although heavy industry was slower in maturing, iron manufacture and shipbuilding began to develop about the year 1910. The Yawata Iron Works, a Government enterprise, was the centre of iron manufacture in Japan in those days, and the domestic production of iron ships of the 20,000–30,000 tons class became feasible. During World War I, the Japanese economy experienced an unprecedented boom. The metallurgical and chemical industries in particular attained remarkable development. p 301 (15) p 304 (22)

As industrialization progressed, a large number of industrial workers were recruited from the rural agricultural population. In the textile industries, female workers outnumbered male workers. Their working conditions were generally poor. The long working hours and the low wages often became a social problem.

Thus Japan took her first steps towards becoming a modern industrial country. In the field of industry, modernization was achieved in the short period of about half a century, as compared with the century and more that most of the advanced capitalist nations in the West had taken to complete the same process of economic transformation. The rapidity of the development in Japan was the result of grafting large-scale mechanized industries imported from the Western advanced nations on to Japan's traditional handiwork industries. The historical conditions of industrialization in Japan left various characteristic marks on the Japanese economy. These conditions produced a conspicuous disequilibrium between industry and agriculture and between major and minor enterprises, an overgrowth of the military and export industries, inferior working conditions, a gap between production and consumption levels, and a limitation of the domestic market.

Japan, Asia and the world

The Meiji Revolution had for the time being eliminated the danger of Japanese territory becoming the target of military operations on the part of the Western powers. However, the general international trend of 'eastern advance of Western powers' was still continuing, and the sense of uneasiness about Japan's relations with foreign countries became nationwide, so far from its being dissipated as a result of the rise of nationalism after the Meiji Revolution. The Meiji regime did adopt the principles of opening the country to foreign intercourse and of maintaining friendly relations with foreign countries as Japan's national policy, but at the same time the Government remained constantly on the watch. It regarded 'all foreign countries as a common enemy of our Empire' (a comment made by Iwakura Tomomi in 1869).

Since Japan's ambition was to become a member of the international community on a footing of equality with other members, the initial concrete objective of her foreign policy, which was pursued throughout the Meiji period, was a revision of the unequal treaties that had been concluded by the Tokugawa Shogunate with various Western countries in the last days of the Shogunate. These treaties provided for unilateral consular jurisdiction and conventional tariff systems. These

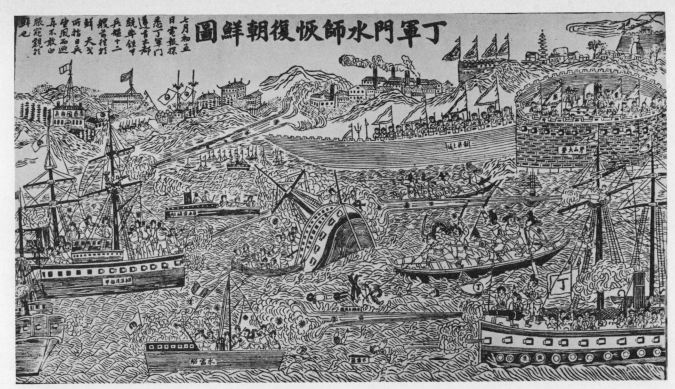

丁軍門水師恢復朝鮮圖

Japan's victory in support of the Korean rebellion of 1894 was a tremendous psychological blow to China. It was the first test of the two countries' newly Westernized forces. In a battle off the Yalu river four out of twelve Chinese ships were sunk with no Japanese losses. China could not at first admit defeat, and popular woodcuts were issued showing her navy 'crushing the Japanese fleet and recovering Korea'. (4)

provisions were damaging for Japan's national prestige and interests. Accordingly the Government repeatedly negotiated for their abolition from the date of the dispatch of the Iwakura Mission. The negotiations encountered difficulties, but in 1894 a new treaty, repealing the consular jurisdiction system and partially revising the conventional tariff system, was concluded between Japan and Britain, and then new treaties providing for similar revisions were concluded with other Western countries. (The conventional tariff system was finally abolished in 1911.)

p 301 (16) These factors created a general pattern of foreign-policy debate in Japan which was to last until 1945. Anti-government factions generally advocated aggressive and dynamic foreign policies, whereas the Government and its supporters insisted on a relatively prudent approach, in deference to the necessity for a *rapprochement* with the Great Powers. The opposition was animated in many cases by a sentiment in favour of the 'development of Asia' – the idea that Japan must collaborate with China and Korea in coping with the Western powers. The Government's policy favoured a 'break with Asia' – the idea that Japan must join the Western powers in dealing with the Asian countries, even at a sacrifice of China and Korea. However, even these seemingly contradictory ideas often fused into one when they were applied to specific issues. Collaboration with Korea and China was considered possible only on condition that Japan should take the lead in paving the way for internal

reforms in these neighbouring countries. Thus the argument for the 'development of Asia' turned out to be little different from the argument for the 'break with Asia'. In short, the course followed by Japan after the Meiji Revolution was for Japan to break away from Asia, with 'Asian development' as the great Japanese objective.

p 302 (17) In 1894 Japan went to war with China over the Korean question, and her victory in this war put her in possession of a colonial empire on the Western pattern. However, the speedy joint intervention of France, Germany and Russia, which forced Japan to renounce annexations in Manchuria at China's expense, brought home to the Japanese the difficulty for a backward imperial Japan of launching out on the rough seas of competitive imperialism as a lonely adventurer. Herein lay the principal reason for the Japanese government's maintenance of its basic policy of co-operation with Britain and with the United States.

China's defeat by Japan drew the Western powers' covetous eyes towards China. They now began to compete with each other keenly for China's territorial spoils. Japan, on the other hand, found herself in an ironical position. By excluding Chinese influence from Korea, Japan opened the way for Russian influence to infiltrate there. This development impelled Japan to face a direct confrontation with Russia now in order to secure her own supremacy in Korea.

p 302–3 (18) The logical consequence was Japan's war with Russia in 1904–05. Japan had prepared for this by continuing the Anglo-Japanese Alliance of 1902. In waging this major war, Japan depended largely on loans raised in Britain and the United States for meeting a major portion of her military expenditure. Japan's military victory in this war had considerable effects on the international political situation in East Asia. Japan gained exclusive control of Korea, and she annexed Korea five

'L'Epée de Damoclès'—a cartoon of 1903 illustrates the growing spectre of Japanese military power, provoked into action by Russian interference in Korea and Manchuria. (5)

years later. Meanwhile, Japan stepped into Russia's shoes in southern Manchuria, and this gave Japan a foot-hold for her subsequent continental aggression. Little more than fifteen years after the Sino-Japanese War, Japan found her territory increased from 380,000 square kilometres to 670,000 square kilometres, and she obtained a new sphere of influence that was twice as large. Japan's ardent desire for the construction of a Western-ized empire in the East was thus fulfilled. But, in consequence, there was no longer the common objective for the nation as a whole to pursue. Also, Japan now had to shoulder the new and awkward burden of ruling over an alien people, an enterprise which was beyond her range of experience. Moreover, she was saddling herself with this commitment just at the time when the Western nations, finding themselves confronted with the nationalist movement in Asia, were beginning to feel the weight of 'the white man's burden'.

As a result of the Russo-Japanese War, the Western nations became once more suspicious of Japan. They regarded this newly risen empire in the Far East as a dangerous rival. Japan's emergence as a world power was also a challenge to their sense of racial superiority. The white peoples considered themselves to be the guardians of the future of civilization. Their antipathy towards the Japanese was now accentuated, and the Japanese became the chief target of their 'Yellow Peril' phobia. Shortly after the Russo-Japanese war, the boycott of Japanese immigrants began in the United States and Canada. There were symptoms of antagonism between Japan and the United States, and of a cooling of Anglo-Japanese relations.

Japan joined the Allied Powers in World War I, and as a result of the Paris Peace Conference of 1919 she became one of the Big Five powers of the world. However, the Japanese proposal for the inclusion of a provision for racial equality in the League of Nations Charter was rejected. The Western attitude towards Japan that was reflected in this action intensified Japanese feelings of frustration.

How did the other Asian nations respond to the emergence of this new 'Westernized empire' in the Far East? According to Sun Yat-sen (in a speech made in 1924), by exploding the myth of 'the invincible white man', Japan's victory over Russia had encouraged the Asian peoples to aim at defeating the Europeans and at

developing vigorous movements for independence. However, this expectation that Japan would be a pioneer of Asian liberation was soon disappointed. When, in the midst of World War I, Japan presented the Twenty-one Demands for the extension of her rights and interests in China, and when, as a result of the Paris Peace Conference, Japan acquired Germany's previous rights in Shantung Province, there was a wave of anti-Japanese protests all over China. In the Asian peoples' eyes, Japan was now no longer a liberator; Japan must have given them the impression of being an imperialist aggressor who was as bad as, or in certain cases worse than, the Western powers.

Thus Japan faced the danger of being isolated not only from the Western powers but from the Asian nations too. From the 1920s to the early 1930s, she took part in a series of international disarmament conferences. As a result of these conferences, she renounced some of her special interests in China and adhered to the policies of non-interference in China's domestic affairs and of the strengthening of economic relations. This was an attempt, on Japan's part, to promote collaboration with Britain and with the United States. Perhaps these Japanese gestures also had the wider purpose of extricating Japan from her perilous isolation in the international community of nations.

Westernization versus traditionalism

'The strange thing is that the Japanese today do not want to know anything about their past. What is more, men of culture are even ashamed of it. "Everything was utterly barbarous," someone declared to me. Others, asked by me about Japanese history, flatly declared: "We do not have any history of our own." It is a matter of far greater concern to these representatives of the New Japan to induce foreigners to appreciate Japan's new institutions, however unreasonable they may be, than to appreciate the truly reasonable elements in Japan's own cultural tradition.' These words were written by Dr Erwin Bälz in his diary for 1876. His observations are an interesting index of the attitude of Japanese intellectuals in the early years of Meiji towards the traditional culture of Japan. For them, Japanese culture was simply an object of contempt, and Japanese history before the Meiji Revolution was something that must be repudiated.

In general, however, these earlier Japanese Westernizers were optimistic about Japan's future. They believed in the existence of a common world civilization, and they cherished the optimistic belief that Japan could catch up with the West and would become a modern civilized nation by adopting Western civilization uncompromisingly.

For about twenty years after the Meiji Revolution, there was a spate of Westernization in Japan, and this had a great effect on the way of life of the urban section of the population. They delighted in novelties and were sensitive to Western fashions. On the other hand, there was a marked decline of Japan's own traditional arts; historic monuments such as temples, shrines, and castles were demolished, and many invaluable cultural assets were jettisoned.

Towards the end of the 1880s a reaction against Westernization set in. This originated in popular criticisms of Government leaders for their extravagance and for their infatuation with Western civilization at the expense of the general public. A powerful new current of opinion – calling for the preservation of Japanese national characteristics – was now set in motion in intellectual circles. The supporters of this principle rejected the superficial and uncritical imitation of the West, and looked for their standards of value in Japan's traditional culture. It was here that they found truth, virtue, and beauty. The Government also responded to the new trend and began to encourage the revival of Confucianist thought and the diffusion of nationalist thought. The Imperial Rescript on Education, issued in 1890, declared the Confucianist family ethic to be the true basis of morality. The Japanese state was presented as a family headed by the Emperor. The edict emphasized the spirit of *chuko itchi* (unity of loyalty and filial duty) and of *chukun aikoku* (loyalty and patriotism). This made the Emperor not only the holder of potential sovereign power but also the centre of moral and ethical values for the people. The worship of the Emperor was made a substitute for religion in modern Japan. There was also a revival of state Shintō, which had been employed unsuccessfully as a means of educating the people in the early years of Meiji. This movement was similar to that of the early Meiji era, but now it had a much stronger political colouring as a result of its association with the worship of the Emperor.

The improvement of the educational system brought with it a sharp rise in the percentage of compulsory school attendance after the 1890s, but there was also now less liberalism and more nationalism in the content of education. However, these developments were not necessarily indicative of a uniform return to the traditional spirit of Japan. The new nationalist ideology in Japan was influenced by German ideology, and the supremacy of the state's interests over the individual's rights was inferred from Herbert Spencer's view of society as an organism. It can be said that, even in the later half of the Meiji period, Westernization was still continuing in Japan, though now at a much slower pace.

The road to war

Japan in the 1920s appeared to be stable both in her domestic life and in her foreign relations. The accentuation of the democratic and pacifist trend throughout the world after World War I made itself felt in Japan. The party system made its appearance in domestic politics, and, in foreign relations, a policy of reducing armaments and of international collaboration was pursued under the arrangements made at the Washington Conference (1921–22). Beneath this seemingly stable surface, however, there was an undercurrent that was moving slowly but surely towards a major change in Japan's course.

In the domestic field, those elder statesmen *(genrō)* who, under the Meiji Constitution, had acted collectively in the Emperor's name, died one after another or gradually lost ground under the assault of popular movements. Consequently, it became difficult to maintain a harmonious integration of the various institutions of the state, and sectionalism in government became apparent. Party politics certainly became a routine practice, but the unity of national will could not easily be preserved

The establishment of the party system in the 20th century led to the gradual extension of universal suffrage. A cartoon of 1918, when only about three per cent of the population had the right to vote, shows the unenfranchised threatening to break into the circle of the privileged. (6)

through the medium of the House of Representatives, considering that the principle of popular sovereignty had not been acknowledged. On the other hand, under the influence of the Bolshevik Revolution and under the pressure of the rice riot in 1918, the movement for social reform became vigorous enough to create political instability. Moreover, the world-wide economic depression that started in 1929 had a major impact on Japan. It aggravated the problem of the balance of international payments, and, on the domestic front in Japan, the depression hit agriculture. The impoverishment of the peasants fomented social unrest.

In the field of Japan's foreign relations, Japan's position in China was jeopardized by an upsurge of nationalism in China during and after World War I. In the later 1920s some progress towards national unification was achieved by the Chinese national government. It pursued a 'revolutionary foreign policy' which aimed at a restoration of China's national prestige through the recapture of foreign footholds in China. In particular, the numerous 'special rights' which Japan had been asserting for herself in Manchuria since the Russo-Japanese War became the main target of an intense anti-Japanese campaign by the Chinese. This Chinese movement offended Japanese national susceptibilities, for, in Japanese eyes, Manchuria was a land which had cost the blood of 200,000 Japanese. The Japanese government had been trying to uphold its basic policy, which was a policy of *rapprochement* with Britain and the United States and of abstaining from armed intervention in China. This policy was now denounced as weak, and the opposition to it gradually mounted, mainly in military and right-wing circles. These groups held that pacifist and disarmament policies were calculated to maintain the existing international order which centred on Britain and the United States, and the existing privileged status of the Western Great Powers. The Japanese government's practice of co-operative diplomacy was held to be merely another name for submission to Anglo-Saxon imperialism.

p 302–3 (18)

Another factor that was inimical to Japan's concili-atory policy towards Britain and the United States over the problem of China was the intensification of inter-national economic competition – a result of the develop-ment of the policy of autarky after the great depression. In consequence, many Japanese became increasingly pessimistic about the prospect of peaceful economic development. These various political and economic fac-tors were aggravated by the Soviet Union's endeavour to build up its military strength under the First Five-Year Plan. This Russian move seriously alarmed the leaders of the Japanese Army, and it created acute dis-satisfaction with the government's disarmament policy in the Japanese armed forces as a whole. In this situa-tion, politicians became an immediate target of criticism in the press for their failure to meet the 'internal and external crises' satisfactorily, for their indulgence in the struggle between the parties for political power without regard for the national interest, and for their involve-ment in a series of scandals. This attack aroused popular distrust in the political parties and in the Diet itself.

In the early 1930s there was a rapidly increasing demand in military circles for the liquidation of the party system of politics, for the establishment of some more effective form of domestic government, for the abandonment of co-operative diplomacy, and for the settlement of the Manchurian question by force of arms.

The Manchurian Incident in September 1931 was a turning point. Japan now launched out on diplomatic and military adventures at the risk of being isolated internationally. She withdrew from the League of Nations and from the disarmament conference, and she made war, once again, on China. 'Independence for the Supreme Command' became the slogan of the armed forces. In the early 1930s a series of terroristic attempts at a *coup d'état* were made by representatives of the right wing, including both private citizens and young military officers. Their objective was to bring about a radical change in Japan's political system. The assassination of Prime Minister Inukai in 1932 gave the quietus to government by party cabinets. In 1936 the High Com-mand quashed a rebellion by radical young military officers and purged the armed forces' own ranks with the object of further strengthening the High Command's political influence. The political parties gradually faded away. In 1940 they dissolved themselves and formed a new organization called Taisei Yokusan Kai, or the Imperial Rule Assistance Association. The parliamentary system, based on the existence of 'plural' political parties, now became an empty name. This should not, however, be interpreted as signifying the establishment of a dictatorship by the Japanese High Command on the lines of the contemporary Nazi dictatorship in Ger-many. Between 1930 and 1945 there were as many as sixteen Cabinet changes. There was also intense antagon-ism, within the government, between the military and the bureaucracy. Sectionalism in political leadership had been inherent in the Japanese system of government since the beginning of the Meiji era, and this fundamental evil remained uneradicated.

This point is illustrated by the history of Japanese foreign policy after the Manchurian Incident. On the one hand there were a group consisting of senior

statesmen, court officials, and some diplomats, which attempted to maintain a conciliatory attitude towards Britain and the United States. On the other hand there were the armed forces, the Army in particular, who were trying to impose a policy of independent Japanese action against the Anglo-Saxon powers. Under the stress of this domestic conflict, Japan often appeared to lose all unity of national will in developing her foreign policy. Military action was often precipitated by some unauthorized movement by a unit of Japanese troops or by an accidental clash with foreign troops. The Govern-ment would then declare that its policy was to localize the incident, yet the military operations invariably spread, and none of the people who were officially responsible for the conduct of the war had any general plans or any long views. Japanese politics thus came to be bedevilled by an utter lack of responsibility.

In 1940, when Japan was still deeply involved in her war with China, she concluded a triple alliance with Germany and Italy. She had been impressed by Ger-many's brilliant military successes on the European front in the first phase of World War II. The new alliance was tantamount to a mutual recognition of Japan's and Germany's hegemony in Asia and in Europe respectively. At the same time, Japan began to contemplate conquests in South-east Asia as well as in China. Japan's antagonism to the Anglo-Saxon bloc culminated in a fateful act. In December 1941, she attacked the American fleet in Pearl Harbor and invaded the American, French, British, and Dutch colonial empires in South-east Asia. This reckless adventure was to cost the lives of three million people. p 303 (19,20

Prime Minister Tōjō, who was Japan's leader during World War II, is the only Japanese in the modern history of Japan who has served concurrently as Premier and as Minister of War. Yet even Tōjō, who was often regarded as a dictator, was inhibited by the Constitution from interfering with the prerogatives of the Supreme Com-mand. Nor could he have any say in the appointments to posts in the navy. In order to unify the premiership and the Supreme Command, Tōjō elected to occupy a third post, that of Chief of the General Staff; but this action drew upon him immediate censure for 'violation of the Constitution' and 'encroachment on the Supreme Com-mand'. Tōjō was forced to retire as the tide of war turned against Japan.

This military domination and aggressiveness was con-doned as being a reversion to the Japanese tradition. It was argued that Japan's blind adoption of Western materialistic civilization since the Meiji Revolution had misled the Japanese people into materialism and self-indulgence, and that these deplorable tendencies must be overcome by a moral uplift and by a return to Japan's traditional culture. p 301 (16)

In the early 1940s, anti-foreign feeling in Japan reached its climax. In the Japanese propaganda to Japan's Asian neighbours, the anti-foreign agitation was camouflaged as the 'Great Asia principle'. This idea can be traced back to the argument for the development of Asia in the Meiji period. The Japanese now exhorted all Asian nations to unite under the leadership of Japan for liberating them-selves from their status of slaves of the West and for building an Asia for the Asians. The argument did make

The rising militarism of Japan. At the Yasukuni shrine in Tokyo during the 1930s members of the armed forces pay their respects to the spirits of soldiers and sailors who have sacrificed their lives for their country since the Meiji Restoration. (7)

a great appeal to people who, witnessing the emergence of Nazi Germany, the rise of the Soviet Union as a powerful country, and the upsurge of Asian nationalism, hoped that the previous world order, shaped to suit Anglo-Saxon interests, was now going to be rapidly reorganized. The Great Asia principle was considered the 'greatest cause' for which Japan was to wage war against Britain and the United States. However, the principle was implemented in the policy of the construction of a 'Great East Asia Co-prosperity Sphere', so it was merely a euphemism for the exclusive domination of East Asia by the 'Great Empire of Japan'.

After World War II

The result of World War II was a third 'Western impact' on Japan which gave her as great a shock as Perry's 'black ships' had given her a century earlier. From August 1945 to April 1952, Japan was under foreign military occupation. During the first three years of this occupation, 'demilitarization' and 'democratization' were put into practice all over Japan under the virtual military dictatorship of the American GHQ. Various institutions of the 'Great Empire of Japan' were liquidated. A new Constitution was brought into force. The Emperor was divested of all political power, and sovereignty was invested in the people. War was renounced.

The reforms introduced in post-war Japan include the dissolution of the *zaibatsu* (big business interests), agrarian reform, the abolition of laws and regulations restricting the basic human rights of the people, the liberalization of education, the prohibition of state Shintō, the revival of political parties, and the enactment of legislation for the protection of workers. The Japanese people were not enthusiastic about these reforms, yet there is no doubt that they did accept them positively. What deserves attention here is that, unlike the reforms instituted in the Meiji Revolution, many of the post-war reforms represented a return to the actual practice of pre-war days, especially of the 1920s. This pre-war practice was now either revived in a more thoroughgoing form or was confirmed in principle.

The Japanese had never previously experienced a

defeat in war or occupation of their country by foreign troops; and their unprecedented defeat after World War II shattered their self-confidence. MacArthur's remark that Japan had now become a fourth-rate country aggravated the Japanese people's sense of inferiority. The Japanese had been strongly inclined to rate themselves by the standard of the Westerners' rating of Japan. Like the intellectuals of the early Meiji era, the intellectuals of the immediate post-war days regarded the preceding era as a shameful and barbarous dark age which must be repudiated. In the Meiji period, however, this feeling was accompanied by intense nationalistic and patriotic sentiment. No such sentiment existed in post-war Japan. The United States, which had been looked upon as a brute during the war, was now considered to be an 'apostle of peace and democracy, the liberator of Japan'. However, as American policy for Japan under the occupation began to change from 'demilitarization' and 'democratization' to 'construction of an anti-communist citadel', there was a gradual decline in the 'progressive' intellectuals' admiration of the United States.

p 304 (21)

Since the Meiji Revolution Japan has been oscillating between Westernization and traditionalism. In the post-war years the pendulum was swinging in the direction of Westernization and particularly of Americanization. This tendency declared itself not only in the impersonal form of the political and economic relations between Japan and the United States; it also became apparent in the Japanese people's way of life.

When the occupation came to an end, when Japan regained her independence and re-entered international society, the Japanese gradually began to recover their self-confidence. The country's rapid economic rehabilitation and growth played a major role in this.

At the time of Japan's surrender, many of her cities were in ruins and their industrial plants had been totally demolished. Hiroshima and Nagasaki had suffered the unprecedented disaster of nuclear attack. By 1946 the product of the mining and manufacturing industries had been reduced to less than one-fifth of its pre-war peak, and agricultural production had sunk to two-thirds. Commodity prices soared. In 1948 they were

p 304 (21)

150 times higher than the pre-war level. The Japanese people's life had been ruined, and there had been a severe shortage of food. At the time, a majority of the people must have felt that it would take decades for Japan to revert to her pre-war standards of living and of economic productivity.

Fortunately this expectation proved to be erroneous. Thanks to the policy of austerity that was adopted in 1949, inflation was overcome and economic recovery made progress. This was partly due to the 'special procurement boom' caused by the Korean War. In 1955 industrial production exceeded the pre-war record. At about the same time, technological innovation and capital investment began on a large scale, and after this there was a steady economic growth at an annual rate ranging from 10 to 25 per cent. During the period running from 1955 to 1971, mining and manufacturing production increased eightfold, exports tenfold, and wages fourfold – a notable increase, even when we take into account the rise of about twofold in prices. Industry underwent a major change in structure – from textile to heavy and chemical industries. These two industries, together, came to provide two-thirds of Japan's exports.

p 306 (27)

High buildings appeared in Tokyo and in other major cities; expressways, subways, and the new trunk line were built; and a number of television stations were opened.

Japan's gross national product is now the second largest in the non-Communist part of the world, and Japan has become one of the greatest industrial nations in the whole world. Political and business leaders incessantly refer to the economic power of Japan. This is a delicate way of flattering the people.

p 304–5 (22–24)
p 306 (28)

This rapid economic growth and the concomitant rise in the people's standard of living have produced a 'consumer revolution' and have brought about major changes in the Japanese attitude to life. The consumer revolution has taken the forms of an increase in the consumption of meat, milk, eggs, and processed food-stuffs; increased spending on recreation; and the widespread acquisition of durable consumer goods such as television sets, refrigerators, air-conditioners, and automobiles. The consumer revolution has even spread to rural communities, which in pre-war days had known nothing of these amenities of life. Though the rural communities have lost much of their labour force under the pressure of rapid industrialization in the cities, their rice harvest has been constantly on the increase owing to the progress of agricultural techniques and mechanization. The rise in the price of rice has also helped to improve the economic position of the producer. The picture of the 'poor peasants' is now out of date.

The gap in standards of living between urban and rural communities has been much reduced, and something like a uniform national way of life is coming into existence. Probably this change has been largely due to the rapid development of mass communications and to the resultant circulation of a great deal of information.

The arrival of the mass consumption age has changed the Japanese attitude to life very greatly. The pre-war ideals of thrift and saving, and of self-denial for the sake of the country, have been replaced by an enjoyment of spending and of private life.

However, this rapid economic growth has also produced a number of unhappy effects, such as overcrowding in the major cities, a housing shortage, traffic congestion, a serious increase in the number of fatal traffic accidents, air pollution, and water pollution. The so-called 'public hazard question' is common to all highly industrialized countries, but it has presented a particularly serious problem for Japan, because Japan has been concentrating her efforts on increasing her production-capital but has not kept pace with this in her investment for covering the overhead costs of social health. Japan's rapid urbanization has destroyed the rural community that was unified by family bonds and paternal relationships – the model of order in pre-war Japan – and it has created the urban 'lonely crowd' on a large scale. In the midst of material prosperity, people miss something spiritual. The Sōka Gakkai and other newly established religious organizations began to pullulate in the later 1950s. These organizations have helped to provide a new spiritual basis for life and to reintegrate into the community those members of it who have become alienated from it.

The rapid social changes in post-war Japan have also produced a schism in ethical ideals and a gap between generations. It would be extremely difficult now to descry a national objective of the kind that Japan certainly had in the Meiji period.

p 305 (25)

Immediately after the war, 'the construction of a peace-loving nation' provided an objective for the Japanese to pursue. There was a wide consensus in favour of this, for the entire Japanese people had a bitter memory of the war. A movement for collecting signatures for a memorial demanding the prohibition of nuclear weapons was begun by the private initiative of women's organizations and cultural bodies in 1956. This movement was so successful that, within six months, the signatures of twenty million individuals were collected, and this clearly indicates that the symbolic word 'peace' meant much in post-war Japan. However, the opposition to nuclear weapons, which had started as a non-partisan national campaign, has since fallen into confusion and discord, and this second chapter of the story reflects the grim realities of international politics, while political and factional strife on the home front is a practical commentary on the actual function of 'peace' as a symbol. Meanwhile, such changes in Japan's international environment as the decline of Anglo-American prestige in Asia and the emergence of China as a nuclear power are now exposing Japan to the temptation to turn herself into a political and military great power as well as an economic one. 'Peace' in its passive sense is being taken by the younger generation as meaning simply dullness.

The schism in ethical ideals and the gap between generations are phenomena that are common to all 'advanced' nations in the world, and no satisfactory solution of these problems has been discovered so far. Here is a challenge – and an opportunity – for Japan. Ever since the Meiji Revolution, Japan has been taking the advanced countries of the West as her models in her strenuous endeavours to achieve progress. Today the whole world is confronted by new problems. In facing these common new problems, why should not Japan try to work out original solutions of her own?

XIII REBELLION, REFORM AND REVOLUTION

China, Korea and Vietnam in the modern world

JEAN CHESNEAUX

China is first of all poor and secondly a blank sheet. (yi ch'iung erh pai)

Mao Tse-tung

China's break with her own past during the 20th century has been more far-reaching and more radical than that of any other nation – a distinction particularly surprising in a people so wedded to tradition, as the first half of this book has made clear. Yet in a sense she is right in claiming that only now is she realizing her full potential and discovering her real self. One way of interpreting what has happened is in terms of 'models', successive attempts by China to remould her society by following the example of others believed to be more advanced than herself – first the Japanese model (the *yang-wu* reforms of 1860–1889); then the Western model (the bourgeois revolutionary regime of 1911); finally the Russian model (the CCP before 1927 and the first phase of Communist power after 1949). Each of these models was tried and failed. Only then did China construct a model of her own, and it was done by returning to her own roots, the peasants.

The Chinese Communist Party was founded in Shanghai in 1921. At first its programme followed orthodox Marxist-Leninist principles, according to which revolutions are made by the urban proletariat.

Stalin, moreover, was advising its leaders to co-operate with the Kuomintang, in spite of the fact that right and left wings were becoming irreconcilable. The inevitable clash came in 1927, when Chiang Kai-shek turned on his former allies, massacred as many as he could, and forced the rest to flee to the countryside. Here the young Mao Tse-tung began to test his political thesis. He saw that Marxist-Leninism had to be re-interpreted before it could be applied in China. Asia was not Europe. Working in the mountainous, densely-wooded area of Kiangsi, in south-east China, he built up, together with his military commander, Chu Teh, a force based on the local peasantry. The Chinese Soviet Republic was proclaimed at Juichin, Kiangsi, in November 1931.

More than thirty years after, with the CCP firmly in power, a unit of the People's Liberation Army has returned to the Chinkang Mountains, the first base of the Chinese Revolution, to relive, in the same surroundings, the events of that momentous struggle. It was from this area that, harried by Chiang Kai-shek's armies, the Communists set out on their Long March of 6000 miles to set up a new and permanent base in the north-west. (1)

The German occupation of Kiaochow China paying laborers (wheelbarrow men)

Western dominance in 19th-century China is made explicit in a photograph such as this showing the waterfront of Canton. Over the huddled wooden houses of the Chinese rise the towers of the Roman Catholic Cathedral built by the French in 1860. Canton was one of the 'treaty ports' which the Chinese had been forced to open to foreign trade after the Opium War of 1839–42. 'Unequal treaties' gave European nations and America, and later Japan, extra-territorial rights in these ports as well as legal and commercial privileges. (2)

French imperialism had taken firm hold on Vietnam from the middle of the 19th century, and was moving steadily northwards. War with China broke out in 1884. The result was indecisive, China losing eleven warships at Foochow, but the French failing to hold a strategic area near Hanoi. This woodcut (left) was premature in its celebration of French victory. (3)

Germany seized Kiaochow, part of the Shantung peninsula including the port of Tsingtao, in 1897. In this contemporary drawing, German officers, conspicuously well groomed, supervise the paying of Chinese wheelbarrowmen. Britain, France and Russia were simultaneously moving to take over other parts of China. The dismemberment of the whole empire seemed not far off. (4)

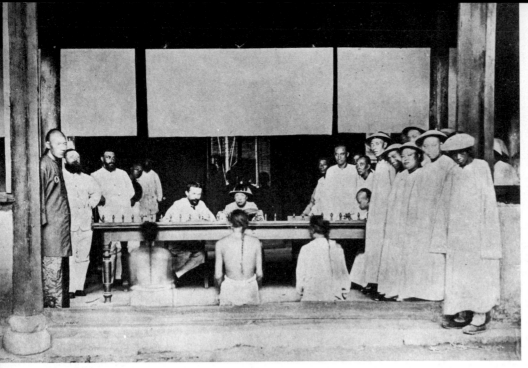

'Semi-colonies' grew up around the treaty ports, where districts known as 'concessions' were administered by Europeans and Chinese residents were obliged to live under European laws. In 1864 'Mixed Courts' were set up, so that cases of dispute between Chinese and Europeans were heard by judges representing both sides (above). Although the unequal treaties worked to the disadvantage of China, they stimulated the growth, on the eastern seaboard, of cities on the Western model. This in turn produced a social class that was new to China, a commercial bourgeoisie anxious to modernize the country by developing Western institutions. The Revolution of 1911 owed much to the support of this class, but it proved to be too insecurely based in China as a whole. (5)

'Destroy the foreigner!' The backlash provoked by the Great Powers' imperialist activities came in 1900 with the Boxer Rising. The Empress Dowager's government, falling back into an extreme reactionary position, first tolerated and then encouraged the Boxers (a secret society so called because they practised physical exercises to harmonize spirit and muscle) when they began their attacks on missionaries and Chinese Christians. Between June and August 1901 the foreign legations at Peking were besieged. But Chinese counsels were themselves divided. The siege was not pressed whole-heartedly. An international force – British, American, German, Japanese – was able to relieve the legations. Below: the army entering Peking. Above: Japanese troops guarding their headquarters. (6, 8)

The missionaries had benefited as much as the traders from the establishment of the treaty ports and the seizure of bases like Kiaochow (the scene of this engraving of about 1900). But they offended the common people by their proselytizing zeal and the governing classes by their pretensions to official status. (7)

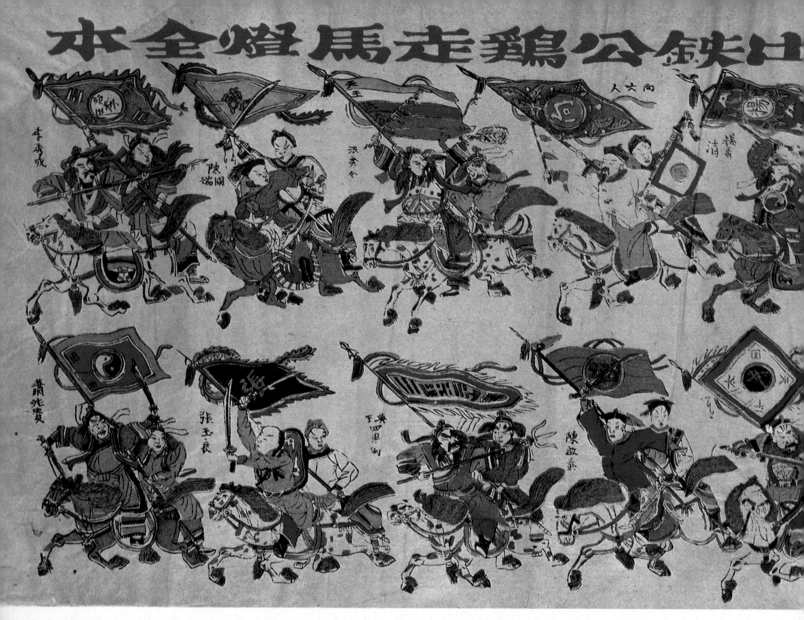

Rebellion from below had been a constant feature of Chinese history, and this is especially true of the period between 1850 and 1870. All the classic symptoms of the 'dynastic cycle' – the violent replacement of one dynasty by another – seemed to be occurring: peasant unrest, separatist movements, secret societies, the breakdown of administration.

The Taiping Rebellion of 1850–64 came closest to destroying the Ch'ing dynasty. For several years the rebels controlled a vast area of central China, including the city of Nanking. This popular print (above) shows the Taiping leaders, known as 'kings'. The founder, Hung Hsiu-ch'uen, is third from the left, top row. What is especially interesting about the movement is its ideology – a mixture of missionary Christianity and Confucianism. In its moral puritanism, egalitarian social policy and emphasis on discipline it can be seen as a forerunner of modern Chinese Communism. (9)

The Boxers, the last major popular movement before 1911, also began as an anti-Ch'ing rebellion but was skilfully turned against the foreigners. These two patriotic prints show the campaign in a somewhat rosy light. Left: Boxer forces attacking the British and French. Right: British prisoners being brought before a Chinese general. (10, 12)

Chinese Christians suffered more than anybody in the rising tide of anti-foreign feeling at the end of the century. In the villages, where local clan meetings still disciplined members, they were often ruthlessly persecuted. Here prisoners are arraigned and punished before the clan elders, with the ancestral tablet behind them (see p. 99, pl. 5). 'If one family in a clan is found secretly worshipping the Pig' (i.e. Christ), says the inscription, 'it will bring disgrace to all of that clan.' (11)

'Western knowledge is purely for practical use' was the slogan of the *yang-wu* movement. Its supporters aimed at following Japan in adapting what was needed from the West while preserving traditional Chinese values. The Foochow Arsenal (above), a factory combined with a naval training school, was built by French engineers in 1867. (13)

Sun Yat-sen, the most widely respected of the exiled revolutionary leaders, had spent twenty-five years of his life organizing resistance from Japan, England, Vietnam and elsewhere. But, like Lenin in 1917, he was taken by surprise when it actually came (opposite). Quickly returning to China from London, he was elected provisional president. In this historic photograph (left) he is seen with his military staff leaving Shanghai to be inaugurated at Nanking, January 1912. The last emperor abdicated a month later. (14)

A second wave of revolution was soon necessary. Sun Yat-sen's successor, Yüan Shih-k'ai, strangled parliamentary government at birth, set up a dictatorship and finally proclaimed himself emperor. Sun's own 'Nationalist Party', the Kuomintang, struggled in vain against a situation in which only military governors, 'warlords', could exercise effective power. In 1919 it was learned that the Versailles Conference had confirmed Japan in possession of the old German Shantung territories. An anti-Japanese student demonstration held on 4 May grew into a nationwide protest. Students in Shanghai (left) initiated a boycott of Japanese goods which lasted until 1922. It was the beginning of a new drive towards nationalism, socialism and 'New Culture'. (15)

The Revolution which had finally toppled the Manchu dynasty was more political than social. Popular exasperation with the government increased until in October 1911 a mutiny in Wuchang suddenly spread through the southern and central provinces. (16)

The warlords who held power after the collapse of the republic in 1916 represented the rich landlord class whose interest it was to maintain the *status quo*. In 1927 Chang Tso-lin, military governor of Manchuria, defeated his rivals and tried briefly to form a government in Peking (below) but was killed the following year by the Japanese. At about this time, Kuomintang policy, under the leadership of Chiang Kai-shek and with the support of industrialists, foreigners and landlords, swung sharply to the right and turned on the CCP, which had concentrated on social revolution. Abortive resistance took place in Nanking, Hunan (under Mao Tse-tung) and Canton. At Canton (right) young Communists were hunted and killed in the street. (17, 18)

To impose unity on China Chiang Kai-shek had to conquer the warlords of the centre and north. The long prepared Northern Expedition was launched in the summer of 1926. In this contemporary illustration Sun Yat-sen, who had died the previous year, is given the place of honour; beneath him, on the horse, is Chiang Kai-shek. At this time the Communists still formed a united front with the Kuomintang and it was they who were the most effective propagandists (below). The people welcomed the new regime, which promised many social and legal reforms. But after the Communist purge, and the subsequent occupation of Peking, it became apparent that nothing had changed. Chiang compromised and conciliated not only the landlords but also the Japanese, who seized Manchuria and began pressing on China's northern frontier. (19, 20)

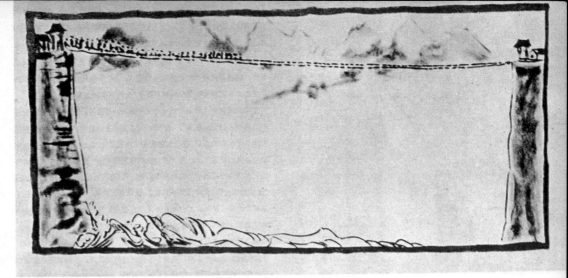

The beleaguered Communists, completely cut off from the outside world, held out for seven years in several scattered areas – one in the north, in Shensi, the two largest in the south, in Kiangsi. Here Chiang Kai-shek's fifth campaign, in 1934, threw nearly a million men against them and forced them to concede that their position was untenable. They decided to withdraw across the whole breadth of China to join their comrades in the north. Ninety thousand (including some women) set out on 16 October 1934. The direct way being barred, they went west as far as the border of Tibet, then swung north. Two sketches done on the march show them (left) crossing the snow-covered Chin-shan mountains and (above) capturing the vital iron chain bridge across the river Tatu, one of the most daring exploits of the whole march. Thirty volunteers clambered across the bare chains (the planks had been removed) and captured the enemy position on the other side. The Long March ended exactly a year after it had begun, in October 1935, when the survivors made contact with the Red Army of Shensi. They had covered 6000 miles. About 70,000 had died or been left behind on the way. Below: the Tatu bridge today is almost a national monument. (21–23)

Nationalist China – as the territory controlled by the Kuomintang was usually called after 1927 – presented a sad picture of betrayal and failure. Much progressive legislation concerning land, the position of women and individual freedom had been passed but only a small proportion was actually carried out. In the absence of social reform power remained with the old landlord class, who lived off rents, paid no taxes and in times of famine bought up more and more land to add to their estates. Communist propaganda had no need to exaggerate the hardships that were endured. Above: Kuomintang tax collectors seize the last animals and grain from a starving family. Right: a symbolic hand grasps the peasants' paddy-field. (24, 25)

Even the urban bourgeoisie abandoned the Nationalist cause when galloping inflation overtook its economy. By 1948 the signs of collapse were clear. Anxious crowds besieged the banks in cities like Shanghai (left). Chinese of every class – peasants, workers, businessmen and intellectuals – went over *en masse* to the Communists. (26)

Red China – 'the liberated areas' – constituted a deliberate and carefully planned attempt to create a new society, one in which China's vast mass of peasants could for the first time in history take charge of their own lives. Ideas and organization were supplied by the Communist Party, but to a very large extent decisions were taken by the people themselves. Every area 'liberated' by the Red Army formed its own Peasants' Union (above). The army itself consisted mostly of peasants fighting (above right) for a cause with which they could completely identify. (27, 28)

To educate the new nation the Communists set up a 'Resistance University' in caves, formerly the grain cellars of landlords, at Yenan. Courses were severely practical: political history, economy, Leninism, strategy, guerrilla warfare, etc. Those who graduated then led the drive to educate the peasantry. (29)

Behind the army were peasants who willingly kept it supplied with food. One of the cardinal points of Red policy was good relations between soldiers and farmers. The Kuomintang army, by contrast, lived by forced exactions and met only non-co-operation and sabotage. (30)

Yenan, the Red capital in the north-western province of Shensi, has become the symbol of modern China. If the soviets of Kiangsi were the cradle of Maoism, Yenan was its nursery. Here land confiscated from the landlords was distributed among the peasants, rudimentary industry was developed, and an ambitious programme of social reorganization set in motion. From here too the struggle was carried on against the Japanese, first in conjunction with the Kuomintang (Chiang Kai-shek having been compelled by his own army to form a united front) but after 1940 in renewed rivalry. It was the heroic age of Chinese Communism, and the 'Yenan spirit' is still a call to revolutionary idealism. The hills in the background are honeycombed with caves, where the people – and the government – lived as a protection against bombing. (31)

'The people's very own army' was something unprecedented in China, where soldiers had come to be regarded as almost the natural enemies of the people. This 1944 poster shows peasants bringing them food and horses; carrying wounded and supplying the camp; sending off a new recruit. At the bottom the serviceman's house is well-maintained and the disabled cared for.

The war against Japan, in spite of its hardships, certainly aided the Communists' cause. Not only, in conquered areas, were the old institutions largely destroyed, but the Communists' experience of guerrilla warfare enabled them to organize units behind the Japanese lines which became centres of 're-education'. When Japan collapsed in 1945, therefore, they were in a favourable position, in spite of the massive aid given to Chiang Kai-shek by the Americans. After another brief attempt at co-operation, the Civil War began again. It was bitterly fought, lasted four years, and ended in 1949 with the complete victory of Communism. (33)

Mao's leadership was confirmed by the Long March. It represented an original development of Marxist-Leninism. As early as 1926, when he wrote his classic *Report on an Investigation into the Peasant Movement in Honan*, Mao had seen that China required a revolutionary movement relying primarily on the peasant rather than the urban worker. Buttressed by a steady stream of theoretical books and pamphlets, tried and tested in Kiangsi and Yenan, Mao's brand of Communism proved to be the blueprint for a new way of life – one which uprooted almost every feature of the Chinese tradition and yet (to Mao and his followers) embodied 'all that was precious in China's past from Confucius to Sun Yat-sen'. Left: Mao in Yenan, about 1940, chatting with a group of peasants. (32)

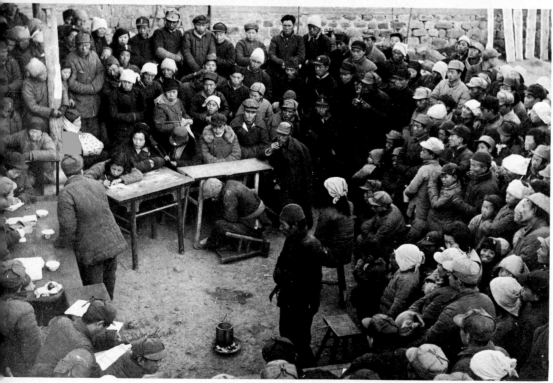

The drive for industrialization in the 1950s led to the building of such vast steelworks as that of Anshan, in Manchuria (above), begun by the Japanese and enlarged with Russian help. By 1960 it was producing nearly five million tons of steel per year and was the object of intense national pride. (37)

Peasant co-operatives also followed Russian models, as indeed did the propaganda posters designed to popularize them. Below: three stages of the Socialist transformation of agriculture symbolized by bridge building – the individual peasant, the mutual aid team and the agricultural producers' co-operative, 'the bridge to a prosperous, happy future'. (38)

The reaction to Russian-style management came first in 1958, second during the Cultural Revolution of 1966, when it was subjected to vigorous criticism from below. Posters were displayed (this factory is at Shen-yang) and long discussions held, taking the political theories of Mao Tse-tung as their text, but production actually went up. (39)

A Chinese 'line', not an imitation of something else but a genuinely new form of society, gradually emerged in 1958 and 1966. Agriculture and industry, instead of being segregated and separately controlled, were merged, each supplying the needs of the other on a regional basis, the new unit being the commune. The commune, said Mao, 'includes industry, agriculture, culture, trade, military affairs . . . people of all trades and professions. The countryside is urbanized, the city ruralized. . . . New changes have come to society *as a whole*'. The last decade has vindicated the change. Above: fields in the Mao P'ing Commune, Kiangsi Province. Left: painting by an assistant enginedriver showing small-scale commune industry. Below: painting by a peasant captioned 'Fertilizer is piled into mountains and sent out to the fields'. (40–42)

The Cultural Revolution was in essence a people's rebellion led by Mao and the radical left, against the Party that was ruling China in their name. Those in power were accused of forming a privileged class, as in Russia. Mao himself encouraged the rebels (details of the inner Party struggle are still unknown) and issued his own poster headed 'Bombard the Headquarters', a crucial document which led to the formation of militant student groups, the Red Guards. The Party's Central Committee hastily adopted the Revolution as its own policy, but the chorus of criticism grew, creeping up the hierarchy until it touched everyone but Mao. Party authority, hitherto absolute, disintegrated. In its place Revolutionary Committees were set up at all levels. The crowd (opposite) is celebrating the formation of one such committee. (43)

肥料堆成山
送到田里边

Korea was divided in 1945, a Communist regime being installed in the north and a US-sponsored right-wing government under Syngman Rhee in the south. In June 1950 the North launched a war of liberation against the South. Above left: the People's Army entering Taejon. American forces under General MacArthur (seen, above, with Rhee) were able to halt the advance and push back the Communists, who then called upon Chinese help. In 1953 a truce restored the *status quo*. (44, 45)

North Korea today has freed itself from the old landlord class and from Japanese imperialism. Peasants and workers share in its remarkable economic recovery (left: a reading class in a North Korean village, and below: scenes in a building plant and a chemical works). Even so, the Party remains authoritarian, allowing little initiative from below. (46–48)

In Vietnam the end of World War II allowed colonial rule to be re-imposed in the south – in its early stages (above) using the Japanese to enforce it – but found Communism well entrenched in the north. The war against France, led by Ho Chi Minh and General Giap (second and fourth from the left, above) ended in victory at Dien Bien Phu in 1954. The Geneva Conference then provisionally divided the country (until elections, which were never held) into a Communist North and a non-Communist South. From its very beginning the Southern regime depended on US political and military support. Since then the struggle of the NLF led by Communists against the authoritarian Saigon government has occupied the world stage. In its early phase they relied on captured weapons (right) but North Vietnam, Russia and China were gradually drawn in. America saw herself as engaged in a crusade against Communist aggression. To the Communists the picture seemed all too familiar: a corrupt privileged class being kept in power by foreign aid while a heroic guerrilla army fought for equality and justice. Below: North and South in the early 1970s. In Hoa Binh Province an open-air class in physics is held in the school of agriculture. In Saigon a 'Coca-Cola culture' flourishes that represents all the vices of capitalism with none of its virtues. (49–53)

China looks to the land for her future as she has done in the past. The peasant is still the foundation of the state, but a continuous effort is being made not to allow a gulf to open again between those who work the land and those who administer and govern it. The new Communes are models of social equality and shared responsibility. Model of models is Tachai, in northern Shansi. The land here was particularly barren and difficult, and the villagers met with a series of natural catastrophes. Yet they succeeded in extending cultivation, raising production and inventing new systems of organization. The painting (below) shows the new village and in the background the terraces which were so laboriously built on the desert hills. (55)

'**Learn from Tachai'**, written in the background of the poster (above), is now a slogan for the rest of China. In the worker's hand is Mao Tse-tung's *On Contradictions*. Mao's popular books distil Communist philosophy in simple, easily remembered phrases for people inexperienced in abstract thinking. After the previous chapters of this book, Maoism can be convincingly seen as a continuation of the Chinese ethical tradition, which has always stressed the inviolability of the moral law and the subordination of the individual to the community. Mao's achievement has been to create a society in which that ethical tradition at last has some chance of being worked out in practice. (54)

*China, Korea and Vietnam
in the modern world*

JEAN CHESNEAUX

The turning-point from reform to revolution in the 1940s is symbolized by the burning of the land-deeds, the records of traditional China. As the Communist armies freed the country first from the Japanese, then from the Kuomintang, the peasants themselves took an active part in the redistribution of the land and the organizing of a new society. (1)

CHINA IN THE EARLY 19TH CENTURY was by no means the 'sleeping giant' that Napoleon had called her. She was being shaken by a major crisis in which may be observed all the classic symptoms of the 'dynastic cycle', though accompanied this time by some entirely new elements. Agrarian unrest was on the increase, bringing with it renewed activity of the secret societies; the administration was proving incompetent and corrupt; and the Manchu dynasty of the Ch'ing seemed to be in danger of losing the mandate of Heaven, just as the T'ang, the Sung, and the Ming had done before it. The danger was all the greater because the dynasty was an alien one and was unpopular on that account. This crisis of the old order was, moreover, further aggravated by the population explosion, by the growth of intellectual radicalism among scholars who disapproved of the regime, by the rise of proto-capitalism as manufacturing developed, and finally by the fact that China was not, like Japan, sealed off from the outside world. The immense success of American crops such as tobacco and ground-nuts, which had been introduced into Macao by the Portuguese in the 16th century and which had subsequently spread throughout a country that was reputedly 'closed' and 'stagnant', shows that China was capable of evolving through contact with the West without falling under its domination. However, this internal crisis at the beginning of the 19th century never had time to come to a head: the shock of the Opium Wars rudely upset the free interplay of the historical forces then confronting each other at the very heart of Chinese society, and prevented specific solutions from being reached by this means.

China at the crossroads
The Opium Wars (1839–42 and 1856–60) were in fact representative of the clash between two qualitatively different societies after the one had made a unilateral intrusion into the historical development of the other. The outcome of these wars put the West in a position of strength based on force, which was to govern its relations with China for close on a century: it was the period of gunboat diplomacy, the Franco-Chinese War, the expedition against the Boxers, and so on. The result-

322 (3)
p 323
(6,8)

ing imbalance is reflected in the 'unequal treaties' providing for concessions, extraterritorial rights, and foreign control of the Chinese Customs, which were all to the advantage of the West.

p 322 (2)
p 323 (5)

It was therefore hardly a question of 'confrontation', definable in terms of 'challenge' and 'response' (J. K. Fairbank), bringing together two parties in a voluntary exchange of views and on an equal footing. Relentless Western expansion resulting from the Industrial Revolution obliged China to develop in conjunction with the West. In other words, she was forced into a position of dependence on a historical process whose causes were quite alien to her at that time. The result was that China's own natural line of development was completely and abruptly broken off – not, as Western historians too often assert, given the benefit of a severe, though ultimately salutary, shock which is supposed to have roused her from her age-long lethargy.

It is for this reason that the Opium Wars, which, in a short view, were merely a series of border incidents of little military significance (except for the sack of Peking in 1860), undoubtedly form the starting point of modern Chinese history, and this is commonly accepted by Chinese historians. The Wars had the effect of checking the internal crisis that was brewing for traditional China. For a time they worked in favour of the *ancien*

341

régime, which it was in the interest of the Western powers to preserve for the sake of its submissiveness in negotiation. This was a constant pattern. The West supported the imperial government against the Taiping, Yuan Shih-k'ai against Sun Yat-sen, and the Kuomintang (Nationalist Party) against the Communists. Ironically enough, it was this very policy which guaranteed that the movement inaugurated by the Opium Wars should end in a crisis for the *ancien régime* even more radical than the one that was impending in 1820: total political collapse in 1911 and total social collapse in 1949.

The easy victories gained by the West provoked three different kinds of reaction. First, both the prestige and the political authority of the dynasty were weakened, leading to a wave of popular movements that were unprecedented in scale, though generally the rebels were not clearly aware that their actions had any connection with Western pressure on China. This is true of the Taiping Rebellion affecting central China (1850–64), the Nien uprising in the north (1853–68), and the Muslim insurrections in the north-west and south-west (1853–77). There was in addition a whole series of minor rebellions so widespread that from 1850 to 1870 not one of the eighteen provinces was regarded by the imperial authorities as being secure. They nonetheless succeeded in maintaining the upper hand, since the peasant revolts, though powerful, were unco-ordinated, and they shared no vision of a new future.

A second reaction was ultra-conservatism. People clung to tradition and the past as bastions against Western pressure. This feeling was widespread in court circles, but was also common among the provincial gentry and the masses. Among those who suffered from this conservative proto-nationalism on the part of the local gentry and the peasants were the foreign missionaries, both Catholic and Protestant, as was shown in the riots of 1860–70 and in the Boxer Rising.

p 323 (7)
p 323 (6,8)
p 324–5 (10,12)

The Japanese model
The ruling cliques of the Empire, however, adopted a third course of action. They sought to adapt themselves to the new conditions created by Western penetration, and so to carry out a controlled modernization. The efficacy of Western methods was recognized, but they hoped to limit their application to certain specific fields such as technology or diplomacy, while the essential principles of the *ancien régime* in its social and political aspects could continue unchanged. This was the *yang-wu* movement (the management of Chinese affairs by Western methods). It lasted roughly from 1860 to 1885, and represents the last consistent effort of the ruling classes of the old China to salvage their ascendancy and, with it, all the traditional social structure. These statesmen, some of whom, like Tseng Kuo-fan, Tso Tsung-t'ang, and Li Hung-Chang, were men of great distinction, and were not slow to point to a precedent and a model: Japan and the Meiji Revolution. The ruling classes in Japan had certainly managed to keep their authority and political hegemony after 1868, as we have seen in Chapter XII; but they had done so by changing the forms of their power and taking the lead in a modernizing movement which included the building of a modern transport system, the creation of new industries, the adoption of

p 326 (13)

modern education, and the development of a monetary economy.

Following the Japanese model, the supporters of *yang-wu* were prepared to accept the system of unequal treaties and to collaborate with the West. They deferred, for example, to the advice of a man such as Robert Hart, the famous Inspector-General of the Imperial Customs of China, an Englishman who in reality acted as a kind of 'General Resident' for the Western powers in China (using the term in the sense it had in India in the 19th century). They established a Foreign Office and sent the first Chinese diplomats to the West (a hitherto unknown practice, since the Emperor, being the Son of Heaven, occupied a position of pre-eminence and could therefore admit no other ruler to a footing of equality). They founded modern military arsenals, invited the West to provide officers to train the Chinese army, opened up mines, built textile factories equipped with machinery from the West, and sent the first batches of Chinese students abroad. They also set up 'translation centres' for the country-wide distribution of Western text-books on natural science, international law and medicine. This collective enterprise had as its slogan *Chung-hsüeh wei t'i; Hsi-hsüeh wei yung*: 'Chinese wisdom is the foundation of society; Western knowledge is purely for practical use.'

The advocates of *yang-wu* were not the only Chinese to seek, in some measure at least, a solution from the West for their country's problems. Paradoxically, this was precisely what the leaders of the great peasant rebellion of the Taiping had already done. Between 1850 and 1860 these people were professing a primitive form of agrarian Communism, but combined with features taken from Christianity. The latter included the Ten Commandments, baptism, and the divinity of Christ, whose younger brother Hung, their founder, claimed to be. These simple-minded peasants were making fumbling efforts to possess themselves of the religious 'secrets' to which they attributed the superiority of the West.

p 324– (9)

The *yang-wu* movement, however, was doomed to failure, like the syncretist endeavours of the Taiping before it. The Japanese model was unworkable in China for a variety of reasons. For one thing, the moving spirits of the *yang-wu* did not have so free a hand as the makers of the Meiji Revolution. The latter had been able to break down the feudal structure and destroy the political power of the daimyō, but the Chinese advocates of *yang-wu* were bound by the overriding necessity of preserving the existing social order. Unlike the Japanese reforms, the *yang-wu* movement failed to create a true modern bourgeoisie. In fact just the opposite. The new industrial enterprises and the merchants operating them came under the control of the Confucian bureaucracy, whose traditional power was consequently strengthened. Again, the Meiji revolutionaries had introduced monetary taxation throughout the country, and had transformed their feudal economic system into a capitalist one; but the advocates of *yang-wu* made hardly any changes in China's traditional economy. It was only where Western activity penetrated, that is to say in limited areas and at certain levels, that any modification took place.

The failure of the *yang-wu* movement was also a reflection of China's international status. The West had

A meeting of the foreign community in the concessions of Shanghai. Large areas in the so-called treaty ports were leased from China by Britain, France and others. Under the 'extraterritorial' system they were allowed to rule by European laws, and Chinese living there became virtual foreigners in their own country. (2)

refrained on the whole from interfering with the Meiji experiments: Japan's significance was too marginal, and her importance for the world market too slight, for the West to feel any necessity or advantage in tightening its political and economic control over her when the 19th century was drawing to a close. But China was a very different proposition. As the expansionist pressure from Europe increased, the West was no longer satisfied with the successes obtained at the time of the Opium Wars. *Yang-wu* policy was based on the supposition that a lasting settlement was possible with the West, within the framework of the unequal treaties of 1842 and 1860: but this hope was shattered by the Franco-Chinese War of 1884–85 and by renewed pressure from Russia and Britain, in north-east and in south-west China respectively. These pressures on the part of foreign powers became general when the 'break-up' and the 'battle of the concessions' set in between 1896 and 1900.

A further proof that the Japanese model had no real relevance for China was presented by the failure of the modernist reforms of the scholar K'ang Yu-wei, another great admirer of Japan. He tried in 1898 to introduce a programme of innovation, but he encountered the hostility of the reactionaries and popular indifference. This Confucian scholar, an ardent reformer and enlightened monarchist, was forced to abandon office barely a 'Hundred Days' after his appointment.

The Western model

For the next third of a century and more, it was the European, and not the Japanese, model that attracted the ruling circles in China, or at least those among them who desired it to transform their country.

It was a bitter, and in the end a mortal, blow to the two-thousand-year-old Chinese Empire when, at the beginning of the century, the West began to make fresh and even more imperious demands. The requirements of financial expansion were more pressing than the political determination to underpin China's *ancien régime*. Taking advantage of the easy victory gained over China in 1895 by an already modernized Japan, the Great Powers acquired very large mining and railway concessions, as well as 'spheres of influence' and 'leased territories', and at the same time they tightened their control over Chinese state finances. Certain state revenues were henceforth paid directly into the great foreign banks in China as security against the various 'debts' and 'indemnities' which China had under duress agreed to owe or to pay to the West. The dynastic crisis could no longer be postponed as it had been between 1860 and 1870 as a result of the *yang-wu* movement. This crisis produced some classical features: that is to say, some of the 'preliminary indications of dynastic collapse', such as agrarian unrest, renewed activity of the secret societies, deterioration of the administration and of the maintenance of public works, weakening of central authority, and a general sense of the imminent 'rupture of the Mandate'. But the new crisis was also partly traceable to some novel phenomena. For the first time in Chinese history the collapse of the dynasty made way for a regime of a totally different kind: a Republic, proclaimed by the young revolutionary conspirators in October 1911. The Revolution of 1911 seemed to be the triumph of a new ideology and a new type of political organization – the Revolutionary Party. Traditional China knew nothing of political parties in the true sense, being used only to the rivalries between cliques of courtiers and mandarins and the turbulent activities of esoteric secret societies.

The Revolution of 1911 was not merely the direct outcome of renewed pressure from the West: it was also the expression of certain new political and social forces such as the commercial bourgeoisie, the modern intelligentsia, and even the budding industrial proletariat. The Republicans were to a large extent their spokesmen.

The new bourgeoisie was a descendant of the traditional merchant class that had dealt in salt and tea, of the compradores (Chinese agents of the Western firms), and of the mandarins who had founded the State enterprises launched at the time of the *yang-wu* movement and had subsequently branched out into business of their own. This class was active mainly in the big 'Treaty Ports'. It adopted Western modes of living in the matter of clothes, entertainment, and education, and it organized itself in powerful Chambers of Commerce. But its economic base was weak. It lacked capital and and business acumen, and its activities did not amount to much except in the field of light industry.

The modern intelligentsia, too, made its appearance at the end of the 19th century. It was composed of doctors, journalists, professors, students, engineers, and

22 (3)

22 (4)

p 321 (1)

p 323 (5)

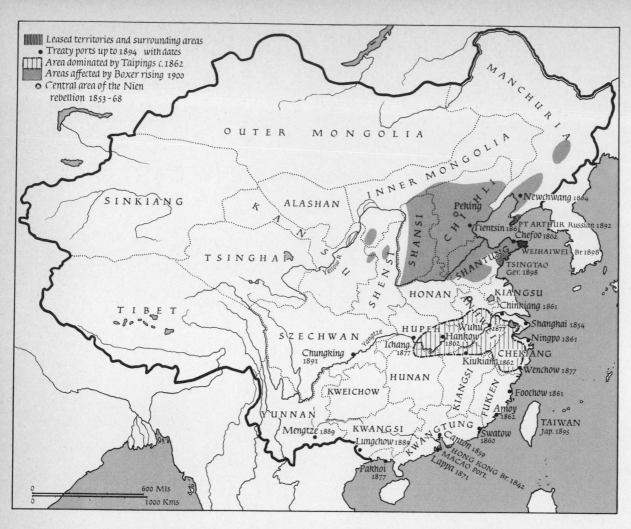

China during the late 19th and early 20th centuries, showing the treaty ports, leased territories, and areas of Taiping and Boxer control. (3)

p 326
(14)
p 328
(19)

writers. Of the three most prominent personalities of the period – Sun Yat-sen, Liang Ch'i-ch'ao, and Ch'en Tu-hsiu – the first was a doctor, the second a journalist, and the third a professor. Besides these several categories, there was the military intelligentsia, in particular the officers of the 'New Army'. They too were acquainted with the modern world in the field of military science. Like the 'Free Officers' in Egypt in 1952, they were deeply concerned with national resurgence, and they played a major role in the preparation and the success of the 1911 Revolution.

Lastly, the proletariat had come into being with the advent of extensive modern industry, not only foreign, but also Chinese. It was concentrated in a small number of important centres like Shanghai and Wuhan. Despite their wretched conditions, bad pay, and poor training, these workers showed considerable spirit. By 1920 they numbered about one and a half million, of whom more than half were employed by British or Japanese interests in China. They formed their own trade unions, organized strikes, and asserted their own social identity.

Even so, these new classes, which were the product of the Western penetration of China, still counted for little by comparison with the mass of the peasants and the political and social authority of the old ruling classes; for as a social force the *ancien régime* survived its political demise in 1911. Neither the bourgeoisie, nor the intelligentsia, nor even the proletariat out of its own resources, was in a position to exercise anything like a hegemony that could make a mark on history. Not only were they a small minority, living on the periphery; but their position

in the old society remained largely what it had always been. Many of the bourgeoisie and the intelligentsia retained their links with the old world of agrarian notables and landowners. As for the workers, many of these were peasants living only temporarily in the towns.

This explains the failure of attempts to introduce into China a political system on the Western pattern: there was no definite social basis that was strong enough to support them. Sun Yat-sen himself – one of those Chinese who, in Mao's words, 'desperately sought from the West the solution to the problems of their country' – was symbolic of this irrelevance of Western political systems to Chinese realities. This admirer of Montesquieu and Henry George, and author of an ambitious political system (Three Principles, Five Functions, etc.), achieved only a short-lived and geographically marginal control over the affairs of China. The list of failures in the political Westernization of China between 1911 and 1949 is a formidable one.

The Constitution of 1911, for example, was an attempt to introduce into China a system based on Anglo-Saxon democratic practice, with a cabinet, a parliamentary majority, and so on. It remained officially in force for almost fifteen years, and during this period the 'Republican Government' of Peking enjoyed diplomatic (and financial) recognition by the Powers. In reality, however, it was the rival factions of warlords who exercised the power, and parliamentary assemblies, ministers, and presidents of the Republic were all meekly subservient to them. Nothing came, either, from the federal solution

344

by which some intellectuals in 1920 hoped to put an end to this inter-provincial strife. Its advocates were thoroughly conversant with Swiss constitutional law and with the theory of states' rights in the USA, but they were powerless to impose their ideas on the warlords and so to transform China into a federation of autonomous provinces.

We could go on adding to this list of attempts to graft Western ideologies on to the living organism that was China. Our list would include the anarchism of Kropotkin and Reclus, which between 1910 and 1920 had won an enthusiastic following among some young Chinese intellectuals in contact with the West; social democracy, advocated between 1930 and 1940 by Carsun Chang and Chang Tung-sun, the founders of the tiny Chinese Social Democrat Party; and German and Italian Fascism, which by 1935 was having considerable influence on some leaders of the Kuomintang and on members of Chiang Kai-shek's immediate entourage. None of these grafts was successful, and none of them was anything more than a barren incident in the political history of modern China.

p 327
(16)
From a cultural point of view also, the period between the Republican Revolution of 1911 and the advent to power of the Communists in 1949 is marked by the fascination which the West had for many young Chinese. The mandarin reformers of 1860–80 had found it sufficient to allot a 'utilitarian' role *(yung)* to Western knowledge, and they had continued to regard traditional Chinese learning as the 'foundation' *(t'i)* of society; the new generation talked of 'integral Westernization'. This was the attitude of the young revolutionary philosopher T'an Ssu-t'ung, who was bitterly opposed to the *ancien régime* in its entirety. Though far more of a radical than K'ang Yu-wei, he supported his reform movement in 1898, and when K'ang was overthrown by the reactionaries, T'an was one of the six martyrs who suffered in the repression.

'Mr Science' and 'Mr Democracy'

By 1915, Western culture had acquired a prestige illustrated by the two symbolic figures 'Mr Science' and 'Mr Democracy', the two experts who were said to be on their way to ailing China's bedside with the appropriate remedies. This idea was pioneered by Professor Ch'en Tu-hsiu, the founder of *New Youth*, a magazine that was passionately dedicated to criticizing traditional China and praising 'modern culture', which was not at that time differentiated from Western culture. Then followed the May Fourth movement of 1919, whose promoters were enthusiastic over their discovery of the new Western ideologies, from Marx to Bertrand Russell, and from Bakunin to Tolstoy and Dewey. Out of this movement Chinese Marxism was born, and Ch'en Tu-hsiu was the first Secretary-General of the Chinese Communist Party, founded in 1921. By this step, the Westernizing movement succeeded for the first time in implanting something that was viable in Chinese life, and in building up a historically significant institution that was capable of transforming the old China; but the movement achieved this at the cost of its own survival, for Communism is both a historical part of the West and a political force dedicated to the destruction of Western values. Indeed, this

The special edition of the radical 'New Youth' magazine, published in Peking in May 1919. It was devoted to Marxism, and contained a contribution by Li Ta-chao, later a founder member of the Chinese Communist Party. (4)

implanting of Marxism in China raised very complex problems, resulting in two entirely conflicting versions of Chinese Communism – a subject to which we will return.

Whatever its political consequences and its role in the formation of Chinese Communism, the May Fourth movement, in so far as it was an attempt to promote the acclimatization of an alien culture, attracted the interest of only a very small section of Chinese society: namely the Westernized intellectuals. These people, who lived in Shanghai and the other large modern cities, were familiar with the world of the intelligentsia and the Chinese bourgeoisie, but knew little of the industrial proletariat, and nothing at all of the peasants (who, for their part, knew nothing of them). It was only after the outbreak of war with Japan, when writers and artists participated in the Yenan Forum (convened in the guerrilla bases in 1942), that contact at a deeper level became possible between the peasants and the professional thinkers.

Medicine is a case in point of this incompatibility between what the West had to offer and the Chinese reality to which it had to be applied. Since the end of the 19th century, modern medicine in the form of vaccines, antisepsis, hospital treatment, and surgery had been practised in the Treaty Ports and in a small number of isolated places in the interior where there were missionary hospitals. Some Chinese doctors, such as the famous Wu Lien-teh, had attracted numbers of followers who were experts in modern medical practice. But the Chinese doctors who had this modern training preferred to remain in the towns where they had studied. They were assured of finding there a remunerative Chinese clientele with a Westernized mode of life similar to their own. The bulk of the rural population, and indeed most of the town-dwellers too, continued to have recourse to traditional doctors, who practised acupuncture and moxibustion and possessed an empirical pharmacopoeia of surprising richness. In Communist China, since 1949, an attempt has been made to introduce modern medicine into the country districts and at the same time to incorporate in it a number of the empirical techniques of traditional medicine, such as the study of the pulse and of the effects of mineral medicaments.

p 135 (6)
p 136 (9)
p 137 (11)
p 140 (18)

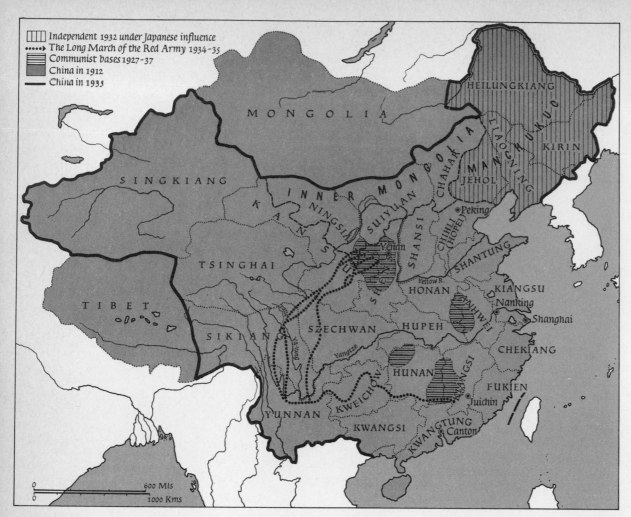

China between 1912 and 1937, showing the scope of the Japanese infiltration, the Communist bases and the route of the Long March. (5)

The same lack of consistency and balance characterized the Chinese economy as it underwent 'modernization' during the first half of the 20th century. A 'modern' sector came into being in the shape of partly mechanized mines, textile and food industries, a railway system and steam shipping lines, and big banking. Business in the great ports and their hinterland was predominantly capitalist. But capital enterprise was responsible for only a very small proportion of China's consumer products. Besides being limited in size, the modern sector occupied only a geographically peripheral position. It developed appreciably only on the coast, in the north-east, and at certain places in the Yangtze basin. The pattern of the railway system, with its lines radiating from peripheral poles, illustrates the priority for the modern economy of external communications over domestic interregional traffic. The whole interior of China, which in practice meant almost all the peasantry, was thus isolated. The agrarian system based on the traditional ground-rent, combined with usury and the customary labour levy, continued in force.

p 139
(17)

p 330
(24,25)

Even the modern sector had by no means freed itself from the old economic system. In the factories the quasi-feudal relations between workers, contractors, and foremen were of greater importance than the cash-nexus. The modern bourgeoisie clung to land ownership and often depended for its income more on ground-rents than on its investments in capitalist enterprise. Thus the modern sector was isolated from the main body of the Chinese economy, and therefore was doomed to be hardly more than an appendage of the world capitalist system.

Many of the chief capitalist enterprises were Japanese or British. Even those which were Chinese-owned were dependent on foreign capital, technicians, equipment and maintenance of plant, and, in some cases, also on foreign markets.

In short, the Western model was no more successful in China at the beginning of the 20th century than the Japanese model had been in the 19th. The elements of Westernization – whether in the form of ideologies, political systems, private life, or the organization of the economy – never penetrated beyond the fringes, but were confined to border regions or to social minorities, of which Shanghai was both the centre and the symbol. The 'modern' elements had no influence on the peasants, and indeed no relevance to them. These Western solutions were incapable of solving the real problems of China as a political and social entity, which were the warlords, the landlords, the monopoly of culture and power by a privileged minority, moral and material poverty, and the country's dependence on the Great Powers, who were all this while profiting from the unequal treaties.

Communism: the Russian model

The Communist movement raised new problems for China; it also offered a new ideology and set in motion new historical processes. But the solution of those problems, the success of that ideology, and the effectiveness of those processes still depended on a fundamental adjustment of them to the Chinese situation, and on their relevance to the Chinese community as a whole and not only to its elite or its fringe elements. This was as true for the period of revolutionary struggle (1921–49) as for the period of construction of a socialist China (from 1949 onwards, and particularly during the major crisis of the Cultural Revolution).

From its foundation in 1921 to its triumph in 1949, the struggles of the Chinese Communist Party (CCP) passed through several distinct phases. There were the workers' protests in isolation (1921–23), the United Front with the bourgeoisie and the Kuomintang to suppress the northern warlords (1924–27), the formation of insurgent zones in southern China (the Kiangsi Soviets, 1927–34), the Long March (1934–35), the organization of anti-Japanese resistance in the guerrilla bases of northern China (1937–45), the attempt to form a coalition government with the Kuomintang (1945–46), and the resumption of the conflict with the Kuomintang (1946–49). During these successive phases, a number of fundamental choices had to be made, and the diversity of the responses revealed the existence of two diametrically opposed versions of the Chinese Communist movement. Simplified labels for these are the Comintern version and the Yenan version.

p 327 (17,18) 328–9 (21–3) 21 (1)

One question at issue was the part to be played in revolutionary strategy by the working class and the peasantry respectively. In China, the Communist movement had been started by intellectuals who were deeply convinced of the validity of what had happened in Russia, and therefore it had begun by emphasizing the privileged role of the industrial proletariat – the class which, as the victim of capitalism, was deemed to have the historical mission of overthrowing capitalism. Like the other members of the Comintern, even those in only slightly industrialized countries, the CCP busied itself between 1920 and 1925 with forming unions, organizing strikes, and arousing the class-consciousness of the proletariat. These workers' campaigns attained considerable proportions, as for example in the case of the sixteen-month boycott-strike directed from Canton against Hong Kong in 1925–26. But when the rupture between the Kuomintang and the CCP came in the spring of 1927, the workers' movement was crushed in a few weeks. From then on, it was the peasantry which provided the chief social support for the Communist revolution. Living as it did in a natural environment, away from centres of political and military repression, the peasant class was capable of a sustained effort such as could not be achieved by the workers in the towns, who were dependent on their wages, and who could not afford to wait. This transference of the revolutionary mandate to the peasants was the policy of a new group of leaders, to which Mao belonged, while those who, like Li Li-san and Liu Shao-ch'i, favoured the working-class approach, preferred to continue their activities in the industrial centres, as they had done before 1927.

p 332 (32)

Another issue was that of the relative merits of armed struggle and the political struggle of the masses. Here again, a more original answer superseded the 'classical' one. Until 1927 the CCP, whether acting alone, or through the big workers' unions, or in collaboration with its allies of the Kuomintang, had been bent on promoting powerful political risings such as the May Thirtieth movement of 1925 in Shanghai. But it was only after 1927 that, under Mao's influence, the Party came to

Between 1927, when the Party broke with the Kuomintang, and 1935, the date of the Long March, Chinese Communists were divided between those who followed Mao to the remote countryside and more traditional Marxists who tried to promote urban revolution. In this woodcut of the early thirties, called 'Strike', the banner in the foreground reads 'Workers and peasants, rise up'. (6)

accept the idea of a protracted armed struggle, supported by the peasantry alone. The principles of revolutionary civil war, already outlined at the time of the Kiangsi Soviets, were vindicated in the anti-Japanese guerrilla zones from 1937 onwards, and they ensured the final victory in 1948–49: the large towns held by the Kuomintang were surrounded by the rising tide of peasants.

p 327 (18)

Yet another question centred on the form of the relationship between the party leadership and the revolutionary masses. Confronted with a form of political action for which their own tradition offered them no precedent (except for the old secret societies and the clandestine republican groups which had evolved largely from them), the Chinese Communists had at the outset modelled themselves closely upon the Bolsheviks. The CCP was based on the democratic centralism of Lenin, and in its turn provided the pattern for wider organizations such as the youth movement and the unions. It was the organizer of the great popular movements of 1925 and 1926 in southern China. After the collapse of the strategic alliance with the Kuomintang in 1927, the central organization of the Party continued in existence, but with its strength considerably diminished, for it had lost the power to mobilize popular forces, even in the towns, and was in any case weakened by internal rivalries. From 1927 onwards, first in the Kiangsi Soviets and later in the guerrilla bases of Yenan, a quite

In the Communist liberated areas, where the majority of peasants were illiterate, elections were carried out by the electors depositing beans in a bowl. The candidates stand with their backs to the bowls so as not to know who is voting for them. (7)

different system of relations was introduced between the avant-garde and the masses. The leadership of the Party, and to an even greater extent its middle echelon, relinquished its position of complete hegemony. From then on it worked in conjunction with the People's Army. Under this new arrangement the army formed an essential link between the professional revolutionaries and the popular movement. Here again the originality of Maoism showed itself, though its effect was to draw a further distinction between the 'red' zones (guerrilla bases) and the 'white' zones (urban areas where armed struggle was not possible). The army acted as a new type of political organization in the 'red' zones, while clandestine activity on more traditional lines continued in the 'white' zones.

Another fundamental issue for Chinese Communism was the national question – the national heritage and national 'mandate'. The Chinese Communists were on the whole indifferent to these problems before 1937, even during the period of the Kiangsi Soviets (which may be regarded as the initial phase of Maoism); but by reason of the priority that they gave, during the war, to popular resistance against Japan, they found themselves committed to a much more uncompromising assertion of their national character. Chinese public opinion came to regard them as the defenders of the national interest, whereas the delaying tactics and military passivity of Chiang Kai-shek seemed to prove his indifference to it. The Communists laid claim at the same time to Chinese cultural heritage ('from Confucius to Sun Yat-sen', declared Mao in calling for a critical re-evaluation of 'all that is precious in China's past'). A sense of the continuity of China's history began to play its part in a complex of attitudes that, before, had been virtually centred on Moscow and on the world Communist movement.

p 331
(27,28,
30)

p 333
(33)

p 328
(19)

p 340
(54)

In these circumstances, what form were the internationalist aspirations of militant Chinese Communists to take? Once again, the CCP gave such differing answers to the question that they hardly seemed to come from the same movement. One answer took the form of proletarian internationalism of the most classic kind, such as was formulated during the heyday of the Comintern. Chinese delegates were present in Moscow at the conferences of the international Communist movement, and internationalism was identified with unconditional solidarity with the Soviet Union. This attitude characterized the Chinese Communists until 1927. Indeed, these bonds of solidarity with Moscow remained strong even after that, not only in the traditional party organization, but also in the guerrilla bases. This is evident in the letter from Mao to those fighting for the cause in the Spanish War, expressing regret that Chinese volunteers were unable to join the International Brigades. But during the Yenan period the internationalism of the Chinese Communists was enriched by a new element: a special relation of solidarity with the popular movements in colonial countries. Emphasis was given at that time to the existence of special bonds between the combatants at Yenan and the revolutionary movements in such countries as Vietnam, Korea, and India. Some of the militants involved in these movements, including among others Ho Chi Minh, were in fact in the guerrilla bases during the war with Japan.

Even before they came to power, therefore, the Chinese Communists, or at any rate the dominant section of them, had already retreated some way from the 'model' offered by the Bolshevik party, its strategy and its social and cultural orientation. Yenan, a remote and scattered little township in the backward mountain area of the north-west, was the symbol of all these new tendencies and the nucleus round which they crystallized. The great port of Shanghai, on the other hand, which was the main centre of the Chinese working population and was for many years the headquarters of the Central Committee, had been the rallying point for the more classical revolutionary tendencies, and was more directly linked with the experience and organization of the Comintern (with which it could communicate more easily than could Yenan). It was no accident that Shanghai continued to perform, during the development of Communism in China, the same function as it had performed for the Westernizing tendencies of the bourgeoisie between 1900 and 1930: the role of transmitter of foreign ideas. European Communism, like the other foreign ideas, failed to become naturalized among the Chinese masses, and, through the intermediary of the guerrilla bases, they evolved their own, quite different, version.

p 334
(34,35)

p 339
(50)

p 331
(29)

p 332–
(31)

p 330
(26)

Moscow versus Yenan

From 1949 onwards, the tradition of Yenan and the tradition of the Comintern continued to conflict, at first discreetly and then more openly as time went on. An initial period of 'classicism', during which the Soviet model was closely adhered to, was followed by the abrupt changes of course and the quite original choices of 1956–58: accelerated collectivization, people's communes, the Great Leap Forward, and the 'general line'. The setback suffered by these bold efforts brought about a partial

p 336
(40–2)

p 340
(55)

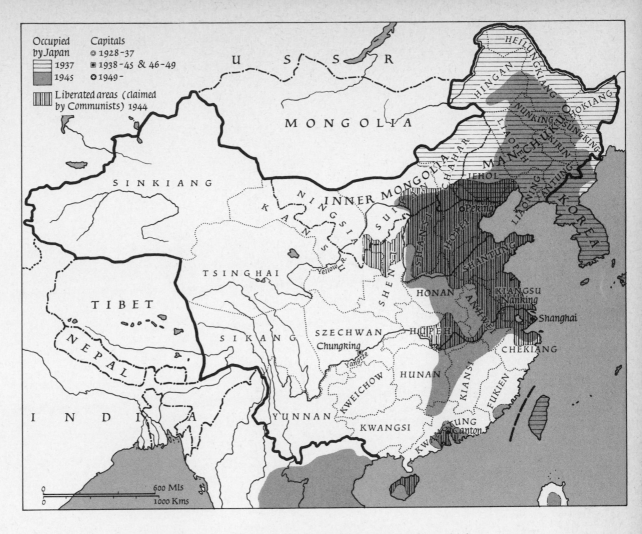

P 335
(39)

P 337
(43)

China, 1935–49, showing the extent of Japanese occupation. The 'liberated areas' were actually a loose conglomeration of nineteen areas only partially controlled by the Communists and not connected. (8)

Occupied by Japan
☐ 1937
■ 1945

Capitals
◎ 1928–37
■ 1938–45 & 46–49
○ 1949–

▦ Liberated areas (claimed by Communists) 1944

return to the Soviet model between 1962 and 1965, a phase during which the conflict between the two lines seems to have been particularly acrimonious until the explosion of that major crisis, the Cultural Revolution. The Cultural Revolution (1966–69) put a decisive end to the conflict by simultaneously eradicating both the remaining traces of the Soviet model and its advocates.

In the 1950s, the influence of the Soviet model had been particularly marked where political structure was concerned. Public life, from the capital down to the rural localities, was controlled by the dual instrument of Party and Government, the Party being the ultimate authority. A Constitution, adopted in 1954 and differing from the Soviet Constitution only in minor details, established the machinery of government: it laid down the functions of the President of the Republic, provided for the periodical election of members to the National Assembly, and so on. The Party continued to adhere strictly to the principles of proletarian internationalism and democratic centralism; it convened its Eighth Congress in 1956. Its members constituted a privileged elite that enjoyed material advantages: educational opportunities for their children, social power, and control over the admission of new members – in fact an authentic Communist 'establishment' after the model of Stalinist Russia. The legitimacy of the power of the Party, of its operation, and of its members, was deemed to have been fixed once and for all, and to be henceforth beyond dispute.

The same classicism characterized economic methods. Priority was given to central planning, to capital invest-

ment, and to heavy industry, a policy which was accompanied by close co-operation with the other socialist countries and particularly with the Soviet Union. These countries were pursuing the same general economic policy, and co-operation was facilitated by the similarity of their priorities; for the industrial sector offers far greater possibilities for the exchange of technicians and the supply of plant than is possible, say, for agriculture. Economic policy abroad was in complete harmony with plans for economic development at home. The Five-Year Plan of 1953–57 was the expression of this trend, and its symbol was Anshan, the vast steel complex in the north-east. It is significant that the propaganda magazines published in Peking at that time were much given to advertising these large and important enterprises – tall blast furnaces, huge dams, and so on. Every large town in China acquired its permanent exhibition centre for displaying the economic achievements of the Soviet Union: these buildings were perfect examples of the over-ornate Soviet architecture of the 1950s, and they have their exact replicas in Warsaw, Budapest, and elsewhere.

The influence of the Soviet model was equally obvious where the army was concerned. The tradition of Yenan, that of a people's army in close contact with the people whom it served, was lost. Instead, the army, now stationed in barracks, became isolated and began to develop increasingly ponderous structures of its own. Even the honorary rank of marshal was created, which was something quite alien to the atmosphere in the guerrilla bases before 1949, and emphasis was placed on

P 335
(37, 38)

P 331
(29)

P 332–3
(31)

conventional heavy armament such as aircraft and armoured cars. The same Soviet influence was evident in the most widely divergent aspects of social life. An instance of this was the system of library classification. Before 1949 this was the decimal classification used by the Library of Congress in Washington, which had been introduced into China by the Kuomintang. It was now replaced by the Soviet system, though this was no better suited to Chinese books.

There are, however, two points to be observed which will to some extent correct the impression of total and mechanical imitation of a model imported from abroad. The first point is that China had scarcely any other choice open to her in 1949–50, inasmuch as the West deliberately turned its back on her and became hardened in this attitude by her entry into the Korean War, in which she was implicated almost before her new regime was established, and certainly contrary to her wishes and expectations. Secondly, it was Liu Shao-ch'i's group and its associates who were the most actively engaged in following the Soviet example. It was no mere coincidence that Liu fathered the Constitution of 1954, or that he played the principal role at the Eighth Party Congress, from which Mao was, politically, absent; or again that Po I-po, who was in charge of the economy at the time of the Five-Year Plan, employed methods very similar to those used by the heads of the Soviet economy. These were the men who were to come under attack in the Cultural Revolution. They were a group of prominent figures who stood for the adoption of Soviet methods of organization, but this does not mean that they were unconditional supporters of the Soviet Union itself; and in this they differed from another group, led by Wang Ming, a high-ranking Chinese official of the Comintern at the Stalin period. This explains how it was that Liu Shao-ch'i's group was able to endorse the policy of rupture with the Soviet Union in 1960 and at the same time to pursue a policy that was close to the Soviet model – a policy subsequently swept away by the Cultural Revolution.

The tradition of Yenan was the inspiration for the progressive break with the Soviet model. In this, Mao seems to have played the leading part. It was Mao who insisted on forwarding the 'rising tide' of socialism in the countryside in 1955–56, and on analysing 'contradictions within the people' in 1957, on launching the Great Leap Forward and the people's communes in 1958, and on calling for the vigorous prosecution of the Cultural Revolution in 1966–67. This fresh orientation led to a reversal of priorities. The emphasis was now placed on the basic importance of agriculture instead of heavy industry, which thus lost the favoured position that it had enjoyed since the Stalin period. This led also to a greater liberty of action being allowed to local initiative, and to the mobilization of the masses by political means instead of relying on technical knowledge alone (a phase of the 'red versus expert' controversy). Social needs could be defined far more consciously and definitely than is possible in a consumer society, and moral considerations could be given precedence over material incentive. In all these points there is an obvious contrast with the Soviet model, both in its Stalinist version and in its Kosyginist version, though the contrast with the latter alone is insisted on by Peking today. The change has been no less radical in the political sphere. The problem of the relation between governors and governed has been faced frankly for the first time in the history of socialist countries, and a solution has been sought through an unprecedented procedure. A minority group within the Establishment has initiated a 'disestablishment' operation, relying on popular forces which it has released against the established order, with all the attendant risks that such a strategy implies.

Korea and Vietnam

Throughout the course of their histories down to the present time, Korea and Vietnam offer striking resemblances, which have been outlined in Chapter VII. Both were 'tributary kingdoms' of the old Chinese Empire, and were deeply impregnated by its influence in the form of Confucianism, imperial institutions, and so on. Both fell subsequently and at about the same time, under the colonial rule of Japan in the one case and of France in the other. Both were victims of Great Power rivalry and of the confrontation between the socialist camp and that headed by the United States, and both found themselves divided into a socialist North and a South linked to the 'Free World'. In Vietnam this situation dates from the Geneva Conference of 1954, and in Korea from the Panmunjon Agreements in 1953. The parallel has become still more striking since the crisis in the Communist international movement that has produced the split between Moscow and Peking. The regimes in Hanoi and P'yong'yang are in fact the front rank of Communist 'non-alignment'. They refuse to give their unconditional support to either the Chinese or the Soviet line. South Korea and South Vietnam offer the contrasting spectacle of countries whose society is superficially Westernized, with its American cars, television, and Coca-Cola, but whose authoritarian regimes owe their survival entirely to political, and above all military, aid from the United States. In fact Vietnam and Korea, to judge by their development during the past century, confirm the conclusion that has been suggested by the study of China. The countries of the Far East are impervious to the influence of an artificially imported Western model, whether this is introduced through colonial rule or by more modern means. This resistance to foreign models is so intense that it has declared itself even towards socialist societies enjoying such prestige as the Soviet Union and China.

Until the end of the 19th century, Korea was an isolated country imprisoned within the archaic structures of the 'Asian mode of production'. This was characterized by the absence of private ownership of the land, and by the despotic power wielded by the Yi dynasty and the political class in its entourage. Japanese colonial rule transformed the country into a source of raw materials obtained from mines in the north, of food products from the rice-growing south, and of labour: millions of Koreans emigrated to Russia, Siberia, China, and especially to Japan. This intensive exploitation could, however, hardly be called modernization in the true sense of the term. The peasants now worked for the great Japanese colonialist companies, and for the new landowners, who were in political collaboration with the colonial regime; the old aristocracy had disappeared without trace, but the workers were still coolies in all but name. The totalitarian methods of direct administration and ruthless exploitation practised by Japan did not create conditions favourable for the growth of an intelligentsia or a modern bourgeoisie, and the few representatives of these classes emigrated to China or the United States.

This colonial regime collapsed with the Japanese Empire in August 1945, though not as a result of internal crisis or the activities of the national movement, which certainly could not claim this defeat of the colonizers as the triumph of intense or prolonged struggle by the people. The moderate nationalists, who had been monarchists until the death of the last king of Korea in 1919, consisted of nothing more than a few groups of exiled intellectuals like Syngman Rhee. Nor had the Communists ever succeeded in forming a true political party with its roots in social reality. They had expended themselves in strife between factions that were affiliated either to the Comintern or to the different versions of the Chinese Communist movement, or even to a Japanese Communist Party which was itself in a divided and enfeebled state. After the occupation of the country by the Soviet army in 1945, these conflicting factions rapidly gave way to a highly authoritarian Communist regime of a very 'Stalinist' kind, whose position was made even stronger by the Korean War. However, under Kim Il Sung, Communist Korea has progressively detached itself from the Soviet Union, but without making any decided approach to China. Communist Korea's watchword is the independent line (*jiu-che*, 'through self'), and this appears to be producing remarkable results in the economic field, though it shows no signs of allowing to popular initiative from below the same scope that it has in China, thanks there to the Yenan tradition. The incident involving the *Pueblo*, the American ship captured in 1968 by the North Koreans, illustrated the degree of independence achieved by North Korea from both Moscow and Peking.

The Northern regime appeared to have no very strong popular support in the South. There the only opposition to the dictatorial power of Syngman Rhee and the politico-military factions which succeeded him was of a very limited nature and was confined chiefly to the students. It did not present any radical challenge to the principles of this society, which is based on free enterprise and is intimately connected with the particular form of civilization represented by the United States. This relative stability of the pro-American regimes in Seoul has the same historical explanation as the rigid, authoritarian nature of the political system which has been built up in North Korea since 1945. The harsh colonial regime imposed by the Japanese, which was itself the successor of extremely archaic 'Asian' political structures, has prevented the establishment in Korea of popular traditions of political struggle and the formation of a native Korean political experience and sense of citizenship. This point is further illustrated by the very character of the Korean War, which was a curious 'enclave' of European military history in Asia. It was a 'non-Asian' war inasmuch as it was fought on a 'front' and was waged between two politico-military machines

that were each in control of a solid block of territory. By contrast, the Asian wars of the 20th century – in China (1937–45), Vietnam, the Philippines, and Malaysia alike – have been people's wars in which the opposing forces have been enmeshed over the whole area of the disputed territory.

This is the fundamental difference between the histories of Korea and Vietnam in the 20th century. The similarities already mentioned are equally fundamental; but Vietnam's distinctive feature is the richness of the political experience of her people, and the lofty character, the dynamism, and the persistence of the people's struggles throughout the French colonial period, and even before that.

The pre-colonial history of Vietnam had in fact already been shaped to a considerably larger extent than that of Korea by the sensitivity and the initiative of the people. The wars of resistance to Chinese rule and to subsequent Chinese attempts at re-conquest in the 10th and 13th centuries, between 1418 and 1427 and again in 1789, had had the effect of mobilizing the masses of the peasantry. They rose again in the Tay-Son peasant war at the end of the 18th century and brought into power a rebel dynasty which had restored unity to the country after it had been torn apart by two centuries of feudal rivalry. Traditions of popular resistance such as these helped the national movement in Vietnam to maintain a constant pressure during the whole colonial period and to refuse to accept the loss of independence as an

French colonial rule brought profound economic and social changes in its train. The extraction of coal and non-ferrous metals, the establishment of rubber plantations, the production of rice on a commercial scale for export, the building of a network of railways, and the development of large ports such as Saigon and Haiphong created a whole modern sector in the economy. But this could not exist in isolation from the traditional sector, and the countryside began to be directly affected by the new economic conditions such as an expanding market and the progressive collection of taxes in monetary form. The peasants were the ultimate source from which the colonial authorities financed the modern sector with loans, subsidies, and investment and tax benefits. To the already heavy land-tax were added the 'three beasts of burden': the state (i.e. French) monopolies of opium, salt, and spirits.

The former ruling classes – the landowners and the mandarins – were by this time ranged on the side of the colonial system. They took advantage of its support to consolidate their economic power over the peasants. New social classes were, however, beginning to make their appearance. Though the Vietnamese commercial bourgeoisie was 'stunted' (according to Tran Duc Thao) by reason of the tight control exercised by colonial capitalism over such vital sectors of the economy as production and trade, the proletariat, comprising miners, dockers, factory and railway workers, was by this time a force to be reckoned with. To these should be added the coolies in the plantations, who were peasants no longer despite the nature of their work. Other classes that had developed considerably were the intelligentsia and the petty bourgeoisie, who were a requisite for the efficient functioning of the colonial system. These consisted of

p 338 (45)

p 338 (44)

p 338 (46–8)

American troops come to Vietnam—and leave it, in coffins, piloted by Death. (9)

office workers and junior administrative officials, journalists, writers, and industrial technicians. All these social strata were to play a considerable part in the various stages of the national movement, though not all were to prove equal to resolving its inherent contradictions.

In its early stages the struggle against the colonial regime was in fact waged solely by the peasants. These were organized and inspired by a few rural Confucian scholars who had refused to follow the example of the monarchy and throw in their lot with the French. But these 'scholars' rebellions' were backward-looking. They invoked Confucian loyalty to a monarchy, but this had already bowed to foreign rule, and had therefore nothing constructive to offer. In the second phase, the leadership of the national movement passed into the hands of the petty bourgeoisie, the intellectuals, and other 'Westernized' classes, but they also came up against a contradiction they were unable to resolve – namely that the West, which for them meant France, was at once their model and the master to be overthrown. It was the desire of these moderates – men like Phan Boi Chau and Phan Chu Trinh – to liberate Vietnam from French rule, but they were at the same time convinced of the need for Vietnam to break with her past and to modernize herself on the French pattern, for instance in the fields of education and economic development. In the third stage, the leadership of the national movement devolved upon the Vietnamese Communists. It was they who, by means of the Viet-Minh Front, infused courage into the struggle against Japan and in 1945 proclaimed the restoration of Vietnamese independence in the shape of the Democratic Republic of Vietnam. It was they who waged the war against France for eight years (1946–54) and achieved the historic victory of Dien Bien Phu. Thereby, in the eyes of Vietnamese public opinion, they acquired a degree of prestige and national status which has few parallels among the other Communist parties of

P 339
(49)

P 339
(50)

Asia. Since 1954 their resistance to American penetration of the South, and from 1965 onwards to American attempts to bring the North to heel, have served only to enhance this prestige and status.

It was this domestic record that finally encouraged the Vietnamese Communists to 'rely above all on their own strength' (a favourite slogan), and to stop blindly following the example of the Soviet Union or China, as they had previously done in several fields (as when they had attempted a Chinese-style agricultural collectivization in 1955, and when they had tried to adopt the Soviet formula of economic centralization and concentration on heavy industry in 1958–60). The Vietnamese Communists maintain cordial relations with both China and the Soviet Union, but at the same time they preserve complete freedom of action for themselves.

It will be apparent that the evolution of the countries of Eastern Asia since the 19th century has been marked by a long and patient seeking after an inner historical logic and national identity. Neither the Japanese nor the Western model succeeded in gaining a real hold in China. The French colonial regime and Japanese colonial power alike failed to impose lasting structures on Vietnam and Korea. Neither regime was able to withstand the shock of World War II. This search for identity has continued in spite of these countries' membership of the world Communist system (the word bloc is definitely misleading). They were attracted at first by the Soviet model, and then by the Chinese one, but they subsequently turned to a more national form of Communism that was closer to their own historical experience and to the needs of their people.

To Western eyes these countries may look very strange and very remote. But they have not resigned themselves to the prospect of living in isolation indefinitely. That they were isolated for such a long time, under such a severe quarantine, was because a large part of the outside world was not willing to let them follow a course of their own, and has even gone to the length of active interference in an attempt to impose on them its own type of civilization. An example of this is the massive use in Vietnam of chemicals such as DDT which are legally banned in the West as being a danger to the natural environment. It is an established fact that in certain areas of South Vietnam the rice plantations will not yield again for twenty years, and the forests for a hundred, even if the fighting were to come to an end now.

Hence there is in these countries no illusion as to the possibility of compromise with societies which not only are interventionist but are themselves in the throes of such acutely traumatic experiences as the revolt of youth, the crisis of the institution of the family, a surfeit of technology, the ruin of the natural environment, and obsessions with money. This dichotomy remains, whether or not a US President visits Peking, whether or not the Vietnam genocide at last comes to an end. The West, in its own clumsy and chaotic fashion, is also in search of its identity. The sophisticated half of the world will be able to reach a satisfactory settlement with the other, unsophisticated, half only when it succeeds in coming to terms with itself. When one day they each come to the end of their quest, East and West will perhaps prove Kipling wrong by meeting at last.

LIST AND SOURCES OF ILLUSTRATIONS

*The page on which an illustration appears is shown by the first set of numerals,
its plate or figure number by the second. Sources of photographs are given in italics*

I Signs and Meanings

17 1. *The Eighteen Scholars (Calligraphy)*; painting on silk, Sung dynasty. *National Palace Museum, Taipei, Taiwan*

18–19 2. Oracle bone, 1400–1100 BC. *Courtesy the Trustees of the British Museum, London*
3. Wooden strips from Yumen, AD 100. *Courtesy the Trustees of the British Museum, London*
4, 5. Ritual bronze vessel, early Chou dynasty. *Courtesy the Trustees of the British Museum, London*
6. Number one of ten stone drums; ink rubbing, Ch'in dynasty. *Courtesy Wango H. C. Weng Collection, New York*
7. The burning of the books and the burying alive of the scholars in the Ch'in dynasty, from a Ch'ing album. *Bibliothèque Nationale, Paris*
8. Part of the *Diamond Sutra*, AD 868. *Courtesy the Trustees of the British Museum, London*
9. Movable wooden printing block with Buddhist texts and carvings. *Museum für Völkerkunde, Berlin*

20 10. Letter by Mi Fei, Sung dynasty. *National Palace Museum, Taipei, Taiwan*
11. *Pine and Mountains in Spring*, attributed to Mi Fei; painting on paper, Sung dynasty. *National Palace Museum, Taipei, Taiwan*

21 12. Section of handscroll of bamboo, by Hsü Wei, 16th century. *Courtesy of the Smithsonian Institution, Freer Gallery of Art, Washington D.C.*
13. Illustration of landscape with figures, attributed to Wang Ching-ming; watercolour on silk, 16th-century copy of book dated AD 1323. Victoria and Albert Museum, London. Photo *Eileen Tweedy*

22 14. *The Thousand Character Essay* by Wen Cheng-ming; ink on paper, Ming dynasty. *National Palace Museum, Taipei, Taiwan*
15. Imperial order to General Yo Fei by Sung emperor Kao-tsung; 12th century. *National Palace Museum, Taipei, Taiwan*
16. Examination cells near Canton, 19th century. Photo *courtesy Church Missionary Society, London*

23 17. Yü Chih-ting: *Gathering of Literary Men at Ch'eng-nan*, detail; colour on silk, Ch'ing dynasty. Tokyo National Museum, Japan

18. Street scene, Kiu-kiang, China, from J. Thomson *Illustrations of China and its People*, London 1873. Photo *Thames and Hudson archives*
19. A peasant's spare time school; woodcut by Ku Yuan, from *Ku Yuan Mu-k'o Hsüan-chi*, Peking 1952. Photo *R. B. Fleming*
20. Front page of the newspaper, *Renmin Ribao*, 9 August 1966. Photo *R. B. Fleming*

24 21. Poster from Literacy Campaign in Liberated Areas, 1940s. From Tsou Ya and Li P'ing-fan, *Chiehfang-ch'ü mu-k'o*, Peking 1962. Photo *R. B. Fleming*
22. Children in school, from *China Pictorial*, No. 6, 1970
23. Students at Tsinghua University. Photo *Frank Fischbeck (Camera Press, London)*

25 *1. The component brushstrokes of the character yung, by C. Su*

26 *2. Comparison of oraclebone characters with modern*
3, 4. The process of papermaking, from T'ien-kung K'ai-wu, by Sung Yinghsing, 1637. Photo R. B. Fleming
5. The production of ink, from Chung-kuo pan-huahsuan, Peking 1960. Photo R. B. Fleming

27 *6. Styles of script, by Wu Shih-ch'ang*
7. Page from the encyclopaedia San-ts'ai t'u-hui compiled by Wang Ch'i and Wang Ssŭ-i, 1607. Photo R. B. Fleming

28 *8. Rotatable case for storage of founts of movable type, from Nung Shu, by Wang Chên, 14th century. Photo R. B. Fleming*
9. Grass writing from Chinese Calligraphy, by Driscoll and Toda, 1935

II 'The Middle Kingdom'

33 1. Scroll showing Emperor K'ang Hsi's tour of inspection in the South; silk, Ch'ing dynasty. *Musée Guimet, Paris*

34 2. Portrait of Chao K'uangyin, silk. *National Palace Museum, Taipei, Taiwan*
3. Prime Minister of China, Ho-k'un, 18th century. *Metropolitan Museum of Art, New York*
4. Village scene, from *The Cultivation of Rice*; Ch'ing dynasty. *Bibliothèque Nationale, Paris*

5. Street scene in Pien-ching, detail from the *Ch'ing-ming shang-ho-t'u* (scroll), by Chang Tse-tuan, 12th century. Palace Museum, Peking. Photo *Eileen Tweedy*

35 6. Transportation of salt by water, from *T'ien-kung k'aiwu* by Sung Ying-hsing, published 1637. British Museum, London. Photo *R. B. Fleming*
7. Cutting a canal at Chungmon, from *Hung Hsueh Yin Yuan T'u Chi*. British Museum, London. Photo *John Freeman*
8. Detail of a family of donors from a Buddhist painting on silk, Tun-huang Caves, Kansu, AD 983. *Courtesy the Trustees of the British Museum, London*

36 9. Bronze ritual vessel, Shang dynasty. *Courtesy the Trustees of the British Museum, London*
10. Boy on a frog; bronze, Chou dynasty. *The Brooklyn Museum, N.Y.*
11. Ceremonial implement: a jade blade mounted in bronze, inlaid with turquoise; Shang dynasty. *Courtesy of the Smithsonian Institution, Freer Gallery of Art, Washington D.C.*

37 12. Painted shell showing a horse-drawn chariot; Late Chou. *Gift of Homer H. Tielke, Jr, in honour of the fortieth anniversary of Mr and Mrs Homer F. Tielke, Sr. Cleveland Museum of Art, Cleveland, Ohio*
13. Detail from a ceremonial wine vessel; bronze, Warring States Period. *Center of Asian Art and Culture, The Avery Brundage Collection, San Francisco*
14. Chao Po-chu: Entry of first Han emperor, Liu Pang, into Ch'ang-an; silk, 12th century. *William Amory Gardner and Annie A. Hough Funds, Boston Museum of Fine Arts, Mass.*

38 15. Landscape picture; rubbing from tiled door of Western Han tomb, excavated in 1959 at Nan-kuan, Cheng-chou, Honan province
16. Farm cottage; pottery model, Han dynasty. Photo *Kadokawa Publishing Company*
17. Manor house; pottery model, Han dynasty. *Rockhill Nelson Museum, Kansas City*
18. Battle on a bridge; stone rubbing from Wu family shrine, Chia-hsiang, Shan-

tung, Han dynasty. From *Chin-shih-so*. Photo *Eileen Tweedy*

39 19. Market scene, moulded brick from Szechwan. Szechwan Provincial Museum, China. Photo *Eileen Tweedy*
20. Hunting and agriculture scene; rubbing of a tomb tile from Szechwan. Szechwan University Museum, China. Photo *Eileen Tweedy*
21. Grain-pounding with tilt hammers; rubbing of a tomb tile from Szechwan. Szechwan Provincial Museum, China. Photo *Eileen Tweedy*
22. Salt industry in Szechwan; rubbing of a moulded brick. Szechwan Provincial Museum, China. Photo *Eileen Tweedy*

40 23. Chao Po-chu: An imperial palace of the Han period; silk, Sung dynasty. *National Palace Museum, Taipei, Taiwan*
24. Soldier kneeling with shield; grey pottery, Han dynasty. Photo *Kadokawa Publishing Company*
25. Chinese coin box; Han dynasty. *Royal Ontario Museum, Toronto*

41 26. Emperor T'ai-tsung of the T'ang; painting on silk, Ching dynasty. *National Palace Museum, Taipei, Taiwan*
27. Noble lady; San Ts'ai pottery, T'ang dynasty. *Courtesy the Trustees of the British Museum, London*
28. Examination of county magistrates; from a colour album, Ch'ing dynasty. *Bibliothèque Nationale, Paris*

42 29. Emperor Hsüan-tsung's journey to Shu, after Li Chao-tao; ink and colour on silk, T'ang dynasty. *National Palace Museum, Taipei, Taiwan*
30. The retinue of Chang I-ch'ao; detail of a wall painting, late T'ang dynasty. From the Tun-huang Caves, Kansu, China. Photo *R. B. Fleming*
31. The Ta-ming palace, detail, attributed to Wang Chen-p'eng; ink on paper, Yuan dynasty. *John M. Crawford Jr Collection, New York*

43 32. *Ten Kings of Hell*, detail; paper, T'ang dynasty. From the Tun-huang Caves, Kansu, China. *Courtesy of Trustees of the British Museum, London*
33. Butcher's shop; wall painting, T'ang dynasty. From the Tun-huang Cave

357

CHINA

KOREA

DATE	DYNASTY	HISTORY	CULTURE	
500	CHOU	*The Book of Documents* (c. 1000 onwards) Chou rulers involved in continuous internal Introduction of iron Beginning of canal construction	*The Book of Poetry* Kuan-tzu (b. 645): Legalist school Confucius (551–479) Lao-tzu	
400 300	(WARRING STATES PERIOD)	Growth of large cities: Lin-tz'u, Hsia-tu, Han-tan, etc.	Mou-tzu (?468–376) *Songs of Ch'u* (c. 350 BC–AD 140) Chuang-tzu (b. c. 369) Mencius (372–289) Tsou Yen (305–240): Five Elements school Hsün-tzu (?313–238)	Korea divided into three kingdom
200	CH'IN	Burning of the books (213) Building of the Great Wall Paper first manufactured		
100	EARLY HAN	Beginning of professional civil service Emperor Wu (140–87) Ch'ang-an capital	Confucianism supreme (136) Music Department established (c. 120)	Emperor Wu of China annexes Korea (109/108)
BC AD				Kingdom of Silla founded; Three Kingdoms period begins (57) Confucianism introduced
100	LATER HAN	Emperor Ming (58–75) Chinese settlement in South China Rebellion of Yellow Turbans (184) Introduction of Buddhism	Chang Ling: The Way of the Five Bushels of Rice (143)	State of Karak (42–562)
200 300		China invaded by nomadic tribes from the north Fall of Ch'ang-an (316) Population shifts south of the Yangtze	Juan Chi (210–63) Neo-Taoism (220–420) Lu Chi (261–363)	Chinese rule ends (313) Chinese Buddhism introduced
400	SIX DYNASTIES	North China unified under the Northern Wei (Toba Turks)		
500 600	SUI	Emperor Yang Chien (589–604) Emperor Yang-ti (604–18) Examination system assumes final form Capital re-established at Ch'ang-an	T'an-luan (476–542): Pure Land school Chih-i (538–97): T'ien-t'ai school Chi-tsang (549–623): Chung-lun school Tu-shun (557–640): Hua-yen school Hsüan-tsang (596–664): Wei-shih school Northern School of Gradual Enlightenment Southern School of Sudden Enlightenment	Koguryŏ and Paekche conquered Silla: Korea re-unified
700 800	T'ANG	Hsüan Tsung (712–56) An Lu-shan's rebellion (755) Emperor Hsien-tsung (805–20) First printed book (868) Invention of gunpowder (before 10th C.) China divided into ten states	Wang Wei (701–61) Li Po (701–62) Tu Fu (712–70) Han Yü (768–819) Po Chü-i (772–846)	Gishō, founder of Kegon Buddhis in Korea (624–702)
900 1000	FIVE DYNASTIES	Invasion of the Khitan from the north Capital established at Kaifeng Wang Hu-shih (1021–86) Movable type used by c. 1030	Neo-Confucianism flourishes Ch'eng I (1033–1107): School of Principle	Koryŏ dynasty begins (935)
1100	NORTHERN SUNG	Explosion of Crab Nebula observed (1054) Invasion of the Jurchid from the north Jurchid expelled from Peking Huang-ho changes course: millions drown	Kiangsi school of poetry Su Shih (1037–1101) Chou Pang-yen (1056–1121) Lu Hsiang-shan (1139–93): School of the	
1200	SOUTHERN SUNG	Mongols under Genghis Khan invade Khubilai Khan (1279–94) Marco Polo in China	Chu Hsi (1130–1200) Mind Kuan Han-ch'ing (c. 1220– c. 1300) Ma Chih-yüan (c. 1250– c. 1325)	
1300	YUAN	Chu Yüan-chang (1368–98) Cheng Ho's voyages (1405–33)	Wang Shih-fu: *The Western Chamber*	Mongol domination (1231–1356)
1400				Koryŏ dynasty ends (1392) Yi (Choson) dynasty begins Phonetic alphabet developed Buddhism repressed
1500	MING	Portuguese arrive in China Arrival of Jesuits: Matteo Ricci in Peking 1600	Wang Yang-ming (1472–1529) Wu Ch'eng-en (c. 1506–82): *Journey to the West (Monkey)* Hsü Wei (1521–93)	Rise of Neo-Confucianism Korean painting flourishes
1600		Invasion of the Manchus Emperor K'ang-hsi (1662–1722) Treaty of Nerchinsk (1689)	Wang Cheng-ming (1522–67) Wang Fu-chih (1619–92) Final version of the *Water Margin* (begun 13th century)	Japan invades Korea (1592) Manchus invade and occupy Korea (1627)
1700 1800	CH'ING (MANCHUS)	Emperor Yung-cheng (1722–36) Emperor Ch'ien-lung (1736–95)	Ts'ao Chan (c. 1716–63): *Dream of the Red Chamber*	
1900		Opium Wars (1839–42, 1856–60) Taiping Rebellion (1850–64) Boxer Rising (1900)	K'ang Yu-wei (1858–1927) Fung Yu-lan (b. 1895) Abbot T'ai-hsü (1898–1947)	Treaty with Japan (1876) Treaty with USA (1883) Anti-court revolts (1882, 1884)
	KUOMINTANG CCP	1911 Revolution CCP founded (1921) Long March (1934–35) People's Republic of China (1949)	Maoist philosophy and literature	Korea annexed by Japan (1910) Democratic Republic (1945) Korean War (1950–53)

VIETNAM

JAPAN

VIETNAM	HISTORY	CULTURE	PERIOD OR SHOGUNATE	DATE
				500
			JOMON PERIOD	400
				300
…nam conquered by the Ch'in (207) …nd becomes Chinese colony				200
				100
			YAYOI PERIOD	BC AD
	Bronze Age			100
…dhism takes root in north Vietnam …nese intellectuals emigrate to …ietnam				200
	Iron Age	First mention of Japan in Chinese history Introduction of Chinese script		300
				400
			UJI ('CLAN') PERIOD	500
		Buddhism introduced (552)		
	Transition from clan to imperial system First Japanese embassy to China (607) Coup d'état by Fujiwara; Taika reforms (645) Emperor Temmu (671) Capital established at Nara (710) Land reclamation policy initiated (724) Capital established at Heian (Kyoto) (794) Fujiwara Yoshifusa (804–72)	Adoption of Chinese calendar (604) Six Schools of Nara (625–736) Kakinomoto no Hitomaro (d. 707) *Kojiki* (712) *Nihon shoki* (720) *Manyoshū* completed (777) Kūkai (774–835) Tendai and Shingon sects introduced Ariwara no Narihira (825–80) Ki no Tsurayuki (?859–945) *Kokinshū* (905) *Engishiki* (927) *Tosa Diary* by Tsurayuki (935) *Gossamer Years* (954–74) *Tales of Ise* Murasaki Shikibu (978–1016?): *Tale of Genji*	TAIKA PERIOD	600
…reased cultural exchanges with …China			NARA PERIOD	700
			HEIAN PERIOD	800
…tnam ceases to be Chinese colony …939) …h dynasty (968)				900
	Records Office established by Emperor Go-Sanjo (1069) Cloister government begins (1086) Hogen and Heiji insurrections (1156, 1160) War between Taira and Minamoto (1180–85) Yoritomo inaugurates Shogunate (1192) Go-Toba's struggle with Shogunate (1221) Attempted Mongol invasions (1274, 1281)		(FUJIWARA PERIOD)	1000
		Fujiwara Shunzei (1114–1204) Teika (1162–1241) Rinzai school of Zen (1191) *Shin Kokinshū* (1205) Ippen (1239–89) *Tale of the Heike* (1225) Sōtō school of Zen (1227)	TAIRA PERIOD	1100
…ngol invasions (1280s)			KAMAKURA PERIOD	1200
	Go-Daigo (1318–39) Yoshimitsu (1368–94) Ashikaga Takauji (1338–58) becomes Shogun Two imperial courts unified (1392)	Nō plays (14th and 15th centuries) Sōgi (1421–1508) Sesshū (1420–1506)	NAMBOKUCHO PERIOD	1300
…r with China (1418–27)			ASHIKAGA SHOGUNATE (MUROMACHI)	1400
	Warring States (Sengoku) begins (1467) Nobunaga (1534–82) Hideyoshi (1583–98) Portuguese land in Japan (1543) Edo (Tokyo) Shogunate capital (1590) Tokugawa Ieyasu (1603–16) Shimabara Rebellion (1637–38) 'Floating World'	Francis Xavier comes to Japan 'Christian century' (1549–1639) Genroku period Saikaku (1642–93) Bashō (1644–94) Kabuki plays Monzaemon (1653–1725) Yosa Buson (1716–83) Motoori Norinaga (1730–1801) Katsushika Hokusai (1760–1849) Shintō revival	MOMOYAMA PERIOD	1500 / 1600
…y-son peasant war (1771–86) …nchu invasions under Ch'ien-lung …1788–89) …nese suzerainty (1802) …tnam becomes French protectorate …1884)	Commodore Perry arrives in Japan (1853) Meiji Restoration (1868) War with China (1894–95) War with Russia (1904–05) Manchurian Incident (1931) Attack on Pearl Harbor (1941)	Takizawa Bakin (1767–1847) Andō Hiroshige (1767–1858) Modern Japanese novel and film	TOKUGAWA SHOGUNATE (EDO)	1700 / 1800
…r with France (1946–54) …r between North and South begins …1954)			MEIJI RESTORATION	1900

BIBLIOGRAPHY

On East Asia as a whole the standard work is *A History of East Asian Civilization* by John K. Fairbank, Edwin O. Reischauer and Albert M. Craig, divided into two volumes:
- I *East Asia, The Great Tradition* (Boston, 1958)
- II *East Asia, The Modern Transformation* (Boston and London, 1965)

I Signs and Meanings
CHAO YUEN REN *Mandarin Primer* (Cambridge, Mass., 1948)
COEDES, G. *Les Peuples de la Péninsule Indochinoise* (Paris, 1962)
EGEROD, SØREN 'Review of W. A. C. H. Dobson: Late Archaic Chinese', *Acta Orientalia*, Vol. XXV, 1–2 (Copenhagen, 1959)
FORREST, R. A. D. *The Chinese Language* (London, 1965)
GRIFFIS, WILLIAM E. *Corea: The Hermit Nation* (New York, 9th edn, 1911)
KARLGREN, BERNHARD *Analytic Dictionary of Chinese and Sino-Japanese* (Paris, 1925)
The Chinese Language (New York, 1949)
'Grammata Serica Recensa', *Bulletin of the Museum of Far Eastern Antiquities*, Vol. XXIX (Stockholm, 1957)
Philology and Ancient China (Oslo, Leipzig, Paris, London, and Cambridge, Mass., 1926)
Religion i Kina, Antiken (Stockholm, 1964)
KRATOCHVIL, PAUL *The Chinese Language Today* (London, 1968)
MASPERO, GEORGES *L'Indochine*, Vol. I (Paris and Brussels, 1929)
MICHEL, ABEL DES 'Mémoire sur les origines et le caractère de la langue Annamite', *Mémoires présentés par divers Savants à l'Académie des Inscriptions et Belles-Lettres*, Vol. X (Paris, 1887)
MILLER, ROY ANDREW *The Japanese Language* (Chicago, 1967)

II 'The Middle Kingdom'
BALAZS, E. *Chinese Civilization and Bureaucracy* (London and New Haven, Conn., 1964)
ELVIN, M. *The Pattern of Chinese History* (London, 1973)
GERNET, J. *Daily Life in China on the eve of the Mongol Invasion* (London, 1962)
Le Monde Chinois (Paris, 1972)
HO, P. T. *The ladder of success in Imperial China* (New York, 1964)
HUCKER, C. O. *The Traditional Chinese State in Ming Times* (Tucson, 1961)
LOEWE, M. *Everyday Life in Early Imperial China* (London, 1968)
YI-FU TUAN *China* (London, 1970)

III Beyond the Wall
BADDELEY, J. F. *Russia, Mongolia, China* (London, 1919)
BAWDEN, C. R. *The Modern History of Mongolia* (London, 1968)
CARRUTHERS, D. *Unknown Mongolia* (London, 1913)
FRITERS, G. M. *Outer Mongolia and its International Position* (Baltimore, 1949, and London, 1951)
GROUSSET, RENÉ (trans. Sinor and MacKellar) *Conqueror of the World* (London, 1967)
(trans. Anthony Watson-Gandy and Terence Gordon) *The Rise and Splendour of the Chinese Empire* (London, 1952)
HEISSIG, W. *A Lost Civilisation, The Mongols Rediscovered* (London, 1966)
LATTIMORE, OWEN *Inner Asian Frontiers of China* (New York, 1940; reprinted 1951)
Studies in Frontier History (Paris–The Hague and London–New York, 1962)
LEGG, STUART *The Heartland* (London, 1970)
PHILLIPS, E. D. *The Mongols* (London, 1969)

IV The Path to Wisdom
CHAN, WING-TSIT *Religious Trends in Modern China* (London and New York, 1953)
Comp. and trans. *A Source Book in Chinese Philosophy* (London and Princeton, NJ, 1963)
CHAN, WING-TSIT, ISMA'IL RAGI AL FĀRŪQĪ, JOSEPH M. KITAGAWA and P. T. RAJU, comps. *The Great Asian Religions: An Anthology* (London and New York, 1969)
CHANG, CARSUN *The Development of Neo-Confucian Thought*, 2 vols. (New York, 1957 and 1962)
CH'EN, KENNETH *Buddhism in China: A Historical Survey* (Princeton, NJ, 1964)
CHU HSI (trans. Wing-tsit Chan) *Reflections on Things at Hand: The Neo-Confucian Anthology* (London and New York, 1967)
CHUANG-TZU (trans. Burton Watson) *The Complete Works of Chuang Tzu* (London and New York, 1968)
CONFUCIUS (trans. Arthur Waley) *The Analects of Confucius* (London and New York, 1938)
FUNG YU-LAN (trans. Derk Bodde) *A History of Chinese Philosophy*, 2 vols. (Princeton, NJ, 1952–53)
GRAHAM, A. C. *Two Chinese Philosophers: Ch'eng Ming-tao and Ch'eng Yi-ch'uan* (London, 1958)
HUI-NENG (trans. Wing-tsit Chan) *The Platform Scripture: The Basic Classic of Zen Buddhism* (New York, 1963)
LAO-TZU (trans. Wing-tsit Chan) *The Way of Lao Tzu* (Indianapolis, NY, 1963)
MENCIUS (trans. D. C. Lau) *Mencius* (Harmondsworth and Baltimore, 1970)
WANG YANG-MING (WANG SHOU-JEN) (trans. Wing-tsit Chan) *Instructions for Practical Living* (London and New York, 1963)

V The Empirical Tradition
BERNARD, HENRI S. J. *Matteo Ricci's Scientific Contribution to China* (Peiping, 1935)
HO PENG-YOKE *The Astronomical Chapters of the Chin Shu.* (The Hague, 1966)
KWOK, D. W. Y. *Scientism in Chinese Thought, 1900–1950* (New Haven, Conn., 1965)
MIKAMI YOSHIO *The Development of Mathematics in China and Japan* (Leipzig, 1913)
NAKAYAMA, SHIGERU *A History of Japanese Astronomy* (Cambridge, Mass., 1969)
NEEDHAM, JOSEPH *The Grand Titration: Science and Society in East and West* (London, 1969)
Science and Civilisation in China (Cambridge, England, 1954–)
SIVIN, NATHAN *Chinese Alchemy: Preliminary Studies* (Cambridge, Mass., 1968)
WYLIE, ALEXANDER *Chinese Researches* (Shanghai, 1897)
YABUUTI KIYOSI 'Indian and Arabian Astronomy in China', *Zinbun-kagaku-kenkyūsyo, Kyoto University* (Kyoto, 1954)
YAMATA KEIJI 'The Science and Technology of Contemporary China', in R. Van Voorhis, ed., *China and the Great Cultural Revolution* (Tokyo, 1969)

VI Worlds and Language
HSIA, C. T. *The Classic Chinese Novel* (New York, 1968)
HUNG, WILLIAM *Tu Fu, China's Greatest Poet* (Cambridge, Mass., 1952)
LIN YUTANG *The Gay Genius* (New York, 1947). A biography of Su Shih
LIU, JAMES J. Y. *The Art of Chinese Poetry* (London and Chicago, 1962)
The Chinese Knight-Errant (London and Chicago, 1967)
The Poetry of Li Shang-yin (Chicago, 1969)
LIU WU-CHI *An Introduction to Chinese Literature* (Bloomington, Ind., 1966)
WALMSLEY, L. C. and D. B. *Wang Wei, the Poet-Painter* (Rutland, Vt, 1968)
WATSON, BURTON *Early Chinese Literature* (New York, 1962)
YOSHIKAWA KŌJIRŌ (trans. Burton Watson) *An Introduction to Sung Poetry* (Cambridge, Mass., 1967)

Translations from Chinese literature
Sources of the quotations in Professor Liu's chapter are given on p. 14
Other recommended translations of works mentioned in the text:
BREWITT-TAYLOR, C. H. *Romance of the Three Kingdoms* (Shanghai, 1925; reprinted Rutland, Vt, 1959)
CHANG YIN-NAN and L. C. WALMSLEY *Poems of Wang Wei* (Rutland, Vt, 1958)
EGERTON, CLEMENT *The Golden Lotus* (London, 1939; reprinted New York, 1962)
FRODSHAM, J. D. *The Poems of Li Ho* (Oxford, 1970)
GRAHAM, A. C. *Poems of the Late T'ang* (Harmondsworth, 1965)
HAWKES, DAVID *A Little Primer of Tu Fu* (Oxford, 1967)
HIGHTOWER, J. R. *The Poetry of T'ao Ch'ien* (Oxford, 1970)
HSIUNG, S. I. *The Romance of the Western Chamber* (London, 1935)
JACKSON, J. H. *Water Margin* (Shanghai, 1937)
WALEY, ARTHUR *Monkey* (London 1942, New York 1944)
WANG, C. C. *Dream of the Red Chamber* (New York, 1958)
YANG HSIEN-YI and GLADYS YANG *Selected Plays of Kuan Han-ch'ing* (Shanghai, 1958)

VII Chinese Culture Overseas

Korea
HULBER, H. B. *History of Korea* (London, 1905, revised edn 1962)
MICHAEL, F. H. and TAYLOR, C. E. *Korea, its Land, People and Culture of all Ages* (Seoul, 1960)
OSGOOD, C. *The Koreans and their Culture* (1951)

Vietnam
BUTTINGER, JOSEPH *Vietnam: A Political History* (London, 1969)
CHESNEAUX, JEAN *Contribution à l'histoire de la Nation Vietnamienne* (Paris, 1956)
LÉ THÀNH KHÔI *Le Viêt-nam, Histoire et Civilisation* (Paris, 1955)

Tibet
BUSHELL, S. W. 'The Early History of Tibet from Chinese Sources' in *Journal of the Royal Asiatic Society* n.s. XII (London, 1880)
LI TIEH-TSENG *Tibet, Today and Yesterday* (New York, 1960)
RICHARDSON, H. E. *Tibet and its History* (London, 1962)

ROCKHILL, W. W. *The Dalai Lamas of Lhasa and their Relations with the Manchu Emperors of China* (1910)

SHAKABPA, T. *Tibet, A Political History* (1967)

SNELLGROVE, D. L. and RICHARDSON, H. E. *A Cultural History of Tibet* (London, 1968)

VIII Feudal Japan

BROWN, D. M. *Money Economy in Medieval Japan* (New Haven, Conn., 1951)

DORE, R. P. *Education in Tokugawa Japan* (London, 1965)

HALL, J. W. *Japan from Prehistory to Modern Times* (New York and London, 1970)
Government and Local Power in Japan, 500 to 1700 (Princeton, NJ, 1966)

JOUON DES LONGRAIS, F. *L'est et l'ouest. Institutions du Japon et de l'Occident comparées* (Paris and Tokyo, 1958)

McCULLOUGH, H. C. *Yoshitsune: A Fifteenth Century Japanese Chronicle* (Stanford, Calif., 1966)
The Taiheiki. A Chronicle of Medieval Japan (New York, 1959)

MORRIS, I. *The World of the Shining Prince: Court Life in Ancient Japan* (London, 1964)

REISCHAUER, E. O. Chapter on Japanese feudalism, in R. Coulborn, ed., *Feudalism in History* (Princeton, NJ, 1956)

SANSOM, GEORGE B. *A History of Japan.* 3 vols (Stanford, Calif., and London, 1958–1963).
Japan, a Short Cultural History (New York and London, rev. ed., 1962)

SHELDON, C. D. *The Rise of the Merchant Class in Tokugawa Japan, 1600–1868* (Locust Valley, NY, 1958)

SHINODA, M. *The Founding of the Kamakura Shogunate, 1180–1185* (New York, 1960)

SMITH, T. C. *The Agrarian Origins of Modern Japan* (Stanford, Calif., 1959)

TOTMAN, C. *Politics in the Tokugawa Bakufu, 1600–1843* (Harvard, Mass., 1967)

TSUKAHIRA, T. *The Sankin Kotai System of Tokugawa Japan* (Harvard, Mass., 1966)

WEBB, H. *The Imperial Institution in Tokugawa Japan* (New York, 1968)

IX Cult and Creed

ANEZAKI MASAHARU *A History of Japanese Religion* (London, 1930; Tokyo, 1963)

ASTON, W. G. *Shinto: The Way of the Gods* (London, 1905)

DUMOULIN, HEINRICH *A History of Zen* (London, 1964)

ELIOT, SIR CHARLES *Japanese Buddhism* (London, 1935, 1959)

HOLTON, D. C. *The National Faith of Japan: A Study in Modern Shinto* (London, 1938)

KITAGAWA, J. M. *Religion in Japanese History* (New York, 1966)

NAKAMURA HAJIME *The Ways of Thinking of Eastern Peoples* (Tokyo, 1963)

SUZUKI, D. T. *Essays in Zen Bud-*

dhism 1–3 (London, 1950–53)

VISSER, M. W. DE *Ancient Buddhism in Japan* (Leiden, 1935)

X A Literature of Court and People

BOWNAS, GEOFFREY, and ANTHONY THWAITE *Penguin Book of Japanese Verse* (Harmondsworth, Middx., 1964)

BROWER, ROBERT H., and EARL MINER *Japanese Court Poetry* (Stanford, Calif., 1961)

KEENE, DONALD *Anthology of Japanese Literature* (New York, 1955, and Harmondsworth, Middx., 1968)
Landscapes and Portraits (Tokyo, 1971)
ed. *Twenty Plays of the Nō Theatre* (New York and London, 1970)
trans. *Chūshingura* (New York and London, 1971)
trans. *Essays in Idleness: The 'Tsurezuregusa' of Kenkō* (New York and London, 1967)
trans. *Major Plays of Chikamatsu* (New York and London, 1961)
Manyōshū (New York and London, 1969)

MORRIS, IVAN, trans. *The Life of an Amorous Woman* (London and New York, 1963)
trans. *The Pillow Book of Sei Shōnagon* (London and New York, 1967)

NOBUYUKI YUASA, trans. *The Narrow Road to the Deep North* (Harmondsworth, Middx., 1966)

SEIDENSTICKER, E. G., trans. *The Gossamer Years* (Tokyo, 1964)

WALEY, ARTHUR, trans. *The Tale of Genji* (London and New York, 1935)

XI Europe goes East

APPLETON, WILLIAM W. *A Cycle of Cathay: The Chinese Vogue in England* (New York, 1951)

BOXER, C. R. *The Christian Century in Japan, 1549–1650* (Berkeley, Calif., and London, 1951)

DERMIGNY, LOUIS *La Chine et l'occident: le commerce à Canton au XVIIIᵉ siècle, 1719–1833*, 3 vols (Leiden, 1964)

DUNNE, GEORGE H., S.J. *Generation of Giants: The Story of the Jesuits in China* (Notre Dame, Ind., 1962)

FU LO-SHU *A Documentary Chronicle of Sino-Western Relations 1644–1820*, 2 vols (Tucson, Ariz., 1966)

GALLAGHER, LOUIS J., S.J. *China in the Sixteenth Century: The Journal of Matthew Ricci, 1583–1610* (New York, 1953)

GILMORE, MYRON P. *The World of Humanism, 1453–1517* (New York and Evanston, Ill., 1962)

HUDSON, G. F. *Europe and China: A Survey of Their Relations from the Earliest Times to 1800* (London, 1931)

KEENE, DONALD *The Japanese Discovery of Europe, 1720–1830* (Stanford, Calif., rev. edn 1969)

LACH, DONALD *The Century of Discovery* (Chicago, 1965)

LATOURETTE, KENNETH SCOTT *A History of Christian Missions in China* (London, 1929)

LEVENSON, JOSEPH R., ed. *European Expansion and the Counter-Example of Asia, 1300–1600* (Englewood Cliffs, NJ, 1967)

PARRY, JOHN H. *The Age of Reconnaissance* (London and Cleveland, Ohio, 1963)

ROWBOTHAM, ARNOLD H. *Missionary and Mandarin: The Jesuits at the Court of China* (Berkeley, 1942)

SANSOM, GEORGE B. *The Western World and Japan* (New York and London, 1950)

XII A New Role for Japan

AKITA, GEORGE *The Foundations of Constitutional Government in Japan, 1868–1900* (Harvard, 1965)

ALCOCK, SIR RUTHERFORD *The Capital of the Tycoon: A Narrative of Three Years' Residence in Japan* (London, 1863)

BEARDSLEY, RICHARD K., *et al.*, eds., *Village Japan* (Chicago, 1959)

BEASLEY, W. G. *The Modern History of Japan* (London, 1964)
The Meiji Restoration (Stanford and London, 1973)

BLACKER, CARMEN *The Japanese Enlightenment: A Study of the Writings of Fukuzawa Yukichi* (Cambridge, 1964)

BUTOW, R. *Tojo and the Coming of the War* (Princeton, 1961)
Japan's Decision to Surrender (Stanford, 1954)

CONROY, F. H. *Japan's Seizure of Korea, 1868–1910* (Philadelphia, 1960)

CRAIG, ARTHUR *Chōshū in the Meiji Restoration* (Harvard, 1961)

CROWLEY, JAMES B. *Japan's Quest for Autonomy, 1930–1938* (Princeton, 1966)

DORE, R. P. *Land Reform in Japan* (Oxford, 1965)
City Life in Japan (Berkeley and London, 1958)

DUUS, PETER *Party Rivalry and Political Change in Taishō Japan* (Harvard, 1968)

EMBREE, JOHN F., *Suye Mura: a Japanese Village* (Chicago, 1958)

FEIS, HERBERT *The Road to Pearl Harbor* (Princeton, 1950)
Japan Subdued: The Atomic Bomb and the End of the War in the Pacific (Princeton, 1961)

HACKETT, R. F. *Yamagata Aritomo in the Rise of Modern Japan, 1838–1922* (Harvard, 1971)

HIRSCHMEIER, J. *The Origins of Entrepreneurship in Meiji Japan* (Harvard, 1964)

IKE, NOBUTAKA *The Beginnings of Political Democracy in Japan* (Baltimore, 1950)

IRIYE, AKIRA *After Imperialism: The Search for a New Order in the Far East, 1921–1931* (Harvard, 1966)

JANSEN, MARIUS *Sakamoto Ryōma and the Meiji Restoration* (Princeton, 1961)

KAWAI, KAZUO *Japan's American Interlude* (Chicago, 1960)

LEVINE, S. B. *Industrial Relations in Postwar Japan* (Illinois, 1958)

LOCKWOOD, WM. W. *The Economic Development of Japan, 1868–1938* (Princeton, 1954)

MARUYAMA, MASAO *Thought and*

Behaviour in Modern Japanese Politics (Oxford, 1963)

MAXON, YALE C. *Control of Japanese Foreign Policy, 1930–1945* (Berkeley, 1957)

MILLER, FRANK L. *Minobe Tatsukichi, Interpreter of Constitutionalism in Japan* (Berkeley, 1964)

NAJITA, T., *Hara Kei in the Politics of Compromise, 1905–1915* (Harvard, 1967)

OGATA, SADAKO N. *Defiance in Manchuria; the Making of Japanese Foreign Policy, 1931–1932* (Berkeley, 1964)

REISCHAUER, E. O. *The United States and Japan* (Harvard, 1965)
Studies in the Modernization of Japan (Princeton, 1965–1971). 6 vols., ed. by Jansen, Dore, Ward, Lockwood, Morley and Shively.

TOTTEN, G. O. *The Social Democratic Movement in Pre-war Japan* (Yale, 1966)

WILSON, GEORGE M. *Radical Nationalist in Japan: Kita Ikki, 1883–1937* (Harvard, 1969)

XIII Rebellion, Reform and Revolution

CHESNEAUX, J. *Vietnam* (Paris, 1968)

CHESNEAUX, J., and M. BASTID *La Chine. Des guerres de l'opium à la guerre franco-chinoise, 1840–1885* (Paris, 1969)

CHESNEAUX, J., C. BOUDAREL, and D. HEMERY, eds. *Tradition et révolution au Vietnam* (Paris, 1970)

CHOW TSE-TSUNG *The May Fourth Movement* (Cambridge, Mass., 1960)

CROOK, I. and D. *Revolution in a Chinese Village* (London, 1966)

FAIRBANK, J. K., and TENG SSU-YU *China's Response to the West: A Documentary History, 1839–1923* (New York, 1966)

GRAY, J., ed. *Modern China's Search for a Political Form* (London, 1969)

HAN SU-YIN *Memoirs (The Crippled Tree; A Mortal Flower; Birdless Summer)*, 3 vols (London, 1965–8)

HINTON, W. *Fanshen: A Documentary of Revolution in a Chinese Village* (New York, 1966)

HO PING-TI, TANG TSOU, eds. *China in Crisis*, 3 vols (Chicago, 1968)

LEE CHONG-SIK *The Politics of Korean Nationalism* (New York, 1962)

MAO TSE-TUNG *Selected Works*, 4 vols (Peking, 1960)

NEEDHAM, J. 'The Past in China's Present', *The Centennial Review*, 1960

SCHRAM, S. *Mao: Basic Tactics* (London, 1966)

SCHURMANN, F., and O. SCHELL *China Readings*, 3 vols (London, 1967)

SMITH, R. *Vietnam and the West* (London, 1969)

SNOW, E. *Red Star over China* (London, rev. edn 1969)
The Other Side of the River (London, 1963)

SUN YAT-SEN (trans. Frank W. Price) *San Min Chu i: The Three Principles of the People* (Taipei, 1953)